The Sequence

The Sequence

*Unveiling the Six Sequences
in the New Testament That Prove the
Post-Armageddon, Premillennial Resurrection*

STEVEN R. BATES

WIPF & STOCK · Eugene, Oregon

THE SEQUENCE
Unveiling the Six Sequences in the New Testament That Prove the Post-Armageddon, Premillennial Resurrection

Copyright © 2024 Steven R. Bates. All rights reserved. Except for brief quotations in critical publications or reviews, no part of this book may be reproduced in any manner without prior written permission from the publisher. Write: Permissions, Wipf and Stock Publishers, 199 W. 8th Ave., Suite 3, Eugene, OR 97401.

Wipf & Stock
An Imprint of Wipf and Stock Publishers
199 W. 8th Ave., Suite 3
Eugene, OR 97401

www.wipfandstock.com

PAPERBACK ISBN: 979-8-3852-1459-4
HARDCOVER ISBN: 979-8-3852-1460-0
EBOOK ISBN: 979-8-3852-1461-7

VERSION NUMBER 10/08/25

Scripture quotations marked (NRSV) are from the New Revised Standard Version Bible, copyright © 1989 the Division of Christian Education of the National Council of the Churches of Christ in the United States of America. Used by permission. All rights reserved.

Scripture quotations marked (KJV) are taken from The Authorized (King James) Version. Rights in the Authorized Version in the United Kingdom are vested in the Crown. Reproduced by permission of the Crown's patentee, Cambridge University Press

Contents

Preface | vii
Introduction: Unveiling the Six Sequences | ix

1. Sequence in 1 and 2 Thessalonians | 1
2. Sequence in the Olivet Discourse | 37
3. The Thirteen Conversations in Revelation | 67
4. First Sequence in Revelation, Part 1:
   Through the Sixth Trumpet (6:1—9:21) | 82
5. Second Sequence in Revelation: *The Two Witnesses (11:1–13)*
   First Sequence in Revelation, Part 1 (cont.):
   The Seventh Trumpet (11:15-19) | 136
6. Third Sequence in Revelation: *The Woman, the Child, and the Dragon (12:1-6)*
   Fourth Sequence in Revelation, Part 1: *The War in Heaven to the Woman's Escape (12:7-17)* | 157
7. Fourth Sequence, Part 2:
   The First and Second Beasts (12:18—13:18) | 211
8. Fourth Sequence, Part 3: *Mount Zion to the Worship around God's Throne (14:1—15:4)* | 245
9. First Sequence, Part 2: *The Seven Bowls (15:5—19:10)* | 273
10. First Sequence, Part 3: *The Lord's Return and the First Resurrection (19:11—20:6a)* | 328
11. First Sequence, Part 4: *The Millennium and the Final Judgment (20:6b-15)* | 363

12 First Sequence, Part 5: *The Second Resurrection and the New Jerusalem (21:1—22:5)* | 391

Conclusion: Truth and Error | 413
Appendix A: Chart Showing the Complete Reconciliation of the Six Sequences | 421
Appendix B: Proof That Daniel's Seventieth Week Has Nothing to Do with End Times | 460
Bibliography | 485

Preface

Today's Typical Academic Book in eschatology will often provide the reader a brief history of the various positions in this particular branch of theology followed by why certain positions should be considered the more attractive options. *This is not that book.* Instead, over the course of the following twelve chapters, you will be presented six sequences from the three major sources in the NT regarding the subject, i.e., Paul's letters to the Thessalonians, the Olivet Discourse, and John's visions in Revelation, and through a careful reconciliation of those six sequences, I will show that there's only one sequence of end times, which I have labeled "The Post-Armageddon, Premillennial Resurrection." Had any other sequence of end times been correct, whether pretribulationism, pre-wrath, mid-tribulationism, historic premillennialism, postmillennialism, a-millennialism, preterism, or any other sequence that one could possibly imagine, then the proponents of that postulation should be able to take the same six sequences from Scripture and reconcile them precisely with one another, paragraph by paragraph, sentence by sentence, and word by word, and prove whatever sequence they propose. But no one will ever attempt such an endeavor because it's theoretically impossible. Scripture's six sequences only confirm one sequence and it is the one which has been presented in *The Sequence.*

I have labeled the six sequences as follows: Sequence in 1 and 2 Thessalonians, Sequence in the Olivet Discourse, First Sequence in Revelation (Parts 1–5), Second Sequence in Revelation, Third Sequence in Revelation, and, finally, Fourth Sequence in Revelation (Parts 1–3). If the thought of the four sequences in Revelation seem unfamiliar, there's a good reason: To my knowledge, not only have the four sequences in

Revelation never been addressed, but they've never been identified. When this unfortunate shortcoming is coupled with the all-too-often misinterpreted sequences assumed to be present in the Olivet Discourse and 1 and 2 Thessalonians, the current lack of consensus within eschatology is the inevitable result. Written with the academic and non-academic in mind, *The Sequence* seeks to alleviate the current confusion within eschatology by correctly identifying the six sequences present within the New Testament and thereby prove that Christ and the apostles only advocated one sequence of end times.

S. Bates

Introduction

Unveiling the Six Sequences

Several years ago, a well-known Christian apologist made the statement, "There is a crisis in eschatology." To those unfamiliar with the word, he was simply saying there is a crisis originating from within the biblical study of end-time events. According to the apologist, the crisis existed because he believed there had been a significant and credible criticism leveled against Christ's own words concerning the timing of his return and that criticism has essentially gone unaddressed. He also contended that most in the church did not take the crisis seriously. The indictment continued by saying that this unaddressed criticism, which began with the great European theologians of the late nineteenth and early twentieth centuries, has resulted in great harm to the reputation of Christ, his words, and therefore to the reputation of Scripture in general.[1] I suppose that the conclusion that one is to take away from this indictment is that many in the church would rather remain in a cocoon, believing whatever they wish rather than confronting this supposed credible and formidable attack on Christ and his words. A case in point by the apologist is that one of the favorite passages theologians are eager to highlight against the prophecies of Christ centers on the presumed miscalculation from the Lord in the following passage:[2]

"From the fig tree learn its lesson: as soon as its branch becomes tender and puts forth its leaves, you know that summer is near. So also, when you see all these things, you know that he is near, at the very gates. Truly I tell you, this generation will not pass away until all these things

---

1. Sproul, *Last Days according to Jesus*, 17–23.
2. Sproul, *Last Days according to Jesus*, 24–25.

INTRODUCTION

have taken place. Heaven and earth will pass away, but my words will not pass away" (Matt 24:32–35).

The apologist pointed out that the theologians, when citing this passage, claimed that Christ was certain that he would return during his generation, and since he did not return, they confidently assert that he was a mistaken and disillusioned prophet. And as the reasoning continued, since he was mistaken about the sequence surrounding his own return, then his teachings elsewhere cannot be trusted, and thereby, the theologians believe they have successfully impugned the integrity of Christ and Scripture in one fell swoop. Even C. S. Lewis, in his collection of short essays *The World's Last Night*, said concerning this passage, "It is certainly the most embarrassing verse in the Bible."[3] But I beg to differ. The text is not embarrassing in the least. Sure, if one were to only read this passage out of context as it stands alone in the above illustration, one might conceivably believe that Jesus was speaking about returning during his own generation, which would naturally have included him and his disciples on the Mount of Olives that night, and therefore the prediction would have been proof that he had miscalculated his return. But as the reader will soon learn, Jesus not only addressed his disciples in the Olivet Discourse, but he also addressed a second group that night, and that was the future Jewish "reader" of the discourse in the last generation, who will witness a series of events presented by Christ, beginning with the apocalyptic abomination of desolation and continuing through the appearance of the Son of Man and the gathering of the saints. When Jesus said "this generation" in Matt 24:32–35, he was only referencing the last generation of the Jewish reader who would one day witness that entire sequence of apocalyptic events, beginning with the abomination of desolation. He absolutely knew that his generation and the generation of the future Jewish "reader" were not the same, and therefore he was never mistaken. In fact, concerning the generation of Jesus and the disciples, after telling the disciples that they would hear of wars and rumors of wars, Jesus consoled his little band of followers, telling them that there was no need to be alarmed because "the end is not yet" (Matt 24:6). In other words, the end will not take place in their generation. The belief that Jesus thought he would return in his own generation was simply one assumed by theologians who lacked the proper understanding of several texts that revealed Christ's cognizance of the times and seasons. This notion that

---

3. Lewis, *World's Last Night and Other Essays*, 98.

INTRODUCTION

Jesus mistakenly thought he would return during his generation was not a miscalculation by Christ, but rather was one by certain theologians as well as those who were misled by their errant postulations.[4]

If the passage in Matthew serves as the centerpiece for "the crisis in eschatology," then I believe we need not be overly concerned, at least as it pertains to a perceived threat to the integrity of Christ's words on end times or to the reputation of Scripture. However I do concede there is a type of crisis in eschatology, but it is not from past theologians, but rather it's because of the current lack of proper eschatological teaching from within the church. The crisis is easily evidenced by the many and varied disagreements concerning the return of Christ and the resurrection and rapture of the saints, especially as they pertain to their placement in the sequence of end times. You may speak with ten people and come away with ten opinions. But should this be the norm? Either Scripture has somewhere revealed the truth of the sequence of end-time events or it has not. And if it has, one would certainly believe that the sequence must be obtainable, and if it is obtainable, one must also believe that it is the Lord's will that it should be determined.

In order to do this, I invite you to accompany me on a brief journey, beginning with Paul's short stay with the Thessalonians and the examination of his two subsequent letters addressed to them, then reviewing Christ's intimate discussion with his disciples on the Mount of Olives, and eventually arriving on the Isle of Patmos, where a disciple named John saw visions of the future while in the Spirit. Why these three stops? Although short sequences of end times are scattered throughout the Old and New Testaments, it is within these three sources where the greatest quantity of future events are placed in their proper chronology—and it is done so on several occasions. As you and I travel together from Thessalonica to Jerusalem, and from Jerusalem to the Isle of Patmos, I hope that you will sense some of the protective nature of Paul and the parental concern he possessed for his children in the faith at Thessalonica, the solemnity and gravity of the hour as Jesus sits surrounded by his zealous but naive disciples on the Mount of Olives, and the awe-struck, almost adrenaline-like induced excitement of John as he sees one fantastic scene after another, standing in the presence of the Father, the Son, and the Holy Spirit, as well as myriads and myriads of heavenly angelic beings. Sometimes the journey will be accompanied by straightforward and

---

4. Schweitzer, *Quest of the Historical Jesus*, 356–57.

familiar commentary and, at other times, the discussions might suddenly become unfamiliar and uncomfortably complex. Either way, I hope that you will not take anything for granted, but rather do as the Bereans when they heard Paul's teachings for the first time:

"For they welcomed the message very eagerly and examined the scriptures every day to see whether these things were so" (Acts 17:11b).

My advice to do as the Bereans is because I'm sure you have read studies of end times where an author said this will happen and then this will happen, but without any detailed biblical explanation. Of course, what the author said might sound factual and indisputable because you've heard it countless times before, but nevertheless, the claims are presented without scriptural substantiation. I hope to prevent that from happening here. As we proceed step by step in our study, I want you to understand scripturally why any event falls at a certain point in the sequence and, if you had previously thought or been taught that event should appear elsewhere, I hope you will be thoroughly convinced of its newfound location in your mind before turning the page.

During the study, when we come to a new topic or an event for the first time in a certain passage, I will not necessarily reveal everything that will eventually be written on the subject. As an example, when we come across the Day of the Lord in 1 and 2 Thessalonians, I will not discuss the voluminous information about the Day that is yet to come from our study in the Olivet Discourse and Revelation. Likewise, even within Revelation, when we come across the subject of the 144,000 Jewish remnant in Rev 7, we will not exhaust our discussion on the subject before gathering additional information when we see them again in Rev 14. Furthermore, I will never attempt to prematurely convince you of any event's final place in the end-time sequence, especially if the passage under discussion doesn't supply the needed information to make such a decision. Rather, I will only place the event in the sequence when sufficient information has been gathered. Remember, I want you, the reader, to gradually progress in the knowledge of the subject or event as we together collect information in increments, from passage to passage. Because of this approach, you will note several times throughout the book, I will say concerning any question that might arise that we must wait for more information before determining the correct answer. The needed information might be on the next page or the next chapter, but either way, if a question has been brought up, I can assure you an answer awaits. Again, my goal is for you to experience the process of determining the

INTRODUCTION

correct sequence of end-time events, step by step, without someone just presenting a sequence without biblical substantiation. In essence, I have purposed this book twofold: Certainly to present the correct sequence of end times, hence the title of the book, but also to provide one the ability to determine the correct sequence by seeing familiar passages with a new and fresh perspective.

You will soon realize that there are many tables and lists—lots of them! If I were trying to impress you with style, there would be zero. But my goal is not necessarily to provide you with an eloquent treatise, but rather to provide you with any means possible to learn the fail-safe process of deductive reasoning in order to determine the correct sequence of end times, and to do that, lists and tables seemed an effective way to assist in that regard. As an example, a common use of the charts and tables will be to periodically provide the reader a list of three or four options for answers to certain questions that inevitably present themselves in the process of determining the sequence. Next, the incorrect options will be eliminated one by one by the use of some common sense and deductive reasoning until the correct answer remains (this process of reasoning is called *reductio ad absurdum*).[5] The technique is so successful, that many biblical questions that have seemed heretofore unanswerable will be solved quite easily by this method. It is my contention that almost without exception scriptural passages have only one correct interpretation and, whether it is successfully discovered or not, the correct interpretation is close at hand, waiting to be pursued with as much vigor and determination as one can possibly muster. And if successful, the reward will be the correct sequence of end times as well as delivering the church from the real "crisis in eschatology."

The three sources will yield six sequences. As stated in the preface, I have labeled the six sequences as follows: Sequence in 1 and 2 Thessalonians, Sequence in the Olivet Discourse, First Sequence of Revelation (Parts 1–5), Second Sequence in Revelation, Third Sequence in Revelation, and, finally, Fourth Sequence in Revelation (Parts 1–3). And although the overwhelming content of this study is devoted to the four sequences in Revelation, the two determined from 1 and 2 Thessalonians and the Olivet Discourse are no less important. In fact, if the believer had only the sequence derived from Paul's two letters or the one from the Lord's Olivet

---

5. In logic, *reductio ad absurdum* is the form of argument that seeks to establish the truth of a claim by showing that opposing views will lead to absurdity or contradiction.

Discourse, he or she would possess sufficient knowledge of the end times. But for Scripture to provide all six is almost too good to be true.

The following is a schematic showing the relationship of the time periods covered by the six sequences from the perspective of the abomination of desolation and Christ's return:

Table Introduction.1. The Relationship of the Six Sequences			
		<——1 & 2 Thessalonians——>	
	<————The Olivet Discourse————>		
	<—————1st Sequence in Revelation—————>		
<-2nd Seq. Rev->			
<-3rd Seq. Rev->			
	<————4th Sequence in Revelation————>		
^			^
Abomination of Desolation			Christ's Return

Although a few sequences contain more events than others, at no time will any of the six contradict each other. All of the events within one sequence will align perfectly with those of the remaining five. In this regard, the relationship between the sequences may be said to compare to a harmony of the Gospels: All are unique, yet all agree.

The format of the book is as follows: At the end of each of the twelve chapters, with few exceptions, a chart will reflect the determined sequence of events gathered from the passages of Scripture addressed within that particular chapter. Of course, each chart will vary in size, depending upon the number of sequences represented (from one to six), as well as the number of events covered within the chapter. At the end of the twelve chapters, however, the reader will be pleased to find "Appendix A: Chart Showing the Complete Reconciliation of the Six Sequences," which reconciles all of the end-time events determined from each of the sources; this final chart will span approximately forty pages.[6] Concerning the sources themselves, the study will follow the pattern of many commentaries, whereby the verses under discussion, e.g., from 1 Thess 4 and 5, 2 Thess 1 and 2, the Olivet Discourse, and Rev 4–22, will be shown as extracts followed by commentary as well as auxiliary verses in regular print. Furthermore, since the primary purpose of this study is to

6. See p. 421.

INTRODUCTION

determine the sequence of end times as opposed to writing an in-depth commentary, per se, some verses may be accompanied by sparse commentary because they have been deemed to have no bearing on the end-time sequence. And, finally, unless otherwise noted, all quoted Scripture will come from the New Revised Standard Version, abbreviated NRSV.

Now, with the two letters from Paul in one hand, and logic and reasoning in the other, let's determine the end-time sequence Paul expected to witness and subsequently passed along to a newly formed, somewhat confused, little church. Our first stop is Thessalonica.

CHAPTER 1

Sequence in 1 and 2 Thessalonians

AT A CERTAIN POINT in their lives, someone brought the good news to the Thessalonians that they had the opportunity to be placed in a right relationship with the Creator of the universe, and this most gracious opportunity had been provided by a man that had been crucified several years earlier in the distant city of Jerusalem, and as proof of this wonderful news, the man, Jesus Christ of Nazareth, had been raised from the dead three days after his crucifixion. When another man, the one who brought this good news, entered their city, onlookers were no doubt filled with some curiosity and compassion because of the appearance of the diminutive figure, who was carrying fresh wounds and bruises from a recent and severe beating because he had brought the same gospel to a previous city. Of course, the man was none other than the apostle Paul. Individuals of the city receiving his entourage took him in and tended to his wounds, wounds that both he and his partner, Silas, received while in the Roman colony of Philippi, just north of Thessalonica.

Over a period of the next three sabbaths, Paul began to present the Thessalonians with some of the basic foundational teachings of Christianity. He probably began with his personal testimony and shared how he had heard the voice of the risen Jesus Christ on the road to Damascus and saw a light brighter than the sun, leaving him blind for three days. Perhaps he shared details of his and Silas's most recent arrest and ordeal of being severely beaten in Philippi and imprisoned before a miraculous earthquake swung the doors open of a dark and dingy jail cell (1 Thess 2:2). Eventually, however, he began to teach on faith, love, holiness, and the expected soon return of the man whom he had seen on the road to Damascus—the same one who had been crucified on a cross in Jerusalem and resurrected three days later—the man, Christ Jesus.

After a few days of fellowship and teaching, just as they had seen Paul arrive on the dusty road leading into the city, there came the urgent moment that he had to leave the city. Paul, with his life threatened by some jealous Jews that had followed him from Philippi, coupled with some ruffians from Thessalonica, was ushered out of town by the brothers under the cover of darkness. But, thankfully, he does not leave the Thessalonians as he found them. Many are now born-again, basking in the joy of the Holy Spirit and having a brand new outlook on the future. Now, as they return to the rigors of everyday life, they have an added bounce in their step and a wonderful anticipation accompanying their daily routine: They are now eagerly waiting for the return of the One from heaven whom Paul had preached and taught about for the past several weeks.

However, in the weeks and months to follow, there was a gradual and increasing anxiety spreading throughout the little church: What will happen to the recently departed relatives and friends who have died in Christ since the apostle left? Paul had been made aware of this news because Timothy, one of Paul's young assistants, had been sent on a mission to assess the state of the community's well-being and had just come back from visiting them and relayed to the apostle their anxiety-filled questions (1 Thess 3:1–6). Paul carefully listens to his assistant and responds to the newly formed band of believers by writing them a letter. A few paragraphs into the letter, he addressed their specific concern for those who had recently died:

> But we do not want you to be uninformed, brothers and sisters, about those who have died, so that you may not grieve as others do who have no hope. For since we believe that Jesus died and rose again, even so, through Jesus, God will bring with him those who have died. For this we declare to you by the word of the Lord, that we who are alive, who are left until the coming of the Lord, will by no means precede those who have died. For the Lord himself, with a cry of command, with the archangel's call and with the sound of God's trumpet, will descend from heaven, and the dead in Christ will rise first. Then we who are alive, who are left, will be caught up in the clouds together with them to meet the Lord in the air; and so we will be with the Lord forever. Therefore encourage one another with these words. (1 Thess 4:13–18)

As mentioned, the possibility that one or more church members had died since Paul's departure seems to be the issue, but for the members to be so uninformed as to what will eventually happen to them seems curious. When present with them, surely one would think that Paul had described what will happen to the dead in Christ as well as to those who are alive and left when the Lord returns. Perhaps Paul didn't emphasize the fate of the dead in Christ as much as he did the living because he was very cognizant of the fact that the Thessalonians did not have any relatives who had previously died in Christ prior to his visit, since he was the first one to present the gospel to them. And as far as the new converts were concerned, Paul may not have been overly concerned about the unexpected demise of any of them because he fully expected the soon return of Christ. Here are two verses that reveal Paul's expectation:

1. "For this we declare to you by the word of the Lord, that we who are alive, who are left until the coming of the Lord, will by no means precede those who have died" (1 Thess 4:15).
2. "Then we who are alive, who are left, will be caught up in the clouds together with them to meet the Lord in the air . . ." (1 Thess 4:17a).

Although he obviously wasn't, Paul believed he was going to be among the ones who would be alive and left until the coming of the Lord. The word translated "coming" is from the very familiar Greek word *parousia*. Therefore, Paul fully expected to still be alive at the *parousia* of Christ. And since Paul believed that he and the Thessalonians would be living at the Lord's return, this assumption could very well be the reason for his sparse teaching on the subject of the resurrection of the dead to the new converts. When this assumption is coupled with the Thessalonians' presumed lack of general knowledge on the subject of the Jewish belief in the resurrection of the dead, it becomes very easy to understand the predominantly gentile church's state of confusion on the subject.

The Resurrection and Rapture of the Saints

Whatever the circumstances, Paul now addresses the scenarios of both the dead and the living at Christ's return. He assured the Thessalonians that there is nothing to worry about. Good things will happen to the dead in Christ at his *parousia* even before good things happen to the living. Notwithstanding the apostle's teaching on the subject while with them, the new converts now receive the full impetus of Paul's knowledge concerning the timing associated with the gathering of the dead in Christ and the gathering of those who are living at the resurrection event. The dead in Christ will be gathered first—then the living. At some point near or at the Lord's *parousia*, Christ will descend, the dead will be raised, and then the living will be caught up in the air with them to meet the Lord in the air. Here's the brief sequence of events surrounding the gathering of the saints:

Table 1.1. Events Surrounding the Gathering of the Saints in 1 Thess 4:16–17	
1. A cry of command	4. Jesus descends from heaven
2. The archangel's call	5. The dead in Christ rise first
3. The sound of God's trumpet	6. Then those who are alive and left are caught up together with them to meet the Lord in the air

Notice that I didn't say this series of events describes the *parousia* of the Lord, but rather "the gathering" of the saints. Why? Because that's the way Paul worded it. He did not necessarily say that the gathering of the saints and the *parousia* are one and the same; he simply said at the time of the Lord's *parousia*, there will be two groups of saints: those who are still living at the moment of the *parousia* and those who have already died prior to the *parousia*. He then proceeds to describe how both groups will be gathered to the Lord: First the dead in Christ, then the living. Again, he never committed to the fact that the *parousia* and the gathering occur simultaneously. When researching how Paul dealt elsewhere with the subject of the resurrection's timing in relation to the *parousia*, the following is what the apostle later told the Corinthians:

"For since death came through a human being, the resurrection of the dead has also come through a human being; for as all die in Adam, so all will be made alive in Christ. But each in his own order: Christ the first fruits, then at his coming, those who belong to Christ" (1 Cor 15:21–23).

To the Thessalonians he said the resurrection-event would not occur "until" the *parousia* (1 Thess 4:15), and to the Corinthians, he said the resurrection would occur "at" the *parousia* (1 Cor 15:23). Whether "until the *parousia*" or "at the *parousia*," either phrase technically indicates that the resurrection event will occur in close proximity, time-wise, to the coming of the Lord, but not necessarily simultaneously with the coming. Therefore, one is left with the nagging question of what is the exact relationship between the *parousia* of the Lord and the resurrection of the saints. Here are the only three possibilities:

Table 1.2. Relationship between the Coming of the Lord and the Resurrection/Rapture Event
Option #1: The resurrection/rapture event will occur before the coming of Christ.
Option #2: The resurrection/rapture event will occur simultaneously with the coming of Christ.
Option #3: The resurrection/rapture event will occur after the coming of Christ.

When Paul told the Thessalonians that the resurrection would not occur "until the coming" and then later told the Corinthians that the resurrection would occur "at the coming of the Lord," little did the apostle realize that he was leaving open the possibility for many differing and opposing opinions with these statements. How so? Today, there are those who believe each of the above options. And the proponents for each option are adamant that they, alone, are correct. But as was stated in the introduction of this study, only one option can be correct. Now, it's a matter of finding it. Unfortunately, Paul will not satisfactorily clarify the precise relationship between the *parousia* and the gathering of the saints in either 1 or 2 Thessalonians, but thankfully, before we finish our study in 2 Thessalonians, at least one of the three options will be eliminated. And of course, somewhere in our later study of Revelation the correct option will be positively identified.

After Paul told the Corinthians that the resurrection would occur "at" the *parousia*, he then shared with the church the same teaching he had given the Thessalonians, and that was of the two-part gathering of the saints—but this time he added the revelation of a spectacular miracle accompanying the event:

"Listen, I will tell you a mystery! We will not all die, but we will be changed, in a moment, in the twinkling of an eye, at the last trumpet. For the trumpet will sound, and the dead will be raised imperishable, and we will be changed. For this perishable body must put on imperishability, and this mortal body must put on immortality" (1 Cor 15:51–53).

Not only will the saints be caught up together to meet the Lord in the air, but they will receive glorious and indestructible new bodies. Furthermore, those who are living at the *parousia* will not be required to go through death's door in order to receive this glorified body! As the living saints are still standing and breathing, God will instantly transform their natural bodies into glorified bodies. Note that Paul's phrase "in the twinkling of an eye" specifically applies to the instant "transformation" (Greek: *allagēsometha*) from the natural body to the glorified body; it doesn't necessarily have anything to do with the speed with which the saints will be gathered or caught up, which may, or may not, be a rapid event.

For whatever reason, the miracle of the glorified body was not divulged to the Thessalonians as it was to the Corinthians. However, when one combines Paul's revelations of the resurrection-event given to both churches, they are almost too much to fathom: At some point in close proximity to the *parousia* of the Lord, whether before, simultaneously, or after, the saints will be gathered and caught up to meet the Lord in the air, with brand new, glorified bodies! And lest one forgets, Paul expected to be among the living saints, at the time of the *parousia*.

The Day of the Lord

Having allayed their concerns for those who have died, Paul next turns to their second concern: What about the times and seasons? Not only did the Thessalonians want to know what was going to happen to their loved ones who had passed away, but they wanted to know when all of these events were going to take place. Here's Paul's answer:

> Now concerning the times and the seasons, brothers and sisters, you do not need to have anything written to you. For you yourselves know very well that the day of the Lord will come like a thief in the night. When they say, "There is peace and security," then sudden destruction will come upon them, as labor pains come upon a pregnant woman, and there will be no escape! But you, beloved, are not in darkness, for that day to surprise you like a thief; for you are all children of light and children of the day; we are not of the night or of darkness. So then let us not fall asleep as others do, but let us keep awake and be sober; for those who sleep sleep at night, and those who are drunk get drunk at night. (1 Thess 5:1–7)

Before delving into his answer, it seems that one can detect a slight reprimand in Paul's first few words: "you do not need to have anything written to you." Whatever Paul is about to say in the letter, one gets the impression that he thought he covered this part of the subject sufficiently when he had visited them. Nevertheless, he said, "For you yourselves know very well that the day of the Lord will come like a thief in the night. When they say, 'There is peace and security,' then sudden destruction will come upon them, as labor pains come upon a pregnant woman, and there will be no escape!" Instead of responding by saying the return of Christ and the gathering of the saints will happen at such and such a time, Paul instead speaks of the Day of the Lord. Why the switch from speaking one moment about the coming of the Lord and the gathering of the saints, and the very next moment, he brings up the Day of the Lord? Are they the same? When Paul said the Day of the Lord will come like a thief in the night, did this mean that the coming of the Lord will come like a thief in the night, or that the resurrection of the saints will come like a thief in the night, or perhaps was Paul separating the arrival of the Day of the Lord from the arrival of the coming of Christ, and perhaps, even from the arrival of the gathering of the saints? Here, we are not only faced with the question of when the Day of the Lord will arrive, but what is the Day of the Lord? Concerning the latter, Paul said the Day will bring sudden and unexpected destruction upon "them" when they are saying there is peace and security. Just from this one statement, one knows that God will bring destruction upon those whom he deems worthy of destruction at a time when they naively believe nothing will happen to them. This scenario is similar to the days of Noah and Lot, when God sent judgment and wrath against the unrighteous when they least expected it. Concerning the question as to when the Day will come in the sequence of end times, in order to make things somewhat easier to analyze and since Paul has already indicated that the coming of the Lord and the gathering of the saints will occur at approximately the same time, let's for the time being temporarily consider the coming of the Lord and resurrection of the saints as one unit, occurring at the same time, and then see how the Day of the Lord might possibly relate time-wise to that one unit. Here are the options:

Table 1.3. Relationship between the Day of the Lord and the Coming of the Lord and the Resurrection of the Saints
Option #1: The Day of the Lord arrives before the coming of the Lord/resurrection of the saints.
Option #2: The Day of the Lord and the coming of the Lord/resurrection of the saints occur simultaneously.
Option #3: The Day of the Lord arrives after the coming of the Lord/resurrection of the saints.

Before making any hasty decisions, we can make a few preliminary observations concerning option #3, which suggests that the Day of the Lord arrives after the coming of the Lord/resurrection of the saints. Since the Thessalonians were obviously inquisitive about the timing of the end-time events, why would Paul begin by describing in detail the onset of the Day of the Lord, if it were a separate event that occurred after the coming of the Lord and resurrection of the saints, in which the resurrection and rapture event, in particular, would necessarily place the Thessalonians already caught up to be with the Lord, perhaps even up to heaven? In other words, why would Paul attempt to comfort the Thessalonians, who were obviously anxious about the times and seasons of end-time events, by addressing an end-time event, i.e., the Day of the Lord, that would not affect them in the least? In that same vein of reasoning, notice that Paul even told the Thessalonians that they were not in darkness for the Day to surprise them, and furthermore, they belonged to the Day of the Lord. One must admit, these are strange descriptions by Paul of the relationship between the Day of the Lord and the Thessalonians, if Paul knew they will be in heaven while the Day is commencing on the earth. If the Thessalonians are in heaven while the Day is occurring on the earth, then how could the Thessalonians belong to the Day? Something sounds amiss.

With just these simple deductive reasonings, the probability that Paul taught that the Day of the Lord will arrive after the coming of the Lord and resurrection of the saints seems unlikely. However, it's still prudent to gather more evidence before completely eliminating option #3.

The Armor of God and That Evil Day

After the apostle encouraged the Thessalonians to keep awake and be sober after having discussed the Day of the Lord, he commanded them to put on the armor of God:

> But since we belong to the day, let us be sober, and put on the breastplate of faith and love, and for a helmet the hope of salvation. (1 Thess 5:8)

Then, in the very next sentence, Paul gives one of the greatest promises in all of Scripture, not to mention one of the most commonly used verses by many to defend a myriad of stances regarding the sequence of end times:

SEQUENCE IN 1 AND 2 THESSALONIANS

> For God has destined us not for wrath but for obtaining salvation through our Lord Jesus Christ, who died for us, so that whether we are awake or asleep we may live with him. Therefore encourage one another and build up each other, as indeed you are doing. (1 Thess 5:9–11)

Paul clearly said that the believer is not the object of God's wrath. Case closed. There's no reason to argue the point. If Paul is confident of the certainty of the statement, then we must also be confident. But why would Paul tell the Thessalonians to put on the breastplate of faith and for a helmet the hope of salvation immediately after discussing the Day of the Lord, a day which clearly initiates God's wrath against the unrighteous, unless perhaps the righteous need some sort of added protection against what the Day brings? But that doesn't make any sense, especially since Paul immediately followed the instruction to wear the breastplate and helmet with the promise that the believer is not destined for God's wrath. So what are we missing? The answer to our mystery is found in Paul's similar instruction that he later gave to the Ephesians:

"Therefore take up the whole armor of God, so that you may be able to withstand on that evil day, and having done everything, to stand firm. Stand therefore, and fasten the belt of truth around your waist, and put on the breastplate of righteousness. As shoes for your feet put on whatever will make you ready to proclaim the gospel of peace. With all of these, take the shield of faith, with which you will be able to quench all the flaming arrows of the evil one. Take the helmet of salvation, and the sword of the Spirit, which is the word of God. Pray in the Spirit at all times in every prayer and supplication. To that end keep alert and always persevere in supplication for all the saints" (Eph 6:13–18).

By the time Paul wrote to the Ephesians, his earlier use of the illustration of a simple armor of God to the Thessalonians—the breastplate of faith and love and the helmet of salvation—had developed into a full-fledged, detailed armor of God. Now the armor included the belt of truth, the breastplate of righteousness, shoes to enable one to proclaim the gospel of peace, the shield of faith, the helmet of salvation, and last but not least, the sword of the Spirit, which is the word of God. Although there is more detail, make no mistake, it's the same armor of God that the Thessalonians were instructed to wear. But unlike the letter to the Thessalonians, Paul reveals in the letter to the Ephesians the reason for the armor. Although truth, righteousness, the readiness to witness, faith, and the word of God should be worn every day during the life of the believer, still, as he did to the Thessalonians, Paul applies the phrase in an apocalyptic sense—in preparation for the end times. How can one be sure of that? By a third illustration. See how he spoke to the Romans about the last days and the armor of God:

"Besides this, you know what time it is, how it is now the moment for you to wake from sleep. For salvation is nearer to us now than when we became believers; the night is far gone, the day is near. Let us then lay aside the works of darkness and put on the armor of light; let us live honorably as in the day, not in reveling and drunkenness, not in debauchery and licentiousness, not in quarreling and jealousy. Instead, put on the Lord Jesus Christ, and make no provision for the flesh, to gratify its desires" (Rom 13:11–14).

Whether it's a nondescript armor to the Thessalonians, a detailed armor to the Ephesians, or just simply putting on the armor of light to the Romans, Paul was constantly urging the church to put on the armor of God in preparation for a period that lies on the distant horizon. Although the reader may have overlooked it, in the correspondence to the Ephesians Paul named the period (italics used for emphasis):

"Therefore take up the whole armor of God, so that you may be able to withstand on *that evil day*, and having done everything, to stand firm" (Eph 6:13).

The armor of God is to be worn in preparation for what the apostle refers to as "that evil day." And when that day comes, believers are not told to run or cower in fear, but rather, to stand their ground.

So how are we to view this "evil day" alongside the Day of the Lord? Although both days lie in the future, as it stands at this point in our study, we don't know if the two periods are congruent, overlap, or are completely separate periods. However, we do know that the character of each day is different from the sheer fact of their labels: The Day of the Lord is just, righteous, and holy. After all, it's God's Day. We've learned that the Day will come like a thief in the night and bring wrath and destruction upon the unrighteous, who clearly deserve it. But not so the righteous: They are instructed not to fear the Day or any wrath that may accompany it because the righteous are not destined for God's wrath, but rather for obtaining salvation through the Lord Jesus Christ. On the other hand, "that evil day" is, for lack of a better term, evil! And despite the believers' covering and promised protection from God's wrath during the Day of the Lord, Paul, almost with a sense of extreme urgency, implores the saints to put on the armor of God in preparation for what lies ahead during "that evil day."

The Revelation of Jesus Christ

When receiving the first letter, one of the leaders of the congregation probably stood up in front of the congregation and read the much anticipated note from the hand of Paul, and after it was read the church's anxiety soon subsided. Although undergoing tremendous persecution, there was now the comfort of knowing that the departed loved ones would surely be seen again, and that newfound knowledge, coupled with Paul's in-depth teaching on the glorious resurrection and rapture of the saints, as well as being given the promise that God's wrath was not their destiny, gave the church the fortitude to stand on her own two feet, only depending on the guidance and comfort of the Holy Spirit.

Although, the first letter brought invaluable answers to many of their questions, the Thessalonians continued to undergo severe persecution and suffering, which, upon reflection, may have been the reason behind the recent deaths which prompted the need for the initial letter in the first place. But now Paul learns that there is a new anxiousness spreading throughout the little church because of a recent misunderstanding of Paul's teaching on the sequence of end-time events, specifically concerning his last subject of the letter, the Day of the Lord. Once Paul decided on how he would handle the situation, he began his introduction to the second letter by reviewing the events surrounding the church's most anticipated event, the revelation of Jesus Christ, also known as the *parousia*:

> Therefore we ourselves boast of you among the churches of God for your steadfastness and faith during all your persecutions and the afflictions that you are enduring. This is evidence of the righteous judgment of God, and is intended to make you worthy of the kingdom of God, for which you are also suffering. For it is indeed just of God to repay with affliction those who afflict you, and to give relief to the afflicted as well as to us, when the Lord Jesus is revealed from heaven with his mighty angels in flaming fire, inflicting vengeance on those who do not know God and on those who do not obey the gospel of our Lord Jesus. These will suffer the punishment of eternal destruction, separated from the presence of the Lord and from the glory of his might . . . (2 Thess 1:4–9).

After assuring the Thessalonians that he was well aware of their present suffering, he reminded them that one day justice would prevail. He said when Jesus is revealed from heaven with his angels in flaming fire, that the Lord will bring relief, or rest, to both him and them, as well as affliction to those who have afflicted the church and the apostle. Again, in no uncertain terms, Paul expected to weather whatever preceded the revelation of Jesus Christ and therefore to be alive and waiting for the Lord at his return. The relief that Paul expects is translated from the Greek word *anesin* and can be translated repose, freedom, liberty, ease, rest, or, as translated by the NRSV, relief. Whatever the precise meaning Paul had in mind, one can be sure that the apostle expected good things at the Lord's revelation.

Paul's expectation that he and the Thessalonians will receive relief or rest or ease at Christ's *parousia* happens to eliminate one of the three options concerning the question of the time-relationship between the coming of the Lord and the resurrection of the saints, presented in the first letter. Here was that earlier table:

Table 1.2. Relationship between the Coming of the Lord and the Resurrection/Rapture Event
Option #1: The resurrection/rapture event will occur before the coming of Christ.
Option #2: The resurrection/rapture event will occur simultaneously with the coming of Christ.
Option #3: The resurrection/rapture event will occur after the coming of Christ.

If the resurrection and rapture truly occurred before the appearance of the Lord, as option #1 suggests, then the saints would have already received their glorified bodies, as per 1 Cor 15:50–53, and would therefore be in no need of relief, or rest, or ease—or any other translation of the word *anesin*—at the Lord's coming. Whether in heaven or on earth, glorified, indestructible, immortal bodies do not need anything, especially relief or rest or ease. Natural bodies need rest. That the saints, according to Paul, will be in a position to need and receive this "relief" at the coming of the Lord necessarily means the saints have not received their glorified bodies prior to the *parousia*, therefore proving the resurrection has not occurred prior to the *parousia*, thereby eliminating option #1. (Technically option #1 was already eliminated by something Paul said in the first letter. When the apostle proclaimed, "For this we declare to you by the word of the

Lord, that we who are alive, who are left until the coming of the Lord, will by no means precede those who have died," he clearly indicated that the resurrection and rapture of the saints will not occur prior to the Lord's *parousia*, which in and of itself eliminated option #1.)

Paul's statements in 1 and 2 Thessalonians leave only the possibility that the resurrection/rapture will occur simultaneously with the coming of Christ (option #2) or after the coming (option #3). As indicated earlier, Paul will not further distinguish between these two options during the remainder of the second letter; therefore we will have to wait until our studies in the Olivet Discourse and Revelation before determining the answer.

Next, Paul continues to describe the scenario of the revelation of Christ by saying that the saints will glorify and marvel at Christ when they initially see him:

> . . . when he comes to be glorified by his saints and to be marveled at on that day among all who have believed, because our testimony to you was believed. To this end we always pray for you, asking that our God will make you worthy of his call and will fulfill by his power every good resolve and work of faith, so that the name of our Lord Jesus may be glorified in you, and you in him, according to the grace of our God and the Lord Jesus Christ. (2 Thess 1:10–12)

Notice the stark difference between the roles of the angels (1:7–8) and that of the saints at the Lord's *parousia* (1:10). Whereas the Lord's accompanying angels will obviously be bent on war at the revelation of Christ, the saints, on the other hand, will attempt to take in the never-before-seen spectacle as they marvel at the appearance of Jesus, while simultaneously giving him glory. It should go without saying that the heavenward gaze of the saints juxtaposed with the downward, earthly glare of the angels yields quite a contrast and therefore the roles held by both groups should never be confused. Since no one thinks the angels will take the place of the saints, who are clearly portrayed as looking upward and marveling at Christ's appearance, I ask you, Why would anyone believe the saints could possibly take the place of the angels, who are clearly described as the ones accompanying Jesus at his revelation, in flaming fire no less, and bent on war?

Great Expectations

Of course, neither Paul nor the members of the little church would be alive to see the *parousia* of the Lord Jesus. Paul and the Thessalonians have long since gone on to be with the Lord, but that does not change one very significant fact: Whatever Paul "expected" would happen to him and the Thessalonians "will" happen to the last generation of believers living at the time of the Lord's return. The logic is elementary, but for some reason it is difficult for many to grasp. Although Paul didn't know for certain the exact relationship between the timing of his own death and the coming of the Lord, one must never forget that Paul knew the correct sequence of end times and that was true whether he was part of the last generation or not. Early in his ministry, which was when Paul wrote to the Thessalonians, it is quite evident that the apostle thought he would be living at the Lord's *parousia*. Therefore, in Paul's mind, he fully expected to be united with Jesus by way of the rapture and not by the resurrection. However, as his ministry progressed, the moment came when Paul understood that his earlier expectations were not to be. This is very clear from his final words to Timothy:

"As for me, I am already being poured out as a libation, and the time of my departure has come. I have fought the good fight, I have finished the race, I have kept the faith. From now on there is reserved for me the crown of righteousness, which the Lord, the righteous judge, will give me on that day, and not only to me but also to all who have longed for his appearing" (2 Tim 4:6–8).

Instead of living through the end-time persecution that would lead up to the moment of Christ's coming and the time that God would bring relief to him and the Thessalonians, Paul came to the realization that he was going to die a martyr before the glorious event of the revelation of Jesus Christ. In the following passage, one can see how his expectations had already changed from the time he wrote 1 and 2 Thessalonians to the time he wrote Philippians:

"I want to know Christ and the power of his resurrection and the sharing of his sufferings by becoming like him in his death, if somehow I may attain the resurrection from the dead" (Phil 3:10–11).

Instead of expecting to be raptured, he now places all of his hope in the resurrection.

Paul Addresses the Day of the Lord a Second Time

The salutation and introductory remarks concerning the revelation of Christ are over, and now comes the occasion for the second letter. For some reason, perhaps a slight misunderstanding of Paul's closing remarks in the first letter, or a memory loss of certain details of the apostle's teaching when he had visited them, or some false teaching from an outsider, or most likely, a combination of all three, the Thessalonians had come to believe that the Day of the Lord had arrived. Here's Paul's response:

> As to the coming of our Lord Jesus Christ and our being gathered together to him, we beg you, brothers and sisters, not to be quickly shaken in mind or alarmed, either by spirit or by word or by letter, as though from us, to the effect that the day of the Lord is already here. Let no one deceive you in any way; for that day will not come unless the rebellion comes first and the lawless one is revealed, the one destined for destruction. He opposes and exalts himself above every so-called god or object of worship, so that he takes his seat in the temple of God, declaring himself to be God. Do you not remember that I told you these things when I was still with you? (2 Thess 2:1–5)

Unless we know the exact meaning of the Day of the Lord as well as the sequence of events that Paul taught the Thessalonians, then the fact that they thought the Day had arrived doesn't help us comprehend the problem with which they presented Paul. Nevertheless, regardless of our comprehension of the problem, Paul did not believe their error was insurmountable. He simply told them that it was impossible that the Day had arrived because the rebellion and the revealing of the man of lawlessness must first occur. It appears that Paul suspected that much of the misunderstanding was simply because the Thessalonians had forgotten these two facts, because he subsequently said, "Do you not remember that I told you these things when I was still with you?" Despite whatever they were thinking and despite whatever may have caused it, Paul's simple reminder of these two facts apparently resolved the misunderstanding. (Don't you wish every theological problem could be resolved so easily!)

Still, what were they actually thinking? Today, some have suggested that the Thessalonians thought they had missed the coming of the Lord, missed the resurrection and rapture of the church, and were now about to face whatever perils the Day of the Lord might bring. In other words, they thought they had been "left behind"![1] It's an interesting theory, and a surprisingly popular theory as well, but nevertheless, it is impossible. The Thessalonians didn't think the Lord had returned or the resurrection and rapture had occurred, any more than you and I think that today; they were not ignorant. Just as you and I have not seen Jesus light up the sky, neither had the Thessalonians; just as you and I have not noticed any missing relatives or friends in the faith, neither had the Thessalonians. And just as you and I have not noticed some great vacuum in society because of the sudden disappearance of the church from the earth's population, neither had the Thessalonians. Furthermore, if the little church had truly thought they had missed the rapture, what did they think of the apostle Paul and his entourage concerning the rapture? After all, were not the Thessalonians in constant correspondence with Paul through his assistant, Timothy? If the Thessalonians thought they had missed the rapture, what must they have thought of poor Timothy and Paul and his helpers, who were still canvassing the earth and spreading the good news of Christ? (Of course, I am being facetious.) However, the fact remains that the Thessalonians knew they hadn't missed the rapture any more than Paul had. Their thinking that the Day of the Lord had arrived meant something, but "the missed-the-rapture theory" wasn't it.

What Did Paul Teach concerning the Day?

Recall back in the first letter, when Paul initially brought up the subject of the Day of the Lord while addressing the question of the times and seasons, we were unsure of the sequence of the Day of the Lord in relation to the coming of the Lord and the resurrection of the saints. When preparing to examine that relationship, we had suggested that the coming of Christ and the gathering of the saints should be temporarily considered as one unit, just for the sake of simplicity. Here were the options:

---

1. Walvoord, *Rapture Question*, 240.

Table 1.3. Relationship between the Day of the Lord, and the Coming of the Lord and the Resurrection
Option #1: The Day of the Lord arrives before the coming of the Lord/resurrection of the saints.
Option #2: The Day of the Lord and the coming of the Lord/resurrection of the saints occur simultaneously.
Option #3: The Day of the Lord arrives after the coming of the Lord/resurrection of the saints.

We were already highly suspicious of option #3, questioning why Paul would have chosen to alleviate the concerns of the Thessalonians as to the times and seasons of end-time events by first describing the Day of the Lord, if indeed the Day occurred after the coming of the Lord and resurrection of the saints. It was surmised that, if that were the case, Paul's response would have been nonsensical, discussing an event that would take place on earth only after the Thessalonians were safely in heaven. Now, this most recent dilemma, in which the Thessalonians believed the Day of the Lord had actually arrived, all the while knowing that Jesus had not appeared and the saints had not been resurrected and raptured, proves once and for all that option #3 is indeed impossible. Despite any misunderstanding the Thessalonians may have encountered, they could never have mistakenly believed that the Day had arrived if Paul had truly taught that the coming of Christ and the resurrection of the saints preceded the Day of the Lord. It's one thing to forget that the rebellion and the revealing of the man of lawlessness preceded the Day of the Lord, but no one could possibly forget that the coming of Christ and resurrection of the saints preceded the Day of the Lord, if that's what Paul had actually taught! Would you forget? I know I wouldn't! Therefore it is certain that Paul never taught that the coming of the Lord and resurrection of the saints preceded the Day of the Lord, and with that, option #3 is officially eliminated.

Turning to option #2, which suggests that the three events—the Day of the Lord, the coming of the Lord, and the resurrection of the saints—occur simultaneously (which is a very popular theory), is one that can now be eliminated as well, and very similarly for the reasons that option #3 was eliminated. The fact that the Thessalonians could honestly and legitimately think the Day of the Lord had arrived, and yet all the while know: (1) that the Lord had not appeared in the skies, (2) the dead had not been resurrected, and (3) they themselves had not been raptured and received their glorified bodies proves that Paul could not have taught that those three events occurred simultaneously. Had Paul taught such a doctrine, and the Thessalonians were still somehow incomprehensibly misled into believing that the Day had arrived, the apostle would have simply told the Thessalonians in his second letter that the Day had obviously not arrived because, as they could very well see, the Lord had not appeared and they were still walking around in their natural bodies. But Paul didn't give this simple response for one good reason: He never taught that the three events occur simultaneously. Therefore, option #2 is now eliminated.

Only option #1 remains. The only way the Thessalonians could have conceivably believed that the Day of the Lord had arrived, all the while knowing that Jesus had not appeared and the saints had not been raptured, was if Paul had taught that the Day of the Lord preceded the coming of the Lord and the resurrection of the saints, which is exactly what he taught. When that fact is fully comprehended and then coupled with Paul's reminder that the rebellion and the revealing of the man of lawlessness must precede the Day of the Lord, one can finally ascertain the sequence taught by Paul:

1. The Rebellion and the Revealing of the Man of Lawlessness
2. The Day of the Lord
3. The Coming of Christ and the Gathering of the Saints

By forgetting Paul's teaching that the rebellion and the revealing of the man of the lawlessness must precede the Day of the Lord, the community was easily led to believe the Day had arrived in the midst of their suffering. And what did the Thessalonians expect the Day to bring? Good things or bad things? Unlike what is consistently taught today, which is that the Thessalonians were extremely worried that they had missed the rapture and had fallen into the throes of the Day of the Lord, instead, the Thessalonians were actually cautiously optimistic about the prospect of the Day's arrival. As stated above, from Paul's first letter they knew that the Day would bring destruction and wrath upon the unrighteous like a thief in the night, and therefore the newly formed community understandably surmised that God's overwhelming destruction levied against their persecutors would necessarily bring some measure of relief from their present sufferings. That's not to say they weren't somewhat shaken in mind or alarmed, as Paul implied in 2 Thess 2:2. Certainly when one believes the world as they know is soon coming to an end, there's going to be some anxiety. But despite whatever calamities the Thessalonians thought might accompany the Day, they were still filled with joy at the prospect that they were about to receive at least some measure of relief from their present suffering, and even more importantly, they knew the Day would bring them one step closer to the return of Christ. But as we all well know, the Day had not arrived. Now, Paul had the unpleasant task of letting the Thessalonians know that relief from their present suffering was not just around the corner. However, before bluntly telling them that they were mistaken about the Day's arrival and dashing their misguided hopes of a soon deliverance from suffering, a response that could have done irreparable harm to the weaker converts and, not to mention, cause an embarrassing situation for the entire new community, Paul wisely and tactfully reminded them in the letter's introduction of the glory that one day awaited them, and that was the magnificent and glorious revelation of Jesus Christ. Like a skilled counselor, he told them good news before gently telling them that their expectation of the Day's arrival was unfounded, which was sure to bring the community no little measure of disappointment.

The Man of Lawlessness and That Evil Day

It's now quite apparent why Paul admonished the Thessalonians to put on the armor of God in the first letter. As earlier surmised, and rightfully so, the Thessalonians did not have to put on the armor of God in preparation for the wrath brought by the Day of the Lord, because almost within the same breath, Paul clearly stated that they were not destined for that wrath. And, of course, the believer obviously doesn't need the armor of God in preparation for the appearance of Christ nor the gathering of the saints. (That statement was almost too embarrassing to write!) It is certain that Paul told the believers—specifically, the Thessalonians, the Ephesians, and the Romans—to put on the armor of God in preparation for the period of time corresponding to the rebellion and the revealing of the man of lawlessness, a period of time that we now know arrives before the Day of the Lord. Because of the Lord's many revelations to the apostle, Paul was surely privy to the atrocities that will be perpetrated by the man of lawlessness once he is revealed, and that's doubtless why the apostle called this period of persecution against the saints "that evil day." Observe:

1. The Rebellion and the Revealing of the Man of Lawlessness (*that evil day*)
2. The Day of the Lord
3. The Coming of Christ and the Gathering of the Saints

In retrospect, the Thessalonians were correct when they supposed that their suffering would end or at least be greatly reduced at the arrival of the Day of the Lord. But where they were mistaken was having the assumption that they were going to be alive at the Day's arrival. They were not. And since Paul and the Thessalonians were not part of the last generation, they were never going to experience the suffering caused by the man of lawlessness during "that evil day" nor were they ever going to experience any possible relief from suffering brought by the Day of the Lord or the later manifestation of Christ.

The Man of Lawlessness and the Rebellion

Now, concerning the two events that Paul said must precede the Day of the Lord, which are the rebellion and the revealing of the man of lawlessness, Paul says very little about the rebellion. This could indicate that Paul might have considered the rebellion a subject he had already sufficiently discussed when he was with them and he simply did not think it necessary to address it a second time. Whether that's the case or not, one knows that the rebellion, whatever the meaning, will precede the Day of the Lord. Observe:

"Let no one deceive you in any way; for that day will not come unless the rebellion comes first and the lawless one is revealed, the one destined for destruction" (2 Thess 2:3).

It is commonly agreed upon that when Paul used the word "rebellion" he was referencing a mass falling away of the saints in the last days. The thought is seemingly in line with Christ's words in the Olivet Discourse, although there, technically, the Lord was not speaking of a falling away from the faith in the end-times, but rather a falling away immediately following the martyrdom of the apostles:

"Then they will hand you over to be tortured and will put you to death, and you will be hated by all nations because of my name. Then many will fall away, and they will betray one another and hate one another" (Matt 24:9–10).

In Matthew's account, Jesus employed the word *skandalisthēsontai*, which is here translated "will fall away," as it certainly carries the meaning of a deserting or falling away from the faith. In a later confirmation of the word's meaning, Peter used the same word in a response to Jesus:

"Peter said to him, 'Though all become deserters because of you, I will never desert you'" (Matt 26:33).

The words "deserters" and "will never desert you" come from the same Greek root word used above in Matt 24:9, 10. In essence, Peter was telling the Lord although others may backslide because of fear of persecution, or fear of ridicule, or even love for the things of this world, I will never leave or forsake you.[2]

In the following, Jesus again uses the word when interpreting the meaning of the following portion of the familiar parable of the sower and the seed:

"Other seed fell on rocky ground, where it did not have much soil, and it sprang up quickly, since it had no depth of soil. And when the sun rose, it was scorched; and since it had no root, it withered away" (Mark 4:5–6).

In the above, Jesus said that because some seed fell on rocky ground where it didn't have much soil, that when the sun came up, the seed sprang up quickly before any root could be developed, resulting in the plant being scorched and withering away. Later, the Lord compared the seed to how some people respond to hearing the good news:

"And these are the ones sown on rocky ground: when they hear the word, they immediately receive it with joy. But they have no root, and endure only for a while; then, when trouble or persecution arises on the account of the word, immediately they fall away" (Mark 4:16–17).

Christ's point cannot be missed: This particular group of people received the good news immediately and with joy. There's nothing out of the ordinary with that scenario. That's the testimony of most believers. But here's the problem: Having joyfully committed to the Lord, this group doesn't do what it takes to become established in the Lord, and because of that, the moment persecution or trouble comes (and it will come), they fall away because they are not established in the faith. Again, the word Jesus used for "fall away" in the parable is *skandalizontai*. It carries the same meaning for those who fell away from the faith after the apostles were killed and for Peter who temporarily fell away on the night of Christ's betrayal.

2. Of course, as it turns out, Peter did exactly that on the night of Jesus' betrayal (Matt 26:69–75).

Had Paul used *skandalisthēsontai* in 2 Thess 2:3, there would be little doubt that he was talking about a certain falling away from the faith because of a weakness of some sort prior to the Day of the Lord. But he didn't. Instead, the apostle used the word *apostasia*, which has a significantly different meaning. The word is derived from *apó* meaning "away from" and *histémi* meaning "to stand." Rather than falling away from the faith because of trouble or persecution, *apostasia* conveys a more sinister connotation that literally means "to deliberately leave a previous standing," and for that reason it is very often translated "revolt" or "rebellion." In other words, the person in question leaves the faith not necessarily because he or she was driven away by suffering or persecution, but rather, they "chose" to leave the faith of their own volition. But why would someone leave the faith voluntarily in the last days? Paul reveals the reason as he uses the same Greek derivative in his first written correspondence to Timothy:

"Now the Spirit expressly says that in later times some will renounce the faith by paying attention to deceitful spirits and teachings of demons, through the hypocrisy of liars whose consciences are seared with a hot iron. They forbid marriage and demand abstinence from foods, which God created to be received with thanksgiving by those who believe and know the truth" (1 Tim 4:1–3).

Here, the Holy Spirit said this particular group, unlike the group referenced by Christ during the apostolic age, will be deceived into falling away in the last days by deceitful spirits and demonic teachings. The Greek *apostēsontai*, translated here as "renounce," connotes a deliberate refusal of the truth because of deception by evil spirits. Therefore, it appears that when Paul was writing to Timothy, he was reiterating what he had previously told the Thessalonians, and that is that in the last days there will be a rebellion—a falling away from the faith because of deception. And what was the only difference Paul made to his two addressees? To Timothy, the rebellion in the last days will be directly caused by deception from spirits and demonic teachings; to the Thessalonians, he specifically implies the rebellion will be caused by deception from the man of lawlessness (2 Thess 2:9–12).

In the end, one is sure to know that people in every generation have fallen from the faith because of fear caused by persecution and suffering. This just comes with the territory. The addressees of the author of Hebrews are a perfect example. In their minds, contending for their faith in Christ had become too much of a burden because of the severe suffering that had accompanied Christianity. However, the author reminded them of their earlier fortitude:

"But recall those earlier days when, after you had been enlightened, you endured a hard struggle with sufferings, sometimes being publicly exposed to abuse and persecution, and sometimes being partners with those so treated. For you had compassion for those who were in prison, and you cheerfully accepted the plundering of your possessions, knowing that you yourselves possessed something better and more lasting. Do not, therefore, abandon that confidence of yours; it brings a great reward. For you need endurance, so that when you have done the will of God, you may receive what was promised" (Heb 10:32–36).

Although falling from the faith because of persecution is no excuse, it still happens. However, in the last days, Paul describes an aberration. There will occur a conscious and deliberate mass exodus from the Christian faith because of demonic deception, rather than persecution as one might expect. Nevertheless, whether someone falls away because of persecution (*skandalizontai*) or deception (*apostasia*), the result is the same: they were never part of the elect. The words of the apostle John come to mind:

"They went out from us, but they did not belong to us; for if they had belonged to us, they would have remained with us. But by going out they made it plain that none of them belongs to us" (1 John 2:19).

In other words, persecution or deception will never cause the elect to fall away from the faith.

The Man of Lawlessness and the Temple

Unlike the rebellion, Paul addresses the second prerequisite to the Day of the Lord, the revealing of the man of lawlessness, in quite some depth. Again, here's the text:

"Let no one deceive you in any way; for that day will not come unless the rebellion comes first and the lawless one is revealed, the one destined for destruction. He opposes and exalts himself above every so-called god or object of worship, so that he takes his seat in the temple of God, declaring himself to be God" (2 Thess 2:3–4).

Of all the apocalyptic passages penned by the apostle Paul, few have caused more consternation, speculation, and debate than the above two verses. Some have even doubted Paul's authorship of the second letter because of the difficulty these and other verses present within the epistle, which is quite alarming to say the least.[3] The controversy comes from Paul's statement that the future man of lawlessness, who will be revealed to the church before the arrival of the Day of the Lord, will enter the temple of God and declare himself to be God. But the obvious conundrum is that today there isn't a temple for the man of lawlessness to enter. Herod's Temple, the one standing in Jerusalem when Paul penned the statement, has long since been destroyed. However, according to many, that fact poses no problem because it is asserted that when Paul gave that statement to the Thessalonians, he was never referencing Herod's Temple, but instead was referring to a future temple that was yet to be built. According to the theory, simply because Herod's Temple was torn down by the Romans in AD 70, coupled with the fact that there must be a temple in existence for the man of lawlessness to enter in order to fulfill Paul's prophecy, confirms the fact that Paul must have been referring to a future rebuilt temple. But was that actually what Paul was thinking? When Paul spoke of the man entering the temple, was he indeed referring to a future rebuilt temple or was he referring to Herod's Temple, or, perhaps, was he speaking of neither? We need to determine this answer because the entire premise of a future rebuilt Jewish temple predominately rests on these two verses.

Before exploring any options for the temple that Paul may have been referencing, let's summarize what we know to this point: First and foremost, God had revealed to Paul that the man of lawlessness was going to enter a certain temple and declare himself to be God. Secondly, since Paul continued to believe that he and the Thessalonians were soon to witness the revealing of the man, one would assume that Paul believed that this particular temple, wherever it sits, was already in existence. At least, that seems logical. Now, with that brief clarification, let's examine three possible options that Paul may have been referencing when speaking about the temple that the man of lawlessness would one day enter:

Table 1.4. Options for the Temple That the Man of Lawlessness Will Enter
Option #1: Herod's Temple
Option #2: A rebuilt temple during Paul's lifetime
Option #3: A rebuilt temple in the distant future, after Paul's death

Let's examine each:

3. Best, *First and Second Epistles to the Thessalonians*, 50–59.

Option #1: Paul was referencing Herod's Temple

It is impossible that Paul was referencing Herod's Temple. Why? Because if he was, Paul made a mistake—and a big one at that! As stated above, the temple was torn down in AD 70 and since the man was not even born by the time of the destruction, the man of lawlessness was never going to lay eyes on Herod's Temple, much less enter it. Unless Paul was completely wrong in his declaration to the Thessalonians, and the Scripture was in error (which it wasn't), Herod's Temple was not the one that God revealed to Paul.

Option #2: Paul was referencing a rebuilt temple during his lifetime

This option required Paul to believe that Herod's Temple would be torn down and another one rebuilt in time for the man of lawlessness to enter it before the Lord appeared, all within Paul's remaining lifetime. Since Paul was perhaps in his mid to upper forties when he wrote the letters to the Thessalonians (ca. AD 52–53),[4] can one truly entertain the thought that Paul expected that there would be time enough for Herod's Temple to be destroyed and another one rebuilt from the ground up—all before the Lord returned during the apostle's lifetime? One must admit that sounds preposterous, especially since Herod's Temple was reported to have taken over forty-six years to construct (John 2:20) and that wasn't even from the ground up, but rather the new construction used the existing foundation of the second temple, which was Zerubbabel's Temple.[5] But even more importantly, one knows that Paul was not referencing a temple rebuilt during his lifetime because it too never happened! Had Paul's prophecy referenced a temple that was supposed to be rebuilt during his lifetime, Paul and the Scripture would have been in error, which again, is impossible.

Option #3: Paul was referencing a rebuilt temple in the distant future—after his death

This is certainly the option with the greatest following today. If ten ministers preach on end times, five are going to talk about the temple that is

---

4. Goodwin, *Harmony of the Life of St. Paul*, 80.
5. Frame, *Commentary on Thessalonians*, 257.

soon to be rebuilt in Jerusalem. The talk goes something like this: The temple plans are drawn, finances are set aside, the temple utensils are hidden away, the search for a red heifer is actively underway, etc. But as were the first two options, this one is also impossible. As indicated earlier, even after the Lord revealed to Paul that the man of lawlessness would enter a certain temple and declare himself to be God, Paul continued to believe that he and the Thessalonians were about to witness the revealing of the man, necessitating the fact that Paul believed the man of lawlessness was alive and would soon enter the temple in question that God had revealed to Paul. This proves the fact that Paul knew the mysterious temple was already in existence and not a hypothetical temple to be built in the distant future, at some point after the apostle's death. Therefore, the third option, despite its overwhelming popularity, must be eliminated.

A Fourth Option

Since Paul was not referencing Herod's Temple, nor a rebuilt temple during his lifetime, nor a rebuilt temple after his death, is there a fourth option, where Scripture elsewhere tells of this same man of lawlessness entering a certain temple and speaking arrogantly? There is one place:

"As I watched, thrones were set in place, and an Ancient of Days took his throne, his clothing was white as snow, and the hair of his head like pure wool; his throne was fiery flames, and its wheels were burning fire. A stream of fire issued and flowed out from his presence. A thousand thousands served him, and ten thousand times ten thousand stood attending him. The court sat in judgment, and the books were opened.

"I watched then because of the noise of the arrogant words that the horn was speaking. And as I watched, the beast was put to death, and its body destroyed and given over to be burned with fire. As for the rest of the beasts, their dominion was taken away, but their lives were prolonged for a season and a time" (Dan 7:9–12).

Having determined that the temple referenced by Paul had to be in existence during the apostle's lifetime, we now turn to the only two temples of God in existence during that period: Herod's Temple and the temple of God in heaven, referenced by Daniel in the above text. Herod's Temple has already been eliminated as the temple that Paul was referencing because it no longer exists. The future man of lawlessness would never enter it. Therefore, when Paul told the Thessalonians that the man would enter the temple of God, the only temple in existence that Paul could have possibly been referencing was the temple of God in heaven. In fact, the majority of Paul's knowledge of the man entering the temple came from this text in Dan 7. In the passage, Daniel tells of a beast and a "little horn" being brought into the temple of God, into the presence of the Ancient of Days to face judgment just before being cast into the fire. The reader will later learn that this beast and little horn are none other than the beast and the false prophet of Revelation, who will be brought before the Father immediately after the Battle of Armageddon, just before being cast into the lake of fire. The scene is unique to all of history, as this pair of reprobates are the only two personalities that will be cast into the lake of fire one thousand years before anyone else. Just from this simple observation, one knows that since the beast of Daniel is the beast of Revelation, then the little horn of Daniel must be the false prophet of Revelation. Additionally, in our later studies of Revelation, it will be easily proven that since the beast will be released out of the bottomless pit and the little horn was described with human attributes, the beast is an angel and the little horn is a man. And therefore, since Paul's man of lawlessness is obviously a man, then the man of lawlessness and the little horn and the false prophet are all one and the same. Observe:

Table 1.5. The Beast Will Later Be Proven to Be an Angel and Both the Little Horn and the False Prophet Will Be Proven to Be a Man

	The Angel	The Man
Dan 7	The beast	The little horn
2 Thess 2	———	The man of lawlessness
Rev 13 and 20	The beast	The false prophet

As the beast and the little horn were escorted into the temple of God by the attending angels and the little horn was then made to sit before the Father, Daniel said he watched because of the arrogant words that he was speaking (Dan 7:11). What could the man possibly have been boasting about in front of the Father? Did the man boast about his intelligence? Did he brag about his miraculous power? his appearance? Unfortunately for us, Daniel doesn't disclose what he heard the man say. But Paul does. Paul said once the man enters the temple and is seated before the Father, the man will speak arrogantly and bizarrely, claiming that he himself is God! Those are the hidden words that Daniel heard and that caught his attention. Surely, the bombastic words of the deranged man in heaven only echoed what the man had already been claiming back on earth.

Notice Daniel didn't say the beast spoke arrogantly in front of the Father, but only the little horn. This indicates that the beast will stand by quietly and submissively in front of the Father while the man of lawlessness will be the only one speaking arrogantly in front of the Ancient of Days. Why the difference in behavior between the beast and the little horn? Although both personalities are equally evil and guilty before the Lord, as proven by the fact that both will receive the same sentence to the lake of fire at the same time, the angelic beast is certainly more cognizant of the holiness and majesty of the One seated on the throne, simply because he, as an angel, is more knowledgeable of the spirit world; the little horn doesn't have a clue. One is reminded of Peter's words describing the difference between the knowledge of angels and the knowledge of men concerning the glorious ones in heaven:

"Bold and willful, they are not afraid to slander the glorious ones, whereas angels, though greater in might and power, do not bring against them a slanderous judgment from the Lord. These people, however, are like irrational animals, mere creatures of instinct, born to be caught and killed. They slander what they do not understand, and when those creatures are destroyed, they also will be destroyed, suffering the penalty for doing wrong" (2 Pet 2:10b–13a).

This passage lets one know that there is a greater potential for men, rather than angels, to slander the unknown things as well as the unknown ones in heaven. Quite simply, the beast knows more than the false prophet. As a further example of this discrepancy of knowledge, although the angelic beast and Satan will be the ones who supply the power behind the miracles performed by the little horn, the man somewhere along the way will come to believe that he is the source of the power, contributing to his psychotic belief that he is actually God. By the time he is captured and brought into the temple of God in heaven, the man's god-complex will be so severe, and his mind so deranged, that he will actually dare to speak boldly and arrogantly in front of the Father, claiming to be God. Daniel was stunned. The scene is surreal.

SEQUENCE IN 1 AND 2 THESSALONIANS

A Fifth Option?

Despite the fact that the majority of Paul's knowledge concerning the future man of lawlessness and his entry into the temple of God came from Dan 7, many mistakenly believe that when Paul said the man will "enter the temple," the apostle wasn't actually talking about a real temple but was instead speaking metaphorically, revealing a mystery to the Thessalonians that the man would one day enter "the church" in some capacity rather than an existing temple.[6] Adherents to this belief cite the following words to the Corinthians by Paul for support:[7]

1. "Do you not know that you are God's temple and that God's Spirit dwells in you? If anyone destroys God's temple, God will destroy that person. For God's temple is holy, and you are that temple" (1 Cor 3:16–17).

2. "Shun fornication! Every sin that a person commits is outside the body; but the fornicator sins against the body itself. Or do you not know that your body is a temple of the Holy Spirit within you, which you have from God, and that you are not your own? For you were bought with a price; therefore glorify God in your body" (1 Cor 6:18–20).

3. "Do not be mismatched with unbelievers. For what partnership is there between righteousness and lawlessness? Or what fellowship is there between light and darkness? What agreement does Christ have with Beliar? Or what does a believer share with an unbeliever? What agreement has the temple of God with idols? For we are the temple of the living God" (2 Cor 6:14–16a).

True, the apostle did tell the Corinthians that they were the temple of God, but that was because he was reminding them that the Holy Spirit dwelled within them, and therefore, certain ones in their community should stop living unrighteously and instead return to living a life of holiness.

Nevertheless, there's no written evidence that Paul ever verbalized that same statement—the statement that the believer's body was a temple of the Holy Spirit—to the Thessalonians. Unlike some in the Corinthian church, the Thessalonians seemed for the most part to be living a life of

---

6. Frame, *Commentary on the Epistles of St. Paul to the Thessalonians*, 256.
7. Beale and Campbell, *Revelation*, 217.

sanctification. The following is a sampling of Paul's commendations to the Thessalonians:

1. "And you became imitators of us and of the Lord, for in spite of persecution you received the word with joy inspired by the Holy Spirit, so that you became an example to all the believers in Macedonia and in Achaia. For the word of the Lord has sounded forth from you not only in Macedonia and Achaia, but in every place your faith in God has become known, so that we have no need to speak about it" (1 Thess 1:6–8).

2. "But Timothy has just now come to us from you, and has brought us the good news of your faith and love" (1 Thess 3:6a).

3. "Finally, brothers, we ask and urge you in the Lord Jesus that, as you learned from us how you ought to live and to please God (as, in fact, you are doing), you should do so more and more" (1 Thess 4:1).

4. "Now concerning love of the brothers and sisters, you do not need to have anyone write to you, for you yourselves have been taught by God to love one another; and indeed you do love all the brothers and sisters throughout Macedonia. But we urge you, beloved, to do so more and more" (1 Thess 4:9–10).

As one can see, the Thessalonians and the Corinthians presented two different scenarios to Paul: The Thessalonians were doing well and the apostle urged them to keep up the good work; on the other hand some of the Corinthians were living according to the flesh, not by the Spirit. It was in this context that Paul told the Corinthians that their bodies were individually as well as corporately considered to be the temple of God.

Now, the question remains: Did Paul repeat the illustration of the temple and the church to the Thessalonians? Who knows? Maybe he did or maybe he didn't. Obviously, if he didn't, they couldn't be expected to make the connection between the temple and the church in 2 Thess 2:4, if that's indeed what Paul intended, correct? However, for argument's sake, let's assume that when Paul visited Thessalonica (Acts 17:1–9), somewhere during the stay he told them that their bodies were the temple of the Holy Spirit. Here's my question to you: Since it's apparent that the Thessalonians were already confused concerning Paul's earlier teachings surrounding (1) the future rebellion, (2) the future revealing of the man of lawlessness, and (3) the future Day of the Lord, can one honestly believe that the apostle would then proceed to write so obtusely and metaphorically to an already befuddled congregation of new converts by telling them that the future man of lawlessness will one day enter "the temple of God" instead of plainly saying the man will one day enter "the church," if the latter is indeed what Paul actually meant? Wouldn't that be a strange approach by the apostle in a letter written specifically for the sake of clarification? One would think that Paul would have erred on the side of caution in the second letter by plainly writing what he meant, leaving no room for misinterpretation. What if some of the Thessalonians didn't remember all the words of the apostle's several oral dissertations, one of which may have included the statement that they were now the temple of God, and because of that lack of remembrance, they mistakenly believed the apostle was implying that the man would enter the still-standing Herod's Temple in Jerusalem instead of the church? In that scenario, things have gone from bad to worse concerning the Thessalonians' confusion! I don't think Paul would have allowed that confusion to germinate, do you? And because of that simple reasoning, one can be certain that the apostle chose his words very carefully, telling his recipients exactly what he wanted them to hear: Had Paul wanted to convey to the Thessalonians that the man would one enter the church, he would have plainly said "The man will enter the church." But he didn't. Instead he said that the man of lawlessness will enter "the temple of God," which happens to be the same temple of God in heaven that Daniel had already revealed to his recipients.

The Man of Lawlessness and the Restrainer

Next, Paul explains why the man of lawlessness has not been revealed as of yet, but assures the Thessalonians that after he is revealed and completes his allotted time on earth, he will then come to a sure and dreadful end:

> And you know what is now restraining him, so that he may be revealed when his time comes. For the mystery of lawlessness is already at work, but only until the one who now restrains it is removed. And then the lawless one will be revealed, whom the Lord Jesus will destroy with the breath of his mouth, annihilating him by the manifestation of his coming. (2 Thess 2:6–8)

Concerning who or what is restraining the man of lawlessness from being revealed, there are no lack of speculations. One of the more popular ones is the restraining presence of the church, and specifically, the restraining presence of the Holy Spirit within the church. The theory goes as follows: Once the church is raptured, in essence taking with it the restraining presence of the Holy Spirit, then the man can finally be revealed to the world.[8] Again, the theory is impossible. According to Paul, not only will the church be present on the earth at the revealing of the man of lawlessness, but one now knows the church will be present on the earth at the time of the man's demise, when the Lord destroys the man "with the breath of his mouth, annihilating him by the manifestation of his *parousia*," the same *parousia* that Paul and the Thessalonians expected to witness:

"For this we declare to you by the word of the Lord, that we who are alive, who are left until the *parousia* of the Lord, will by no means precede those who have died" (1 Thess 4:15).

In other words, Paul has clearly indicated that the saints of the last generation will be present for each of the three milestones of the man of lawlessness' public life:

1. His revealing
2. His reign
3. And his demise[9]

Therefore, since "the restrainer" is not the vacated church nor the vacated Holy Spirit, then who or what might Paul have been referencing when speaking of the man's restrainer? When analyzing the text, it does seem that Paul had previously identified the restrainer to the Thessalonians, whoever he is, as proven by the phrase, "And you know what is now restraining him." But for reasons known only to Paul, he chose not to bring further attention to the restrainer's identity in the letter. Therefore,

---

8. Walvoord, *Rapture Question*, 244–45.

9. Notice that when Paul describes the Lord's encounter with the man at the *parousia* (2 Thess 2:8), the translations of "destroy" and "annihilate" certainly give one the impression that at the manifestation of Christ the man of lawlessness will be utterly destroyed on the spot. However, when reviewing the phrase "will destroy with the breath of his mouth, annihilating him by the manifestation of his coming," one should be aware that the Greek word *anelie*, translated "will destroy," is better translated "will take up" or "will take away." Likewise, the Greek word *katargēsei*, translated "annihilating," is more accurately translated with the meanings: nullify, will do away with, bring to nought, or render inoperative. Rather than completely destroying the man of lawlessness at the *parousia*, the Greek text indicates that Jesus will instead take him out of the way, rendering him inoperative by the manifestation of his coming. These observations will later be reaffirmed when John sees the beast and false prophet only captured at the Battle of Armageddon, rather than annihilated (Rev 19:20).

in a text such as this one, when a satisfactory answer is not readily apparent, it's always beneficial to look for a passage elsewhere in Scripture that might describe the scenario in question. Again, the book of Daniel comes to our rescue. In the following, an angel tells Daniel that, in the future, a powerful servant of God will arise just before a time of great anguish:

"At that time Michael, the great prince, the protector of your people, shall arise. There shall be a time of anguish, such as has never occurred since nations first came into existence. But at that time your people shall be delivered, everyone who is found written in the book" (Dan 12:1).

The reader will later learn that the setting for the above passage, in which Michael arises just as the Jewish remnant is being delivered out of the city of Jerusalem, is an event known as the abomination of desolation. Is it possible that this text in Daniel identifies Michael as the restrainer and that, at some point after the abomination of desolation, after the Jewish people have been safely delivered out of the city, God finally directs the Archangel Michael to refrain from keeping the man of lawlessness at bay, thus permitting the man to be revealed? Perhaps. It does seem plausible from this passage that the words "At that time Michael, the great prince, the protector of your people, shall arise" might mark the approximate period of time when Michael begins to no longer restrain the angelic beast from channeling his miraculous powers through the man, by which the man will then be revealed. The timing is certainly spot on. If indeed the archangel has been assigned the task of restraining the man, it is sure to be one of Michael's easier assignments from the Lord.

The Revealing of the Man of Lawlessness

Since it has been proven that the temple in which the man of lawlessness will one day enter is God's temple in heaven, then obviously the popular expectation that the man of lawlessness will be revealed to the world by entering a rebuilt temple in Jerusalem and offering an unclean sacrifice upon its altar is rendered fictitious. Since that is the case, then how might the man truly be revealed? In Paul's concluding remarks of the man of lawlessness, the apostle reveals the answer:

> The coming of the lawless one is apparent in the working of Satan, who uses all power, signs, lying wonders, and every kind of wicked deception for those who are perishing, because they refused to love the truth and so be saved. For this reason God

sends them a powerful delusion, leading them to believe what is false, so that all who have not believed the truth but took pleasure in unrighteousness will be condemned. (2 Thess 2:9–12)

Miracles will reveal the man.[10] Enabled by the power of the enemy, the man of lawlessness will perform miracles, signs, and wonders that will mesmerize the world, deceiving them into believing that he is some kind of deity. Note that Paul does not include the righteous in this deception. Only the unrighteous will be deceived. These are the ones who are perishing and who refuse to love the truth and refuse to be saved. The saints, on the other hand, will see through the man's charade and will not fall for his deception because they will do as the Holy Spirit has implored, and that is to put on the armor of God so that they will be able to stand against the wiles of the devil on that evil day (Eph 6:10–17). In fact, it is precisely because the saints will not be deceived by the man's miracles and claims of deity that Paul calls this period "that evil day." How so? As one will soon learn, when the saints refuse to acquiesce and obey the man's demands to worship the beast, he will predictably commit evil acts against the saints by retaliating against them and putting them to death.

Closing Thoughts: Reflections on the Hypothetical Temple

After the sacrifice of his Son on the cross, God was never again going to accept the levitical priesthood as the representative of his people, and therefore he was never again going to manifest himself in the temple's Holy of Holies. As the Hebrew author indicated, the old covenant, its temple, the furnishings of the temple, and the sacrificial offerings surrounding the temple had served their purpose:

"In speaking of 'a new covenant,' he has made the first one obsolete. And what is obsolete and growing old will soon disappear" (Heb 8:13).

And the temple did soon disappear, literally, in AD 70 with the Roman destruction of Jerusalem and the sanctuary. As God would have it, for those individuals who wanted to believe in Christ after his resurrection but yet couldn't let go of Judaism or the temple, God was going to help deliver them of that temptation by allowing the temple to be completely destroyed, never to be heard from again. The Lord would now directly

---

10. Actually one miracle in particular will reveal the man, and that miracle is disclosed in Rev 13.

meet the believer whenever and wherever they were willing to worship the Lord in spirit and truth, just as Christ told the woman at the well:

"Jesus said to her, 'Woman, believe me, the hour is coming when you will worship the Father neither on this mountain nor in Jerusalem. You worship what you do not know; we worship what we know, for salvation is from the Jews. But the hour is coming, and is now here, when the true worshipers will worship the Father in spirit and truth, for the Father seeks such as these to worship him. God is spirit, and those who worship him must worship in spirit and truth'" (John 4:21–24).

And, thankfully, it's been this way for two thousand years and counting. But because most do not understand that the prophecy of Paul concerning the man of lawlessness and the temple of God, as confirmed by Daniel, is a reference to "the final judgment of the man in God's temple in heaven" rather than to "the revealing of the man in a make-believe temple on earth," their expectation of the future has severely clouded their better judgment to the extent that they mistakenly believe that an earthly temple must be built in Jerusalem at all costs in order to fulfill Paul's prophecy in 2 Thess 2:4, despite the fact that a rebuilt temple goes against everything Christ accomplished on the cross and everything the New Testament teaches. Today, when Christians try to organize preparations for the building of a temple in Jerusalem for the sole purpose of providing a place for the man of lawlessness to enter in order to fulfill Scripture, despite their good intentions, their efforts are meaningless, irrelevant, and, worse yet, potentially harmful to any meaningful testimony they may have for the Jewish people. The idea that Christians would encourage Jewish non-believers in Jerusalem to build a temple in order to participate in Judaistic sacrifices and ceremonies is akin to Christians spreading the old news of Moses and the law, rather than the good news of Jesus Christ and grace.

∼

The following is the end-time sequence that Paul expected to witness and subsequently passed along to the Thessalonians:

Table 1.6. Sequence in 1 & 2 Thessalonians
1. The Rebellion and the Revealing of the Man of Lawlessness (2 Thess 2:3–12)
2. The Day of the Lord (1 Thess 5:1–11)
3. The Return of the Lord and the Resurrection and Rapture of the Saints (2 Thess 1:5–12 and 1 Thess 4:13–18)
It is to be determined whether these two events are simultaneous or separate.

CHAPTER 2

Sequence in the Olivet Discourse

LEAVING THESSALONICA, WE MOVE to Jerusalem. As we survey the Scripture leading up to the crucifixion, one sees Jesus and the disciples walking through the streets of the city, soon to take the path that leads to the base of the Mount of Olives, and then up the side of the mountain to doubtless where Jesus and the disciples often gathered for prayer. It is there that we will hear Jesus impart the sequence of end times in its most profound simplicity, in a way that has never been heard before or since.

As Jesus and the disciples exited the temple, the Master was already keenly aware that he had entered the valley of the shadow of death, edging closer to his appointment with the cross. However, the disciples were at the opposite end of the spectrum, completely oblivious to the horrific scourging and beating that lay ahead for Jesus, as shown by how they were nonchalantly admiring the beauty of the temple:

> As Jesus came out of the temple and was going away, his disciples came to point out to him the buildings of the temple. Then he asked them, "You see all these, do you not? Truly I tell you, not one stone will be left here upon another; all will be thrown down." (Matt 24:1–2)

Just as Jesus predicted, Jerusalem would fall to the Roman army forty years later, at which time each of the temple stones would be torn down, leaving not one stone upon another.

Later that evening, Jesus and the disciples eventually made their way down to the Kidron Valley, through the grove of olive trees, and then up the Mount of Olives, where Jesus sat down and began to share the sequence of end-time events that awaited the elect of God. These words were not to be forgotten after his crucifixion and resurrection, and for that reason, Jesus waited until the very end to share the sequence. Undoubtedly, many of the disciples were still reeling from Jesus' shocking words about the destruction of the temple and naturally assumed that it would trigger the end of the world:

> When he was sitting on the Mount of Olives, the disciples came to him privately, saying, "Tell us, when will this be, and what will be the sign of your coming and the end of the age?" Jesus answered them, "Beware that no one leads you astray. For many will come in my name, saying, 'I am the Messiah!' and they will lead many astray. And you will hear of wars and rumors of wars; see that you are not alarmed; for this must take place, but the end is not yet. For nation will rise against nation, and kingdom against kingdom, and there will be famines and earthquakes in various places; all this is but the beginning of the birth pangs." (Matt 24:3–8)

The reason that the disciples knew to ask Jesus when he was coming back was because Jesus had previously told them of his departure and subsequent return:

"Do not let your hearts be troubled. Believe in God, believe also in me. In my Father's house are many dwelling places. If it were not so, would I have told you that I go to prepare a place for you? And if I go and prepare a place for you, I will come again and will take you to myself, so that where I am, there you may be also" (John 14:1–3).

Although Jesus told the disciples that he was going away, he promised them that he would return. In their minds, it would have been a predictable next step to combine something as traumatic as the temple's destruction with Christ's return from heaven and the end of the age, because up until their time with Christ the temple and Judaism had been the center of the disciples' world. If not the end of the age, what else could explain the destruction of the cultural and religious center of God's people? The disciples were naturally apprehensive and wanted to know when this catastrophe concerning the temple would take place. Instead of a direct answer, Jesus began by predicting a future filled with an uncharacteristic increase in national upheavals such as wars and rumors of wars, as well as an increase in common, naturally occurring phenomenons, such as famines and earthquakes, saying that they were but the beginning of the birth pangs. He then zeroed in on the fate of those around him:

> Then they will hand you over to be tortured and will put you to death, and you will be hated by all nations because of my name. Then many will fall away and they will betray one another and hate one another. And many false prophets will arise and lead many astray. And because of the increase of lawlessness, the love of many will grow cold. But anyone who endures to the end will be saved. And this good news of the kingdom will be proclaimed throughout the world, as a testimony to all the nations; and then the end will come. (Matt 24:9–14)

However long the disciples' lighthearted mood lingered after leaving the temple, it now came crashing to a halt. They would die as martyrs. With the possible exception of John, all would be put to death for the sake of Christ. James would be first; others would soon follow. Then, Jesus said many would "fall away" (Greek: *skandalisthēsontai*) from the faith.[1] But then the Lord gave a promise of hope saying anyone who endured to the end would be saved and that the good news would be proclaimed throughout the world. Then the end would come. If one did not know any better, this would have been a fitting place to end the discourse: The disciples would die as martyrs, the gospel would be preached around the world, and once the world heard the good news, the end would come. But the Lord's discourse was only getting started, as mysteries were about to be unveiled.

Let the Reader Understand

Next comes the most significant transition in the Olivet Discourse, which, if not recognized, will render any attempt at correctly interpreting the discourse a complete failure. Prior to this verse, Jesus addressed his disciples. However, beginning with the mention of "the desolating sacrilege standing in the holy place," Jesus addresses the enigmatic "reader":

> So when you see the desolating sacrilege standing in the holy place, as was spoken by the prophet Daniel (let the reader

---

1. The period of falling away immediately after the deaths of the apostles should not be confused with the period of falling away on the distant horizon, which will be characterized by the increase of deception and lawlessness. As you well recall from our study in 2 Thessalonians, Paul described the future "falling away" as the rebellion, i.e., the apostasy (Greek: *apostasia*).

understand), then those in Judea must flee to the mountains; the one on the housetop must not go down to take what is in the house; the one in the field must not turn back to get a coat. Woe to those who are pregnant and to those who are nursing infants in those days! Pray that your flight may not be in winter or on a sabbath. (Matt 24:15–20)

It is certain that the Lord's disciples existed approximately two thousand years ago, but what about "the reader"? Past or future? Although there are mixed opinions, only one can be correct. Despite whichever one turns how to be right, we can all agree that "let the reader understand" is a very unexpected and strange phrase to find in the Lord's narrative, or anyone's narrative, for that matter. No one when speaking to others all of a sudden inserts a phrase such as this into their dialogue. The phrase was certainly added by the author of the gospel, and is not among the original words spoken by the Lord during the discourse. It does indicate, at least from the perspective of the author of the gospel, that the Lord's dialogue beginning with the phrase "let the reader understand" was directed toward others who will later read the Lord's recorded words of the discourse as opposed to the disciples who were present at the discourse and hearing it in real time. And not only will "the reader" read the discourse at a later date, but he or she will also witness a mysterious event that Jesus identifies as "the desolating sacrilege standing in the holy place" (Matt 24:15). Also, just from Christ's subsequent phrase "those in Judea" (Matt 24:16), one knows that the readers, whoever they might be, will be living in and around Jerusalem when they witness this particular sacrilege, or abomination, as it is sometimes called.

Now to the all-important question: Why would Jesus withdraw his focus from the disciples and address a group of readers who were not present, who would one day witness an unknown event only identified as the abomination of desolation? And why would he begin to warn them that when they see this abomination, they are to flee Jerusalem as quickly as possible? Jesus even indicated that many of these readers might be at a physical disadvantage and could find it difficult to successfully escape the site of the abomination unless they pray and ask for God's help (Matt 24:20). Circumstances that could place some of the readers at a distinct disadvantage are that the abomination might occur on the Sabbath, or in winter, or some of the women readers might be pregnant or nursing infants (Matt 24:19–20). In short, the Lord doesn't want the future readers to take any chances; they are to immediately flee at the first sight of the abomination because Jesus, for whatever reason, is concerned for their physical safety. And this begs another question: Why was Christ so concerned about the physical safety of these absentee-readers, when he obviously did not voice the same precautions for the physical safety of his disciples who were standing next to him? After all, had he not just prophesied that their lives would end in martyrdom (Matt 24:9)? And yet Jesus did not once encourage any of the disciples to flee Jerusalem in order to escape their adversaries. Perplexing, to say the least.

The Series of Events Following the Abomination

Curiously, Jesus only gives two characteristics of the desolating sacrilege: That it will be standing in the holy place, and it is the one described by Daniel. (Note: The phrase *hesto en topō hagiō*, translated "standing *in* the holy place," can also be translated just as accurately "standing *on* the holy place" or "standing *at* the holy place." This may sound inconsequential now, but later the notation will prove significant.) Other than these two descriptions, Jesus gives no specific details surrounding the event to the reader, such as who will commit the abomination, or what heinous act comprises the abomination. It's almost as if Christ expects the reader to be aware of the fact that Daniel referenced three abominations of desolation (compare Dan 9:27, 11:31, and 12:11) and the reader should somehow be cognizant of which of the three the Lord had in mind. Whether that is the case or not, it is certain that Jesus believes the reader will recognize the abomination as soon as he or she sees it, and because of that, they will then know that they are to immediately flee.

After describing some of the possible extenuating circumstances that the readers might encounter at the time of the abomination of desolation, and what they are to do or not do, the Lord reveals a series of events that will immediately follow this mysterious abomination of desolation:

> For at that time there will be great suffering, such as has not been from the beginning of the world until now, no, and never will be. And if those days had not been cut short, no one would be saved; but for the sake of the elect those days will be cut short. Then if anyone says to you, "Look! Here is the Messiah!" or "There he is!"—do not believe it. For false messiahs and false prophets will appear and produce great signs and omens, to lead astray, if possible, even the elect. Take note, I have told you beforehand. So, if they say to you, "Look! He is in the wilderness,"

do not go out. If they say, "Look! He is in the inner rooms," do not believe it. For as the lightning comes from the east and flashes as far as the west, so will be the coming of the Son of Man. Wherever the corpse is, there the vultures will gather.

Immediately after the suffering of those days the sun will be darkened, and the moon will not give its light; the stars will fall from heaven, and the powers of heaven will be shaken. Then the sign of the Son of Man will appear in heaven, and then all the tribes of the earth will mourn, and they will see "the Son of Man coming on the clouds of heaven" with power and great glory. And he will send out his angels with a loud trumpet call, and they will gather his elect from the four winds, from one end of heaven to the other. (Matt 24:21–31)

By connecting each of the events subsequent to the abomination, beginning with the greatest suffering in the history of the world and continuing to the gathering of the elect with such words and phrases as "for at that time," "those days," "then," and "immediately after," Jesus indicated that the uninterrupted string of events comprise one series of events. Observe:

Table 2.1. Sequence of the Uninterrupted String of Events Given by Christ	
The Events	**The Connecting Words or Phrases in Context**
1. The Abomination of Desolation	"When" you see the desolating sacrilege standing in the holy place (24:15).
2. The Greatest Suffering in History	"For at that time" there will be great suffering, such as has not been from the beginning of the world until now, no, and never will be (24:21).
3. Days of Suffering Are Shortened	And if "those days" had not been cut short, no one would be saved (24:22).
4. Deception by False Messiahs and False Prophets	"Then" if anyone says to you, 'Look here is the Messiah!' or 'There he is!'—do not believe it (24:23).
5. Heavenly Signs	"Immediately after" the suffering of those days the sun will be darkened, the moon will not give its light, the stars will fall from heaven . . . (24:29a).
6. God Shakes the Heavens	"And" the powers of heaven will be shaken (24:29b).

Table 2.1. Sequence of the Uninterrupted String of Events Given by Christ	
The Events	The Connecting Words or Phrases in Context
7a. The Son of Man Appears	"Then" the sign of the Son of Man will appear in heaven, and "then" all the tribes of the earth will mourn, and they will see the Son of Man coming on the clouds of heaven with power and great glory (24:30).
7b. The Elect Are Gathered	"And" he will send out his angels with a loud trumpet call, and they will gather his elect from the four winds, from one end of heaven to the other (24:31).

Every event is connected to the previous and subsequent event. Furthermore, not only will the events comprise one series of uninterrupted events, but Jesus later indicated to the reader that the entire series of events will occur within one generation:

"Truly I tell you, this generation will not pass away until all these things have taken place. Heaven and earth will pass away, but my words will not pass away" (Matt 24:34–35).

It's easy to get bogged down in the minutiae of certain details that are irrelevant. There always seems to be much speculation as to whether Jesus was speaking of his own generation or another, or perhaps, how long or short was a particular generation that may have been brought into the discussion. But whether a generation is forty, fifty, or a hundred years is inconsequential as to what Jesus was saying. The generation Jesus was speaking about had nothing to do with his generation nor with any other generation marked by a significant historical event, such as when Israel became a nation in 1948, or when the city of Jerusalem was retaken in the Six-Day War in 1967. Jesus simply told "the reader" of the generation that sees the prophesied series of events begin to take place, starting with the abomination of desolation, that their generation will not pass away until all the subsequent events also have taken place: the period of the greatest suffering in history, the shortening of that great suffering, the subsequent period of deception, the heavenly signs, the powers of heaven being shaken, the appearance of the Son of Man, and the gathering of the saints. In other words, the generation of the reader who witnesses the abomination of desolation is the generation that will witness the appearance of the Son of Man and the gathering of the saints. Jesus meant nothing more and nothing less.

What more needs to be said? Jesus' sequence of end-time events is almost too simple. In fact he even said at one point in the discourse, "But be alert; I have already told you everything." Therefore, since Jesus said the entire series of events will occur within one generation and since there hasn't been any semblance of an abomination of desolation in Jerusalem followed by each of the particular events in the series, then there's no further explanation needed to prove that the series of events that Jesus prophesied to "the reader" on the Mount of Olives two thousand years ago still remains unfulfilled.

The Greatest Suffering in History

Despite the fact that it has been proven that the series of events is future and will lead up to the appearance of the Son of Man and the gathering of the saints, many attempt to force the series of events back into the past. Rather than a future abomination of desolation, or a future period of the greatest suffering in history, or the future heavenly signs, etc., the same believe that all the events listed by Christ during the Olivet Discourse have already occurred. Adherents to this belief system are called *preterists*.[2] As an example, *preterists* believe the abomination of desolation refers to the desolation of Jerusalem associated with the aftermath of the destruction of Jerusalem and the temple by the Romans in AD 70. Furthermore, they believe the entire subsequent series of events that Jesus prophesied also occurred immediately following Jerusalem's destruction, including what the Lord called the greatest suffering in history:

> For at that time there will be great suffering, such as has not been from the beginning of the world until now, no, and never will be. (Matt 24:21)

According to the *preterists*, this period of suffering was fulfilled by the suffering and death of the Jewish inhabitants during the Roman invasion. Granted, the Roman invasion of Jerusalem produced death and suffering, but was it the greatest suffering in the history of the world, or ever will be? Certainly not. The invasion of AD 70 is said to have

---

2. The term comes from the Latin word *praeter*, which is a prefix denoting that something has passed.

produced perhaps as high as one million casualties. Even if the estimate is correct the number of casualties wouldn't be considered the greatest suffering in Jewish history, much less the history of the world. As most are aware, six million Jews were tortured and systematically murdered in World War II by mass shootings, starvations, and gas chambers. This genocide alone killed almost two-thirds of all European Jews during the 1930s and forties. True, the Roman invasion of AD 70 was horrific, but it didn't compare to the Jewish casualities of WWII, at least numerically. No matter how much one may attempt to equate Jesus' statement of the "greatest suffering in the history of the world" to the fall of Jerusalem in AD 70, the endeavor is futile, and, not to mention, shows a lack of belief in the veracity of Christ's words. Anyone believing Jesus was referencing the Roman invasion of Jerusalem in Matt 24:21, quite frankly, cannot be taken seriously.

When Christ said the period following the abomination of desolation would be the greatest suffering in the history of mankind, not only should one consider that the Lord was prophesying a period of suffering worse than that of WWII when 6 million Jews and 70 million non-Jews died, but one should understand that Jesus was prophesying a period of suffering worse than the combined periods of WWI and WWII when a total of approximately 125 million men, women, and children died. Again, Jesus said it will be the worst period of suffering in history.

The Suffering of Those Days Will Be Shortened

Confirming the fact that Jesus was not speaking in hyperbole when he spoke of the suffering, the Lord then said if those days were not shortened, "no one would be saved":

> And if those days had not been cut short, no one would be saved; but for the sake of the elect those days will be cut short. (Matt 24:22)

When the Greek phrase *ouk an esōthē pasa sarx* is more closely examined, it actually states that "no flesh would be saved," conveying the thought that if those particular days of suffering were not stopped, the whole human race would be wiped out, including non-Christians and Christians alike. In other words, the slaughter wouldn't stop at 125 million casualties, which, as stated above, was the combined death toll of WWI and WWII, but it would progress to one billion, two billion, three billion, four billion, etc., until the whole human race was annihilated. Therefore, God must and will put a stop to it. And why will God intervene? Jesus said God will shorten those days of suffering *for the sake of the elect*. And who are the elect? Simply, the elect are the people of God. They have been chosen to live with God for eternity. Paul said that God has already chosen the elect from the foundation of the world. In the following, note some of Paul's descriptions of the chosen:

1. "Blessed be the God and Father of our Lord Jesus Christ, who has blessed us in Christ with every spiritual blessing in the heavenly places, just as he chose us in Christ before the foundation of the world to be holy and blameless before him in love. He destined us for adoption as his children through Jesus Christ, according to the good pleasure of his will, to the praise of his glorious grace that he freely bestowed on us in the Beloved" (Eph 1:3–6).

2. "For those whom he foreknew he also predestined to be conformed to the image of his Son, in order that he might be the firstborn within a large family. And those whom he predestined he also called; and those whom he called he also justified; and those whom he justified he also glorified" (Rom 8:29–30).

3. "But God's firm foundation stands, bearing this inscription: 'The Lord knows those who are his'" (2 Tim 2:19a).

Despite however one chooses to look at it, the fact is that one is either part of the elect or not.[3] According to Paul, the die has already

---

3. Many believers have trouble accepting the fact that God has already chosen the elect before the foundation of the world. Nevertheless, this is what Scripture teaches. Indulge me, if you will, in a little vignette: Imagine that you have been brought into the throne room of the Father himself, similarly to John's experience in Revelation. And imagine that the Father asked you if you believe that he was omniscient, knowing all things. You replied that you do. Next, he spoke to you concerning two people in your life, say, a coworker and a distant relative, and the Father said that one is part of the elect and one isn't; however, he didn't tell you which is which. Now, here's my question to you: Will the coworker or the distant relative do anything whatsoever to prove God's statement incorrect, thereby altering God's elect, while simultaneously destroying his attribute of omniscience? Not a chance. What God knows, he knows. Whoever of the two is not part of the elect will ultimately choose a path other than with God, and the one who is part of the elect will at some point call on the Lord and persevere in the faith. The reader may then pose the question that since God has mercy on whomever he chooses and hardens the heart of whomever he chooses (Rom 9:18), then what is one to do? Well, according to Peter, pursue God and live a life of holiness. In short, live as though you are part of the elect. Observe (italics used for emphasis): "For this very reason, you must make every effort to support your faith with goodness, and goodness

been cast. If one comes to a place in his or her life where they confess Christ and continue to abide in the Lord until death, then that person is part of the elect, and has already been chosen before the foundation of the world. But if one dies before being brought into a right relationship with God, then that individual was never part of the elect.

It is with this backdrop that one will be able to understand why God must stop the astronomical death count for the sake of the elect. Remember, Jesus indicated if the worldwide sufferings and killings that follow the abomination were allowed to go unchecked, the result would inevitably affect the elect. But how? One might ask, if a person is in a right relationship with God and then are suddenly killed during this future, post-abomination holocaust, just as the disciples were killed in the first century, how would that affect the elect? Answer: It wouldn't. When Jesus said "but for the sake of the elect those days will be cut short," he was only referencing that part of the elect who have not yet made a confession of Christ. During any point in time, the elect consist of those who have already been brought into a right relationship with God, as well as those who are yet to be brought into that relationship. But because this latter group is just as much a part of the elect chosen from the foundation of the world as the first group, they too will inevitably be brought into a right relationship. God will see to it. Hypothetically, if God allowed the mass slaughter during the post-abomination holocaust to go unchecked, everyone would be killed according to Jesus, including the elect who have yet to be credited the righteousness of Christ. But that scenario is impossible. God won't permit it. When Christ said the time of suffering will be cut short for the sake of the elect, one sees God in action, making sure that everyone he has chosen from the foundation of the world will be physically protected in order to see the day that he or she calls on the name of the Lord—even if God has to go to the extraordinary length of shortening the days of the greatest suffering in the history of the world.

---

with knowledge, and knowledge with self-control, and self-control with endurance, and endurance with godliness, and godliness with mutual affection, and mutual affection with love. For if these things are yours and are increasing among you, they keep you from being ineffective and unfruitful in the knowledge of our Lord Jesus Christ . . . Therefore, brothers and sisters, *be all the more eager to confirm your call and election*, for if you do this, you will never stumble. For in this way, entry into the eternal kingdom of our Lord and Savior Jesus Christ will be richly provided for you" (2 Pet 1:5–8, 10–11).

Although it is true that God has already chosen the elect before the foundation of the world, still, God promises an individual, through the writings of Peter, if one pursues a life of sanctification and holiness in Christ until the very end, that person will never stumble and will thereby confirm their pre-foundation-of-the-world call and election.

Identity of the Reader

With the understanding that God will stop the global holocaust for the part of the elect that has not yet confessed, we finally have enough information to answer one of our original questions: Why was the "reader" that Jesus addressed during the Olivet Discourse told to physically escape the city of Jerusalem in the last generation, while the disciples were never encouraged to flee from persecution during Christ's generation? Hopefully, with this recent explanation of the two groups of the elect, the answer is readily apparent: Within the future Jewish readers of the Olivet Discourse that Jesus addressed will be God's last-generation Jewish elect, who, at the time they witness the abomination of desolation, have not yet made a confession for Christ. Therefore, Christ indirectly instructed "the elect" by directly instructing "the reader" to flee Jerusalem and escape physical death at the abomination in order that he or she may later call on the name of the Lord. As the previous sentence indicated, every "reader" that Christ addressed in the Olivet Discourse will not be part of the elect. In fact, even every "reader who escapes Jerusalem" at the time of the abomination of desolation, according to Joel, will not be part of the elect:

"I will show portents in the heavens and on the earth, blood and fire and columns of smoke. The sun shall be turned to darkness, and the moon to blood, before the great and terrible day of the Lord comes. Then everyone who calls on the name of the Lord shall be saved; for in Mount Zion and in Jerusalem there shall be those who escape, as the Lord has said, and among the survivors shall be those whom the Lord calls" (Joel 2:30–32).

Joel didn't say "all" the survivors shall be those whom the Lord calls but rather he said "among the survivors" shall be those whom the Lord calls. In other words, there will be some who see the abomination, escape Jerusalem, but are not part of the elect. Next question: How will a person who escapes Jerusalem at the abomination know if they are among those whom the Lord has chosen before the foundation of the world? Answer: When the Lord calls someone, the elect will respond to his call, by calling on the Lord themselves. And according to Joel, in this particular instance, the Jewish elect will call on the Lord when they see the heavenly signs. As discussed earlier, if God has chosen someone from the foundation of the world, a time will surely come when that individual will respond to God's call and confess Christ at some point during their lifetime.

Looking again at Rom 8:29–30, where Paul traces the steps of salvation, the progression from being foreknown and predestined by God to later being justified and glorified is bridged by God's call and the believer's responding faith and confession, which is when Christ's redemptive work on the cross is actually applied to the individual. The following two passages of scripture bring attention to the Lord's call and the elect's response, respectively:

1. "For many are called, but few are chosen" (Matt 22:14).

2. "Because if you confess with your lips that Jesus is Lord and believe in your heart that God raised him from the dead, you will be saved. For one believes with the heart and so is justified, and one confesses with the mouth and so is saved. The scripture says, 'No one who believes in him will be put to shame.' For there is no distinction between Jew and Greek; the same Lord is Lord of all and is generous to all who call on him. For, 'Everyone who calls on the name of the Lord shall be saved'" (Rom 10:9–13).

Whether God's call comes to an individual by the preaching of the gospel,[4] a testimony by a friend, reading the Scripture, reading a devotional book, or any number of other ways, a person knows they have been "chosen by God before the foundation of the world" if he or she responds favorably to his call and perseveres in the faith. Here are the steps of salvation:

Table 2.2. The Steps of Salvation	
God's Part (Rom 8:29-30)	**Man's Part** (Rom 10:9-13)
1. God foreknew the elect (before the foundation of the world).	
2. God predestined the elect (before the foundation of the world).	
3. God calls many (during the life of an individual).	
	4. Only the elect respond to God's call by faith and confession.
5. God justifies the elect.	
6. God glorifies the elect.	

4. As an example, the Thessalonians were "called" by God through Paul's "preaching of the gospel" (2 Thess 2:14).

Not only does God do his part, but he facilitates man's part as well: He supplies the faith by which the elect make confession. In other words, the believer can't take credit for anything! Here's Paul's explanation to the Ephesians (italics used for emphasis):

"For by grace you have been saved through faith, *and this is not your own doing; it is the gift of God*—not the result of works, so that no one may boast" (Eph 2:8–9).

Although Jesus instructed the last-generation Jewish readers (of the Olivet Discourse) to escape Jerusalem when they see the abomination of desolation, not all the inhabitants of Jerusalem will escape (Luke 21:24). And, as stated, even among those who successfully escape, not all will later make a confession of Jesus Christ. But those who escape and later confess Christ are the elect of God. These are the ones that Jesus actually set out to reach among the "readers" of the Olivet Discourse.

Strength to Escape?

Now that one knows the identity of the reader, let's apply this knowledge to an all too often misunderstood passage (italics used for emphasis):

"Be on guard so that your hearts are not weighed down with dissipation and drunkenness and the worries of this life and that day catch you unexpectedly, like a trap. For it will come upon all who live on the face of the whole earth. Be alert at all times, *praying that you may have the strength to escape all these things that will take place, and to stand before the Son of Man*" (Luke 21:34–36).

Many mistakenly believe this passage is directed to the saints of the last generation who are already in a right standing with the Lord, and furthermore, that it is a reference to the rapture of the living saints at the time of the resurrection. But neither belief is correct. At this point in the Olivet Discourse, Jesus is still addressing the Jewish "reader" of the last generation who will need to escape Jerusalem at the time of the abomination. Although Luke does not specifically record the phrase "let the reader understand," we know when examining a harmony of the Synoptic Gospels, i.e., Matthew, Mark, and Luke, Jesus is still addressing the reader in this part of the discourse which specifically concerns the need for watchfulness by the last-generation Jewish "reader." The following chart compares the corresponding scriptural references of the Synoptic Gospels in the latter part of the discourse, which deal with (1) the Lord's return, (2) the fig tree, and (3) the need for watchfulness:

Table 2.3. Harmony of the Lord's Closing Remarks in the Olivet Discourse

	Matthew	Mark	Luke
1. The Lord's return:	24:30–31	13:26–27	21:27–28
2. The fig tree:	24:32–35	13:28–31	21:29–33
3. Need for watchfulness:	24:36–44	13:32–37	21:34–36

In the third section, i.e., the need for watchfulness, the Lord urges the reader to always be on the alert, especially with a keen eye on the abomination of desolation in the account of Matthew and Mark, and on the armies that will surround Jerusalem in the account of Luke. Jesus told the last-generation Jewish "reader" to be prepared to escape Jerusalem at the moment either of these events occur. Of the three accounts, Luke is the only one that quotes Jesus as telling the reader to pray that one have the strength to escape all these things so that one may stand before the Son of Man. In other words, just as Matthew and Mark record that one should pray that the escape may not be in winter or on the Sabbath,[5] similarly, Luke records, "pray that you have strength to escape all these things." When gathering each of the Lord's words in this section of the discourse, one comes away with the following: If you are pregnant or nursing, pray that you have strength to escape! If you find yourself trapped on your rooftop, pray that you have strength to escape! If it's too cold or too hot or too anything, pray that you have strength to escape! Jesus is simply urging the last-generation, Jewish, unsaved "reader" to pray to God for help so that he or she might have the physical strength to run for their lives—because if they escape, they might be among the elect and therefore stand before the Son of Man.

To suppose that Christ is encouraging one who is already in a right relationship with God to pray for physical strength to escape all the things that are coming upon the world and therefore, in essence, to pray to have strength to be included in the rapture is to misinterpret the text as well as grossly misunderstand the gospel. Once a person is born-again and is in a right relationship to God, neither Jesus nor the apostles ever instruct a believer to pray for physical strength to stand before the Lord,

---

5. Jesus knew that anyone in the last generation that was actively practicing Judaism would be hesitant to travel too far on the Sabbath (compare Exodus 20:8-11 and Acts 1:12); therefore he urged the "reader" to pray that his or her escape may not fall on the Sabbath (Matt 24:20).

because physical strength has nothing to do with standing before the Son of Man and has nothing to do with salvation and certainly has nothing to do with being raptured. If anyone is to be raptured and ultimately stand before the Son of Man, it will only be because one has confessed Christ and thereby been credited the righteousness of Christ. Anything beyond Christ's righteousness, at least as it concerns salvation or the rapture, is as Isaiah declared: "like filthy rags" (Isa 64:6).

On the Mount of Olives, the reason the Lord did not urge the disciples to run for their lives in the face of adversity was because they were already in a right relationship with the Lord. All they needed to do was follow the same instructions that Paul would later give the Ephesians, the Thessalonians, and the Romans, and that was to put on the whole armor of God so that they would be able to stand firm in Christ in that evil day. It is the Jewish part of the elect—who have not yet confessed Christ—who will ultimately need to pray for strength to escape at the moment of the abomination of desolation, not the part of the elect who have already confessed Christ. If the Lord shows great concern for one's physical safety in the face of persecution, as he did for the future Jewish "reader" of the Olivet Discourse, then one might need to reevaluate their relationship with Christ. But when a believer is already in a right standing with the Lord and then happens to face persecution, as did the disciples during the days of Christ or the saints during "that future evil day," the Lord expects that individual to stand firm in the faith and never waver. The days of praying for physical strength are over.

Deception Follows the Greatest Suffering

Once the last-generation Jewish reader flees Jerusalem at the sight of the abomination of desolation, and then, later, God miraculously ends the greatest suffering in the history of the world for the sake of the elect, the danger is not over. And what was this second threat? After God ends the period of the greatest suffering, Jesus warned the reader that false messiahs and false prophets will then pop up everywhere, producing great signs and miracles and claiming to be or to have seen the Messiah. In order to convince "the reader" that none of these people are the Messiah nor have seen the Messiah, Jesus said his return will not be a secretive event and seen only by a few, but rather, when the Son of Man does return, everyone will see him. Observe:

> Then if anyone says to you, "Look! Here is the Messiah!" or "There he is!"—do not believe it. For false messiahs and false prophets will appear and produce great signs and omens, to lead astray, if possible, even the elect. Take note, I have told you beforehand. So, if they say to you, "Look! He is in the wilderness," do not go out. If they say, "Look! He is in the inner rooms," do not believe it. For as the lightning comes from the east and flashes as far as the west, so will be the coming of the Son of Man. Wherever the corpse is, there the vultures will gather. (Matt 24:23–28)

Why is Jesus giving this warning? Because when "the reader" escapes Jerusalem at the abomination and reaches safety outside of the city, the Lord wants the reader to remain hidden and protected. The Lord's reasoning is obvious: If a reader successfully escapes Jerusalem at the abomination and then reaches a safe exile, but later comes out of hiding because someone said they had seen the Messiah, and thereby, that person gets himself or herself killed, then that reader was never part of the elect. In order to prevent this scenario from happening, Jesus warned "the reader" that once he or she reaches safety, don't come out for any reason—even if some say they are the Lord or that they've seen the Lord.

Christ Indicates a Second Period of Suffering

With Christ's warning of future deception caused by false messiahs and false prophets now accomplished, the Lord next prophesies the appearance of heavenly signs. Since Jesus had just finished speaking about deception, one would expect the Lord to say, "Immediately after the deception of those days, the sun will be darkened, and the moon will not give its light, etc., etc.," but instead he says the following:

> Immediately after the suffering of those days the sun will be darkened, and the moon will not give its light; the stars will fall from heaven, and the powers of heaven will be shaken. (Matt 24:29)

Curiously, instead of saying "Immediately after the *deception* of those days," Jesus said "Immediately after the *suffering* of those days." Of what suffering was the Lord speaking? He couldn't have been referencing the greatest suffering in the world because remember Jesus said God will end that particular suffering (Matt 24:22). Furthermore, when Jesus brings up the subject of false messiahs and false prophets, although he mentions their ability to perform signs and wonders, he doesn't give any indication that they will cause any type of suffering. Again, here's the passage:

"For at that time there will be great suffering, such as has not been from the beginning of the world until now, no, and never will be. And if those days had not been cut short, no one would be saved; but for the sake of the elect those days will be cut short. Then if anyone says to you, 'Look! Here is the Messiah!' or 'There he is!'—do not believe it. For false messiahs and false prophets will appear and produce great signs and omens..." (Matt 24:21–24a).

Logically, if the greatest suffering in the history of the world has been ended by God prior to the appearance of the false messiahs and false prophets, then Jesus must be referencing a "second period of suffering" that will promptly end at the heavenly signs. Observe:

Table 2.4. Jesus Indicates Two Periods of Suffering				
1. Abomination of Desolation (Matt 24:15)	2. Greatest suffering in history (Matt 24:21)	3. God ends the greatest suffering in history for the sake of the elect (Matt 24:22)	4. Period of Deception: False messiahs and false prophets claim to be or to have seen the Messiah + A 2nd Period of Suffering (Matt 24:23–29a)	5. Heavenly Signs (Matt 24:29b)

Because of the words of Jesus, or rather, the lack of his words, one is not yet sure who or what causes this second wave of suffering. Nevertheless, he does seem to indicate that the suffering is congruent with the period of deception caused by the signs and wonders of false messiahs and false prophets. Whether one has assumed correctly in this assessment remains to be seen.

Paul Also Spoke of a Period of Deception and Suffering

Where have we recently read of someone who will deceive others by performing signs and wonders in the last days? As you well know, Paul described a certain deception that will be caused by the man of lawlessness just prior to the arrival of the Day of the Lord (italics used for emphasis):

"The coming of the lawless one is apparent in the working of Satan, who uses all power, signs, lying wonders, and every kind of wicked *deception* for those who are perishing, because they refused to love the truth and so be saved. For this reason God sends them a *powerful delusion*, leading them to believe what is false, so that all who have not believed the truth but took pleasure in unrighteousness will be condemned" (2 Thess 2:9–12).

Could it be that the period of deception caused by the man of lawlessness prior to the Day of the Lord is the same period of deception prophesied by Jesus that will appear prior to the heavenly signs? Perhaps. The answer will depend largely in part on the relationship between Jesus' reference to the heavenly signs and Paul's reference to the Day of the Lord. If it turns out that Jesus and Paul were referencing the same period, we may have come across at least one of the causes for the second wave of suffering. Remember, since we had learned that the man of lawlessness will come to a point whereby he will truly believe that he is God (2 Thess 2:4), it was easily postulated that just as the unrighteous will be deceived by the man's miraculous powers into bowing down and worshiping him, the saints, in contrast, will not be deceived by his powers and therefore will refuse to bow down and worship the man. And for this, one might easily surmise that they will be punished—even executed. The following chart reflects the proposal that the man of lawlessness is in someway connected to the second wave of suffering:

Table 2.5. The Second Period of Suffering: Includes the Man of Lawlessness?				
1. Abomination of Desolation (Matt 24:15)	2. Greatest suffering in history (Matt 24:21)	3. God ends the greatest suffering in history for the sake of the elect (Matt 24:22)	4. Period of Deception: False messiahs and false prophets claim to be or to have seen the Messiah + A 2nd Period of Suffering (Matt 24:23–29a) includes the Man of Lawlessness?	5. Heavenly Signs (Matt 24:29b)

Next, in order to solidify the notion that the man of lawlessness is associated with the second period of suffering, one must first determine if there is an alignment of the time frames between Christ's "heavenly signs" in the Olivet Discourse and Paul's "Day of the Lord" in the letters to the Thessalonians.

The Heavenly Signs and the Day of the Lord

As already indicated, Jesus said that immediately after the second period of suffering will come supernatural signs in the heavens (Matt 24:29). Few apocalyptic events serve such a significant milestone of end times as the appearance of the heavenly signs. Although there may be slight variations in their description throughout the Scripture, the gist is always the same: The sun and moon will become darkened and "the stars" will fall from the skies. Since Jesus indicated that suffering and deception will precede the heavenly signs, what does Scripture say follows the signs? According to Joel and Isaiah, the Day of the Lord (italics used for emphasis):

1. "I will show portents in the heavens and on the earth, blood and fire and columns of smoke. The sun shall be turned to darkness, and the moon to blood, before the great and terrible *day of the Lord* comes" (Joel 2:30).

2. "See, the *day of the Lord* comes, cruel, with wrath and fierce anger, to make the earth a desolation, and to destroy its sinners from it. For the stars of the heavens and their constellations will not give their light; the sun will be dark at its rising, and the moon will not shed its light" (Isa 13:9–10).

That's clear enough. But looking again at the Olivet Discourse, what did Jesus say would follow the heavenly signs? If not careful, it's easy to assume that Jesus said the heavenly signs would immediately be followed by the appearance of the Son of Man, leading one to conclude that the Day of the Lord is synonymous with the appearance of the Son of Man. It's an honest mistake and unfortunately it's a common mistake. But Jesus didn't say the heavenly signs will be followed by the appearance of the Son of Man. Rather he said the heavenly signs will be followed by "the powers of heaven being shaken." Again, the Lord's exact words:

"Immediately after the suffering of those days the sun will be darkened, and the moon will not give its light; the stars will fall from heaven, and the powers of heaven will be shaken" (Matt 24:29).

Since Joel and Isaiah said the heavenly signs will be followed by "the Day of the Lord" and Jesus said the heavenly signs will be followed by "the shaking of the powers of heaven," then could it be that the Day of the Lord is synonymous with the shaking of the powers of heaven, rather than the appearance of Christ? Absolutely! That's exactly the case. In the following passages, notice how the author of Hebrews and Isaiah confirm that the Day of the Lord is characterized by the shaking of heaven as well as the earth (italics used for emphasis):

1. "See that you do not refuse the one who is speaking; for if they did not escape when they refused the one who warned them on earth, how much less will we escape if we reject the one who warns from heaven! At that time his voice shook the earth; but now he has promised, '*Yet once more I will shake not only the earth but also heaven.*' This phrase, 'Yet once more,' indicates the removal of what is shaken—that is created things—so that what cannot be shaken may remain" (Heb 12:25–27).

2. "The earth is utterly broken, the earth is torn asunder, *the earth is violently shaken*. The earth staggers like a drunkard, it sways like a hut; its transgressions lies heavy upon it, and it falls, and will not rise again. *On that day the Lord will punish the host of heaven in heaven, and on earth the kings of the earth*" (Isa 24:19–21).

3. "Therefore *I will make the heavens tremble, and the earth will be shaken out of its place, at the wrath of the Lord of hosts in the day of his fierce anger*" (Isa 13:13).

Each of the above passages are references to the Day of the Lord—not to the manifestation of Jesus Christ. The conclusion is simple but its importance cannot be overstated: When Jesus uttered the words "the powers of heaven will be shaken" as coming after the heavenly signs and before the appearance of the Son of Man, he was specifically referencing the rather lengthy period of the Day of the Lord. And if this precision of the Lord's words is not recognized and accounted for, regrettably, the correct sequence of end times given by Christ will be lost to the reader. Therefore, rather than needlessly wondering what Christ meant by the phrase "the powers of heaven will be shaken," a better question is Why did the Lord spend so little time on the subject of the Day in the Olivet Discourse? Believe it or not, the answer can be deduced from a little side journey where a Canaanite woman approaches Jesus and requests that he cast a demon out of her daughter:

"Jesus left that place and went away to the district of Tyre and Sidon. Just then a Canaanite woman from that region came out and started shouting, 'Have mercy on me, Lord, Son of David; my daughter is tormented by a demon.' But he did not answer her at all. And his disciples came and urged him, saying, 'Send her away, for she keeps shouting after us.' He answered, 'I was sent only to the lost sheep of the house of Israel.' But she came and knelt before him, saying, 'Lord, help me.' He answered, 'It is not fair to take the children's food and throw it to the dogs'" (Matt 15:21–26).

Most know the outcome: After Jesus attempted to dissuade her, she responded with, "Yes, Lord, yet even the dogs eat the crumbs that fall from their masters' table." And with that amazingly astute reply, Jesus healed her daughter. Here's the point: Although Jesus died for the sins of the whole world, his earthly ministry was directed "only to the lost sheep of the house of Israel" (v. 24). Although his earthly ministry would necessarily include the night of the Olivet Discourse, the ministry, somewhat surprisingly to many, included the lost sheep of the house of Israel—in the last generation! As proven throughout this study, Jesus spent the majority of the discourse addressing the last-generation Jewish "reader" because he knew that within this group was to be found the last-generation Jewish "remnant," which, although part of a different generation, was still part of the lost sheep of Israel. Therefore, he warned them centuries in advance to flee Jerusalem at the moment of the abomination, and then, once they were in a safe hiding place, they were to stay put because soon various false messiahs and false prophets would appear, performing extraordinary signs and wonders and claiming to be or to have seen the Messiah. Christ knew that if his warnings were heeded, many of the readers would later call on the name of the Lord at the sight of the heavenly signs, just as prophesied by the prophet Joel. In hindsight, the Lord's mission during the Olivet Discourse was twofold that night: to prepare the disciples for suffering and death, and to help the future Jewish remnant get to the point of conversion. Jesus knew that the subject matter of the Day of the Lord was not pertinent to the disciples nor to the last-generation Jewish elect. How so? The Day would arrive well after the disciples had passed, and when the Day does finally arrive during the last generation, the Jewish elect will be tucked away in safety.

Reconciliation of the False Messiahs and Prophets with the Man of Lawlessness

So what are we left with? Jesus described a period of deception and suffering that follows the greatest suffering in history yet precedes the Day of the Lord, during which false messiahs and false prophets will produce great signs and wonders, and Paul described a period of deception and suffering, whereby a certain man of lawlessness will deceive the unrighteous as well as persecute the righteous, leading up to the Day of the Lord. It is obvious that Jesus and Paul spoke of the same period. And how should Christ's and Paul's words be reconciled? After God shortens the days of the greatest suffering in history, and false messiahs and false prophets begin to appear like ants at a picnic, the man of lawlessness will emerge from among them at some unknown point in time. However, rather than just deceiving the unrighteous with signs and wonders, as will be the *modus operandi* of the false messiahs and false prophets, the man of lawlessness will additionally initiate a period of persecution of the saints. Observe:

Table 2.6. Jesus' Period of Deception and Second Period of Suffering Corresponds to Paul's Period of Deception and Persecutions Caused by the Man of Lawlessness

Jesus:	Abom. of desolation (Matt 24:15)	Greatest suffering in history (Matt 24:21)	Greatest suffering ends (Matt 24:22)	Deception by false messiahs and false prophets (Matt 24:23–28)	"Second" period of suffering of those days (Matt 24:29a)	Heavenly signs appear (Matt 24:29b)	God shakes the powers of heaven (Matt 24:29c)
Paul:					New deception and persecution begin with the revealing of the man of lawlessness (2 Thess 2:3–12)	"They" will be saying there is peace and security when the Day of the Lord arrives (1 Thess 5:3)	The Day of the Lord arrives (1 Thess 5:4–11)

Peace and Security?

The above reconciliation explains Paul's curious comment in 1 Thess 5:3 that "they will be saying there is peace and security" at the arrival of the Day of the Lord. Despite the fact that the world will have gone through a period of the greatest suffering in history, at some point God will end it. This will be followed by deception from false messiahs and false prophets, which, in turn, will be followed by more deception but also persecution of the saints by the man of lawlessness. Hopefully one can see that as the unrighteous are deceived into submitting to the demands of the man of lawlessness, he will spare their lives, which will therefore lead them to enjoy a false sense of peace and security, causing them to utter the heretofore inexplicable proclamation that "there is peace and security." In their minds, as long as the man only persecutes and kills the righteous, the unrighteous will feel safe and secure.

Question: Since one can see that Paul spent some time warning the Thessalonians about the coming of the man of lawlessness, even warning them to put on the "armor of God" because of the coming of "that evil day," have you ever wondered why Jesus didn't do likewise, and also warn "the reader" about the coming persecution from the man of lawlessness and "that evil day," rather than doing as he did, which was just warn "the reader" of the coming deception by the many false messiahs and false prophets? Perhaps, the reason is that, similar to the fact there was no need for Jesus to discuss the details of the Day of the Lord with "the reader" because he knew that "the reader" will be tucked away somewhere in safety outside of Jerusalem during the Day, Jesus also knew that "the reader" will simultaneously be hidden away during "the evil day" perpetrated by the man of lawlessness. (Whether this is the case or not, our upcoming study in Revelation will soon disclose the answer.)

Appearance of the Son of Man

After the heavenly signs and the shaking of the powers of heaven, Jesus said the Son of Man will appear. Not only is Christ's appearance the climax of the Day of the Lord, but it is the climax of human history:

> Then the sign of the Son of Man will appear in heaven, and then all the tribes of the earth will mourn, and they will see "the Son of Man coming on the clouds of heaven" with power and great glory. (Matt 24:30)

This is the moment for which the saints have been waiting and hoping. Here, again, are the words of Paul:

"For it is indeed just of God to repay with affliction those who afflict you, and to give relief to the afflicted as well as to us, when the Lord Jesus is revealed from heaven with his mighty angels in flaming fire, inflicting vengeance on those who do not know God and on those who do not obey the gospel of our Lord Jesus. These will suffer the punishment of eternal destruction, separated from the presence of the Lord and from the glory of his might, when he comes to be glorified by his saints and to be marveled at on that day among all who have believed, because our testimony to you was believed" (2 Thess 1:6–10).

Christ's manifestation will be the most glorious and spectacular event in the history of the world—at least from the believers' perspective. Not so much from the unrighteous. When Jesus said "all the tribes of the earth will mourn" he was revealing the reaction of the unrighteous. To be honest, the fact that there are any unrighteous alive and left at the manifestation of Christ after the shaking of the powers of heaven, also known as the plagues and judgments of the Day of the Lord, boggles the mind. Look at the words of Isaiah, when describing the aftermath of the Day of the Lord (italics used for emphasis):

"I will put an end to the pride of the arrogant, and lay low the insolence of tyrants. *I will make mortals more rare than gold, and humans than the gold of Ophir.* Therefore I will make the heavens tremble, and the earth will be shaken out of its place, at the wrath of the Lord of hosts in the day of his fierce anger" (Isa 13:11b–13).

Hopefully one can see that after God has distributed his many terrible and severe judgments among the unrighteous inhabitants of the earth, none of the remaining survivors will be saying "there is peace and security" at the moment of Christ's appearance, as they will at the initial appearance of the heavenly signs. Although the Day of the Lord and the manifestation of Christ are inextricably intertwined, as the manifestation of Christ is certainly the climax of the Day of the Lord, the two are not one and the same.[6]

The Gathering

After describing the Son of Man's appearance, Jesus next describes the gathering of the elect:

> And he will send out his angels with a loud trumpet call, and they will gather his elect from the four winds, from one end of heaven to the other. (Matt 24:31)

This is a clear reference to the resurrection and rapture of the saints. Don't be misled into thinking that the resurrection of the elect is somehow different than the resurrection of the saints, or that the elect refer to the Jews while the saints refer to the church. The elect and the saints are one and the same, and the elect are composed of both Jews and gentiles. Recall an earlier passage:

"Because if you confess with your lips that Jesus is Lord and believe in your heart that God raised him from the dead, you will be saved. For one believes with the heart and so is justified, and one confesses with the mouth and so is saved. The scripture says, 'No one who believes in him will

---

6. Unless one understands the simple fact that the manifestation of Christ occurs at the end of the Day of the Lord rather than its beginning, the correct sequence of end times will always be unobtainable for that person.

be put to shame.' For there is no distinction between Jew and Greek; the same Lord is Lord of all and is generous to all who call on him. For, 'Everyone who calls on the name of the Lord shall be saved'" (Rom 10:9–13).

If God is going to deal differently with the Jews in the last generation than he does now with the Jews and gentiles in this generation, then someone forgot to tell Paul. Although the apostle does reveal a mystery that the last-generation Jewish remnant will only confess Christ after the full number of gentiles has come in (Rom 11:25), it will be the same confession, of the same Name, leading to the same salvation, and resulting in the same resurrection. As Paul said, "There is no distinction between Jew and Greek." If you hear any teaching to the contrary, discard it. It is a false teaching.

At the moment of the gathering, note that Jesus said he will send out his angels with a loud trumpet call (Matt 24:31). Paul references the same trumpet:

"For the Lord himself, with a cry of command, with the archangel's call and with the sound of God's trumpet, will descend from heaven, and the dead in Christ will rise first. Then we who are alive, who are left, will be caught up in the clouds together with them to meet the Lord in the air; and so we will be with the Lord forever" (1 Thess 4:16–17).

Next, Jesus said that his angels will gather his elect from the four winds, from one end of heaven to the other. One might ask, Why did Jesus only reference heaven in this passage? Did not Paul say that the gathering would include those who are alive and left on the earth as well as the souls of the saints from heaven? Here again are the words of Paul:

"But we do not want you to be uninformed, brothers and sisters, about those who have died, so that you may not grieve as others do who have no hope. For since we believe that Jesus died and rose again, even so, through Jesus, God will bring with him those who have died. For this we declare to you by the word of the Lord, that we who are alive, who are left until the coming of the Lord, will by no means precede those who have died" (1 Thess 4:13–15).

Although Matthew only records Jesus saying that his angels will gather the elect from one end of heaven to the other, in the following Mark records the entirety of Christ's statement, citing the gathering of the saints from both heaven and earth, which is a certain reference to the gathering of the righteous souls from heaven, as well as those who are alive and left on the earth:

"Then he will send out the angels, and gather his elect from the four winds, from the ends of the earth to the ends of heaven" (Mark 13:27).

Mark's added detail revealed that Jesus was well aware of the rapture event, but it was Paul who was the one chosen to unveil the details of the mystery to the church, and specifically, to the Thessalonians and the Corinthians. And only to the latter, as you know, did the apostle add the revelation of the glorified body.

In the following, notice that when Jesus finally reached the subject of the appearance of the Son of Man and the gathering of the saints, he, like Paul, mentioned the appearance of the Son of Man before mentioning the gathering of the saints, possibly lending credence to the notion that the return of the Lord and the gathering of the saints are two separate events, and that the coming of Christ precedes the resurrection and rapture of the saints (ellipses are placed for emphasis):

1. The words of Jesus: "Then the sign of the Son of Man will appear in heaven, and all the tribes of the earth will mourn, and they will see 'the Son of Man coming on the clouds of heaven' with power and great glory . . . . And he will send out his angels with a loud trumpet call, and they will gather his elect from the four winds, from one end of heaven to the other" (Matt 24:30–31).

2. The words of Paul: "As to the coming of our Lord Jesus Christ . . . and our being gathered together to him . . ." (2 Thess 2:1a).

The one-two relationship continues to be a real possibility; however, as we have consistently maintained to this point, until a passage either confirms or refutes the one-two order, we will continue to consider the two events as one unit, if only for the sake of simplicity.

Closing Thoughts: Two Addressees but One Sequence

When Jesus gave his Olivet Discourse about two thousand years ago, he knew that subsequent generations of the Jewish people would read it and wonder if they were the generation in question—the one that would witness the apocalyptic abomination that will cause the desolation of their city, the city of Jerusalem. He told the Jewish reader who witnesses this abomination that it will be followed by a series of consecutive events: a period of the greatest suffering in history, a sudden and miraculous end to the suffering, a period of deception by false messiahs and false prophets, a second period of suffering, the appearance of supernatural heavenly signs, the shaking of the powers of heaven (the Day of the Lord), and finally, the Son of Man's appearance and the gathering of the elect. However, when one reflects back on Paul's sequence determined from 1 and 2 Thessalonians, one sees that the apostle did not discuss the abomination, the period of the greatest suffering in history, the sudden and miraculous end to that suffering, nor the specific emergence of false messiahs and false prophets. Instead, he began with the period of deception and persecution perpetrated by a certain man of lawlessness, and then, without skipping a beat, resumed with the exact events prophesied by Christ: the Day of the Lord, the coming of the Lord, and the gathering of the saints. Why the difference? Simply, the intentions of Jesus and Paul were different. Jesus started at the very beginning—with the abomination of desolation—so as to prepare the readers for the physical escape that was direly needed in order for them to preserve life so that later they could confess the name of Jesus Christ. Although he did not reveal to the reader the heinous act comprising the abomination, Jesus knew the reader would recognize it when it was seen. Next, after having escaped the dangers of the abomination-event and finding a safe refuge away from Jerusalem, Jesus again warns the readers not to come out from where they are hiding because certain false messiahs and false prophets will try to lure them out into the open, whereby, once again, an attempt will be made upon their lives. When analyzing Christ's words, one clearly sees the Lord endeavoring to protect the physical life of the future Jewish reader twice: first, at the moment of the abomination, and, secondly, after the reader has reached a safe refuge outside of Jerusalem.

Paul, on the other hand, did not set out to give his addressee, the Thessalonians, a complete one-two-three sequence in either one of his letters. No doubt, the apostle had already accomplished that task when he had personally visited the Thessalonians during his second missionary journey (Acts 17:1–9). Rather than repeating himself in the letters, Paul simply responded to the pressing questions and issues that the Thessalonians presented him. In the first letter, one learns that the church had questions about those who had already died in Christ; Paul responded with a treatise on the resurrection and rapture. They also wanted to know the times and seasons of the end-time events; he responded with an exposition on the unexpectancy of the Day of the Lord. In the second letter, Paul dealt with the Thessalonians' belief that the Day had arrived, saying that that scenario was impossible because the rebellion and the revealing of the man of lawlessness had not yet occurred. It is because of these unique circumstances that one has to closely analyze Paul's many responses in order to ascertain the correct sequence.

∼

The simplicity of the sequence of the Olivet Discourse was a welcome respite from the somewhat tedious task of determining Paul's understanding of the sequence. However, in the end both sequences agreed perfectly with each other:

Table 2.7. Reconciliation of the Sequences in the Olivet Discourse and 1 & 2 Thessalonians	
Sequence in the Olivet Discourse	**Sequence in 1 & 2 Thessalonians**
1. Abomination of desolation (Matt 24:15)	
2. Greatest suffering in history (Matt 24:21)	
3. God ends the greatest suffering in history. (Matt 24:22)	
4. Deception begins with false messiahs and false prophets (Matt 24:23–28)	
5. There is a second period of suffering: "Immediately after the suffering of those days . . ." (Matt 24:29a)	New deception and persecution begin with the revealing of the man of lawlessness. (2 Thess 2:3–12)
6. Heavenly signs appear. (Matt 24:29b)	"They" will be saying there is peace and security at the coming of the Day of the Lord. (1 Thess 5:3)
7. God shakes the powers of heaven. (Matt 24:29c)	The Day of the Lord arrives. (1 Thess 5:4–11)
8a. The Son of Man appears. (Matt 24:30)	The Return of the Lord (2 Thess 1:5–12)
8b. The elect are gathered from the ends of heaven. (Matt 24:31)	The Resurrection and Rapture of the Saints (1 Thess 4:13–18)
It is still to be determined whether these two events are simultaneous or separate.	

CHAPTER 3

The Thirteen Conversations in Revelation

NEXT AND FINAL STOP: the Isle of Patmos. As we leave the Mount of Olives and head toward the Mediterranean coast, we board a ship in Caesarea and sail to a tiny prison island off the coast of Ephesus. The journey is long, about a thousand miles from the port of Caesarea. But it will be well worth the trip if one hopes to retrieve the last four end-time sequences. It is on the Isle of Patmos that a prisoner resided about two thousand years ago, a disciple by the name of John, who often prayed and sought the face of the Lord while confined on the island. While praying in the Spirit on one particular day of the week, one that John identified as the Lord's day, Jesus appeared to the disciple (Rev 1:9–20), and spoke to him concerning the conditions of seven local churches with the instructions to relay each message to the appropriate church (Rev 2:1—3:22). But the divine visitation did not end there. After the Lord's appearance, John was apparently whisked up to heaven and God's throne room:

> After this I looked, and there in heaven a door stood open! And the first voice, which I had heard speaking to me like a trumpet, said, "Come up here, and I will show you what must take place after this." At once I was in the spirit, and there in heaven stood a throne, with one seated on the throne! (Rev 4:1–2)

To say that John must have been dumbfounded is an understatement. As he gazed at the entire area, his eyes became fixed in the direction that seemed to be the center of everything—where the Lord was sitting on his throne. Never mentioning any details of the Lord's visage, John only described the beautiful rainbow-like colors and hues surrounding his throne:

> And the one seated there looks like jasper and carnelian, and around the throne is a rainbow that looks like emerald. Around the throne are twenty-four thrones, and seated on the thrones are twenty-four elders, dressed in white robes, with golden crowns on their heads. Coming from the throne are flashes of lightning, and rumblings and peals of thunder, and in front of the throne burn seven flaming torches, which are the seven spirits of God; and in front of the throne there is something like a sea of glass, like crystal. (Rev 4:3–6a)

The scene must have been quite intimidating to John because accompanying the beautiful colors and hues above the throne and the tranquil sea of glass below the throne were the deafening sounds of thunder and blinding flashes of lightning emanating from its direction. He then noticed what appeared to be twenty-four men surrounding the throne, identified only as "elders," wearing white robes and golden crowns on their heads, as they too were seated on individual thrones.

What could John have been thinking? One minute he's on the Isle of Patmos praying as he usually does everyday and then, soon afterwards, he finds himself in heaven's throne room surrounded by bright flashes of vibrant, chromatic lights and loud, unfamiliar sounds. Although the scene was extraordinarily beautiful, the experience must have been unbelievably unsettling, to say the least! Was John's body transported up to heaven or just his spirit? Mind you, the Lord could have done it any way he pleased. Compare John's experience to that of Paul's:

"It is necessary to boast; nothing is to be gained by it, but I will go on to visions and revelations of the Lord. I know a person in Christ who fourteen years ago was caught up to the third heaven—whether in the body or out of the body I do not know; God knows. And I know that such a person—whether in the body or out of the body I do not know; God knows—was caught up into Paradise and heard things that are not to be told, that no mortal is permitted to repeat. On behalf of such a one I will boast, but on my own behalf I will not boast, except of my weaknesses. But if I wish to boast, I will not be a fool, for I will be speaking the truth" (2 Cor 12:1–6a).

Although Paul too had been caught up to heaven, he did not know whether he had been taken bodily or just in the spirit. Either way, of one thing Paul was certain: He was not allowed to share any of what he saw or heard while in the third heaven (2 Cor 12:4). Fortunately for us, unlike the instructions given to Paul, John was not prohibited from sharing any of his experiences, and so the narrative continues:

> Around the throne, and on each side of the throne, are four living creatures, full of eyes in front and behind: the first living creature like a lion, the second living creature like an ox, the third living creature with a face like a human face, and the fourth living creature like a flying eagle. And the four living creatures, each of them with six wings, are full of eyes all around and inside. Day and night without ceasing they sing, "Holy, holy, holy, the Lord God the Almighty, who was and is and is to come."
> And whenever the living creatures give glory and honor and thanks to the one who is seated on the throne, who lives forever and ever, the twenty-four elders fall before the one who is seated on the throne and worship the one who lives forever and ever; they cast their crowns before the throne singing,
> "You are worthy, our Lord and God, to receive glory and honor and power, for you created all things, and by your will they existed and were created." (Rev 4:6b–11)

In addition to the twenty-four elders were four strange-looking supernatural creatures surrounding God's throne. The sight of the elders and creatures worshiping and singing around the throne must have been indeed perplexing for John, but the sacred atmosphere probably wasn't. The worship that was directed toward the Lord was no doubt the one part of this heavenly experience that made John feel somewhat at ease. The disciple knew what it was like to come into the sacred presence of God. Often in the Spirit, John had experienced that same sacred presence in his prayer life (Rev 1:10).

Looking closely at the creatures, John no doubt quickly identified the four as the same seen by the prophet Ezekiel:

"As I looked, a stormy wind came out of the north: a great cloud with brightness around it and fire flashing forth continually, and in the middle of the fire, something like gleaming amber. In the middle of it was something like four living creatures. This was their appearance: they were of human form. Each had four faces, and each of them had four wings. Their legs were straight, and the soles of their feet were like the sole of a calf's foot; and they sparkled like burnished bronze. Under their wings on their four sides they had human hands. And the four had their faces and their wings thus: their wings touched one another; each of them moved straight ahead, without turning as they moved. As for the appearance of their faces: the four had the face of a human being, the face of a lion on the right side, the face of an ox on the left side, and the face of an eagle; such were their faces. Their wings were spread out above; each creature had two wings, each of which touched the wing of another, while two covered their bodies" (Ezek 1:4–11).

The four angels that Ezekiel saw accompany the Lord on his journey to the earth were the same John now saw standing around God's throne in heaven. Why the slight difference in the description by the two men? As one can see, Ezekiel's descriptions are much more detailed, describing the creatures from head to foot. When speculating why Ezekiel described four faces on each creature while John described just one, perhaps John was only describing the one face he saw on each creature from where he was standing in the throne room. In Ezekiel's vision, the creatures are in constant, rapid movement, which would have given Ezekiel ample opportunity to see the creatures from many angles, whereas in John's vision they seem to be stationary, standing around God's throne. Or perhaps, God just simply cloaked the true appearance of the creatures in a slightly different manner to each prophet. Either way, one knows that Ezekiel was led by the Holy Spirit to describe in detail the appearance of the four while John was led to concentrate on the frequent manner in which they worshiped the Lord. In the end, these are the same four angels that are always seen in Scripture surrounding God and his throne, whether on earth or in heaven.

The First Conversation and the Scroll

At some moment during this seemingly dreamlike experience, John noticed that the One who was seated on the throne had something in his right hand:

> Then I saw in the right hand of the one seated on the throne a scroll written on the inside and on the back, sealed with seven seals; and I saw a mighty angel proclaiming with a loud voice, "Who is worthy to open the scroll and break its seals?" And no one in heaven or on earth or under the earth was able to open the scroll or to look into it. (Rev 5:1–3)

As soon as John noticed the scroll, he saw "a mighty angel" step forward and proclaim with a very loud and authoritative voice, asking who was worthy to open the scroll. John quickly glanced toward as many individuals as possible, whose attention had been suddenly captivated by the same startling presence of the imposing angel. At first it appeared to John that the scroll in the Father's hand would remain sealed because no one present would step forward and approach the Father and receive the scroll from his hand. And the simple reason was that no one was worthy. The four living creatures were not worthy, nor were the twenty-four elders. Suddenly John began to weep:

> And I began to weep bitterly because no one was found worthy to open the scroll or to look into it. Then one of the elders said to me, "Do not weep. See, the Lion of the tribe of Judah, the Root of David, has conquered, so that he can open the scroll and its seven seals."
>
> Then I saw between the throne and the four living creatures and among the elders a Lamb standing as if it had been slaughtered, having seven horns and seven eyes, which are the seven spirits of God sent out into all the earth. He went and took the scroll from the right hand of the one who was seated on the throne. (Rev 5:4–7)

And then something amazing happened! Out of this extraordinary and surreal scene engulfing John—this scene filled with sounds of the crackling of thunder and blinding flashes of lightning, with the vivid colors of reds, greens, yellows, and blues permeating the entire throne room, and with strange creatures covered with multiple faces and hundreds of eyes—one of the twenty-four elders actually stepped out of this cacophony of sights and sounds and spoke to John! When that happened, John then suddenly saw what appeared to be a Lamb standing near the throne where the Father was seated. What was the significance of the elder's encounter? The answer is extraordinary! When someone in the throne room approached John and conversed with him, that meant that John wasn't just in some dream-like trance back on earth where he was seeing a vision of heaven's throne room, but at least his spirit was actually in God's throne room in the here and now. However, even John may not have been aware of that fact the moment it happened. Compare John's experience to Peter's, when the apostle also didn't know whether he was seeing a vision, or something very real:

"The very night before Herod was going to bring him out, Peter, bound with two chains, was sleeping between two soldiers, while guards in front of the door were keeping watch over the prison. Suddenly an angel of the Lord appeared and a light shone in the cell. He tapped Peter on the side and woke him, saying, 'Get up quickly.' And the chains fell off his wrists. The angel said to him, 'Fasten your belt and put on your sandals.' He did so. Then he said to him, 'Wrap your cloak around you and follow me.' Peter went out and followed him; he did not realize that what was happening with the angel's help was real; he thought he was seeing a vision" (Acts 12:6–9).

Peter didn't know it at the time, but the moment the angel engaged the apostle, i.e., tapped him on the side and spoke to him, that interaction confirmed that the experience was real and not just a simple vision. Only later did Peter catch on:

"After they had passed the first and the second guard, they came before the iron gate leading into the city. It opened for them of its own accord, and they went outside and walked along a lane, when suddenly the angel left him. Peter came to himself and said, 'Now I am sure that the Lord has sent his angel and rescued me from the hands of Herod and from all that the Jewish people were expecting'" (Acts 12:10–11).

Similarly to Peter, perhaps John too thought he was only seeing "a vision" of God's throne room, of the rainbow, of the four living creatures, and of the twenty-four elders, and that he couldn't walk up to any of them and actually touch them or converse with them because this whole experience was only a two-dimensional image created and sent by God. But the moment an elder came up to John and engaged him, that interaction, like that between Peter and the angel, like that between Paul and those in the third heaven, confirmed that at least part of what John was seeing and hearing was in the disciple's present moment.

But we still have unanswered questions. How much of what John was seeing was in the here and now, and how much was still possibly a vision of the future? The following are three possible options:

1. John was taken up to heaven on one particular Lord's day, where he and everyone in the throne room *saw Jesus in real time* open a scroll that revealed scenes of the future.
2. John was taken up to heaven, where he and everyone in the throne room *saw a vision of Jesus* opening the scroll in the future.

3. John was *carried into the future* where he saw everyone in the throne room, as Jesus opened the scroll.

Let's begin by addressing option #3: John was carried to a time in the distant future, to the precise moment that Jesus was about to open the scroll and unleash all of the trumpet and bowl plagues upon the earth. This is time-travel. And one might be surprised how many Christians believe that, beginning with the view of the throne room in chapter 4, John traveled to the future just like Marty McFly (Michael J. Fox) did in the movie *Back to the Future*. But the fact is that John didn't travel to the future in any chapter of Revelation simply because no one can travel time. John, like everyone who has ever been born, was confined to his own present time period. Granted, by the Lord's enablement, John could see things in the future or the past, as well as hear conversations in the future or the past, but he could never travel to another time period. He couldn't travel a hundred years into the future or a hundred seconds into the past no more than you and I can. John couldn't get up on Sunday morning and be transported to Wednesday evening two thousand years later and carry on a conversation with someone on that day. That is fictional time travel and only takes place in the movies or in science-fiction novels. Your past is your past and your future remains in the future, and you must wait for your future to come to you just as someone sits at a railway station and patiently waits for the train to arrive. Paul touched on the subject in his sermon to the Athenians:

"From one ancestor he made all nations to inhabit the whole earth, and he allotted the times of their existence and the boundaries of the places where they would live, so that they would search for God and perhaps grope for him and find him—though indeed he is not far from each of us" (Acts 17:26–27).

Not only has God allotted our places, but he has allotted our times. We can only exist in the moment of time that the Lord has assigned us. If that is not true, then the above scripture is untrue. Therefore, since time travel is fictional, option #3 must be eliminated.

Now, to option #1 and #2: We must now decide whether John was standing with everyone in the throne room, as they all saw a vision of Jesus opening the scroll in the distant future at which time everyone in the throne room saw terrible plagues unleashed upon an unsuspecting world (option #2), or if John was actually standing with everyone in the throne room, including elders, angels, living creatures, and the Father, as Jesus opened the scroll that very moment, obviously not starting any plagues two thousand years ago, but only revealing scenes of the future (option #1). Is it even possible to decide between the two options? Absolutely! The answer is unequivocally option #1: John stood in the presence of everyone in the throne room that day and watched Jesus as he opened the scroll. How can we be sure? *Because John wept.* Here's the explanation:

Had John only been watching "a future vision" of God holding a scroll (option #2), and at some point began to seriously doubt whether anyone in the vision was going to step forward and take the scroll from the Father's hand, John would never have started weeping because of how he thought the vision might or might not turn out. The thought is absurd. John would have just kept watching the vision to see what was going to happen next, just as anyone else would in that position. However, John cried because he was actually there in the throne room and saw the Father holding the unopened sealed scroll. Somehow, John came to understand that whatever was hidden in the scroll was meant to be revealed not only to him but also to all those standing in the throne room, as well as to the church. But before any of the hidden mysteries of God could be revealed, someone in the throne room had to be worthy enough to approach the Father and receive the scroll from his hand and open it. When no one immediately stepped forward, John was afraid that the scroll would remain sealed, thereby keeping God's knowledge of the church's future hidden. The disciple was deeply grieved. This explains John's emotional response.

With the above reasonings, we have determined that Jesus opened the scroll two thousand years ago, allowing John and all who were present in the throne room to see visions of the future. However the same conclusion could have been reached in short order, by asking you, the reader, three short questions:

1. Have you had the opportunity to see inside the scroll, observing its contents? If you've read Revelation the answer is yes, because when one reads the letter of Revelation the contents of the scroll have been seen.

2. Could the contents of the scroll have been seen unless someone had broken the seals and opened the scroll? The answer is a resounding no, because prior to Christ breaking the seals and opening the scroll, the contents of the scroll remained sealed in the Father's hand

(actually hidden in the Father's mind). Only after Christ opened the scroll were the contents made known.

3. When Christ opened the scroll, did anything happen? Did any plagues or earthquakes occur or did anyone get hurt or killed? Not in the least. Other than the fact that visions of the future were seen, nothing happened. Therefore, the same conclusion has been reached: John actually saw Jesus break open the seven seals two thousand years ago. The seven seals cannot be opened again in the future, giving the false impression that they are being opened for the first time. The contents within the seven seals have already been seen. One can't unsee what one has already seen.

The Remaining Twelve Conversations

The interaction between the elder and John, whereby an elder assured John that the Lamb was worthy to break the seals and open the scroll, was not the only conversation directed toward the disciple that day. After that encounter, John would participate in twelve more conversations recorded in chapters 7 through 22, comprising approximately 35 percent of the content of those chapters, if one includes the settings for the dialogues as well as the dialogues themselves. And the purpose of the conversations? They were provided to help John with his understanding of the visions. As John, along with everyone else in the throne room that day, including angels, elders, and the four living creatures, saw the visions within the scroll for the very first time, the disciple quickly realized that the visions varied in complexity, rendering many of them almost incomprehensible. That's where the conversations come in. When John needed additional explanation concerning a vision, God had an elder or an angel approach the disciple and impart the needed information by way of a conversation. However, God's blessing for John has inadvertently led to unwarranted difficulty for those attempting to understand Revelation, and especially its sequence. Instead of recognizing that these conversations for what they are—assistance for John's benefit two thousand years ago—most everyone mistakenly believes these interactions will occur in the last days along with all the other future events. In other words, instead of rightly understanding that the conversations occurred between the "visions of future events," it is thought that the conversations themselves will also occur in the future! And therein lies the problem. Simply, the events revealed in the visions still lie in the future, while the conversations lie in the past.

Below are excerpts of the thirteen conversations, including their scriptural references as well as a brief description of the occasion for each conversation:[1]

Table 3.1. The Thirteen Conversations	
Scriptural Reference of the Dialogue	**The Occasion for the Conversation**
1st Conversation (Rev 5:5)	Soon after having been swept up to heaven's throne room, John mistakenly thought that no one was worthy to open the seven-sealed scroll or to look into it. Therefore, he began to weep bitterly. It was at this moment that an elder approached John and said, "Do not weep. See the Lion of the tribe of Judah, the Root of David, has conquered, so that he can open the scroll and its seven seals."
2nd Conversation (Rev 7:13–17)	An elder questions John if he knew the identity of the great multitude that he had just seen in the previous vision.
3rd Conversation (Rev 10:4—11:3)	A voice from heaven and a mighty angel speak to John concerning the upcoming vision of the seventh trumpet as well as the future ministry of the two witnesses.
4th Conversation (Rev 14:13)	After seeing a vision of three angelic announcements, John heard a voice from heaven tell him, "Write this: Blessed are the dead who from now on die in the Lord," and the Spirit added, "Yes, they will rest from their labors, for their deeds follow them."
5th Conversation (Rev 16:15)	After John saw the vision of the future pouring of the 6th bowl of God's final wrath, the Lord said in the disciple's hearing, "See, I am coming like a thief! Blessed is the one who stays awake and is clothed, not going about naked and exposed to shame."
6th Conversation (Rev 17:1–2, 7–18)	An angel carried John away in the Spirit, and showed him a vision of a woman sitting on a scarlet beast. While John was scrutinizing the vision, the angel told John about the mystery of Babylon the great and her future fate at the hands of the beast.

1. The initial conversations between John and the Lord on the Isle of Patmos concerning the seven churches recorded in Rev 1–3 have not been included with the thirteen conversations beginning in Rev 5 because this study only pertains to conversations that are deemed essential when determining the future sequence of end-time events.

THE THIRTEEN CONVERSATIONS IN REVELATION

Table 3.1. The Thirteen Conversations	
Scriptural Reference of the Dialogue	**The Occasion for the Conversation**
7th Conversation (Rev 18:4–20)	After again seeing a vision of the future second angelic announcement concerning the fall of Babylon the great, first recorded back in 14:8, John hears another voice from heaven admonish certain future saints with the following: "Come out of her, my people, so that you do not take part in her sins, and so that you do not share in her plagues; for her sins are heaped high as heaven, and God has remembered her iniquities . . ."
8th Conversation (Rev 18:21–24)	After hearing the voice's admonishment, John saw a mighty angel illustrate the fall of Babylon by throwing a stone into the sea and then heard the angel say the fall of Babylon will be just as violent.
9th Conversation (Rev 19:9–10)	After seeing a vision of a great multitude in heaven worshiping God because of two occurrences, i.e., Babylon the great had been judged and the marriage of the Lamb had come, the same mighty angel tells John, "Write this: Blessed are those who are invited to the marriage supper of the Lamb . . . These are true words of God." At that point, John fell down at the angel's feet in order to worship him, but was immediately told, "You must not do that! I am a fellow servant with you and your comrades who hold the testimony of Jesus. Worship God! For the testimony of Jesus is the spirit of prophecy."
10th Conversation (Rev 21:3–4)	As John stood gazing at a vision of the New Jerusalem, a loud voice from the throne said in his hearing, "See, the home of God is among mortals. He will dwell with them as their God; they will be his peoples, and God himself will be with them; he will wipe every tear from their eyes. Death will be no more; mourning and crying and pain will be no more, for the first things have passed away."
11th Conversation (Rev 21:5–8)	Immediately after the loud voice finished speaking, the One seated on the throne told John, "See, I am making all things new. Write this, for these words are trustworthy and true. It is done! I am the Alpha and the Omega, the beginning and the end. To the thirsty I will give water as a gift from the spring of the water of life. Those who conquer will inherit these things, and I will be their God and they will be my children . . ."

Table 3.1. The Thirteen Conversations	
Scriptural Reference of the Dialogue	**The Occasion for the Conversation**
12th Conversation (Rev 21:9, 22:6)	After God gave instructions to John, an angel approached the disciple and told him, "Come, I will show you the bride, the wife of the Lamb," which was a reference to the image of the New Jerusalem. After showing John the details of the image, the angel told John, "These words are trustworthy and true, for the Lord, the God of the spirits of the prophets, has sent his angel to show his servants what must soon take place."
13th Conversation (Rev 22:7–17)	The Father, the Son, and the Holy Spirit, as well as the angel, speak in John's presence as Jesus brings to a conclusion his own words by declaring, "It is I, Jesus, who sent my angel to you with this testimony for the churches. I am the root and the descendant of David, the bright morning star."

Since the thirteen conversations and their settings comprise about one-third of Rev 5–22, that leaves the remaining two-thirds of the text devoted to the actual visions. The two-to-one ratio shouldn't come as a surprise to the reader since the primary reason John was whisked up to heaven in the first place was to see the visions. Now, with the brief introduction of the conversations behind us, it's time to turn to those visions.

The Cardinal Rule When Determining Sequences

Before proceeding to our study of John's visions in the next chapter, one should first be aware that on occasions the disciple will see visions of certain events multiple times in the letter. You might ask, What is the significance of whether John sees an event once, twice, or three times, especially as it relates to determining the correct sequence of end times? *Each time the same event is seen, a different sequence of events is necessarily represented.* In other words, the same event can never appear more than once in any given sequence of events. Therefore, if a single event is seen twice, two sequences are necessarily present; if a certain event is seen three times, then three sequences are present, etc. Because some events in Revelation are indeed seen multiple times, it will be proven that the letter contains four sequences.

The following is an example of an event seen twice. One knows it is the same event because both passages contain identical announcements by the same angel at the same point in time. Here's the twice-seen announcement of "the fall of Babylon the great":

1. "Then another angel, a second, followed, saying, 'Fallen, fallen is Babylon the great! She has made all nations drink of the wine of the wrath of her fornication'" (Rev 14:8).

2. "He called out with a mighty voice, 'Fallen, fallen is Babylon the great! It has become a dwelling place of demons, a haunt of every foul spirit, a haunt of every foul bird, a haunt of every foul and hateful beast. For all the nations have drunk of the wine of the wrath of her fornication, and the kings of the earth have committed fornication with her, and the merchants of the earth have grown rich from the power of her luxury'" (Rev 18:2–3).

When comparing the two scenes of the one announcement, notice that the second one is noticeably longer than the first. It's still the same announcement, but the Lord allowed John to hear the complete announcement in the second account, whereas in the first one, God only allowed John to hear part of it. And as one can easily see, the second scene contains many more details than the first. Nevertheless, both accounts provide unique revelation: In the Rev 14 account, one will later learn that the announcement of Babylon's fall is actually the second of three angelic announcements, but in the Rev 18 account, one will discover that the angelic announcement is preceded by the pouring of the seven bowls of God's final wrath and followed by a great celebration in heaven. This occasional phenomenon experienced by John, where he will see a vision of the same event from different perspectives in different sequences, will inevitably provide the reader added clarity and a deeper understanding of these particular events as one goes about reconciling the many details surrounding them. Hopefully, one can see in this particular example that if the two visions of the same announcement of Babylon's fall are mistakenly thought to represent two different announcements, and then the two scenes are placed in two different slots in a sequence, then, understandably, there will be one too many announcements of the fall of Babylon in that sequence, resulting in—you guessed it—an incorrect sequence.

THE SEQUENCE

Over the next nine chapters of this study (chapters 4–12), the approximately fifty visions recorded in Rev 6–22 will be proven to fall within four sequences. The following chart shows the four sequences with their scriptural references in Revelation, as well as the corresponding chapters of this study (note: As an additional aid to the reader, a section of the chart will precede each of the subsequent chapters, chronicling the study's progression):

Table 3.2. The Reconciliation of the Remaining Nine Chapters of This Study with the Four Sequences in Revelation			
First Sequence (6:1—9:21, 11:15–19, 15:5—22:5)	**Second Sequence** (11:1–13)	**Third Sequence** (12:1–6)	**Fourth Sequence** (12:7—15:4)
Chapter 4 1st Seq., Part 1: Through the 6th Trumpet (6:1—9:21)			
	Chapter 5 2nd Seq.: The 2 Witnesses (11:1–13)		
Chapter 5 (cont.) 1st Seq., Part 1 (cont.): The 7th Trumpet (11:15–19)			
		Chapter 6 3rd Seq.: The Woman, the Child, and the Dragon (12:1–6)	
			Chapter 6 (cont.) 4th Seq., Part 1: The War in Heaven to the Woman's Escape (12:7–17)

Table 3.2. The Reconciliation of the Remaining Nine Chapters of This Study with the Four Sequences in Revelation			
First Sequence (6:1—9:21, 11:15-19, 15:5—22:5)	**Second Sequence** (11:1-13)	**Third Sequence** (12:1-6)	**Fourth Sequence** (12:7—15:4)
			Chapter 7 4th Seq., Part 2: The 1st and 2nd Beasts (12:18—13:18)
			Chapter 8 4th Seq., Part 3: Mount Zion to the Worship around God's Throne (14:1—15:4)
Chapter 9 1st Seq., Part 2: The 7 Bowls (15:5—19:10)			
Chapter 10 1st Seq., Part 3: The Lord's Return and the 1st Resurrection (19:11—20:6a)			
Chapter 11 1st Seq., Part 4: The Millennium and the Final Judgment (20:6b-15)			
Chapter 12 1st Seq., Part 5: The 2nd Resurrection and the New Jerusalem (21:1—22:5)			

CHAPTER 4

First Sequence in Revelation, Part 1
Through the Sixth Trumpet (6:1—9:21)

First Sequence	Second Sequence	Third Sequence	Fourth Sequence
Chapter 4* 1st Seq., Part 1: Through the 6th Trumpet (6:1—9:21)			
	Chapter 5 2nd Seq.: The 2 Witnesses (11:1–13)		
Chapter 5 (cont.) 1st Seq., Part 1 (cont.): The 7th Trumpet (11:15–19)			
		Chapter 6 3rd Seq.: The Woman, the Child, and the Dragon (12:1–6)	

AFTER JESUS STEPPED FORWARD and took the scroll out of the Father's right hand, John stopped weeping. As Jesus opened the seals, one by one, everyone present in the throne room began to see what God had intended for them to see: visions of the future, visions of the church's triumph, visions of the blowing of seven trumpets, visions of the pouring of seven bowls, visions of martyrs, of dragons, of demons, angels, earthquakes, and fires. But understand this, the opening of the seals did not trigger any event that day, as John stood in the throne room. When Jesus broke open the first seal nothing happened other than the fact that those present in God's throne room were enabled to see visions of the future that corresponded to the portion of the metaphoric scroll that was unraveled by the first broken seal. Likewise, when the second seal was broken, nothing happened except those present in the throne room were enabled to see visions of the future that corresponded to the portion of the scroll that was unraveled by that broken seal, and then the third seal, and so on, and so on. Broken seals did not trigger any trumpet-judgment, or bowl-judgment, or anything, for that matter. When Jesus opened the fifth seal, that did not cause any future martyrdom. And when Jesus opened the sixth seal, the sun did not become black, or the moon become like blood, or a great earthquake appear. Rather, the sole purpose of Jesus breaking the seven seals was to enable everyone in the throne room that day, and especially John, to look into the content of the scroll, or rather, into the mind and wisdom of God.

First Four Seals Are Opened: Riders Appear

We begin with one of the most familiar passages in Revelation, commonly known as "the Four Horsemen of the Apocalypse." As Jesus began to break open each of the first four seals, everyone in the throne room immediately began to hear voices and see visions of the future. As each seal was broken the sound of a simple yet authoritative command of "Come!" was heard, followed by the appearance of a brightly colored horse and its rider. As John examined the visions, he soon realized that each command heard in the visions was given by one of the four living creatures. This may have somewhat startled John, especially since the actual living creatures were present in the throne room, surrounding the throne of God, as the visions of those same living creatures and the horseback riders were being displayed with each broken seal! Here are the first four visions of the future:

> Then I saw the Lamb open one of the seven seals, and I heard one
> of the four living creatures call out, as with a voice of thunder,

"Come!" I looked, and there was a white horse! Its rider had a bow; a crown was given to him, and he came out conquering and to conquer.

When he opened the second seal, I heard the second living creature call out, "Come!" And out came another horse, bright red; its rider was permitted to take peace from the earth, so that people would slaughter one another; and he was given a great sword.

When he opened the third seal, I heard the third living creature call out, "Come!" I looked, and there was a black horse! Its rider held a pair of scales in his hand, and I heard what seemed to be a voice in the midst of the four living creatures saying, "A quart of wheat for a day's pay, and three quarts of barley for a day's pay, but do not damage the olive oil and the wine!"

When he opened the fourth seal, I heard the voice of the fourth living creature call out, "Come!" I looked and there was a pale green horse! Its rider's name was Death, and Hades followed with him; they were given authority over a fourth of the earth, to kill with sword, famine, and pestilence, and by the wild animals of the earth. (Rev 6:1–8)

The following is a brief summation of the four riders and their actions:

Table 4.1. The Four Horsemen of the Apocalypse	
The Rider	**The Actions of the Rider**
1. Rider on the White Horse (Rev 6:1–2)	He comes out conquering and to conquer. Furthermore, he is the only rider who was given a crown.
2. Rider on the Red Horse (Rev 6:3–4)	He causes people to slaughter one another.
3. Rider on the Black Horse (Rev 6:5–6)	He causes food and water shortages.
4. Rider on the Pale Green Horse (Rev 6:7–8)	He and his accomplice, Hades, are given authority over a fourth of the earth to kill with sword (war), famine, pestilence, and wild animals.

A fact that will help confirm to the reader that John was seeing visions of the four living creatures and four riders in the future, while the actual four living creatures were present with John in the throne room, is that occasionally when John saw a vision of the future he would qualify what he saw or heard with the Greek word *hōs*, translated "what seemed to be" or "what appeared to be" or something to that effect. He never used that word in any of the thirteen conversations with personalities who were in his presence. Observe (italics used for emphasis):

Table 4.2. Examples of John's Uncertainty in Visions of the Future Expressed in the Word "Seem" or "Appear"
1. "One of its heads *seemed* to have received a deathblow, but its mortal wound had been healed" (Rev 13:3a)
2. "And I saw *what appeared to be* a sea of glass mixed with fire, and those who had conquered the beast and its image and the number of its name, standing beside the sea of glass with harps of God in their hands" (Rev 15:2)
3. "After this I heard *what seemed to be* the loud voice of a great multitude in heaven . . ." (Rev 19:1a)
4. "Then I heard *what seemed to be* the voice of a great multitude, like the sound of many waters, and like the sound of mighty thunderpeals . . ." (Rev 19:6a)

In all four examples, John is attempting to describe visions of the future. As one can see, John struggled to describe what he was seeing and hearing and therefore qualified his description with *hōs*, translated "seemed" (13:3a), "what appeared to be" (15:2), and "what seemed to be" in Rev 19:1a and 6a. Now, with that, let's look again at what John saw and heard when Jesus opened the third seal (italics used for emphasis):

"When he opened the third seal, I heard the third living creature call out, 'Come!' I looked, and there was a black horse! Its rider held a pair of scales in his hand, and I heard *what seemed to be* a voice in the midst of the four living creatures saying, 'A quart of wheat for a day's pay, and three quarts of barley for a day's pay, but do not damage the olive oil and the wine!'" Rev 6:5–6.

Here, we know for a fact that John was seeing a vision of the future because he was having difficulty describing the location of the voice from within the vision, once the third seal was broken open. The voice that John was having difficulty locating could not have been a voice coming from the throne room that day, but rather was a voice that was coming from within a vision of the throne room. Had the voice actually come from someone in the midst of the four living creatures, who were in the throne room with John, then the disciple would have easily known the direction from where the voice came. But the fact that it was a voice coming from within a vision, there was just enough uncertainty from John's perspective that he was not completely sure from where the voice was coming, and therefore he qualified his description with, "I heard *what seemed to be* a voice in the midst of the four living creatures." Here's the point: If John is unsure of what he was hearing or seeing under the third broken seal because it was a vision of the future, then it stands to reason that the visions hidden under the first, second, fourth, fifth, sixth, and seventh seals are also visions of the future, correct?

Zechariah's Similar Visions

As indicated, when the four seals were broken John saw visions of the four living creatures commanding each of the four horseback riders to "Come!" As the chain of events unfolded, it appears that the riders then appeared before the living creatures, after which they quickly left the living creatures and proceeded on a mission of destruction that produced suffering and death on the earth by war, famine, inflation, pestilence, and wild animals (Rev 6:8). The fact that, when the living creatures called out to the horseback riders, they responded indicated the riders comprehended the commandments, thereby proving that the riders were indeed personalities. In choosing whether the riders were human or angelic personalities, the choice can only be angelic because certainly the four living creatures were not commissioning four humans to descend from heaven to the earth and initiate unprecedented global plagues. For additional proof that the riders seen by John were angels and not men, one need look no further than two of Zechariah's eight visions (Zech 1:7—6:8), specifically the first and eighth visions:

The First Vision

"In the night I saw a man riding on a red horse! He was standing among the myrtle trees in the glen; and behind him were red, sorrel, and white horses. Then I said, 'What are these, my lord?' The angel who talked with me said to me, 'I will show you what they are.' So the man who was standing among the myrtle trees answered, 'They are those whom the Lord has sent to patrol the earth.' Then they spoke to the angel of the Lord who was standing among the myrtle trees, 'We have patrolled the earth, and lo, the whole earth remains at peace'" (Zech 1:8–11).

The Eighth Vision

"And again I looked up and saw four chariots coming out from between two mountains—mountains of bronze. The first chariot had red horses, the second chariot black horses, the third chariot white horses, and the fourth chariot dappled gray horses. Then I said to the angel who talked with me, 'What are these, my lord?' The angel answered me, 'These are the four winds of heaven going out, after presenting themselves before the Lord of all the earth. The chariot with the black horses goes toward the north country, the white ones go toward the west country, and the dappled ones go toward the south country.' When the steeds came out, they were impatient to get off and patrol the earth. And he said, 'Go, patrol the earth.' So they patrolled the earth. Then he cried out to me, 'Lo, those who go toward the north country have set my spirit at rest in the north country'" (Zech 6:1–8).

Although Zechariah saw the angelic spirits as riding brightly colored horses in the first vision while in the eighth he saw the spirits as riding in chariots driven by brightly colored horses, one knows that both visions reveal the same four angels who had been commissioned by God to patrol the earth for peace (compare 1:10–11 and 6:7–8). The fact that God slightly altered the images from one vision to the next is irrelevant as to the truth of this observation. Furthermore, whereas both visions revealed the fact that God sent certain angels to patrol the earth for peace, the eighth vision gives the additional revelation as to the direction that each angel patrolled, i.e., one to the north, one to the west, etc.

Differences between Zechariah's and John's Visions

In spite of the similarities between Zechariah's and John's visions, there were dissimilarities: Unlike the angels who were sent to patrol the earth for peace in Zechariah, "the Four Horsemen of the Apocalypse" in Rev 6 were commanded to go and take peace from the earth. Furthermore, an even more significant difference regarding the visions, at least as it pertains to our study, concerns the two prophets: John only saw "the Four Horsemen of the Apocalypse" in *visions of the future*, whereas Zechariah *actually saw the angels—in person*! How do we know that? The presence of conversations. When the angel who was accompanying Zechariah, who had already spoken to the prophet, also conversed with the riders in each vision (compare Zech 1:11 and 6:7), the settings of both the first and eighth visions were then firmly established in the present moment of Zechariah, the accompanying angel, as well as the angelic riders. This observation indicates that God doesn't limit his use of brightly colored, surreal images just for visions of the future, as was the case of "the Four Horsemen of the Apocalypse," but he will, on occasions, use similar images to cloak invisible spirits who happen to be in the actual presence of his prophets—as was the case with Zechariah.

First Four Seals Suggest a Global Holocaust

Although the devastation, suffering, and numbers of deaths caused by "the Four Horsemen of the Apocalypse" are certainly unprecedented, the means by which they will orchestrate the death and destruction are all too familiar. Again, John's vision under the fourth seal:

"When he opened the fourth seal, I heard the voice of the fourth living creature call out, 'Come!' I looked and there was a pale green horse! Its rider's name was Death, and Hades followed with him; they were given authority over a fourth of the earth, to kill with sword, famine, and pestilence, and by the wild animals of the earth" (Rev 6:7–8).

Deaths by sword (war), famine, pestilence (pandemics), and wild animals have always been a common means of the catastrophic loss of life throughout the history of mankind. But even so, John heard something that was almost too incomprehensible. He said that the fourth horseback rider, Death, together with his accomplice, Hades, were given authority over a fourth of the earth to kill by those different means. Assuming the phrase "authority over a fourth of the earth to kill" means a fourth of the population will indeed be killed, then, if one uses the current statistic of the world's population as approximately 8 billion, the death toll would necessarily approach 2 billion! Is that possible? Not only is it possible, but according to the text, it's a *fait accompli*. Of course, you know as well as I do that there's essentially only one way by which two billion deaths could possibly result from a military conflict and that is nuclear war. The following section gives a plausible scenario for the certain, future nuclear war.

The Nuclear War Scenario

At some point in the future, one or more of the precarious peace agreements between certain major military powers will be broken, resulting in the inevitable consequence whereby one of those nations detonates a preemptive nuclear strike triggering, as it stands now, WWIII. Within moments, alliances of each side would doubtless join in with their nuclear weaponry causing a global cascade of nuclear explosions, resulting in an instant catastrophic death toll. With each day of continuous explosions, multiplied millions will be killed. And that's only the beginning of the nightmare. Over the ensuing weeks and months, the resultant nuclear aftermath with its radiation clouds coupled with the millions of unburied bodies would exponentially escalate the death count by way of radiation fallout and a rapidly spreading pandemic, respectively. Furthermore, the inevitable radioactive and viral contamination of water sources and food supplies would lead to global famines and mass starvation, while the hundreds of thousands of recently bombarded and desolated cities would become quickly overrun by wild animals in search of any source of food, including human remains as well as any possible survivors. Two billion deaths will come easily. The scene is grim.

Fifth Seal: Martyrs

While the first four seals revealed the angelic cause behind an obvious nuclear, global holocaust and its aftermath, the broken fifth seal revealed a vision of those who had died in an entirely different manner:

> When he opened the fifth seal, I saw under the altar the souls of those who had been slaughtered for the word of God and for the testimony they had given; they cried out with a loud voice, "Sovereign Lord, holy and true, how long will it be before you judge and avenge our blood on the inhabitants of the earth?" They were each given a white robe and told to rest a little longer, until the number would be complete both of their fellow servants and of their brothers and sisters, who were soon to be killed as they themselves had been killed. (Rev 6:9–11)

Had it not been for John's phrase "I saw under the altar the souls of those who had been slaughtered for the word of God and for the testimony they had given," one would naturally assume that the souls of the righteous seen by the disciple under the fifth seal were the direct result of the nuclear holocaust and its aftermath, i.e., sword (war), famine, pestilence, and wild animals. However, that's impossible since those causes of death cannot be considered martyrdom, per se. Therefore, however the death by martyrdom came about, one must understand that the cause of death must be distinguished from the death caused by the nuclear explosions and the nuclear aftermath.

Notice that when the martyred souls asked the Lord how long it would be before he judged and avenged their blood on the inhabitants of the earth, they were told to wait just a little longer, until the complete number of martyrs would be fulfilled, who were soon to be killed as they had been killed. This verbal exchange indicates that the martyrdom of the saints was nearing an end.

The Two Periods of Suffering Are Confirmed

Question: Where have we recently read of two consecutive periods of suffering that parallel the global holocaust and martyrdom of the saints? Of course the answer is the Olivet Discourse. In it, Jesus said after the abomination of desolation would come the greatest suffering in the history of the world (Matt 24:21), and if God had not shortened the days of that particular suffering that no flesh would survive (Matt 24:22). Next, after that suffering has thankfully been brought to an end, Jesus said a period of deception would begin with false messiahs and false prophets. Then, inexplicably, Jesus said "after the *suffering* of those days will come the heavenly signs" instead of "after the *deception* of those days will come the heavenly signs." Knowing that Christ could not have been referencing the world's greatest suffering, since God had ended that suffering, it was easily determined that Christ had to be referencing a second period of suffering that will, at some point, follow the first period of suffering and immediately precede the heavenly signs. As you well remember, when Christ's prophecy of false messiahs, false prophets, deception, and a second suffering was juxtaposed with Paul's prophecy of deception and suffering caused by the man of lawlessness, it was easily determined that the man of lawlessness will emerge from among the false messiahs and false prophets prophesied by Christ. Here's the earlier chart showing that reconciliation:

Table 2.6. Jesus' Second Period of Suffering Corresponds to the Persecutions Caused by the Man of Lawlessness

Jesus:	Abom. of desolation (Matt 24:15)	Greatest suffering in history (Matt 24:21)	Greatest suffering ends (Matt 24:22)	Deception by false messiahs and false prophets (Matt 24:23–28)	"Second" period of suffering of those days (Matt 24:29a)	Heavenly signs appear (Matt 24:29b)	God shakes the powers of heaven (Matt 24:29c)
Paul:					New deception and persecution begin with the revealing of the man of lawlessness (2 Thess 2:3–12)	"They" will be saying there is peace and security when the Day of the Lord arrives (1 Thess 5:3)	The Day of the Lord arrives (1 Thess 5:4–11)

Although Paul didn't provide any details concerning the first period of suffering, he provided several pieces of invaluable information that paint the scenario of the second period of suffering: Since the apostle clearly indicated that the man of lawlessness will claim deity for himself (2 Thess 2:4), it's quite predictable that the man will demand worship because of that claim. Furthermore, since the apostle revealed that only the unrighteous will be deceived by his miracles (2 Thess 2:9–12), it is certain that they will be the only ones who submit to his demand for worship, and for that acquiescence, he will surely reward them with their lives. On the other hand, the righteous will not be deceived and therefore will not submit to his demands, and because of that steadfast refusal, they will obviously be the ones who suffer the penalty of death.

Perhaps sooner than one might have expected, the first visions of Revelation have confirmed Christ's two periods of sufferings: Christ's "greatest suffering in history" correlates to John's global holocaust perpetrated by "the Four Horsemen of the Apocalypse" (compare Matt 24:21

and Rev 6:1–8), and Christ's second period of suffering correlates to the martyrdom seen by John under the fifth seal (compare Matt 24:29a and Rev 6:9–11). Here's the reconciliation of the two future periods of suffering indicated by Jesus, Paul, and John:

Table 4.3. Jesus' Prophecy of Two Periods of Suffering Affirmed by Paul and John

Jesus:	Abom. of desolation (Matt 24:15)	Greatest suffering in history (Matt 24:21)	Greatest suffering ends (Matt 24:22)	Deception by false messiahs and false prophets (Matt 24:23–28)	Second period of suffering of those days (Matt 24:29a)	Heavenly signs appear (Matt 24:29b)	God shakes the powers of heaven (Matt 24:29c)
Paul:					New deception and persecution begin with the revealing of the man of lawlessness (2 Thess 2:3–12)	"They" will be saying there is peace and security when the Day of the Lord arrives (1 Thess 5:3)	The Day of the Lord arrives (1 Thess 5:4–11)
John:		The Four Horsemen of the Apocalypse will cause 1/4 of earth's population to be killed by war, famine, pestilence, and wild animals (Rev 6:1–8)			The martyred saints are seen under the altar in heaven (Rev 6:9–11)		

What Days Are Cut Short?

The above reconciliation now brings a spotlight upon the earlier quote by Christ in the Olivet Discourse:

"And if those days had not been cut short, no one would be saved; but for the sake of the elect those days will be cut short" (Matt 24:22).

Exactly what days will God cut short? Knowing that the death and destruction orchestrated by "the Four Horsemen of the Apocalypse" will doubtless be a nuclear holocaust of some kind, there are only two possibilities: (1) God will shorten the days of the entire nuclear holocaust, including the initial nuclear warfare as well as the nuclear aftermath of famine, pestilence, and death by wild animals, or (2) God will only shorten the days of the initial nuclear warfare. So which is it? The answer is obviously the second option: that God will only shorten the days of the initial nuclear war. How does one know that? Because the aftermath of the nuclear holocaust—radiation fallout, pestilence, famine, starvation, death by wild animals, etc.—the likes of which will certainly last for months on end, was clearly portrayed as contributing to the deaths of a quarter of the earth's population (Rev 6:5–8), and yet Jesus indicated that "if those days had not been cut short, no one would be saved," implying that God must intervene quickly—perhaps in a matter of days or weeks—in order to stop something that if left unchecked would wipeout the earth's entire population. It should be obvious to the reader that God will miraculously stop the nuclear explosions in order to preserve the unconfessed elect (Matt 24:22); however, the nuclear aftermath, as indicated by the visions under the third and fourth seals, will continue to eat away at the earth's population until a quarter of mankind has been killed. Therefore, one can now confidently assert the following: 1. The nuclear explosions will constitute the first and "greatest" period of suffering, 2. The nuclear aftermath will begin the second period of suffering, and 3. At some point in time, the man of lawlessness will begin killing the saints during the nuclear aftermath.

Here's the updated previous chart:

Table 4.4. God Ends the Nuclear War Caused by the First and Second Riders but the Third and Fourth Riders Then Begin and Continue the Nuclear Aftermath

Jesus:	Abom. of desolation (Matt 24:15)	Greatest suffering in history (Matt 24:21); a global nuclear war begins	Greatest suffering ends (Matt 24:22); God ends the nuclear war, but the nuclear aftermath begins	Deception by false messiahs and false prophets (Matt 24:23–28)	A second period of suffering is in progress (Matt 24:29a)	Heavenly signs appear (Matt 24:29b)	God shakes the powers of heaven (Matt 24:29c)
Paul:					New deception and persecution begin with the revealing of the man of lawlessness (2 Thess 2:3–12)	"They" will be saying there is peace and security when the Day of the Lord arrives (1 Thess 5:3)	The Day of the Lord arrives (1 Thess 5:4–11)
John:		Of the Four Horsemen of the Apocalypse, the 1st and 2nd riders initiate and orchestrate a nuclear war (Rev 6:1–4)	Of the Four Horsemen of the Apocalypse, the 3rd and 4th riders initiate and continue the nuclear aftermath, albeit under the direction of the 1st rider, who is the only one wearing a crown (Rev 6:5–8)		The martyred saints are seen under the altar in heaven (Rev 6:9–11)		

As one can readily see, the modifications indicate that the first and second riders are the invisible forces behind the outbreak of the nuclear war because these riders are described as "conquering" and "causing people to slaughter one another," respectively, whereas the third and fourth riders are presumed to be the invisible forces behind the nuclear aftermath because they are described as initiating food and water shortages, and causing the deaths of a quarter of the earth not only by the war itself but also by its aftermath: "famine, pestilence, and wild animals."[1]

First Vision under the Sixth Seal: An Earthquake, Heavenly Signs, and People Running

When the sixth seal was broken open by Christ, surely John expected to see a single vision just as he had seen under each of the first five broken seals, but instead the disciple saw three visions. Although one might have been unfamiliar with the events seen under the first five seals, the same cannot be said for the first event seen under the sixth seal. Under it, John saw one of the most familiar prophetic events in Scripture, which are the heavenly signs, involving the sun, the moon, and the stars:

> When he opened the sixth seal, I looked, and there came a great earthquake; the sun became black as sackcloth, the full moon became like blood, and the stars of the sky fell to the earth as the fig tree drops its winter fruit when shaken by a gale. The sky vanished like a scroll rolling itself up, and every mountain and island was removed from its place. (Rev 6:12–14)

Have you ever wondered how God might darken the sun and the moon, or seemingly cause the stars in the heavens to fall to the earth? Rather than directly damaging or altering the sun, the moon, and the unlimited canopy of celestial stars, God might just simply block the light of the sun and the moon by an unprecedented thickness of clouds that covers the whole earth. In the following, this is what Ezekiel seems to suggest during his lamentation of Egypt:

---

1. Supporting the scenario presented in the chart is the fact that, as the reader will soon learn, the man of lawlessness will come onto the world stage at just the right moment, promising the inhabitants of the earth an opportunity to purchase the necessary staples of life: food, water, medicine, shelter, clothing, etc., all of which will be in short supply after the initial devastation of the nuclear war and the lingering quagmire of its nuclear aftermath (Rev 13:16–17).

THE SEQUENCE

"When I blot you out, I will cover the heavens, and make their stars dark; I will cover the sun with a cloud, and the moon shall not give its light. All the shining lights of the heavens I will darken above you, and put darkness on your land, says the Lord God" (Ezek 32:7-8).

As far as the phrase "the stars of the sky fell to the earth," that statement should not be taken literally since most know that God made the stars thousands, or, in some cases, millions of times larger than the earth, and therefore the earth couldn't withstand the impact of one star, much less multiple stars. Instead, the Greek phrase *hoi asteres tou ouranou* actually signifies that "the asteroids of heaven" fell to the earth. Of course, this could easily be explained by an unprecedented high activity of meteor or meteorite showers scattered all over the earth.

As to how the appearance of these heavenly signs will affect people in the last days, the following is how Jesus described it:

"There will be signs in the sun, the moon, and the stars, and on the earth distress among nations confused by the roaring of the sea and the waves. People will faint from fear and foreboding of what is coming upon the world, for the powers of the heavens will be shaken" (Luke 21:25-26).

People will faint because they have never seen meteorological activities on this scale. And God will not only bring upheaval and unrest in the skies, but on the earth as well. He will send the greatest earthquake to date, that removes every mountain and island from its place (Rev 6:14). In other words, God will shake the heaven and the earth (Heb 12:26). The resultant "roaring of the seas and the waves" is certainly a reference to the widespread tsunamis and flooding in places that have never experienced these types of catastrophic events. Along with people fainting "from fear and foreboding of what is coming upon the world" John saw an additional reaction:

> "Then the kings of the earth and the magnates and the generals and the rich and the powerful, and everyone, slave and free, hid in the caves and among the rocks of the mountains, calling to the mountains and rocks, 'Fall on us and hide us from the face of the one seated on the throne and from the wrath of the Lamb; for the great day of their wrath has come, and who is able to stand?'" Rev 6:15-17.

John saw people in every walk of life trying to hide in caves and among the rocks and under anything else that might appear to provide some type of protection from the great and terrible Day of God's wrath.

Just from the phrase "for the great day of their wrath has come, and who is able to stand?" (Rev 6:17), one knows that John has just witnessed the initial rumblings of the Day of the Lord. The scene is spectacular, but John was not the first to see it.

Isaiah Saw the Same Scurrying

About seven hundred years prior to John's visions, Isaiah recorded the same scurrying for cover by the unrighteous at the onset of the Day of the Lord. Here are some key excerpts:

"Enter into the rock, and hide in the dust, from the terror of the Lord, and from the glory of his majesty. The haughty eyes of people shall be brought low, and the pride of everyone shall be humbled; and the Lord alone will be exalted in that day . . . . Enter the caves of the rocks and the holes of the ground, from the terror of the Lord, and from the glory of his majesty, when he rises to terrify the earth. On that day people will throw away to the moles and to the bats their idols of silver and their idols of gold, which they made for themselves to worship, to enter the caverns of the rocks and the cleft in the crags, from the terror of the Lord, and from the glory of his majesty, when he rises to terrify the earth" (Isa 2:10–11, 19–21).

Not only did Isaiah see the unrighteous scurrying for cover as did John, but he also saw them discarding their idols of gold and silver and probably anything else that would encumber them in their attempt to escape (Isa 2:20). Today, this could apply to things that only minutes before meant everything to the unrighteous, i.e., houses, cars, lands, money, careers, and anything else that modern man worships. These "idols" will mean nothing on the day that God "rises to terrify the earth" (Isa 2:21).

In Isa 13 the prophet references the other two events seen under the sixth seal—the heavenly signs and the earthquake—completing the trifecta that will transpire at the arrival of the Day of the Lord (italics used for emphasis):

"See, the day of the Lord comes, cruel, with wrath and fierce anger, to make the earth a desolation, and destroy its sinners from it. *For the stars of the heavens and their constellations will not give their light; the sun will be dark at its rising, and the moon will not shed its light.* I will punish the world for its evil, and the wicked for their iniquity; I will put an end to the pride of the arrogant, and lay low the insolence of tyrants. I will make mortals more rare than gold, and humans than the gold of Ophir. Therefore I will make the heavens tremble, *and the earth will be shaken out of its place*, at the wrath of the Lord of hosts in the day of his fierce anger" (Isa 13:9–13).

Note that whereas John said the earthquake will remove every island and mountain out of its place (Rev 6:14), Isaiah simply indicated that the earth itself will be shaken out of its place (Isa 13:13). With either description, it's the same earthquake. Here's the reconciliation of the events from the abomination of desolation until the Day of the Lord prophesied by Jesus, Paul, John, and Isaiah:

Table 4.5. Reconciliation of the Events from the Abomination of Desolation until the Day of the Lord—Prophesied by Jesus, Paul, John, and Isaiah				
The Sequence	**Jesus**	**Paul**	**John**	**Isaiah**
1. Abomination of Desolation	Abomination of desolation (Matt 24:15)			
2. Nuclear War	Greatest suffering in history (Matt 24:21)		Of the Four Horsemen of the Apocalypse, the 1st and 2nd riders initiate and orchestrate the nuclear war (Rev 6:1–4)	
3. The nuclear war ends as the nuclear aftermath begins.	God ends the greatest suffering in the history of the world (Matt 24:22)		Of the Four Horsemen of the Apocalypse, the 3rd and 4th riders initiate and continue the nuclear aftermath, albeit under the direction of the 1st rider, who is the only one wearing a crown (Rev 6:5–8)	

Table 4.5. Reconciliation of the Events from the Abomination of Desolation until the Day of the Lord—Prophesied by Jesus, Paul, John, and Isaiah

The Sequence	Jesus	Paul	John	Isaiah
4. With the nuclear aftermath arise false messiahs and false prophets causing deception.	Deception by false messiahs and false prophets (Matt 24:23–28)			
5. The man of lawlessness emerges from among the false messiahs and false prophets; he deceives the unrighteous and kills the saints.	A second period of suffering is in progress (Matt 24:29a)	At the arrival of the man of lawlessness comes more deception, as well as the targeted persecution of the saints (2 Thess 2:3–12)		
6. Toward the end of the period of martyrdom, which is perpetrated by the man of lawlessness, the souls in heaven are told to wait a little longer until the full number of martyrs has been reached.			Toward the end of the period of martyrdom, the souls in heaven are told to wait a little longer until the complete number of martyrs has been reached (Rev 6:9–11)	

Table 4.5. Reconciliation of the Events from the Abomination of Desolation until the Day of the Lord—Prophesied by Jesus, Paul, John, and Isaiah

The Sequence	Jesus	Paul	John	Isaiah
7. Heavenly Signs	Heavenly signs: 1. Sun is darkened 2. Moon does not give its light 3. Stars fall from heaven (Matt 24:29b)	"They" will be saying there is peace and security when the Day of the Lord arrives (1 Thess 5:3)	Heavenly signs: 1. Sun becomes black as sackcloth 2. Moon becomes like blood 3. Stars fall to the earth (Rev 6:12–13)	Heavenly signs: 1. Sun is dark at its rising 2. Moon does not shed its light 3. Stars do not give their light (Isa 13:10)
8. Great Earthquake			A great earthquake removes every mountain and island from its place (Rev 6:14)	The earth is shaken out of its place (Isa 13:13)
9. The unrighteous attempt to hide.			People hide in caves and among the rocks (Rev 6:15–16)	People hide in caves and among rocks; they throw away their idols of gold and silver (Isa 2:10–21)
10. Day of the Lord	God shakes the powers of heaven (Matt 24:29c)	Day of the Lord (1 Thess 5:4–11)	The great Day of the wrath of the One who sits on the throne and the Lamb arrives (Rev 6:17)	Day of the Lord (Isa 13:9)

Second Vision under the Sixth Seal: Four Angels, the 144,000, and the Mark

Immediately after John saw the heavenly signs, the earthquake, and the unrighteous scurrying for cover, he saw four angels who had been given authority to damage the earth, the sea, and trees. But before executing that power they were told to wait until the servants of their God had been marked with a seal on their foreheads:

> After this I saw four angels standing at the four corners of the earth, holding back the four winds of the earth so that no wind could blow on earth or sea or against any tree. I saw another angel ascending from the rising of the sun, having the seal of the living God, and he called with a loud voice to the four angels who had been given power to damage earth and sea, saying, "Do not damage the earth or the sea or the trees, until we have marked the servants of our God with a seal on their foreheads." And I heard the number of those who were sealed, one hundred forty-four thousand, sealed out of every tribe of the people of Israel. (Rev 7:1–4)

Three questions immediately surface:

1. Who are the four angels who had been given authority to harm the earth, the sea, and the trees?
2. Who are the 144,000 servants of God that the angels were instructed to mark with a seal?
3. What is the significance of the "mark with a seal"?

Let's examine each in turn:

The Four Angels

One will not have to look too far before determining the identity of the four angels who stand at the four corners of the earth. If one glances at the next chapter of Revelation, one will see the narrative of the appearance of the seven angels with their seven trumpets, which officially begins the judgements of the Day of the Lord. Here are excerpts from the description of the first four angels with their four trumpets (italics used for emphasis):

"The first angel blew his trumpet, and there came hail and fire, mixed with blood, and they were hurled to the *earth*; and a third of the earth was burned up, and a third of the *trees* were burned up.... The second angel blew his trumpet, and something like a great mountain, burning with fire, was thrown into the *sea*. A third of the sea became blood.... The third angel blew his trumpet, and a great star fell from heaven, blazing like a torch, and it fell on a third of the rivers and in the springs of water.... The fourth angel blew his trumpet, and a third of the sun was struck, and a third of the moon, and a third of the stars, so that a third of their light was darkened..." (Rev 8:7–12).

With just a quick glance, what do the first four trumpet judgments primarily affect? The earth, the sea, and the trees. And what do the four angels who stand at the four corners of the earth affect? The earth, the sea, and the trees. As the first four angels blow their trumpets in heaven, a second group of four angels will then proceed to cause fires that burn trees and grasses; cause meteors and asteroids to strike the earth, the seas, and the fresh waters; and cause a thick blanket of clouds to block a percentage of the light from the sun, the moon, and the stars. It should be apparent that the four angels who carry out the plagues of the first four trumpets are the four angels who stand at the four corners of the earth and were told to wait before they harm the earth, the sea, and the trees until they have marked with a seal the 144,000 servants of God.

The 144,000

Although the subject of the 144,000 has always been somewhat of an enigma among commentators and one rich with differing opinions, the identity of the 144,000 is quite easy to determine. Initially, one must agree they certainly appear to be Jewish by nationality because John said they came from every tribe of the people of Israel: Judah, Reuben, Gad, Asher, Naphtali, Manasseh, Simeon, Levi, Issachar, Zebulun, Joseph, and Benjamin (Rev 7:5–8). Although Paul might refer to the church, which includes both Jews and gentiles, as the true "Israel of God" in his letters to the Romans and Galatians, he never once described the church as specifically coming from each of the twelve tribes by name, as John lists here (compare Rom 9:1–18 and Gal 4:21–31). Therefore, unless we learn otherwise, let's cautiously assume that the 144,000 servants of God and his Son are Jewish by nationality.

Next, notice the precise moment the four angels were given the instructions to mark the 144,000 Jewish servants: immediately after the appearance of the heavenly signs, the great earthquake, and people scurrying for cover because of the arrival of the Day of the Lord! When has one recently read about some sort of connection between a Jewish group and the appearance of the heavenly signs? It was back during our study of the Olivet Discourse, at which time we cited the following passage from Joel:

"I will show portents in the heavens and on the earth, blood and fire and columns of smoke. The sun shall be turned to darkness, and the moon to blood, before the great and terrible day of the Lord comes. Then everyone who calls on the name of the Lord shall be saved; for in Mount Zion and in Jerusalem there shall be those who escape, as the Lord has said, and among the survivors shall be those whom the Lord calls" (Joel 2:30–32).

God said that when he sends the heavenly signs, i.e., the sun turning to darkness and the moon to blood, then everyone who calls on the name of the Lord shall be saved. And about whom was God speaking? He said in Mount Zion and in Jerusalem there shall be those who escape and among the survivors shall be those whom the Lord calls. Obviously, it is among the survivors of those who escape Jerusalem in the last days that will be the ones who call on the Lord when they see the heavenly signs. And where has one read about a Jewish remnant escaping out of Jerusalem in the last days? In the Olivet Discourse, Jesus admonished the Jews of the last generation to escape Jerusalem at the first sight of the abomination of desolation. Again, here's the text:

"So when you see the desolating sacrilege standing in the holy place, as was spoken by the prophet Daniel (let the reader understand), then those in Judea must flee to the mountains; the one on the housetop must not go down to take what is in the house; the one in the field must not turn back to get a coat. Woe to those who are pregnant and to those who are nursing infants in those days! Pray that your flight may not be in winter or on a sabbath" (Matt 24:15–20).

Here, Jesus urges the Jewish "reader" to hurriedly escape Jerusalem at the first sight of the abomination, so that the Jewish "remnant," which is among the readers, might later come to a place in time when they confess Christ. And "that time" is the appearance of the heavenly signs!

It doesn't take much discernment to understand that the Jewish elect admonished by Christ to flee Jerusalem at the abomination of desolation, and the Jewish elect who will later confess Christ at the sight of the heavenly signs, and the 144,000 Jewish elect who are about to receive an angelic mark on the foreheads because they have just confessed Christ at the appearance of the heavenly signs (who can only now be called "the servants of our God") are all one and the same.

The following reconciliation of the words of Jesus, John, and Joel trace the steps of the 144,000 Jewish remnant from the abomination of desolation to the appearance of the heavenly signs:

Table 4.6. Jesus, John, and Joel Trace the Steps of the 144,000 Jewish Remnant from the Abomination of Desolation to the Appearance of the Heavenly Signs

The Sequence	Jesus	John	Joel
1. The 144,000 Jewish remnant, who are as yet unconfessed, escape Jerusalem at the abomination of desolation.	Jesus urges "the reader" to escape Jerusalem at the sight of the abomination (Matt 24:15)		There shall be those who escape Mount Zion and Jerusalem (Joel 2:32)
2. Nuclear War	Greatest suffering in history (Matt 24:21)	The Four Horsemen of the Apocalypse begin nuclear war (Rev 6:1–4)	
3. The nuclear war ends as the nuclear aftermath begins.	God ends the greatest suffering in the history of the world (Matt 24:22)	Nuclear war ends as the nuclear aftermath begins (Rev 6:5–8)	
4. With the nuclear aftermath arise false messiahs and false prophets causing deception.	Deception by false messiahs and false prophets (Matt 24:23–28)		
5. The man of lawlessness emerges from among the false messiahs and false prophets. He deceives the unrighteous and kills the saints.	A second period of suffering is in progress (Matt 24:29a)		
6. Toward the end of the period of martyrdom, which is perpetrated by the man of lawlessness, the souls in heaven are told to wait a little longer until the full number of martyrs has been reached.		Toward the end of the period of martyrdom, the souls in heaven are told to wait a little longer until the complete number of martyrs has been reached (Rev 6:9–11)	

Table 4.6. Jesus, John, and Joel Trace the Steps of the 144,000 Jewish Remnant from the Abomination of Desolation to the Appearance of the Heavenly Signs

The Sequence	Jesus	John	Joel
7. The 144,000 Jewish remnant calls on the Lord at the appearance of the heavenly signs.	Heavenly signs: 1. Sun is darkened 2. Moon does not give its light 3. Stars fall from heaven (Matt 24:29b)	Heavenly signs: 1. Sun becomes black as sackcloth 2. Moon becomes like blood 3. Stars fall to the earth (Rev 6:12–13)	Among the survivors are those who call on the Lord when they see the heavenly signs (Joel 2:32)
8. A Great Earthquake		A great earthquake removes every mountain and island from its place (Rev 6:14)	
9. The unrighteous hide in caves and among rocks		People hide in caves and among the rocks (Rev 6:15–16)	
10. The Day of the Lord has come.		The great Day of the wrath of the One who sits on the throne and the Lamb has come (Rev 6:17)	
11. The 144,000 Jewish remnant are marked by angels, having confessed Christ at the appearance of the heavenly signs.		The 144,000 Jewish remnant are marked by angels with God's seal (Rev 7:1–8)	
12. The judgments of the Day of the Lord begin.	God shakes the powers of heaven (Matt 24:29c)		

The Mark

Since Joel revealed that it will be at the appearance of the heavenly signs that the last-generation Jewish remnant will give their hearts to the Lord and confess Christ, then by the time John saw the four angels about to mark the 144,000 with a seal (Rev 7:3), the angels' seal had nothing to do with the salvation event. How can one be sure? There are two types of seals referenced in Scripture: one by God, and one by angels. God's seal is the seal of the Holy Spirit and is placed by God at the moment of confession and faith in Christ (italics used for emphasis):

"In him you also, when you had heard the word of truth, the gospel of your salvation, and had believed in him, *were marked with the seal of the promised Holy Spirit*; this is the pledge of our inheritance toward redemption as God's own people, to the praise of his glory" (Eph 1:13–14).

According to Paul, God's seal of the Holy Spirit is placed at the moment of someone's salvation. Angels have nothing to do with this seal because angels have nothing to do with the inner workings of salvation. Salvation is strictly between God and man. In fact, angels are not even permitted to proclaim the good news of salvation, since they have never experienced it and never will. That responsibility has been reserved only for men and women, the recipients of salvation.[2] A good example of this is when an angel appeared to Cornelius, a centurion of the Italian Cohort (Acts 10:3); the angel was not permitted to preach the good news to Cornelius, but could only direct him to Peter, who, in turn, would be the one given the responsibility of bringing the good news of Jesus Christ to the household of the centurion (Acts 10:34–43).

Secondly, there is the seal placed by angels. When John heard the angels' discussion of a seal, this was the seal of which they were speaking (Rev 7:3). And what's its purpose? In short: the physical protection of the believer. Once the 144,000 Jewish remnant confesses Christ at the appearance of the heavenly signs, God will then provide them physical protection from any of his future wrath, just as he does for all of the elect: Jew and gentile, past, present, and future. Recall Paul's promise to the Thessalonians:

"For God has destined us not for wrath but for obtaining salvation through the Lord Jesus Christ, who died for us, so that whether we are

---

2. The author is well aware of Rev 14:6–7 that initially appears to reference an angel proclaiming the gospel of Christ in the last days. However that was only a message to fear and worship God, and since angels are among those who fear and worship God, they too, with God's permission, are allowed to proclaim that particular "eternal gospel." Notwithstanding this fact and, again the point, angels will never experience the salvation provided by Christ and therefore will never have permission to preach the gospel of Jesus Christ—that he was crucified on the cross for the sins of the world and resurrected on the third day for the believers' justification. The privilege of ministering that good news is reserved for the believer.

awake or asleep we may live with him. Therefore encourage one another and build up each other, as indeed you are doing" (1 Thess 5:9–11).

In short, Paul said that the unrighteous are destined for God's wrath; the righteous are not. John saw this glorious truth put into action in the vision under the sixth seal: As soon as the 144,000 Jewish remnant confessed Christ at the appearance of the heavenly signs, God commissioned his angels to mark his newly converted 144,000 Jewish remnant with a seal on their foreheads, thereby protecting them from his wrath which was about to begin with the first trumpet plague. But to be sure, Rev 7 isn't Scripture's only reference to the angelic seal.

Ezekiel Witnessed the Same Mark

During the Babylonian captivity, the Lord carried Ezekiel away in the Spirit and showed the prophet several examples of abominations committed by the Jewish leaders and the people in Jerusalem. After seeing the abominations, Ezekiel heard the following instructions given by the Lord to six angels, and with them was one clothed in linen, with a writing case at his side:

"Then he cried in my hearing with a loud voice, saying, 'Draw near, you executioners of the city, each with his destroying weapon in his hand.' And six men came from the direction of the upper gate, which faces north, each with his weapon for slaughter in his hand; among them was a man clothed in linen, with a writing case at his side. They went in and stood beside the bronze altar.

"Now the glory of the God of Israel had gone up from the cherub on which it rested to the threshold of the house. The Lord called to the man clothed in linen, who had the writing case at his side; and said to him, 'Go through the city, through Jerusalem, and put a mark on the foreheads of those who sigh and groan over all the abominations that are committed in it.' To the others he said in my hearing, 'Pass through the city after him, and kill; your eyes shall not spare, and you shall show no pity. Cut down old men, young men, little children and women, but touch no one who has the mark'" (Ezek 9:1–6a).

Here, one sees God commissioning angels to mark the righteous for physical protection against his upcoming wrath, whereby those same angels are also the ones who will distribute God's wrath against the unmarked. This is the exact scenario in Rev 7. Note also that the passage in Ezekiel illustrates another difference between God's seal and the seal placed by angels: Whereas God's seal of the Holy Spirit is certainly invisible because the Holy Spirit is invisible, the angelic seal is visible . . . at least to angels. In fact, the most important characteristic of the angelic seal is its visibility, in order that angels, whether good or evil, can see the mark and thereby know who are the objects of God's wrath and who are not. However, one might ask, How do we know for certain that evil angels can indeed see the mark? Because, as the reader will soon learn, during the fifth trumpet-judgment evil spirits released out of the bottomless pit will be prohibited from torturing those who have the angelic mark, which necessarily indicates they too will indeed have the ability to see the angelic mark.

Both Ezekiel and John confirm the words of Paul to the Thessalonians: God's people are not destined for wrath. Whether the number of righteous that are to be physically protected are in the hundreds of millions as will be the scene in the last days, or about a million in Israel's exodus from Egypt, or only the number of a righteous remnant left in the city of Jerusalem during the Babylonian captivity, as evidenced in Ezek 9:1–6a, or as little as the size of a single family as was the case with Lot in the narrative of Sodom and Gomorrah, and Noah in the narrative of the flood, God has always protected his people from his wrath. And notice that in each of the preceding examples, God was well able to protect his people while they remained on the earth. To believe that God must first take his people off the planet in order to safely and efficiently protect them from his own wrath is a clear example of not fully appreciating the omniscience and the omnipotence of God. Granted, if you or I were given the responsibility of distributing devastating wrath around the globe against some last-days ne'er-do-wells and scoundrels, it would probably be wise to put some distance between the good and the bad, but thankfully, that has never been an issue with God.

Third Vision under the Sixth Seal: A Great Multitude around the Throne

Finally, John saw the last vision under the sixth seal, which was of a great, innumerable multitude standing with all the angels, the twenty-four elders, and the four living creatures around God's throne in heaven, as they all in unison worshiped God and his Son:

> After this I looked, and there was a great multitude that no one could count, from every nation, from all tribes and peoples and languages, standing before the throne and before the Lamb, robed in white, with palm branches in their hands. They cried out in a loud voice, saying, "Salvation belongs to our God who is seated on the throne, and to the Lamb!" And all the angels stood around the throne and around the elders and the four living creatures, and they fell on their faces before the throne and worshiped God, singing, "Amen! Blessing and glory and wisdom and thanksgiving and honor and power and might be to our God forever and ever! Amen." (Rev 7:9–12)

What is the identity of this great multitude? Some commentators have taught that they are the 144,000 Jews that were referenced in the previous vision. Of course, that's impossible. As proven, the 144,000 are the Jewish remnant of the last generation who will confess Christ at the appearance of the heavenly signs. Needless to say, the recently converted, recently marked 144,000 Jewish remnant standing on the earth immediately after the appearance of the heavenly signs is not the great multitude standing and worshiping around God's throne in heaven immediately prior to the first trumpet judgment. Others have postulated that the great multitude around heaven's throne are the resurrected and raptured church. Proponents of this belief can be further divided into two groups, depending on exactly when they believe the multitude arrived in heaven:

1. Some believe the multitude was resurrected and raptured up to heaven prior to the opening of the first seal. Proponents of this belief-system are called "pretribulationists." Just as the term implies, they believe that the saints will be resurrected and raptured to heaven prior to the tribulation, which they believe begins at the breaking of the first seal.[3]

2. Others believe the multitude was resurrected and raptured up to heaven in between the opening of the sixth and seventh seal, which is known as "the pre-wrath rapture" or "the intra-seal rapture." Again, as the term indicates, these adherents believe that the saints will be resurrected and raptured to heaven after the tribulation of the saints, which they believe coincides with the opening of the sixth seal, but before the dispersal of God's wrath, which they believe begins at the breaking of the seventh seal.[4]

3. Walvoord, *Rapture Question*, 59–76.
4. Kampen, *Sign*, 305–11.

Of course, as concerning the timing of Christ's opening of the seals, hopefully one understands by now that the "intra-seal resurrection and rapture" as well as the "before-the-first-seal resurrection and rapture" are impossible since it has been proven that the seven seals have already been opened, two thousand years ago. The only relationship between the seven seals and the great multitude around the throne is that John saw "the vision" of the future multitude after Christ opened the sixth seal but before Christ opened the seventh seal. Other than that, there is no relationship. Nevertheless, regardless of anyone's lack of understanding of when the seals were opened, the various positions of those who believe the multitude represents the resurrected and raptured church deserve to be addressed. In order to do that, we begin by examining John's second conversation.

Second Conversation: An Elder Asks John the Identity of the Multitude

In the following we have our first example of many to come, where God allows someone to approach John with the express purpose of enlightening him concerning a vision he had just seen or was about to see. In this case, it's one of the twenty-four elders sent to question John concerning the vision of the great multitude that both he and the disciple had just seen. Observe:

> Then one of the elders addressed me, saying, "Who are these, robed in white, and where have they come from?" I said to him, "Sir, you are the one that knows." (Rev 7:13–14a)

After asking him if he knew the identity of the multitude and John indicating that he did not, the elder gave the answer:

> Then he said to me, "These are they who have come out of the great ordeal; they have washed their robes and made them white in the blood of the Lamb." (Rev 7:14b)

The elder said the great multitude had come out of the great ordeal. The Greek phrase *thlipseōs tēs megalēs*, translated "the great ordeal" by the NRSV, is often translated in other Bible translations as the more familiar "the great tribulation."[5] So, out of what great tribulation has the multitude come? One knows the elder cannot be speaking of any tribulation that

---

5. The King James Version is one example.

might be ongoing during the trumpet judgments of the Day of the Lord simply because the trumpets haven't yet started (Rev 8:1–6). Therefore, one knows the elder can only be referencing a period of tribulation prior to the Day of the Lord and its first trumpet. Furthermore, as has been well documented from our studies in the Olivet Discourse and 2 Thessalonians, and now more recently with the visions under the first five seals, one also knows that there will be two distinct periods of suffering prior to the Day of the Lord:

1. The *nuclear war* initiated and orchestrated by the first and second riders of "the Four Horsemen of the Apocalypse."

2. And the *nuclear aftermath* initiated and orchestrated by the third and fourth riders of "the Four Horsemen of the Apocalypse" (as has also been determined, the period of the nuclear aftermath will include at some point *the targeted persecution and slaughter of the saints by the man of lawlessness*).

Because Christ, Paul, and John together confirmed the reality of two future periods of tribulation, one must assume that when the elder told John that these are they who have come out of "the great tribulation," he was doubtless indicating that these are they who have come out of both periods of suffering which include the nuclear war, the nuclear aftermath, and the martyrdom of the saints.

Not the Church

Did you know that when the elder told John that the great multitude had specifically come out of "the great tribulation" he was automatically excluding the millions and millions of saints who have lived and died in the generations prior to the great tribulation? This fact alone proves that the great multitude John saw standing around the throne could not have been the resurrected and raptured church. Had John truly seen the whole church, the great multitude would have been even greater, including all of the saints throughout history and not just the ones who came out during the months or years comprising the great tribulation. Therefore, since the multitude around the throne only represented a portion of the church, one can now understand that the resurrection and rapture was yet to occur, which further indicated that John was only seeing "the souls" of the great multitude. In retrospect, when the elder said, "These are they who have come out of the great ordeal," he wasn't saying these are they who have been resurrected and raptured out of the great tribulation, but rather he was indicating these are they who have "died" during the great tribulation.

Although the above discussion easily proved that the great multitude around the throne was not the resurrected and raptured church, it was unnecessary, nonetheless. Why? Because Paul's expectation of being alive at the *parousia* of Christ has already proven the same point. How so? At the risk of sounding redundant, ask yourself this question: Had the Lord indeed revealed to Paul that the church would be resurrected and raptured prior to the great tribulation of the saints or prior to the Day of the Lord, could Paul still have expected to be living on the earth at the moment of the *parousia*, which Paul himself revealed will be the moment when the man of lawlessness is taken out of the way? Of course not. No matter how one looks at it, the simple fact that Paul expected to witness the capture of the man of lawlessness, which, according to the apostle, will occur after the tribulation, i.e., "that evil day," and after the Day of the Lord, i.e., a day of wrath against the unrighteous, proves that the saints of the last generation will only be resurrected and raptured after the tribulation and after the Day of the Lord.

Glorified Bodies, Righteous Souls, and White Robes

There seems to be some lingering notion that only glorified bodies can wear robes, as opposed to souls or spirits. As the reasoning goes, since the great multitude around the throne were seen wearing robes (Rev 7:9), they must have already received their glorified bodies, proving that the resurrection and rapture had taken place. But the premise is false. Not only can angels, who are spirit beings, wear clothing (Rev 15:6), but the souls of righteous men and women can don clothing just as easily as angels, or men with natural bodies. One has just read where the twenty-four elders were seen wearing white robes (Rev 4:4), and since the elders are distinguished from angels, they are most certainly twenty-four souls of the righteous who will only receive their glorified bodies at the first resurrection, along with the rest of the saints. And lest one forget the vision under the fifth seal, there John saw the souls of the martyred saints each given a white robe (Rev 6:11). Were they expected to hold the robes in their spiritual laps indefinitely until they received glorified bodies?

Of course not. The martyred souls were robed as soon as they received them, and one sees the results of that action later when they, together with all the saints who had died during the great tribulation, were seen "standing before the throne and before the Lamb, *robed in white*, with palm branches in their hands" (Rev 7:9).

Why the Celebration?

After identifying the great multitude as those who had come out of the great tribulation, the elder then described some of their earthly tribulation: With the knowledge that shortages of food and water, and the destruction of the worldwide infrastructure, including homes and shelters, will be the result of the nuclear war and its aftermath, it's easy to understand why the elder said the multitude has experienced hunger, thirst, and scorching heat. Observe:

> For this reason they are before the throne of God, and worship him day and night within his temple, and the one who is seated on the throne will shelter them. They will hunger no more, and thirst no more; the sun will not strike them, nor any scorching heat; for the Lamb at the center of the throne will be their shepherd, and he will guide them to springs of the water of life, and God will wipe away every tear from their eyes. (Rev 7:15–17)

Although their celebration was to be expected, why was the great multitude celebrating and worshiping God and the Lamb at precisely the moment between the appearance of the heavenly signs and the arrival of the first trumpet judgment? Had something significant happened? Absolutely! And the clue to the milestone can be found back in the vision under the fifth seal:

"When he opened the fifth seal, I saw under the altar the souls of those who had been slaughtered for the word of God and for the testimony they had given; they cried out with a loud voice, 'Sovereign Lord, holy and true, how long will it be before you judge and avenge our blood on the inhabitants of the earth?' They were each given a white robe and told to rest a little longer, until the number would be complete both of their fellow servants and of their brothers and sisters, who were soon to be killed as they themselves had been killed" (Rev 6:9–11).

One knows that John saw the martyrs just before the period of martyrdom was about to come to an end because the martyrs were told "to rest a little longer until the number would be complete both of their fellow servants and of their brothers and sisters, who were soon to be killed as they themselves had been killed." But now, in this most recent vision, John sees the great multitude of souls from every nation, from all tribes and peoples and languages, who have died during the great ordeal, joined by millions and millions of angels, the twenty-four elders, and the four living creatures, as all have gathered at this particular moment in order to worship and praise God around his throne. It's difficult to imagine this magnitude of gathering around God's throne, whereby everyone in heaven is seen worshiping and praising the Father and the Lamb in such a wondrous and celebratory fashion, if back on the earth, the slaughter of Christian men, women, and children were still in progress, wouldn't you agree? For this reason alone, it seems certain that the martyrdom of the saints has ended, fulfilling the complete number of martyrs that God has preordained (Rev 6:11). In fact, it is because of this magnificent milestone that the martyred souls have now moved from underneath the altar to join the rest of the saints who also died during the great tribulation, forming the "great multitude that no one could count, from every nation, from all tribes and peoples and languages, standing before the throne and before the Lamb."

An Apparent Discrepancy?

With the above conclusion, we must now address an apparent discrepancy found in our earlier study of 2 Thessalonians (italics used for emphasis):

"For it is indeed just of God to repay with affliction those who afflict you, and *to give relief to the afflicted as well as to us, when the Lord Jesus is revealed from heaven with his mighty angels in flaming fire*, inflicting vengeance on those who do not know God and on those who do not obey the gospel of our Lord Jesus" (2 Thess 1:6–8).

Here, Paul told the Thessalonians that they would receive "relief" (Greek: *anesin*) at the time of the second coming of Christ with his angels in flaming fire, but in our just-completed study, it has been determined that the great multitude of saints around the throne were celebrating the end of the martyrdom of the saints after the appearance of the heavenly signs but before the first trumpet, which is a point in time well before the second coming of Christ. Is our conclusion in Revelation compatible with Paul's statement in 2 Thessalonians? Absolutely! According to Paul, at Christ's return the saints will receive "complete rest and relief" from all of their sufferings and tribulations. But that doesn't change the fact that as early as the heavenly signs, the saints will receive "a measure of relief" from their sufferings because the full number of martyrs has been reached, thus ending the "great" tribulation of the saints. That's not to say that the saints won't continue to suffer and go through a "measure" of tribulation beyond the appearance of the heavenly signs, but, thankfully, without the threat of martyrdom.

Upon reflection, our earlier description of the mindset of the Thessalonians has been proven correct.[6] They knew that when the Day of the Lord arrived, with its overwhelming destruction and wrath poured out upon the unrighteous, the same would necessarily be preoccupied with their own self-preservation, which would automatically bring the Thessalonians some "measure" of relief from their present pain and suffering. But now that one has learned that the Day of the Lord will also bring an end to the martyrdom of the saints, the relief from suffering anticipated by the Thessalonians, had they been part of the last generation, would have been even more than the little community had hoped!

Seventh Seal: The Seven Trumpets

Having seen the last of the three visions under the sixth seal, John now turned back to Jesus and watched him break open the seventh seal. Unexpectedly, the disciple and all those in the throne room had to wait approximately thirty minutes before any new visions appeared:

> When the Lamb opened the seventh seal, there was silence in heaven for about half an hour. (Rev 8:1)

Why the wait? Through the first six seals, the visions seen by John chronicled a period reflecting a time when the enemies of God were granted authority to rule and reign, taking peace from the earth and eventually persecuting and slaughtering the saints. Evil will be rampant during "the great tribulation" and that's why Paul called the period "that evil day." But with the opening of the seventh seal, John is about to see visions that chronicle the Day of the Lord, when God will bring judgment to those who have persecuted and killed his people. Perhaps the Lord thought the thirty minutes of silence was an appropriate interlude

---

6. See pp. 18–19.

to place between the two sets of visions. Whether that was his reasoning or not, after the half hour had passed, the visions resumed. John then saw seven angels given seven trumpets:

> And I saw the seven angels who stand before God, and seven trumpets were given to them. Another angel with a golden censer came and stood at the altar; he was given a great quantity of incense to offer with the prayers of all the saints on the golden altar that is before the throne. And the smoke of the incense, with the prayers of the saints, rose before God from the hand of the angel. Then the angel took the censer and filled it with fire from the altar and threw it on the earth; and there were peals of thunder, rumblings, flashes of lightning, and an earthquake. Now the seven angels who had the seven trumpets made ready to blow them. (Rev 8:2–6)

As the angels stood holding their trumpets, John recognized the first four as the ones who earlier had been instructed to mark the 144,000 Jewish remnant (Rev 7:3). Having completed their task, the four were now permitted to begin harming the earth.[7]

The First Four Trumpets: The Earth Is Harmed

Next, John saw the first angel blow his trumpet as the judgments of the Day of the Lord officially began. Whether the four angels who stand at the four corners of the earth will respond in unison as a quartet to each individual trumpet blast, or perhaps one angel will respond to the first trumpet blast, followed by the second angel who will then respond to the second trumpet blast, then the third angel, etc., is difficult to determine. However one thing is certain: At each trumpet blast in heaven, plagues will appear on earth.

As we begin, note that only during each of the first four trumpet narratives will a brief hypothetical scenario be offered by which God "might" carry out the judgments. However, please remember the conjecture doesn't have anything to do with the sequence of events. Regardless

---

7. Are "the four angels who stand at the four corners of earth" the same angels as "the four winds of heaven" seen by Zechariah in his first and eighth visions, who were sent to patrol the earth for peace (compare Zech 1:7–17 and 6:1–8)? Possibly. It seems perfectly reasonable to think that the four angels commissioned by God to patrol the earth for peace in the past will be the same four commissioned to begin his wrath in the future.

of the means by which God does or does not carry out the first four plagues, the sequence of the plagues are locked into a precise chronological order. Now, with that, here's the first trumpet:

> The first angel blew his trumpet, and there came hail and fire, mixed with blood, and they were hurled to the earth; and a third of the earth was burned up, and a third of the trees were burned up, and all green grass was burned up. (Rev 8:7)

When the first trumpet was blown, a third of the earth, a third of the trees, and all grass was burned up. Unless God just miraculously starts the wildfires *ex nihilo*, how might this plague occur? Well, if nature is any indicator, one would assume the plague would somehow be the result of worldwide lightning strikes. And what might cause the lightning strikes? Here's a possibility: Do you recall the great earthquake that will accompany the heavenly signs (Rev 6:12)? Could an earthquake of that magnitude, which was said to have shaken every mountain and island on the earth from its place, including every volcanic mountain and island, possibly lead to an unprecedented amount of worldwide volcanic activity, which in turn, would consequently release an increased concentration of heat into the atmosphere? And when that heat mixes with the existing cool air, one could easily envision an anomalous amount of worldwide lightning strikes, causing global wildfires. If God does cause the lighting strikes in this manner, then they, coupled with their inevitable high winds, could easily spread enough fires until God's predetermined limit of one-third of the earth was burned, at which time the fires would miraculously abate, thereby preserving the remaining two-thirds of the earth. (Think of the California wildfires, but on a global scale.)

Next, John saw the second angel blow his trumpet:

> The second angel blew his trumpet, and something like a great mountain, burning with fire, was thrown into the sea. A third of the sea became blood, a third of the living creatures in the sea died, and a third of all ships were destroyed. (Rev 8:8–9)

The disciple said he saw "something like a great mountain, burning with fire" that was thrown into the sea. Continuing with the theme of global volcanic activity resulting from the worldwide earthquake, what if the shaken and aggravated, simmering volcanoes, i.e., "burning mountain," erupted all across the globe at the time of the second trumpet, spewing 2,000°F lava, carbon dioxide, and sulfur dioxide into the seas and oceans, poisoning all the sea life that it contacted? This would account for the fact that when John said he saw a great mountain burning with fire being thrown into the sea, he was actually witnessing a scene of burning lava oozing down the side of a mountain, as great portions of the mountain crumbled headlong into the sea. And if that's indeed the circumstance, little would the disciple have known that that same occurrence was happening simultaneously all over the world at the second trumpet, resulting in the destruction of a third of the sea life as well as a third of all oceangoing vessels.

When the third trumpet was blown, most biblical translations read that John said he saw "a great star" fall from heaven, striking the earth. But, as was earlier pointed out, God made the stars thousands and sometimes millions of times larger than the earth. Therefore, one knows that John did not see a literal star fall to the earth; instead, he saw "a great asteroid" hit the earth (Greek: *astēr megas*):

> The third angel blew his trumpet, and a great star fell from heaven, blazing like a torch, and it fell on a third of the rivers and on the springs of water. The name of the star is Wormwood. A third of the waters became wormwood, and many died from the water, because it was made bitter. (Rev 8:10–11)

What was the result of the asteroid's impact? In a word, catastrophic. John said that when the "great star" fell on the earth that a third of the rivers and springs of water became "wormwood" (Greek: *apsinthon*, which means "bitter"). And because the text stated that many died from the bitter water, one knows that the water had somehow become contaminated and poisoned by the asteroid. Some might question how a single asteroid could possibly contaminate a third of the earth's freshwater, rendering the water unfit to drink. However, it might not be as difficult as it initially appears. As it turns out, it might just depend on where God places the impact of the asteroid. As an example, Lake Superior of the Great Lakes contains about 10 percent of the earth's freshwater and Lake Baikal in Russia contains about 20 percent of the earth's freshwater. These two lakes alone hold about a third of the earth's freshwater. Here's the point: When God does choose to strike the earth with a major asteroid in the last days, his purpose of adversely affecting a third of the planet's freshwater might simply be accomplished by destroying two or three of the earth's primary freshwater sources.

Finally, John saw the fourth trumpet blown, which officially brought an end to the plagues that were designed specifically to harm the earth:

> The fourth angel blew his trumpet, and a third of the sun was struck, and a third of the moon, and a third of the stars, so that a third of their light was darkened; a third of the day was kept from shining, and likewise the night. (Rev 8:12)

Could the fourth trumpet judgment be the result of the same asteroid seen during the third trumpet? It's very likely. After the impact of the asteroid, Wormwood, the resultant atmospheric debris and widespread dust-clouds might easily block a third of the light from the sun, the moon, and the stars for an indeterminate period of time. And the effect? No light results in no vegetation; no vegetation means no food; and no food equals starvation. In a word, just like the previous judgments, the result would be catastrophic.

As indicated earlier, the above speculations of how God and his angels might actually carry out the first four trumpet plagues have no bearing on the sequence of end-time events. Whether God uses earthquakes, lightning strikes, volcanoes, asteroids, or dust clouds to enact his judgments, the sequence is the same. As to how God actually will carry out his wrath, only time will tell. This much is certain: Once the plagues begin, fires will be everywhere; a third of the saltwater and freshwater will be poisoned and contaminated; the stench of dead sea life will pollute the fresh air as lifeless sea creatures everywhere begin floating to the surface, littering the seascape just as trash litters a parking lot after a ballgame. And, as if things couldn't get any worse, the skies will become inexplicably dark and vegetation will die, as the sun and moon hide their faces from all of humanity.

Fifth Trumpet: Five Months of Torture

As the darkness from the fourth plague continued to blanket the earth, John next saw an extraordinary sight: an eagle flying in the mid-heaven,[8] warning the inhabitants of the earth about the next three trumpets that the angels were about to blow. Despite the unprecedented devastation against the earth during the first four trumpets and the resultant hardship incurred by the unrighteous, the angel indicated that greater pain and suffering lay ahead:

> Then I looked, and I heard an eagle crying with a loud voice as it flew in midheaven, "Woe, woe, woe, to the inhabitants of the

---
8. The eagle was doubtless a symbolic representation of an angel.

earth, at the blasts of the other trumpets that the three angels are about to blow!" (Rev 8:13)

One will soon learn that the phrase "the inhabitants of the earth," seen here for the second time (Rev 6:10 was the first), will be used by John throughout Revelation as a designation only for the unrighteous, and never for the righteous. When warning the unrighteous of the next three plagues, the eagle identified the plagues as three "woes." The fifth trumpet will release the first woe, the sixth trumpet will release the second, and the seventh trumpet, the third. Here's the first woe:

> And the fifth angel blew his trumpet, and I saw a star that had fallen from heaven to earth and he was given the key to the shaft of the bottomless pit; he opened the shaft of the bottomless pit and from the shaft rose smoke like the smoke of a great furnace, and the sun and the air were darkened with the smoke from the shaft. Then from the smoke came locusts on the earth, and they were given authority like the authority of scorpions of the earth. They were told not to damage the grass of the earth or any green growth or any tree, but only those people who do not have the seal of God on their foreheads. (Rev 9:1–4)

When the trumpet was blown, John saw a star that had fallen to the earth. It is certain that the star is representative of a personality in some way because, in the same verse, John personifies the star by saying that "he" was given the key to the shaft of the bottomless pit. Unless a man can fall from heaven to earth and receive a key to the shaft of the bottomless pit, then one knows that the star is representative of an angel. Once given the key, the angel opened the shaft of the pit, at which time smoke rose, darkening the air and the light from the sun (Rev 9:2). Then, out from the smoke came "locusts" and they were given authority to inflict pain similar to the pain inflicted by a scorpion (Rev 9:3). Next, the locusts were instructed not to damage the grass or the trees of the earth, but only those people who do not have the seal of God on their foreheads (Rev 9:4). The fact that the locusts were given instructions as to who they could or could not harm, and then were expected to comprehend those instructions, proved that the locusts were representative of some type of personality, just as was the star. Furthermore, since the "locusts" had been confined to the bottomless pit, one knows that the personalities were evil because the pit is a place created only for the confinement of evil personalities (compare 2 Pet 2:4–10 and Jude 6–7). Therefore, the question that remains is whether the personalities are evil spirits or, perhaps, evil humans. The answer is quite simple: The locusts must symbolize evil spirits because, had they represented humans confined to the bottomless pit, that would indicate that in some cases, after a person dies, he or she might still be released from confinement in order to roam the earth for a particular reason. But this scenario contradicts Heb 9:27, which states that once a human dies, his or her next appointment is God's judgment, not roaming the earth and torturing other human beings. Here's the text:

"And just as it is appointed for mortals to die once, and after that the judgment..."

In retrospect, the fact that the evil spirits were instructed not to harm anyone who had the seal of God on their foreheads proves the point that was made earlier when discussing the marking of the 144,000 Jewish remnant, and that was that evil angels or spirits have the same ability to see the angelic seal of protection on the foreheads of the righteous, just as God's angels (Rev 7:3).

Next, John reveals two additional restrictions that will be imposed on the demons: Both the time frame and the severity of the harm will have a limit. Observe:

> They were allowed to torture them for five months, but not to kill them, and their torture was like the torture of a scorpion when it stings someone. And in those days people will seek death but will not find it; they will long to die, but death will flee from them. (Rev 9:5–6)

The demons will only be allowed to "torture" the inhabitants of the earth; they will not be allowed to kill them. Furthermore, this torture will only be permitted for five months. Nevertheless, the pain will be so excruciating that the inhabitants of the earth will long to die (Rev 9:6), which seems to insinuate that many will attempt suicide.

God's Drawings of the Demons

Finally, John gets around to describing the appearance of the locusts. Quite frankly, they look hideous. The description includes a conglomeration of locusts, horses, wings, human faces, women's hair, lions' teeth, and iron scales:

> In appearance the locusts were like horses equipped for battle. On their heads were what looked like crowns of gold; their faces

were like human faces, their hair like women's hair, and their teeth like lions' teeth; they had scales like iron breastplates, and the noise of their wings was like the noise of many chariots with horses rushing into battle. They have tails like scorpions, with stingers, and in their tails is their power to harm people for five months. (Rev 9:7–10)

Mind you, this was not how the demons appeared in the spirit realm; rather, this was how God drew them for John's benefit. The following is a list of the locusts' characteristics with the possible symbolism:

Table 4.7. The Locusts of the Fifth Trumpet	
How the Images Appeared to John	**Possible Symbolism of the Images**
1. Crowns of gold on the heads (9:7)	Crowns in Revelation denote authority.
2. Faces like human faces (9:7)	The demons have human-like personalities.
3. Hair like women's hair (9:8)	Perhaps the long unkempt hair, which is seen enveloping a human-like face, connotes a more sinister, animalistic personality, one that is void of any conscience.
4. Teeth like lions' teeth (9:8)	The demons possess the ability to inflict fatal harm.
5. Scales like iron breastplates (9:9)	The demons are indestructible, at least by human standards.
6. Noise like the noise of many chariots (9:9)	The demons have been released and are now on the move.
7. Tails with stingers, like scorpion tails (9:10)	The demons possess not only the ability to kill but also the ability to torture with a pain that stings and lingers like the pain caused by the venom of a scorpion.

Although one might expect that once the evil spirits are released from the bottomless pit, they might immediately begin to randomly and haphazardly torture the unrighteous inhabitants around the earth, but the following verse suggests otherwise:

> They have as king over them the angel of the bottomless pit; his name in Hebrew is Abaddon, and in Greek he is called Apollyon. (Rev 9:11)

FIRST SEQUENCE IN REVELATION, PART 1

By stating that the angel of the bottomless pit is their king, John seems to indicate that the evil spirits will take their marching orders from the angel. His name is *Abaddon* in Hebrew and *Apollyon* in Greek. Both names mean "destruction." The fact that John brought so much attention to this angel now might suggest that the angel given the key to the shaft of the bottomless pit at the beginning of the narrative and the named angel at the end of the narrative are one and the same.

Finally, as John brings to a conclusion his remarks concerning the fifth trumpet, the disciple harkens back to the words of the eagle (Rev 8:13), and proclaims the following:

> The first woe has passed. There are still two woes to come. (Rev 9:12)

Although the severity of the first woe seemed unfathomable, one would assume the next two are worse—if that's possible.

Sixth Trumpet: One-Third of Inhabitants Killed

Five months after the fifth trumpet blast, the demonic torture of the inhabitants of the earth comes to an end. Coming on the heels of that nightmarish ordeal is the second woe. And yes, it's worse; much worse. The sixth trumpet will trigger the release of four evil angels who are bound in the bottomless pit somewhere in the vicinity of the River Euphrates:

> Then the sixth angel blew his trumpet, and I heard a voice from the four horns of the golden altar before God, saying to the sixth angel who had the trumpet, "Release the four angels who are bound at the great river Euphrates." So the four angels were released, who had been held ready for the hour, the day, the month, and the year, to kill a third of humankind. (Rev 9:13–15)

The four angels are presently being held in confinement until a certain month of a year, a certain day of that month, and a certain hour of that day. Unlike the previous plague, where authority was only given to torture the inhabitants of the earth, these angels will be given the authority to kill one-third of those same inhabitants. And although Rev 9:15 reads the seemingly nonspecific "a third of humankind" will be killed, it is certain that those killed during the sixth trumpet holocaust will only consist of the "unrighteousness inhabitants of the earth." Why so? Because the sixth trumpet is part of the Day of the Lord and the judgments of the Day are only for the unrighteous. This is unlike the earlier holocaust perpetrated by "the Four Horsemen of the Apocalypse," which will begin well before the Day of the Lord and include the nuclear holocaust and its aftermath. As one well knows by now, both the righteous and unrighteous will die during that holocaust.[9]

The Troops of Cavalry

Next, after relaying the almost incomprehensible revelation that four unknown angels will be the invisible cause behind the deaths of a third of the unrighteous inhabitants of the earth, John curiously interjects, seemingly out of nowhere, that the sixth trumpet plague will include the participation of an incredibly large number of troops:

> The number of the troops of cavalry was two hundred million; I heard their number. (Rev 9:16)

Without any formal introduction as to who or what comprises the troops, John simply stated they will number two hundred million. Although the disciple gives no indication of the relationship between the four angels and the cavalry, one would assume the vast army is subservient to the four. Question: Could John perhaps assume that we have already been familiarized with the troops and that's why he didn't give more of an introduction to them? Possibly. Nevertheless, whether those were his thoughts or not, the disciple next proceeds to describe the troops:

> And this was how I saw the horses in my vision: the riders wore breastplates the color of fire and of sapphire and of sulfur; the heads of the horses were like lions' heads, and fire and smoke and sulfur came out of their mouths. By these three plagues a third of humankind was killed, by the fire and smoke and sulfur coming out of their mouths. For the power of the horses is in their mouths and in their tails; their tails are like serpents, having heads; and with them they inflict harm. (Rev 9:17–19)

9. When comparing the two holocausts, the death count of the first holocaust will eventually total a quarter of the world's righteous and unrighteous population, or about two billion (assuming one uses the current world census of approximately eight billion). Later, the death count of the sixth-trumpet holocaust will affect one-third of only the unrighteous found within the remaining six billion survivors of the first holocaust, which, technically, would be one-third of less than six billion. As to how much less, no one could possibly know that answer because the percentages of the unrighteous and righteous comprising the original eight billion are unknown. Still, the death toll from each holocaust will doubtless approach two billion causalities.

FIRST SEQUENCE IN REVELATION, PART 1

As one's imagination struggles to keep pace with John's descriptions, one is again faced with a familiar question: Are the two hundred million troops referencing humans or supernatural spirits? Many wholeheartedly believe the army symbolizes a human, natural army, and because of that belief, many assume the military of China or an amalgamation of smaller countries must be in mind here in order to fill the number of such a vast army.[10] In order to begin to determine the true identity of the cavalry of the sixth trumpet, let's compare the "locusts" of the fifth trumpet and the "cavalry" of the sixth trumpet:

Table 4.8. Comparison of the Locusts of the Fifth Trumpet and the Cavalry of the Sixth Trumpet	
Locusts of the 5th Trumpet	**Cavalry of the 6th Trumpet**
1. Appeared as horses (Rev 9:7)	1. Appeared as horses (Rev 9:17)
2. Had teeth like lions' teeth (Rev 9:8)	2. Had heads like lions' heads (Rev 9:17)
3. Had scales like iron breastplates (Rev 9:9)	3. Had breastplates the color of fire, of sapphire, and of sulfur (Rev 9:17)
4. Had tails with stingers like scorpions by which they inflict harm on people for five months (Rev 9:10)	4. Had tails like serpents, having heads, by which they inflict harm (Rev 9:19)
	5. Out of their mouths came fire, smoke, and sulfur, by which they killed a third of the inhabitants of the earth (Rev 9:17–18)

As one can readily see, God drew the same images of personalities in both plagues: Both were visions of horses that had heads and teeth like a lion; both images had breastplates of scales; and both images had tails that inflicted harm on people. In short, the demonic horde of the sixth trumpet is the same demonic horde of the fifth trumpet. The only difference is that during the fifth trumpet plague, the demons will not be permitted to kill the inhabitants, whereas during the sixth trumpet, they will. You might ask, How can one be sure that the demons of the fifth

---

10. Many of those same adherents conflate the "two hundred million cavalry" of the sixth trumpet judgment with the "armies gathered from the nations of the world" of the sixth bowl judgment, which is yet to be addressed (Rev 16:12–16). Suffice to say, without delving into the details of the sixth bowl at the present time, the reader will soon learn that the two armies have nothing in common.

trumpet plague will actually possess the power to kill? By the following passage (italics used for emphasis):

"They were allowed to torture them for five months, *but not to kill them*, and their torture was like the torture of a scorpion when it stings someone" (Rev 9:5).

If they are instructed not to kill, then obviously they will have the ability to kill.

Although only a symbolic drawing, God depicted the demons' "ability to torture" resided in their tails (Rev 9:10, 19), but their "ability to kill" resided in their mouths (Rev 9:17-18). Of course, in reality, the demons' ability to torture and kill had nothing to do with "tails" or "mouths." Again, these were just drawn images of invisible demons by God for John's sake.

As you have no doubt surmised by now, the fact that John had already introduced the demons during the fifth trumpet narrative—even going so far as describing their release out of the bottomless pit, their permission to torture, their appearance, and even their leader—explains why John didn't introduce them during the sixth trumpet narrative.

Joel's Vision of the Cavalry

John is not the only prophet to have seen this great demonic horde. Joel saw them eight hundred years earlier (italics used for emphasis):

". . . for the *day of the Lord* is coming, it is near—a day of darkness and gloom, a day of clouds and thick darkness! Like blackness spread upon the mountains *a great and powerful army comes; their like has never been from old, nor will be again after them in ages to come. Fire devours in front of them, and behind them a flame burns*. Before them the land is like the garden of Eden, but after them a desolate wilderness, and nothing escapes them. *They have the appearance of horses, and like war-horses they charge. As with the rumbling of chariots*, they leap on the tops of the mountains, like the crackling of a flame of fire devouring the stubble, like a powerful army drawn up for battle" (Joel 2:1b-5).

One knows that this is the same, evil army of demons of the fifth and sixth trumpet judgments because, first and foremost, God depicted the demons exactly as he later depicted them to John:

1. The same horses (compare Joel 2:4 and Rev 9:7, 17)

2. The same sound of rumbling chariots (compare Joel 2:5 and Rev 9:9)

3. And the same fire that killed the inhabitants of the earth (compare Joel 2:3 and Rev 9:17–18)

Speaking of fire, look closely again at Joel 2:3: "Before them the land is like the garden of Eden, but after them a desolate wilderness." This confirms what was previously concluded in John's narrative, and that was that the demons were not allowed to use their deadly, destructive fire during the fifth trumpet judgment but were permitted to do so during the sixth trumpet. When fire was not permitted, the land looked like the garden of Eden and the inhabitants of the earth were only tortured, but after its use during the sixth trumpet judgment, the land looked like a desolate wilderness and a third of the inhabitants were killed.

Rebellion Persists

Even the most cynical of minds would think that after having endured the voracious demonic army out of the bottomless pit, at least some of the surviving inhabitants of the earth would repent, but the following passage indicates otherwise:

> The rest of humankind, who were not killed by these plagues, did not repent of the works of their hands or give up worshiping demons and idols of gold and silver and bronze and stone and wood, which cannot see or hear or walk. And they did not repent of their murders or their sorceries or their fornication or their thefts. (Rev 9:20–21)

The rebelliousness of the remaining two-thirds of the inhabitants of the earth is almost incomprehensible. Although God is patient and long-suffering, little do the inhabitants realize that their window of opportunity for repentance is quickly coming to a close.

As John braced himself for the third woe, one can only imagine what the disciple expected. But the mystery would have to be put on hold. Rather than seeing a vision of the seventh angel standing in heaven about to blow his trumpet, John suddenly finds himself on earth with a magnificent looking angel descending toward him from the heavens. The disciple must have wondered how he could have been in the throne room one moment and back on the earth the next; however, the more immediate question racing through his mind was probably who was this angel?

THE SEQUENCE

Concluding Thoughts: The Pattern Continues

As expected, the initial visions of Revelation have confirmed the previously determined sequences from 1 and 2 Thessalonians and the Olivet Discourse. Here's the continuing pattern:

1. *Suffering by the Saints*: Although Jesus said the greatest suffering in the history of the world will start with the abomination of desolation, it was the first visions of Revelation that revealed that the suffering would lead to the deaths of a quarter of the earth's population and would be orchestrated by invisible angels commonly known as "the Four Horsemen of the Apocalypse." Thankfully, Jesus promised that the days of the greatest suffering in history, which will surely be the result of nuclear war, will be shortened by God for the sake of the elect. Nevertheless, the nuclear aftermath will follow as the death toll continues to rise by famine, pestilence, and death by wild animals. At some point during the aftermath, while false messiahs and false prophets are crisscrossing the earth with their many signs and wonders, a man will emerge performing greater signs and greater wonders, who will also begin the targeted persecution of the righteous. Paul refers to him as "the man of lawlessness." By reconciling the words of Christ, Paul, and John, one knows that the period beginning with the nuclear war and continuing through its aftermath as well as the martyrdom of the saints comprise what one of the elders referred to as "the great tribulation of the saints."

2. *Heavenly Signs*: Next, after the man of lawlessness has killed the full number of martyrs, at some unknown point in time, heavenly signs will suddenly appear: The sun will become black, the moon will become like blood, and the stars of the sky will fall to the earth. These supernatural signs will officially mark the arrival of the Day of the Lord. The appearance of the signs will draw two reactions: The unrighteous will become panic stricken, run and hide, and some will even faint (Rev 6:15–17 and Luke 21:25–26), but the 144,000 Jewish remnant, who have been hidden away in the wilderness since the abomination of desolation, will call out to the Lord and confess the name of Jesus Christ (Joel 2:32). God's angels will then mark the 144,000 with a seal that signals to all angels, good and evil, that God's people are to be shielded from his wrath. John then saw a vision of a great multitude of souls worshiping and praising God around his throne because the

full number of the martyred saints will have been reached, thus ending the "great" tribulation of the saints. (Although the full number of martyrs has been reached, it will later be proven that the saints will continue to experience tribulation, but to a lesser degree.)

3. *The Day of the Lord*: After the vision of the great multitude, John saw Jesus open the seventh and final seal. He then noticed that the throne room became eerily silent for about thirty minutes, after which the visions of the future resumed. There appeared a vision of seven angels being given seven trumpets. As the trumpets were blown one by one, plagues occurred on the earth, including global fires, volcanic activities, an asteroid, poisoned waters, and unprecedented darkness. The first four plagues targeted the earth; the next two targeted the inhabitants of the earth. (At this point John has not seen the seventh trumpet.)

4. *The Return of Christ and the Gathering of the Saints*: Although Jesus and Paul have placed the two most anticipated events of the church—the return of Christ and the gathering of the saints—after the Day of the Lord, one must wait for the remaining visions in order to see exactly how they will confirm the sequences of Jesus and Paul.

~

The following is the reconciliation of the three sequences to date, from the abomination of desolation through the sixth trumpet (the newly added events of Rev 6:1—9:21 are italicized):

Table 4.9. Reconciliation of the Three Sequences to Date

The Sequence	Seq. 1 & 2 Thess (1 Thess 4:13–18, 5:3; 2 Thess 1:5–12, 2:3–12)	Seq. Olivet Discourse (Matt 25:15, 21–31; Luke 21:25–26)	1st Seq. Rev, Part 1: Through 6th Trumpet (Rev 6:1—9:21)
1. The 144,000 Jewish remnant, who are yet to confess Christ, escape Jerusalem at the sight of the abomination of desolation.		Jesus urges "the reader" to escape Jerusalem at the sight of the abomination. (Matt 24:15)	
2. The rider on the white horse came out conquering and to conquer. He was commanded by one of the living creatures "to go!"			*Vision seen under the 1st seal: The rider on the white horse came out conquering and to conquer. He was commanded by one of the living creatures "to go!"* (Rev 6:1–2)
3. The 2nd angelic rider appears on a red horse and initiates nuclear war under the leadership of the 1st angelic rider, who is the only rider wearing a crown.		Greatest suffering in the history of the world begins. (Matt 24:21)	*Vision seen under the 2nd seal: The rider on the red horse causes the people on the earth to slaughter one another.* (Rev 6:3–4)
4. God ends the nuclear war for the sake of the elect. If he didn't, no flesh would survive.		God will cut short the days of the greatest suffering in the history of the world for the sake of the elect. (Matt 24:22)	

Table 4.9. Reconciliation of the Three Sequences to Date

The Sequence	Seq. 1 & 2 Thess (1 Thess 4:13–18, 5:3; 2 Thess 1:5–12, 2:3–12)	Seq. Olivet Discourse (Matt 25:15, 21–31; Luke 21:25–26)	1st Seq. Rev, Part 1: Through 6th Trumpet (Rev 6:1—9:21)
5. The 3rd angelic rider causes famine, which initiates the nuclear aftermath.			*Vision seen under the 3rd seal: Rider on the black horse causes famine, which initiates the nuclear aftermath. (Rev 6:5–6)*
6. Death and Hades are given authority to kill 1/4 of the earth's population by the nuclear war as well as its aftermath: famine, pestilence, and death by wild animals.			*Vision seen under the 4th seal: Rider on the pale green horse, who is Death, and his partner, Hades, were given authority to kill 1/4 of the earth by sword, famine, pestilence, and wild animals. (Rev 6:7–8)*
7. During the nuclear aftermath, false messiahs and false prophets appear and bring deception. This deception plants the seeds for "the rebellion."		Deception is caused by false messiahs and false prophets. (Matt 24:23–28)	
8. The man of lawlessness emerges from among the false messiahs and false prophets and continues the deception of the unrighteous, but now begins to target and kill the saints.	At the revealing of the man of lawlessness come more deception of the unrighteousness and the targeted persecution of the saints. (2 Thess 2:3–12)	A second period of suffering is in progress. (Matt 24:29a)	

The Sequence	Seq. 1 & 2 Thess (1 Thess 4:13–18, 5:3; 2 Thess 1:5–12, 2:3–12)	Seq. Olivet Discourse (Matt 25:15, 21–31; Luke 21:25–26)	1st Seq. Rev, Part 1: Through 6th Trumpet (Rev 6:1—9:21)
9. Toward the end of the period of martyrdom, the souls in heaven are told to wait a little longer before God judges and avenges their blood on the inhabitants of the earth until the complete number of martyrs has been reached.			*Vision seen under the 5th seal: Martyrs are seen under heaven's altar, asking God how long will it be before he judges and avenges their blood on the inhabitants of the earth. (Rev 6:9–11)*
10. After the complete number of martyrs has been reached, while the unrighteous are saying there is peace and security, heavenly signs appear, ushering in the Day of the Lord.	After the rebellion and the revealing of the man of lawlessness, while the unrighteous are saying there is peace and security, the Day of the Lord arrives. (1 Thess 5:3a; 2 Thess 2:3)	Heavenly signs appear: 1. Sun is darkened 2. Moon does not give its light 3. Stars fall from heaven. (Matt 24:29b)	*Vision seen under the 6th seal: A great earthquake and heavenly signs appear: 1. Sun becomes black as sackcloth 2. Moon becomes like blood 3. Stars fall to the earth. (Rev 6:12–14)*
11. The unrighteous scurry for cover at the sight of the earthquake and the heavenly signs.	At the arrival of the Day of the Lord, sudden destruction will come upon the unrighteous and there will be no escape. (1 Thess 5:3b)	People are confused by the roaring of the sea and the waves, and faint from fear and foreboding of what is coming upon the world. (Luke 21:25–26)	*The unrighteous are seen scurrying for cover at the sight of the earthquake and the heavenly signs. (Rev 6:15–17)*

Table 4.9. Reconciliation of the Three Sequences to Date			
The Sequence	Seq. 1 & 2 Thess (1 Thess 4:13–18, 5:3; 2 Thess 1:5–12, 2:3–12)	Seq. Olivet Discourse (Matt 25:15, 21–31; Luke 21:25–26)	1st Seq. Rev, Part 1: Through 6th Trumpet (Rev 6:1—9:21)
12. The 4 angels who stand at the 4 corners of the earth are given the authority to harm the earth, but because the 144,000 Jewish remnant has just confessed Christ at the appearance of the heavenly signs, the angels are told to wait until they have marked the remnant with the seal of God.			The 4 angels who stand at the 4 corners of the earth were given the authority to harm the earth but were told to wait until they had marked the 144,000 Jewish remnant with the seal of God. (Rev 7:1–3)
13. The 144,000 are marked with a seal that protects them from the upcoming wrath of God.			The 144,000 Jewish remnant was marked with a seal by God's angels. (Rev 7:4–8)
14. A great multitude who died during "the great tribulation" are seen worshiping around the throne of God because the full number of martyrs has been reached.			A great multitude of saints from every nation were seen standing and worshiping around the throne of God in heaven. (Rev 7:9–17)

Table 4.9. Reconciliation of the Three Sequences to Date

The Sequence	Seq. 1 & 2 Thess (1 Thess 4:13–18, 5:3; 2 Thess 1:5–12, 2:3–12)	Seq. Olivet Discourse (Matt 25:15, 21–31; Luke 21:25–26)	1st Seq. Rev, Part 1: Through 6th Trumpet (Rev 6:1—9:21)
15. The 7 angels who stand before God are given 7 trumpets and they make ready to blow them.			7th seal: *The seven angels who stand before God were given seven trumpets and they made ready to blow them. (Rev 8:1–6)*
16. The judgments of the Day of the Lord arrive with the 1st trumpet judgment: 1/3 of the trees and all grasses are burned up doubtless because of global lightning strikes.		God shakes the powers of heaven. (Matt 24:29c)	1st trumpet: *1/3 of the trees and all grasses were burned up on earth. (Rev 8:7)*
17. The 2nd trumpet judgment: 1/3 of the sea become blood, 1/3 of the living creatures in the sea die, and 1/3 of all ships are destroyed, perhaps from widespread volcanic activity caused by the global earthquake.			2nd trumpet: *1/3 of the sea became blood, 1/3 of the living creatures in the sea died, and 1/3 of all ships were destroyed. (Rev 8:8–9)*
18. The 3rd trumpet judgment: 1/3 of the freshwater becomes poisoned because the earth was struck with the asteroid Wormwood.			3rd trumpet: *1/3 of the freshwater became wormwood, and many died from the water because it was bitter. (Rev 8:10–11)*

Table 4.9. Reconciliation of the Three Sequences to Date			
The Sequence	Seq. 1 & 2 Thess (1 Thess 4:13–18, 5:3; 2 Thess 1:5–12, 2:3–12)	Seq. Olivet Discourse (Matt 25:15, 21–31; Luke 21:25–26)	1st Seq. Rev, Part 1: Through 6th Trumpet (Rev 6:1—9:21)
19. The 4th trumpet judgment: 1/3 of the sun, of the moon, and of the stars are darkened, probably from dust clouds caused by the impact of the asteroid, Wormwood.			4th trumpet: 1/3 of the sun, the moon, and the stars were darkened, and 1/3 of the day and night were kept from shining. (Rev 8:12)
20. The 5th trumpet judgment: Demonic spirits are released out of the bottomless pit and are allowed to torture the inhabitants of the earth for 5 months. Their king is the angel of the bottomless pit.			5th trumpet: Locust-appearing demonic spirits were released out of the bottomless pit and were allowed to torture the inhabitants of the earth for 5 months. (Rev 9:1–11)
21. The 6th trumpet judgment: 4 angels are released from the area of the Euphrates River and they orchestrate the killing of 1/3 of the inhabitants of the earth by means of the same demonic horde seen during the 5th trumpet. They kill 1/3 of the inhabitants by fire, smoke, and sulfur.			6th trumpet: Four angels were released from the area of the Euphrates River and they orchestrated the killing of 1/3 of the inhabitants of the earth, by fire, smoke, and sulfur, using an army of 200 million. (Rev 9:13–21)

CHAPTER 5

Second Sequence in Revelation
The Two Witnesses (11:1–13)

First Sequence in Revelation, Part 1 (cont.)
The Seventh Trumpet (11:15–19)

First Sequence	Second Sequence	Third Sequence	Fourth Sequence
Chapter 4 1st Seq., Part 1: Through the 6th Trumpet (6:1—9:21)			
	Chapter 5* 2nd Seq.: The 2 Witnesses (11:1–13)		
Chapter 5 (cont.)* 1st Seq., Part 1 (cont.): The 7th Trumpet (11:15–19)			
		Chapter 6 3rd Seq.: The Woman, the Child, and the Dragon (12:1–6)	

AFTER JOHN IS LEFT breathless by the vision of the death and anguish caused during the sixth trumpet plague, he certainly must have wondered how the seventh trumpet judgment could possibly be more devastating. But as already indicated, he would have to wait a little longer because, quite unexpectedly, he appears to find himself back on earth watching a mighty angel descend toward him, wrapped in a cloud:

> And I saw another mighty angel coming down from heaven, wrapped in a cloud, with a rainbow over his head; his face was like the sun, and his legs like pillars of fire. He held a little scroll open in his hand. Setting his right foot on the sea and his left foot on the land, he gave a great shout, like a lion roaring. And when he shouted, the seven thunders sounded. And when the seven thunders had sounded, I was about to write, but I heard a voice from heaven saying, "Seal up what the seven thunders have said, and do not write it down." (Rev 10:1–4)

Note that throughout John's visit to heaven, the settings for the visions of the future are constantly changing: One moment, John sees a vision of people everywhere scurrying for cover, trying to run and hide in caves and under the rocks of the earth from the great Day of the Lord, and the next, he sees a vision of a great multitude standing and worshiping around the throne of God in heaven. But now, for the first time it appears that the location of John himself has changed! Or has it? As John saw the angel descending, was the disciple still in heaven seeing a vision of a future angel descending to the earth, or perhaps was John actually back on earth seeing an angel coming down from heaven? Let's determine.

Third Conversation: John Is Told of the Seventh Trumpet and the Two Witnesses

As the angel was seen coming down he gave a great shout, triggering what John described as the sound of the seven thunders. At that precise moment John began to write, but he was quickly prohibited from doing so. That must have caught John off guard since up to this point he had been allowed to record everything he had seen and heard. Next, the angel raised his right hand and swore by him who lives forever and ever:

> Then the angel whom I saw standing on the sea and the land raised his right hand to heaven and swore by him who lives forever and ever, who created heaven and what is in it, the earth

and what is in it, and the sea and what is in it: "There will be no more delay, but in the days when the seventh angel is to blow his trumpet, the mystery of God will be fulfilled, as he announced to his servants the prophets." (Rev 10:5–7)

Still, the question lingers: Was John on the earth seeing a real angel, or was he still in the throne room, seeing "a vision" of an angel? Either way, the angel said that when the day comes for the seventh angel to blow his trumpet the mystery of God will be fulfilled. What mystery of God is the angel referencing? A clue to the mystery is found in a similar passage in Daniel, when an angel in white linen similarly raised his hands toward heaven and swore by him who lives forever:

"One of them said to the man clothed in linen, who was upstream, 'How long shall it be until the end of these wonders?' The man clothed in linen, who was upstream, raised his right hand and his left hand toward heaven. And I heard him swear by the one who lives forever that it would be for a time, two times, and half a time, and that when the shattering of the power of the holy people comes to an end, all these things would be accomplished" (Dan 12:6–7).

Here, Daniel heard the angel clothed in linen swear by the One who lives forever that, after the power of God's saints have been shattered for three and a half years, all these things will be accomplished. Here's a comparison of the two angels:

Table 5.1. The Two Angels Who Swore by the One Who Lives Forever

The Angel in Rev 10	The Angel in Dan 12
1. The mighty angel was wrapped in a cloud.	1. The angel was clothed in linen.
2. He raised his right hand to heaven.	2. He raised his right and left hands to heaven.
3. He swore by him who lives forever.	3. He swore by him who lives forever.
4. He said that in the days that the seventh angel is to blow his trumpet the mystery of God will be fulfilled.	4. He said that after a time, two times, and half a time, the shattering of the power of the holy people will come to an end and then all these things will be accomplished.

If the two angels are referencing the same culmination, one comes away with the following: After a time, two times, and half a time, when the seventh trumpet is blown, the shattering of the power of the holy people will come to an end and then the mystery of God will be fulfilled. As to whether this is an accurate assessment, one must wait and see.

The Moment John Knew Something Was Different

After John saw the angel swearing by the One who lives forever, a critical event occurred that will enable the reader to finally understand what was actually taking place in the narrative. The familiar voice that John had heard earlier spoke again (Rev 4:1), and instructed him to approach the angel standing on the sea and on the land:

> Then the voice that I had heard from heaven spoke to me again, saying, "Go, take the scroll that is open in the hand of the angel standing on the sea and on the land." So I went to the angel and told him to give me the little scroll; and he said to me, "Take it, and eat; it will be bitter to your stomach, but sweet as honey in your mouth." So I took the little scroll from the hand of the angel and ate it; it was sweet as honey in my mouth, but when I had eaten it, my stomach was made bitter. Then they said to me, "You must prophesy again about many peoples and nations and languages and kings." (Rev 10:8–11)

The fact that John approached the angel and engaged him meant that John was actually seeing and conversing with the angel, and was not just seeing a future vision of an angel. Had it been just a vision, as you know, John would not have been able to interact with the angel. Therefore, this is now the third conversation. Furthermore, one also knows that not only was John seeing the angel in real time, but since the angel was descending to the earth, one now understands that John's spirit had actually been, at least temporarily, translated back down to earth from the throne room in order to engage in this conversation with the angel.

Another Proof of John's Encounter with the Angel

Although no other proof is needed to show that the angel was real, there is one additional, subtle confirmation that the reader might find enlightening, and it is found back in the opening sentence (italics used for emphasis):

"*And I saw another mighty angel* coming down from heaven, wrapped in a cloud, with a rainbow over his head; his face was like the sun, and his legs like pillars of fire" (Rev 10:1).

Had John said, "And I saw another angel" without the qualifying "mighty" (Greek: *ischyron*), one would naturally look back at the passages immediately preceding this passage, where John saw two angels blow the fifth and sixth trumpets. And since those were only "visions" of angels, one might rightly question why John was comparing the "real angel" in 10:1 with two visions of angels in 9:1 and 9:13. But, as one would expect, John did not compare the "real angel" with "visions of angels." When one traces back to the last "mighty angel" the disciple encountered, that angel was found at the beginning of John's visit to heaven (italics used for emphasis):

"Then I saw in the right hand of the one seated on the throne a scroll written on the inside and on the back, sealed with seven seals; and I saw *a mighty angel* proclaiming with a loud voice, 'Who is worthy to open the scroll and break its seals?' And no one in heaven or on earth or under the earth was able to open the scroll or look into it. And I began to weep bitterly because no one was found worthy to open the scroll or look into it. Then one of the elders said to me, 'Do not weep. See, the Lion of the tribe of Judah, the Root of David, has conquered, so that he can open the scroll and its seven seals'" (Rev 5:1–5).

The point is obvious: The last "mighty angel" seen by John was also a real, live angel who spoke in the throne room in the disciple's presence, just as the "mighty angel" in Rev 10 spoke in John's presence on the earth. All the other angels referenced in between the mighty angels of Rev 5:1 and Rev 10:1 were only visions of angels.

The Little Scroll

The angel's appearance no doubt seemed quite intimidating to John, and if it were not for the voice from the One who was even more intimidating, instructing the disciple to go up to the angel and take the scroll from his hand, John surely would have never dared approach the angel, and, much less, taken anything out of his hand. But with the voice's command, John did exactly as he was told. When John approached the angel, the angel handed the little scroll to the disciple and told him to eat it. There should be no undue speculation concerning the meaning of the little scroll; it simply symbolized the will of God for John's future, just as the little scroll given to Ezekiel hundreds of years earlier symbolized the will of God for his future:

"But you, mortal, hear what I say to you; do not be rebellious like that rebellious house; open your mouth and eat what I give you. I looked, and a hand was stretched out to me, and a written scroll was in it. He spread it before me; it had writing on the front and on the back, and written on it were words of lamentation and mourning and woe. He said to me, O mortal, eat what is offered to you; eat this scroll, and go, speak to the house of Israel. So I opened my mouth, and he gave me the scroll to eat. He said to me, Mortal, eat this scroll that I give you and fill your stomach with it. Then I ate it; and in my mouth it was as sweet as honey" (Ezek 2:8–10, 3:1–3).

Note that when Ezekiel obeyed the Lord and began to eat the scroll he actually experienced a sweetness in his mouth as would John (compare Ezek 3:3 and Rev 10:10). To preach and prophesy the truth of God surely brought the men pure joy, and therefore the scrolls were sweet as honey as both men accepted God's plan to minister his word. But what are we to say about the bitterness that John also experienced when he swallowed the scroll? It's very likely Ezekiel experienced the same bitterness, although it wasn't recorded. As John and Ezekiel ate the scrolls, there was the certainty that their prophetic message would be rejected by many (Ezek 3:7–11), resulting in God's judgment against the hearers, which would naturally bring sorrow and bitterness to both prophets.

Which Temple?

As soon as John had finished eating the scroll, he was given a measuring rod and told to come and measure the temple of God and the altar and those who worship there:

> Then I was given a measuring rod like a staff, and I was told, "Come and measure the temple of God and the altar and those who worship there, but do not measure the court outside the temple; leave that out, for it is given over to the nations, and they will trample over the holy city for forty-two months." (Rev 11:1–2)

Which temple did the Lord want measured? Was it Herod's Temple? In fact, was Herod's Temple, the one destroyed in AD 70, even standing at the time John received the visions? If it wasn't, then this would obviously indicate that Revelation was written after AD 70. Let's analyze: If not

Herod's, what are the choices? Was John instructed to measure a vision of a future temple that would be built in the latter days? That's exactly what many believe. According to their theory, they believe John was instructed to measure a vision of the same future temple that they believe Paul was referencing in the following statement to the Thessalonians (italics used for emphasis):

"Let no one deceive you in any way; for that day will not come unless the rebellion comes first and the lawless one is revealed, the one destined for destruction. He opposes and exalts himself above every so-called god or object of worship, so that he takes his seat *in the temple of God* declaring himself to be God" (2 Thess 2:3–4).

Recall in chapter 1 of this study that it was proven it was impossible for Paul to have been referencing a rebuilt temple during his lifetime or one in the future, for that matter. As was our reasoning, concerning a temple built during Paul's lifetime, that option was eliminated for the simple reason one was never built during the apostle's lifetime. As to the possibility that Paul was referencing a future temple that would be built after he had passed away, that too was eliminated because of the fact that since Paul believed the man of lawlessness was already in existence and about to enter the temple in question, then Paul had to have known that the temple the man would enter was already in existence. And since there were only two temples of any consequence in existence during the life of Paul—Herod's Temple and God's temple in heaven—and this, coupled with the fact that the man will never enter Herod's Temple because it has since been torn down, then the only temple that Paul could have possibly been referencing was the temple of God in heaven. And, of course, Daniel confirmed this conclusion in a passage describing the man of lawlessness entering God's temple in heaven at the man's judgment (Dan 7:11–12).

Now, back to the temple John was instructed to measure: Although the temple that the man of lawlessness will one day enter and the temple that John was instructed to measure are not necessarily the same temple, the options for each are the same. Again, here's the list:

Table 5.2. The Temple That John Was Commanded to Measure
Option #1: Rebuilt temple during Paul's lifetime
Option #2: Rebuilt temple after Paul passed away
Option #3: Herod's Temple
Option #4: The temple of God in heaven

The first two options can be quickly eliminated because it has been proven these temples have never and will never exist. Likewise, God's temple in heaven, option #4, is also eliminated since the angel told John not to measure the court outside the temple because that area will be given over to the nations as they will trample the area and the city for forty-two months. I think it's safe to say that no area in heaven will be turned over to the nations! Therefore, the only option remaining that correctly identifies the temple that John was instructed to measure was indeed Herod's Temple, option #3.[1]

Why Measure the Temple?

After receiving instruction to measure Herod's Temple and its altar, but not to measure the courtyard around the temple, John was then told the mysterious reason for the omission: The area of the courtyard and beyond will be given over to the nations and they will trample the holy city for forty-two months (11:2b). Therefore, it stands to reason that the area inside the measured lines by John will not be given over to the nations and therefore will be retained for God's purposes, correct? This naturally leads to our next question: How could the area within the lines measured by John be used for God's purposes, especially knowing that the entire temple complex occupying that area would soon be destroyed in AD 70? Answer: Knowing that the structure would soon disappear, God obviously had no interest in the structure itself.[2] Rather, the Lord's future purposes were for the land under the structure. But why? The next verse reveals that answer:

> And I will grant my two witnesses authority to prophesy for one thousand two hundred sixty days, wearing sackcloth. (Rev 11:3)

The Lord told John that he was going to grant his two witnesses authority to prophesy for 1,260 days. And from where would the two

---

1. This determination proves that John's visit to heaven predated AD 70. As to whether John penned the letter of Revelation prior to AD 70, it might be helpful to ask the following: After John's experience in heaven came to an end, did the disciple immediately proceed to record the visions on behalf of the church or did he wait twenty or thirty years before doing so? Of course, the answer is obvious: John doubtless penned the letter prior to AD 70, while the visions were fresh in his mind.

2. The estimation that God had no interest in the structure of the temple should come as no surprise to the reader since the death of his Son on the cross, some forty years earlier, rendered the old covenant obsolete, including the temple (Heb 8–10).

prophesy? From the area given over to the nations or from the area retained by God? Of course, it's the area retained by God. When John was told to measure Herod's Temple two thousand years ago, it had nothing to do with the structure of the temple, but rather, God was decreeing that in the last days, his two witnesses were going to prophesy from atop the Temple Mount, from the very spot where Herod's Temple once stood.

Relationship between the Trampling of Jerusalem and the Witnesses' Ministry

Since Rev 11:2 states that the courtyard outside John's measured boundaries will be given over to the nations and that they will trample over the holy city (Jerusalem) for forty-two months, what might be the time relationship between the forty-two-month trampling of Jerusalem by the nations and the 1,260-day ministry of the two witnesses? Since it's essentially the same length of time, i.e., three and a half years, does that mean the periods are congruent? Not necessarily. In fact, at this point in our study we don't know anything about the time frame of the two witnesses' ministry, but we do know something of the trampling of Jerusalem by the nations, thanks to Luke's account of the Olivet Discourse (italics used for emphasis):

"When you see Jerusalem surrounded by armies, then know that its desolation has come near. Then those in Judea must flee to the mountains, and those inside the city must leave it, and those out in the country must not enter it; for these are days of vengeance, as a fulfillment of all that is written. Woe to those who are pregnant and to those who are nursing infants in those days! For there will be great distress on the earth and wrath against this people; they will fall by the edge of the sword and be taken away as captives among all nations; and *Jerusalem will be trampled on by the Gentiles, until the times of the Gentiles are fulfilled*" (Luke 21:20–24).

Jesus clearly indicated that once the inhabitants of Jerusalem escape the city because of the surrounding armies, then the nations from where these invading armies came will "trample" the city (Greek: *partoumenē*) until the times of the gentiles are fulfilled (Luke 21:24). Similarly in our text in Rev 11, John was told the nations would "trample" the city (Greek: *patēsousin*) for forty-two months (Rev 11:2). Since the moment of the appearance of the surrounding armies in Luke's account is the same moment as the abomination of desolation in Matthew's and Mark's accounts, then one knows that the forty-two-month trampling of Jerusalem will begin approximately at the abomination of desolation. Now, with a clear understanding of the congruency between the moment of the abomination of desolation and the beginning of the trampling of Jerusalem, one only needs to learn the time-relationship between the abomination of desolation and the 1,260-day ministry of the two witnesses in order to finally understand the relationship between the forty-two-month trampling of Jerusalem and the 1,260-day ministry of the two witnesses.

The Identity of the Two Witnesses

Next, after God revealed how long he would allow his two witnesses to minister in the last days, attention shifted to the identity of the two witnesses. They were described to John as the following:

> These are the two olive trees and the two lampstands that stand before the Lord of the earth. (Rev 11:4)

The description that they "are the two olive trees and two lampstands that stand before the Lord of the earth" is perplexing. Thankfully, Zechariah had already been told the same:

"Then I said to him, 'What are these two olive trees on the right and the left of the lampstand?' And a second time I said to him, 'What are these two branches of the olive trees, which pour out the oil through the two golden pipes?' He said to me, 'Do you not know what these are?' I said, 'No, my lord.' Then he said, 'These are the two anointed ones who stand by the Lord of the whole earth'" (Zech 4:11–14).

After Zechariah inquired of the accompanying angel a second time as to the meaning of the two olive trees, the angel finally said the two olive trees represented "the two anointed ones who stand by the Lord of the whole earth." And how does this sparse information help us with their identity? Since the two witnesses are the two olive trees who were standing before the Lord at the time the angel spoke to Zechariah, which was approximately 500 BC, and yet another angel in John's day told the disciple that these same two witnesses will have a ministry in the last days, the end of which they will be killed (Rev 11:7), then, according to the combined information supplied by the two angels, these two men will have lived, as it stands today, at least 2,500 years without ever having died! Now, the only two men recorded in Scripture as having never died are Enoch and Elijah. Therefore, these are the two witnesses; there are no other candidates. But one might argue that the miracles performed by the two witnesses, i.e., the authority to stop the rain, to turn the waters into blood, and to strike the earth with every kind of plague, sound more like the miracles of Elijah and Moses rather than that of Elijah and Enoch, especially since Scripture never recorded Enoch as having ever performed a single miracle.[3] Furthermore, as if to doubly prove the theory, we are reminded that it was Moses and Elijah, not Elijah and Enoch, who appeared on the Mount of Transfiguration with Jesus, as Moses must have represented the law while Elijah clearly represented the prophets. All of that sounds well and good, but as regards to the identity of the two witnesses, those observations are irrelevant. The simple fact is that Moses has died and Enoch hasn't. If Moses were truly one of the two, that would mean that he must die twice, since Scripture has already recorded his death on Mount Nebo, approximately 3,500 years ago (Deut 34:5). If Moses was truly destined to die twice, that would entail that God must supply Moses with a second natural body in order to reappear in the latter days and die a second time, since his first body has long since decayed! However, I don't think God condones reincarnation, do you?

Although no further information is needed to prove the two's identity, still God's word openly declares the identity of one:

"Lo, I will send you the prophet Elijah before the great and terrible day of the Lord comes. He will turn the hearts of parents to their children and the hearts of children to their parents, so that I will not come and strike the land with a curse" (Mal 4:5).

Here, Malachi records God's promise that he will send Elijah back in the last days, before the arrival of the Day of the Lord. Don't let the significance of the short statement go unnoticed: The 1,260-day ministry of Elijah and Enoch will begin at some point prior to the arrival of the heavenly signs and the Day of Lord. (Later, the timing of the two's arrival will be narrowed even further.)[4]

---

3. Charles, *Revelation of St. John*, 281.

4. Despite the fact that two angels specifically told Zechariah and John, respectively, that the two olive trees, the two anointed ones, and the two witnesses are all one and the same, and that they are the ones who stand before the Lord of the earth, some have suggested that the idea of a future 1,260-day ministry of the two witnesses is purely symbolic and the two are actually representative of the church and her role over the past two thousand years. See Wright, *Revelation for Everyone*, 99.

However, that's impossible. The fact that in approximately 500 BC the first angel told Zechariah the two anointed ones were presently in existence eliminates any possibility

SECOND SEQUENCE IN REVELATION

The Ministry and Death of the Two Witnesses

From high atop the Temple Mount, from the exact location of where Herod's Temple once stood, Elijah and Enoch will command the world's attention every day for 1,260 days. The displays of power by the Holy Spirit will be so spectacular that they will be reminiscent of the miracles of Moses at the time of the exodus:

> And if anyone wants to harm them, fire pours from their mouth and consumes their foes; anyone who wants to harm them must be killed in this manner. They have the authority to shut the sky, so that no rain may fall during the days of their prophesying, and they have authority over the waters to turn them into blood, and to strike the earth with every kind of plague, as often as they desire. (Rev 11:5–6)

During their ministry, it is certain that Satan and the inhabitants of the world will desire to kill the prophets (v. 5), but they will be prohibited from doing so because the two will be equipped with the power to defend themselves for the entirety of the 1,260-day ministry by "pouring fire from their mouths." Rather than literal fire this could simply be a reference to the anointed words coming from the mouths of the two, pronouncing instant death upon any and all attackers who threaten their well-being during the 1,260 days (compare Acts 5:9 where Peter pronounces death upon Sapphira).

Next, after briefly describing some of the miracles by the two witnesses, i.e., stopping the rain, turning the waters into blood, and striking the earth with every kind of plague imaginable, without any formal introduction, John references the major antagonist of Revelation:

> When they have finished their testimony, the beast that comes up from the bottomless pit will make war on them and conquer them and kill them, and their dead bodies will lie in the street of the great city that is prophetically called Sodom and Egypt, where also their Lord was crucified. For three and a half days members of the peoples and tribes and languages and nations will gaze at their bodies and refuse to let them be placed in a tomb; and the inhabitants of the earth will gloat over them and celebrate and exchange presents, because these two prophets had been a torment to the inhabitants of the earth. (Rev 11:7–10)

---

that the two symbolized the church, since the birth of the church was still five hundred years in the future.

THE SEQUENCE

Soon after Elijah and Enoch complete their 1,260-day ministry, they will promptly be confronted and killed. And the culprit? John said it is "the beast that comes up from the bottomless pit." The Greek phrase *to thērion to anabainon ek tēs abyssou*, here translated as "the beast that comes up from the bottomless pit," indicates that the beast confronts the two immediately as he is coming out of the pit.[5] Other than the knowledge that the beast will immediately make war against, conquer, and kill the two witnesses soon after they complete their 1,260-day ministry, is there anything else that one knows about the beast? Perhaps more than you think. First, one knows that he is an angel and not a man. As stated earlier, men do not exit the bottomless pit. It's impossible. If a man were ever to darken the door to the bottomless pit, Scripture prohibits him from returning to the earth. According to Heb 9:27, the only thing that awaits him is the judgment—not committing evil deeds on the earth a second time around.

What else does one know about the beast? Well, looking at the text, one would hope that John had given more of an introduction to the murderer of God's two witnesses, rather than almost just casually identifying him as "the beast that comes up from the bottomless pit." This bewilderment on our part is reminiscent of how we initially questioned John's apparent lack of a formal introduction to the two hundred million demons in the sixth-trumpet narrative when he only briefly referenced their number without giving the reader the slightest hint as to their identity (Rev 9:16). Only later, after one realized that John had already introduced the troops during the fifth-trumpet narrative (Rev 9:1–11), did one understand John's apparent lack of introduction in the sixth-trumpet narrative. Could that same situation be going on here? In other words, has John previously introduced the beast to the reader and we've failed to realize it? That's exactly the case (italics used for emphasis):

"In appearance the locusts were like horses equipped for battle. On their heads were what looked like crowns of gold; their faces were like human faces, their hair like women's hair, and their teeth like lions' teeth; they had scales like iron breastplates, and the noise of their wings was like the noise of many chariots with horses rushing into battle. They have tails like scorpions, with stingers, and in their tails is their power to harm people for five months. *They have as king over them the angel of the*

---

5. The verb "coming up," translated from the Greek word *anabainon*, is present participle active and indicates that as the beast is actively coming out of the pit, he proceeds to war against and kill the two witnesses.

bottomless pit; his name in Hebrew is Abaddon, and in Greek he is called Apollyon" (Rev 9:7–11).

At the end of the fifth-trumpet narrative, John referenced "the angel of the bottomless pit." The disciple said he will be the presiding king over all the demonic spirits who blanket the earth during the fifth- and sixth-trumpet plagues. John even identified the angel by his Hebrew name, *Abaddon*, and his Greek name, *Apollyon*. Scripture records the name of no other angel outside of Michael, Gabriel, and Satan. In fact, he is so well known in the invisible world that he is simply referred to as "the" angel of the bottomless pit, which is a place that doubtless incarcerates multiplied millions of angels. For these reasons alone, it is beyond doubt that when John identified the murderer of the two witnesses simply as "the beast that comes up from the bottomless pit," he was again referring to the only personality that he had previously linked with the bottomless pit and that was "the angel of the bottomless pit."

Three and a Half Days

Exactly how will the witnesses be killed? At the end of the witnesses' ministry, the beast will incite the once powerless inhabitants of the earth to storm the Temple Mount, breach the perimeter, and converge upon the two witnesses, as they bravely stand on the spot where they had once defended themselves from all attackers by the power of the Holy Spirit. But now that the ministry has been completed, the Spirit's protection will lift. After the mob mercilessly kills them, the inhabitants of the earth from all the nations and languages will gaze on their dead bodies as they lie lifeless on one of the streets on the Temple Mount (Rev 11:8). Instead of allowing any nearby Christians or sympathetic Jews to properly bury the prophets with the honor and dignity that they deserve (Rev 11:9), the inhabitants of the earth will refuse and instead make sport of the two bodies, doubtless desecrating them in view of the whole world. With unbelievable callousness, the inhabitants will celebrate and even exchange gifts because the two prophets had been such a torment to them (Rev 11:10). However, after three and a half days, while the inhabitants of the earth are still celebrating and dancing in a state of frenzied hysteria, the cold, ashen, blood-stained bodies of the two prophets will begin to stir from where they have been placed for display; their eyes will open, and they will suddenly stand to their feet. Terror will grip the inhabitants, leaving them weak-kneed and panic-stricken, as they cannot believe what they are seeing:

> But after the three and a half days, the breath of life from God entered them, and they stood on their feet, and those who saw them were terrified. Then they heard a loud voice from heaven saying to them, "Come up here!" And they went up to heaven in a cloud while their enemies watched them. At that moment there was a great earthquake, and a tenth of the city fell; seven thousand people were killed in the earthquake, and the rest were terrified and gave glory to the God of heaven. (Rev 11:11–13)

Talk about shock and awe! God will first stun the world by bringing the two witnesses back to life after three and a half days, and then he will doubly shock the world by lifting the two witnesses bodily off the surface of the earth up into the clouds as the inhabitants of the earth are left dazed and dumbfounded. It is at this moment that John said there will be a great earthquake, bringing down a tenth of the city of Jerusalem and killing seven thousand people (Rev 11:13).

Second Sequence in Revelation

Certainly the reader has recognized by now that a sequence of end-time events has been revealed to John by the angel and "the voice." Unlike the previous series of events, which was revealed by visions that began with "the Four Horsemen of the Apocalypse" and continued through the sixth-trumpet plague, this series of events was passed along "verbally" to John. And the explanation? Although the disciple was carried to the actual temple in Jerusalem in order to measure it, the text never indicates that John saw a vision of the two witnesses nor a vision of the beast that came up from the bottomless pit nor a vision of the two witnesses being caught back up to heaven. Therefore it must be assumed that the disciple was only "told" these things, and he, in turn, relayed this information along to us, the readers. Here's the sequence:

Table 5.3. The Second Sequence in Revelation: The Two Witnesses
1. The ministry of the 2 witnesses begins from the Temple Mount (11:3–6).
2. After the 1,260-day ministry of the 2 witnesses ends, the beast will be released out of the bottomless pit and immediately war against, conquer, and kill the 2 witnesses (11:7).

Table 5.3. The Second Sequence in Revelation: The Two Witnesses
3. The dead bodies of the 2 witnesses will lie on a street on the Temple Mount for 3 1/2 days (11:8–10).
4. God will raise the 2 witnesses from the dead and then snatch them back to heaven (11:11–12).
5. God will then send an earthquake which destroys 1/10 of Jerusalem and kills 7,000 people (11:13).

Since one has now been introduced to two sequences in Revelation, one starting approximately at the time of the abomination of desolation and continuing through the sixth trumpet to date (6:1—9:21), and a second one comprising the 1,260-day ministry of the two witnesses (11:3–13), the reader might expect a quick reconciliation of the First Sequence and the Second Sequence in Revelation. However, at this point that's impossible. Until one knows the exact time frame of the 1,260-day ministry of the two witnesses, the reconciliation of the two sequences will have to be put on hold.

John Announces the Passing of the Second Woe

After relaying his third conversation to the reader, John announces the passing of the second woe:

> The second woe has passed. The third woe is coming very soon.
> (Rev 11:14)

Lest one forget, what exactly was the second woe? Of course, it was the sixth trumpet plague that will result in a third of the unrighteous being killed by the two hundred million demons out of the bottomless pit (Rev 9:13–19). However, when one is not aware of the thirteen conversations scattered throughout John's letter, the following is the inevitable mistake: Many believe that the appearance of the mighty angel as well as the 1,260-day ministry of the two witnesses will fall at some point after the sixth trumpet plague and before the seventh trumpet blast. Nothing could be further from the truth. The mighty angel's conversation with John occurred two thousand years ago, and, as far as the two witnesses are concerned, the reader will soon learn that their ministry will have come and gone well before the first trumpet is ever blown. The only relationship between the mighty angel, the two witnesses, the sixth trumpet, and the seventh trumpet is that John spoke to the mighty angel and learned of the two witnesses between the visions of the sixth and seventh trumpets.

John Finally Sees the Vision of the Seventh Trumpet

After John's third conversation, the disciple is finally allowed to see the vision of the seventh trumpet:

> Then the seventh angel blew his trumpet and there were loud voices in heaven, saying, "The kingdom of the world has become the kingdom of our Lord and of his Messiah, and he will reign forever and ever." (Rev 11:15)

At the sound of the trumpet, John heard a very loud celebration in heaven that was absent during the previous six trumpets. From just the few words heard in the celebration, John knew that a milestone of great significance had been reached and that those in heaven were rejoicing over it. The disciple was already aware that he might see something special during the vision of the seventh trumpet because, during the previous conversation, the mighty angel said that the mystery of God would be fulfilled in the days when the seventh angel was to blow his trumpet. Again, here are his words:

"There will be no more delay, but in the days when the seventh angel is to blow his trumpet, the mystery of God will be fulfilled, as he announced to his servants the prophets" (Rev 10:6b–7).

When John heard the celebratory voices contained within the vision of the seventh trumpet, it must have been apparent to him in light of the angel's previous statement that the fulfillment of the mystery of God was the reason for the celebration, and now that he had heard the words, the disciple realized that the fulfilled mystery was that the kingdom of the world had finally become the kingdom of our Lord and of his Messiah! Evidently, the seventh trumpet blast marked the precise moment that the rule and kingdom of the world changed from the hands of someone back to God. In the following passages, look how both Paul and Jesus described the kingdom of the world and its present ruler. In the first one, Paul said that the "god of this world" has blinded the eyes of those who reject the gospel. Of course, he was speaking of Satan and his reign over the inhabitants of the earth. Next, when preparing his disciples for his crucifixion, Jesus spoke similarly concerning the world dominion of Satan (italics used for emphasis):

FIRST SEQUENCE IN REVELATION, PART 1 (CONT.)

1. "And even if our gospel is veiled, it is veiled to those who are perishing. In their case *the god of this world* has blinded the minds of the unbelievers, to keep them from seeing the light of the gospel of the glory of Christ, who is the image of God" (2 Cor 4:3–4).

2. "I will no longer talk much with you, for *the ruler of this world* is coming. He has no power over me" (John 14:30).

According to both texts, Satan is presently the ruler and god of this world. As to whether the future celebration at the seventh trumpet will be because the dominion of the world has been taken from Satan or possibly from someone else remains to be seen; however, one thing is certain, and that is that the dominion of the world will be taken from someone and returned to God at the blast of the seventh trumpet.

Next, after having describing what he "heard" in the vision of the seventh trumpet celebration, John then describes what he "saw and heard":

> Then the twenty-four elders who sit on their thrones before God fell on their faces and worshiped God, singing, "We give you thanks, Lord God Almighty, who are and who were, for you have taken your great power and begun to reign. The nations raged, but your wrath has come, and the time for judging the dead, for rewarding your servants, the prophets and saints and all who fear your name, both small and great, and for destroying those who destroy the earth." (Rev 11:16–18)

With the kingdom of the world having now become the kingdom of the Lord and of his Messiah, John saw the twenty-four elders fall on their faces and worship God, singing that he had taken his great power and begun to reign. And although the nations raged, God's wrath has come as well as the time for the following: (1) judging the dead; (2) rewarding the servants, the prophets, the saints, and all who fear God's name; and (3) destroying those who destroy the earth.[6]

---

6. Because most are unaware that the first resurrection and rapture of the saints are still on the horizon at this stage in the sequence, and instead mistakenly assume that the resurrection has already occurred, many believe that the elders' words "rewarding the servants" is a reference to a particular reward given by God to certain saints for the quality of their service. In the following, Paul, while speaking of his ministry and that of Apollos, cites this enigmatic reward (italics used for emphasis): "According to the grace of God given to me, like a skilled master builder I laid a foundation, and someone else is building on it. Each builder must choose with care how to build on it. For no one can lay any foundation other than the one that has been laid; that foundation is Jesus Christ. Now if anyone builds on the foundation with gold, silver, precious stones, wood, hay, straw—the work of each builder will become visible, for the Day will

An Unexpected Pregnant Woman

After witnessing the vision of the seventh trumpet celebration that included the glorious sights and sounds of the twenty-four elders singing and worshiping around God's throne, John's eyes at some point turned from the elders and glanced toward an unexpected yet magnificent sight standing within the open temple doorway:

> Then God's temple in heaven was opened, and the ark of his covenant was seen within his temple; and there were flashes of lightning, rumblings, peals of thunder, an earthquake, and heavy hail. (Rev 11:19)

In the doorway was the ark of the covenant! Surely John's mind flashed back to the book of Exodus where God instructed Moses to build a sanctuary in the wilderness, with all of its furnishings, including the ark of the covenant (Exod 25:8–9). Doubtless awestruck, John must have wondered what else lay behind the entry of the doorway. Suddenly, the disciple was met with a bevy of lights and sounds, exactly like those he had seen after the seven angels were given their trumpets (Rev 8:5). Just as a display of thunder, lightning, and an earthquake preceded the trumpet plagues, could these same signs now signal the start of a new series of plagues? Perhaps. But before John had a chance to fully ponder the possibility, a most intriguing and spectacular vision materialized before him: one of a pregnant woman clothed with the sun and with the moon under her feet! As his mind must have simultaneously raced with confusion and anticipation, little did John realize that he was about to witness a third sequence of events.

---

disclose it, because it will be revealed with fire, and the fire will test what sort of work each has done. If what has been built on the foundation survives, *the builder will receive a reward*. If the work is burned up, the builder will suffer loss; the builder will be saved, but only as through fire" (1 Cor 3:10–15).

Because of the apostle's clear indication that believers *may or may not receive this particular reward*, one would be hard pressed to think that this was the reward alluded to by the elders at the seventh trumpet celebration, especially since that reward was to be given to all *"the servants, the saints, the prophets, and all who fear God's name."* Therefore, it's obvious that the elders could only have been singing about the upcoming great and climactic reward of the glorified body, which will be given to *all* the saints at the moment of the resurrection and rapture (See Dan 12:13, which equates the resurrection with a reward).

FIRST SEQUENCE IN REVELATION, PART 1 (CONT.)

Concluding Thoughts: A Fulfillment of a Familiar Prophecy?

Is it possible that the 1,260-day ministry of the two witnesses will fulfill a familiar prophecy given by the Lord in the Olivet Discourse? Here's the prophesy:

"And this good news of the kingdom will be proclaimed throughout the world, as a testimony to all the nations; and then the end will come" (Matt 24:14).

It's very often been assumed that Jesus was indicating that once the church finally fulfills the Great Commission, then the end will come. And because of this universal assumption, pastors, evangelists, missionaries, and laymen alike have been fervently canvassing the earth with the gospel ever since Christ uttered the prophecy. Of course believers are commanded to fulfill the Great Commission, as was given by Christ to the disciples:

"And Jesus came and said to them, 'All authority in heaven and on earth has been given to me. Go therefore and make disciples of all nations, baptizing them in the name of the Father and of the Son and of the Holy Spirit, and teaching them to obey everything that I have commanded you. And remember, I am with you always, to the end of the age'" (Matt 28:18–20).

However, the question is not whether the church is obligated to fulfill the Great Commission, but whether Jesus meant that its fulfillment would bring about his return. In other words, did Jesus intend for the saints to suppose that one day a missionary who had been diligently crisscrossing the nations of the globe for decades would finally reach that one last person deep in the Congo of Africa, or possibly in a mosquito-infested village along the Amazon, or, perhaps, high atop a snow covered mountain peak in Mongolia with the good news of the kingdom, and then, and only then, would the end come? The answer is no; this cannot be what Jesus had in mind. Even if a certain generation of ministers and missionaries happens to reach every corner of the entire globe with the gospel, that accomplishment, in and of itself, will not affect the timing of the Lord's return. As proof, Paul said that feat had already been accomplished in his generation (italics used for emphasis):

"And you who were once estranged and hostile in mind, doing evil deeds, he has now reconciled in his fleshy body through death, so as to present you holy and blameless and irreproachable before him—provided that you continue securely established and steadfast in the faith, without shifting from the hope promised by the gospel that you heard, *which has been proclaimed to every creature under heaven*. I, Paul, became a servant of this gospel" (Col 1:21–23).

Here, the Holy Spirit, through the apostle Paul, said the gospel had been thoroughly and efficiently proclaimed in the first generation of the church, and still the end did not come. But what about the second generation? or the third? What about this generation? Whether the church is aware of it or not, the good news of the kingdom has been successfully proclaimed throughout the world in every generation since the first generation (that's more than twenty one-hundred-year generations!). Not one generation has been lacking. How does one know this? Because all of the elect in every generation has been brought into the kingdom of God under the careful guidance and direction of the Holy Spirit. Not one soul has gone missing; not one. And still, the end has not come. Why? Because the end will not come just because the good news of the kingdom has been effectively proclaimed throughout the world in any given generation, as disappointing as that might sound to some. The end will only come, according to Jesus, after the good news of the kingdom has been proclaimed throughout the world *in the last generation*. And who, according to Rev 11, will almost single-handedly accomplish this task? The two witnesses. When Jesus said the good news of the kingdom will be proclaimed throughout the world and then the end will come, could he have been referencing the specific ministry of the two witnesses, when they will command the world stage for 1,260 straight days from high atop the Temple Mount, proclaiming the good news that he is the Messiah as "a testimony to all nations" (Matt 24:14)? Perhaps. If so, that would imply that the Lord considered the murder of the two witnesses as the beginning of the end. If this is indeed the case, perhaps we will soon better understand his reasonings.

CHAPTER 6

Third Sequence in Revelation
The Woman, the Child, and the Dragon (12:1–6)

Fourth Sequence in Revelation, Part 1
The War in Heaven to the Woman's Escape (12:7–17)

First Sequence	Second Sequence	Third Sequence	Fourth Sequence
	Chapter 5 2nd Seq.: The 2 Witnesses (11:1–13)		
Chapter 5 (cont.) 1st Seq., Part 1 (cont.): The 7th Trumpet (11:15–19)			
		Chapter 6* 3rd Seq.: The Woman, the Child, and the Dragon (12:1–6)	
			Chapter 6 (cont.)* 4th Seq., Part 1: The War in Heaven to the Woman's Escape (12:7–17)

THE SEQUENCE

AFTER JOHN SAW THE seventh angel blow his trumpet, followed by the sounds of heaven's jubilation as loud voices announced that the kingdom of the world had become the kingdom of our Lord and of his Messiah, the disciple saw and heard the familiar shakings, sights, and sounds of an earthquake, thunder, and lightning, that had also appeared at the introduction of the trumpet judgments (Rev 8:5). Then suddenly the earthquake and thunder vanished, giving way to visions unlike anything the prophet had ever seen. Filled with fantastic and extraordinary, supernatural creatures, John describes two apparitions appearing in the heavens that were almost cartoonish in appearance:

> A great portent appeared in heaven: a woman clothed with the sun, with the moon under her feet, and on her head a crown of twelve stars. She was pregnant and was crying out in birth pangs, in the agony of giving birth. Then another portent appeared in heaven: a great red dragon, with seven heads and ten horns, and seven diadems on his heads. His tail swept down a third of the stars of heaven and threw them to the earth. Then the dragon stood before the woman who was about to bear a child, so that he might devour her child as soon as it was born. And she gave birth to a son, a male child, who is to rule all the nations with a rod of iron. But her child was snatched away and taken to God and to his throne; and the woman fled into the wilderness, where she has a place prepared by God, so that she can be nourished for one thousand two hundred sixty days. (Rev 12:1–6)

John said a great portent appeared in heaven. The Greek word *sēmeion*, translated "portent," is simply defined as a sign or an omen of some sort. Since most of Revelation is filled with visions of one kind or another, how might one distinguish these "portent-visions" from the other visions of Revelation? One way, other than the fact that John has labeled them as such, might be that they are so fantastic in nature and so unexpectedly unrealistic that even John could hardly believe what he was seeing. Although John could readily see the differences, somehow the disciple had to convey that fact to the reader. Nevertheless, differences aside, the question that concerns us is whether or not these "portents" begin a new sequence. As the reader is sure to be aware, ever since Christ opened the seventh seal (Rev 8:1), the First Sequence of Revelation began to fall within the framework of the blowing of the trumpets: the first angel blew a trumpet in heaven and then a plague occurred on earth;

the second angel blew the next trumpet in heaven, then another plague occurred on earth, and so on and so on. However, the "portents" initially appear to have no direct connection with the trumpet judgments. Even to the causal observer, the portents appear so unlike the trumpet-visions that someone might easily suspect that a different series of events has started, indicating the presence of a new sequence. But these are only subjective observations. As stated in chapter 3, *the objective proof of a different sequence from one series of events to the next is the presence of any event that has already been seen in a previous series of events.* Therefore, as we enter into this strange and unique series of portents, let's remain alert for a possible reoccurring event that will positively confirm our suspicion that we have indeed entered a new sequence of events.

The Woman

One must admit, John's beginning narrative of the outlandish visions seems straightforward enough: As a woman waits patiently for the birth of her child, a menacing-looking dragon stands nearby in order to devour the infant once it is born. Nevertheless, the child is born and lives on the earth for an indefinite period of time before being snatched up to heaven, leaving the dragon empty-handed, as the woman flees into the wilderness. But what does it all mean? Reading a symbolic narrative is one thing, but understanding it is another. What do the woman, the child, and the dragon represent, and what is the meaning of the woman giving birth to the child, and what is the meaning of the child being taken up to heaven? And why did the woman escape into the wilderness? While we ponder this cascade of questions, here's the sequence of the narrative:

Table 6.1. Sequence in the Narrative of the Woman, the Child, and the Dragon
1. A woman appeared and she was pregnant (12:1–2).
2. A dragon appeared. With his tail, he swept down 1/3 of the stars of heaven and threw them to the earth (12:3).
3. The dragon waited in front of the pregnant woman in order to devour the child at its birth (12:4).
4. A male child was born (12:5a).
5. The child was snatched up to heaven and to God's throne (12:5b).
6. The woman fled into the wilderness where she was nourished for 1,260 days (12:6).

As with any of God's visions that might contain symbolism, in order to understand the message he desires to convey, one must first identify as many of the symbolic characters as possible. Sometimes a symbol will be identified within the text, but in many cases, familiarity with those same symbols used elsewhere will prove helpful. That's the case with the first character in the vision: the woman clothed with the sun, with the moon under her feet, and wearing on her head a crown with twelve stars (Rev 12:1). She reminds one of a character in one of Joseph's dreams in Genesis, where his family was depicted as the sun, the moon, and eleven stars:

"He had another dream, and told it to his brothers, saying, 'Look, I have had another dream: the sun, the moon, and eleven stars were bowing down to me.' But when he told it to his father and to his brothers, his father rebuked him, and said to him, 'What kind of dream is this that you have had? Shall we indeed come, I and your mother and your brothers, and bow to the ground before you?'" Gen 37:9–10.

Clearly, one is to understand from the dream that Jacob was represented by the sun, Rachel by the moon, and the eleven brothers of Joseph by the eleven stars. And although John's vision was significantly different than Joseph's dream, still, it seems safe to assume that just as the sun, moon, and stars represented Israel in the dream, they doubtless represent Israel, at least in some way, in the vision.

A Third Sequence Emerges

Next, if we carry the interpretation one step further, since "the woman" was seen fleeing into the wilderness (Rev 12:6), shouldn't one assume that "something closely related to Israel" was seen fleeing into the wilderness? There can be no other conclusion. Now, since this is the case, one cannot help but reflect back on the only other entity we've studied that has fled anywhere and that is the 144,000 Jewish remnant that fled Jerusalem at the appearance of the abomination of desolation. This is one of the most noteworthy events we have studied to date, as evidenced by its multiple references in the Olivet Discourse, in Joel 2, and, by implication, in the First Sequence of Revelation. I say "implication" because, since one has seen the Jewish remnant fleeing Jerusalem just prior to the greatest suffering in history in the Sequence in the Olivet Discourse, then logically, that same flight by the Jewish remnant is implied in the First Sequence of Revelation just prior to the global holocaust caused by "the Four Horsemen of the Apocalypse," since "the global holocaust" and "the greatest suffering in history" have been determined to be one and the same. The following is an abbreviated reconciliation of the Sequence in the Olivet Discourse, the First Sequence in Revelation, and the most recent "Narrative of the Woman, the Child, and the Dragon" showing the flight into the wilderness:

Table 6.2. The 144,000 Jewish Remnant Escapes into the Wilderness

The Sequence	Seq. Olivet Discourse (Matt 24:15–22)	1st Seq. Rev, Part 1: Through 7 Trumpets (Rev 6:1–8)	Narrative of the Woman, Child, and Dragon (Rev 12:1–6)
1. A woman appears and is pregnant.			A woman appeared and was pregnant. (Rev 12:1–2)
2. A dragon appears and with his tail, he sweeps down 1/3 of the stars of heaven and throws them to the earth.			A dragon appeared and with his tail, he swept down 1/3 of the stars of heaven and threw them to the earth. (Rev 12:3)
3. The dragon waits in front of the pregnant woman in order to devour the child at its birth.			The dragon waited in front of the pregnant woman in order to devour the child at its birth. (Rev 12:4)
4. A male child is born.			A male child was born. (Rev 12:5a)
5. The child is snatched up to heaven and to God's throne.			The child was snatched up to heaven and to God's throne. (Rev 12:5b)
6. Abomination of desolation occurs.	Jesus urges "the reader" to escape Jerusalem at the sight of the abomination. (Matt 24:15–20)	The 144,000 Jewish remnant flees into the wilderness (this is implied).	The woman fled into the wilderness where she was nourished for 1,260 days. (Rev 12:6)

Table 6.2. The 144,000 Jewish Remnant Escapes into the Wilderness			
The Sequence	Seq. Olivet Discourse (Matt 24:15–22)	1st Seq. Rev, Part 1: Through 7 Trumpets (Rev 6:1–8)	Narrative of the Woman, Child, and Dragon (Rev 12:1–6)
7. After the abomination of desolation begins the greatest suffering in the history of the world, which is a nuclear war.	The greatest suffering in history begins. (Matt 24:21)	The first two riders of "the Four Horsemen of the Apocalypse" initiate and orchestrate a nuclear war. (Rev 6:1–4)	
8. God ends the nuclear war but the nuclear aftermath follows with its continued death by the preceding nuclear war, as well as death by famine, pestilence, and wild animals.	God shortens the days of the greatest suffering in the history of the world for the sake of the elect. (Matt 24:22)	God ends the nuclear war, at which time the next two riders of "the Four Horsemen of the Apocalypse" initiate and orchestrate the nuclear aftermath. (Rev 6:5–8)	

Since the 144,000 Jewish remnant's escape at the abomination is "implied" in the First Sequence of Revelation, and the "Narrative of the Woman, the Child, and the Dragon" actually contains the event of the 144,000's escape at the abomination, then one knows that the narrative in Rev 12:1–6 has begun a new sequence.[1] Therefore, from here forward, the series of events found within the "Narrative of the Woman, the Child, and the Dragon" will now be labeled the Third Sequence in Revelation. And with that, here are the three sequences to date:

1. The First Sequence in Revelation began with the rider on the white horse and has paused at the end of the seventh trumpet (6:1—9:21, 11:15–19).

---

1. Although the cardinal rule when determining a sequence indicates that one sequence cannot contain the same event twice, this rule is still in effect if one or more of the events in question is "implied" in any series of events.

2. The Second Sequence in Revelation was found within the third conversation, which verbally revealed the series of events surrounding the 1,260-day ministry of the two witnesses (11:1–13).

3. The Third Sequence in Revelation has begun with the "Narrative of the Woman, the Child, and the Dragon" (12:1–6). (Note: Whether v. 6 ends the third sequence is yet to be determined.)

The Child

With the identity of the woman at least partially addressed (whereby one knows that the woman to some extent is related to the 144,000 Jewish remnant), we now turn our attention to the second of the three characters in the narrative: the male child. Initially, the mystery of this symbol seems too simple. Since one knows that the child is "to rule all the nations with a rod of iron" (Rev 12:5) and Rev 19:15 speaks of Christ ruling the nations with a "rod of iron," then the foregone conclusion is that the child must represent Jesus. At least that's the consensus of most commentators. However, one must not overlook the fact that Rev 2:27 tells of Christ also giving to those who conquer the authority to rule the nations with a rod of iron. Here are both texts (italics used for emphasis):

1. "To everyone who conquers and continues to do my works to the end, I will give *authority over the nations; to rule them with an iron rod*, as when clay pots are shattered—even as I received authority from my Father" (Rev 2:26–28a).

2. "From his mouth comes a sharp sword with which to strike down the nations, and *he will rule them with a rod of iron*; he will tread the wine press of the fury of the wrath of God the Almighty. On his robe and on his thigh he has a name inscribed, 'King of kings and Lord of lords'" (Rev 19:15–16).

Although from the above verses it is clear that both Jesus and Christians will one day rule with a rod of iron, still, most scholars continue to believe the child represents Jesus because of two additional assumptions:

1. They believe the image of the dragon waiting to devour the child at birth represented Herod's attempt to kill Jesus by killing all male children under the age of two in the vicinity of Bethlehem soon after Christ's birth (Matt 2:16).

THE SEQUENCE

2. They believe the picture of the child being snatched up to heaven represents Christ's ascension after his resurrection (Acts 1:9).

Those assumptions sound reasonable enough, but how well will they hold up under closer scrutiny? Let's find out. First, let's see whether the child being snatched up to heaven compares favorably with the ascension of Jesus. The Greek word translated "snatched away" in Rev 12:5 is *hērpasthē*, which means "to be caught up" or "raptured." If it sounds familiar, it should. Paul used essentially the same word, *harpagēsometha*, in 1 Thess 4:17 when he said those who are alive and left will be "caught up" in the clouds to meet the Lord in the air. On another occasion Paul used *harpagenta* in 2 Cor 12:2 when the apostle said he knew a person in Christ who "was caught up" to the third heaven when speaking of his personal visions and revelations of the Lord. In all three instances, the subjects are being caught up to heaven not by their own volition or power, but by another source of power. In other words, a greater force is bringing the individuals up, and, of course, that force is the power of God.

Now, let's compare the thought of "being snatched up" by an overwhelming force to Jesus ascending to heaven. In the following, we pick up where Mary Magdalene had been weeping at the tomb of Christ on the third day after the crucifixion. When the Lord appeared to her and called her by name, she recognized him and evidently attempted to hold on to Christ (italics used for emphasis):

"Jesus said to her, 'Do not hold on to me, because *I have not yet ascended* to my Father. But go to my brothers and say to them, "*I am ascending* to my Father and your Father, to my God and your God."' Mary Magdalene went and announced to the disciples, 'I have seen the Lord'; and she told them that he had said these things to her" (John 20:17–18).

Jesus told Mary not to hold on to him because "he had not yet ascended" to the Father. Translated from the Greek *anabebēka*, the word means "I have ascended" or "I have gone up." Instead of an individual being snatched up by another power, the verb *anabainō*, which is the root of *anabebēka*, infers that Jesus himself is the one supplying the power to ascend or go up. Therefore, although the jury is still out for the moment, on first impression, "the child being snatched up to heaven" does not appear equivalent to "Jesus ascending to heaven." In other words, one will be hard pressed to say that Jesus was "snatched up" to heaven at the ascension. Furthermore, the portent gives the impression that the child was snatched away from the grasp of the dragon (Rev 12:5). When Jesus ascended from the Mount of Olives in the sight of the disciples, one can be certain that no one present believed Jesus was being snatched away from the grasp of anyone, least of all, Satan.

The War

The Lord hardly gives John time to digest the scene of the child being snatched up to heaven and the woman fleeing into the wilderness before showing him glimpses of a heavenly battle between the Archangel Michael and the dragon:

> And war broke out in heaven: Michael and his angels fought against the dragon. The dragon and his angels fought back, but they were defeated, and there was no longer any place for them in heaven. The great dragon was thrown down, that ancient serpent, who is called the Devil and Satan, the deceiver of the whole world—he was thrown down to the earth, and his angels were thrown down with him. (Rev 12:7–9)

Because the text containing the scene of the war between Michael and the dragon immediately followed the text containing the child's rapture to heaven and the woman's flight into the wilderness, one might initially have the impression that the war was triggered by one of those two events. Whether that is true or not remains to be seen. But a few things surrounding the war are certain, and that's who the dragon represents, who started the war, and who won it. Although we may still be grappling with the identities of the woman and the child at this point in our study, thanks to the text, we at least know the identity of the dragon: It represents Satan (Rev 12:9). Furthermore, one knows Michael initiated the confrontation and won the war (Rev 12:7–8a). Here again are the pertinent verses:

"And war broke out in heaven: Michael and his angels fought against the dragon. The dragon and his angels fought back, but they were defeated..."

Had Satan initiated the war, the passage would have read something like the following: "And war broke out in heaven: Satan and his angels fought against Michael. But Michael and his angels fought back..." Of course, this is not how the text reads and, because of that, one can be certain Michael initiated the conflict. Furthermore, one also knows Michael won the conflict because it ended with the archangel casting Satan to the earth.

THE SEQUENCE

Next, John heard a voice proclaiming Michael's victory:

> "Then I heard a loud voice in heaven, proclaiming, 'Now have come the salvation and the power and the kingdom of our God and the authority of his Messiah, for the accuser of our brothers has been thrown down, who accuses them day and night before our God. But they have conquered him by the blood of the Lamb and by the word of their testimony, for they did not cling to life even in the face of death. Rejoice then, you heavens and those who dwell in them! But woe to the earth and the sea, for the devil has come down to you with great wrath, because he knows that his time is short!'" Rev 12:10–12.

Notice that not only did John hear the voice proclaim the fact that Satan had been cast down to the earth, but there was another reason for the celebration: The victory of the "brothers" (Greek: *adelphōn*) over Satan "by the blood of the Lamb and by the word of their testimony." It is this second reason that poses a problem for those who believe the child represents Jesus. If one assumes the child being snatched up to heaven represents Christ's ascension, then the proposed scenario necessarily implies that the war between Michael and Satan and heaven's celebratory proclamation soon followed Christ's ascension, correct? But doesn't that scenario place any celebration over Satan's defeat by the brethren prematurely? If the brothers are representative of the saints (and I say "if" with caution), one would think that any celebration of victory over the devil would have been delayed long enough to at least allow the saints some history in defeating the devil by the blood of the Lamb and by the word of their testimony. For Satan's defeat to be proclaimed so soon after Christ's ascension is equivalent to a nation proclaiming victory over another nation only days into a battle that is actually going to continue for years! Nations don't usually do that. Of course, Christ's victory over Satan at the cross was complete, but the majority of the saints' earthly victories over the devil were still to come.

Because of these two preliminary observations—that the event of the child being "snatched up" to heaven (Greek: *hērpasthē*) does not appear equivalent to Christ's ascension (Greek: *anabebēka*), and, secondly, the question of why the voice would proclaim the saints' victory over Satan so soon after Christ's ascension—the theory that the child represents Jesus is seriously called into question. In fact, they strongly suggest that the child does not represent Jesus. True, Jesus ascended to heaven, but certainly no one thinks he was forcefully snatched up to heaven at the ascension, especially because of some supposed threat from Satan. The thought is laughable. Secondly, as just stated, when the voice in heaven proclaimed that "the brethren" had conquered Satan by the blood of the Lamb and by the word of their testimony, if indeed "the brethren" in the context represented the saints, one would assume that any proclamation of the saints' victory over Satan would only come after a long, storied history of the saints' victories over Satan, not when the saints had barely begun their warfare with Satan. Since these two points present seemingly insurmountable difficulties, let's leave open the possibility that the child doesn't represent Jesus. There's still the option that the child is representative in someway of "everyone who conquers and continues to do my works to the end" (Rev 2:26–28).

A Fourth Sequence Emerges

Once Satan realized that he had been cast to the earth by the archangel Michael, the next passage states that he immediately "pursued" (Greek: *ediōxen*) the woman who had given birth to the child, but the woman was given the wings of a great eagle by which she could escape:

> So when the dragon saw that he had been thrown down to the earth, he pursued the woman who had given birth to the male child. But the woman was given the two wings of the great eagle, so that she could fly from the serpent into the wilderness, to her place where she is nourished for a time, and times, and half a time. (Rev 12:13–14)

As one reads about the escape of the woman into the wildernesses, immediately one has a sense of déjà vu. Why so? John has already seen the woman escape into the wilderness! Here's a review of the series of events, beginning with the pregnant woman and continuing through the time she is seen escaping to the wilderness for the second time (italics used for emphasis):

Table 6.3. The Woman's Escape into the Wilderness Is Seen Twice
1. The woman appeared and was pregnant (12:1–2).
2. A dragon appeared. With his tail, he swept down 1/3 of the stars of heaven and threw them to the earth (12:3).
3. The dragon waited in front of the pregnant woman in order to devour the child at birth (12:4).

THE SEQUENCE

Table 6.3. The Woman's Escape into the Wilderness Is Seen Twice
4. A male child was born (12:5a).
5. The child was snatched up to heaven and to God's throne (12:5b).
6. *And the woman fled into the wilderness where she was nourished for 1,260 days* (12:6).
7. War broke out in heaven. Michael and his angels fought against the dragon and his angels, and they fought back (12:7).
8. The dragon and his angels were defeated. They were thrown down to the earth (12:8–9).
9. A voice proclaimed that the devil had been cast to the earth and the brethren had conquered the devil. The earth and the sea were then warned that the devil had come down to them with great wrath because he knows that his time is short (12:10–12).
10. When the dragon saw that he had been thrown down to the earth, he pursued the woman who had given birth to the male child (12:13).
11. *But the woman was given the two wings of an eagle so she could fly from the serpent into the wilderness for a time, and times, and half a time* (12:14).

You may have noticed that we now face a small conundrum. The war in heaven between Michael and Satan (Rev 12:7), which at first appeared to follow the woman's flight into the wilderness where she is nourished for 1,260 days (Rev 12:6), now appears to precede the woman's escape into the wilderness for a time, and times, and half a time (Rev 12:14). Since one sequence cannot contain the same event twice, one knows that the war in heaven cannot both follow and precede the woman fleeing to the wilderness. So which is it? Does the war follow the woman's escape or precede it? Answer: It is certain that the war between Michael and Satan precedes the woman's flight into the wilderness because the text clearly indicates that the woman's flight was a direct result of the war's end (italics used for emphasis):

"*So when the dragon saw that he had been thrown down to the earth, he pursued the woman* who had given birth to the male child. But the woman was given the two wings of the great eagle, so that she could fly from the serpent into the wilderness, to her place where she is nourished for a time, and times, and half a time" (Rev 12:13–14).

The war ended and Satan was cast down; Satan pursued the woman, but she was given the two wings of the great eagle as she fled into the wilderness.[2] It's as simple as one, two, three. By realizing that Rev 12:7–14

2. See Exod 19:4. Just as God enabled the Israelites to flee Egypt "on eagles' wings"

is part of a different sequence than that found within Rev 12:1–6, we can now proceed to label Rev 12:7–14 the Fourth Sequence in Revelation. The following is the initial reconciliation of the third and fourth sequences:

<table>
<tr><td colspan="2">Table 6.4. The First Reconciliation of the Third and Fourth Sequences in Revelation</td></tr>
<tr><td>3rd Seq. Rev: Woman, Child, and Dragon
(12:1–6)</td><td>4th Seq. Rev: Heaven's War to Woman's Escape
(12:7–14)</td></tr>
<tr><td>1. The woman appeared and was pregnant (12:1–2).

2. A dragon appeared. With his tail, he swept down 1/3 of the stars of heaven and threw them to the earth (12:3).

3. The dragon waited in front of the woman in order to devour the child at birth (12:4).

4. A male child was born (12:5a).

5. The child was snatched up to heaven and to God's throne (12:5b).</td><td>1. War broke out in heaven. Michael and his angels fought against the dragon, and the dragon and his angels fought back (12:7).

2. The dragon and his angels were defeated. They were thrown down to the earth (12:8–9).

3. A voice proclaimed that the devil had been cast to the earth and the brethren had conquered the devil. The earth and the sea were then warned that the devil had come down to them with great wrath because he knows that his time is short (12:10–12).

4. When the dragon saw that he had been thrown down to the earth, he pursued the woman who had given birth to the male child (12:13).</td></tr>
<tr><td>The woman fled into the wilderness where she was nourished for 1,260 days (12:6).</td><td>The woman was given the two wings of an eagle so she could fly from the serpent into the wilderness for a time, and times, and half a time (12:14).</td></tr>
</table>

The initial reconciliation of the third and fourth sequences was quite easy; however, while pursuing a more thorough reconciliation, one quickly realizes that the events surrounding the war between Michael and Satan (12:7–9), in the Fourth Sequence, must occur after the events surrounding the birth of the child (12:1–5a), in the Third Sequence. Why? Because Satan could only have swept down his angels out of heaven in anticipation

---

in the exodus he will similarly do so for them when he enables them to flee Jerusalem in the future.

of the child's birth prior to Michael casting those same angels out of heaven permanently. Here's the slight update to the initial reconciliation:

Table 6.5. The Second Reconciliation of the Third and Fourth Sequences

3rd Seq. Rev: Woman, Child, and Dragon (12:1–6)	4th Seq. Rev: Heaven's War to Woman's Escape (12:7–14)
1. The woman appeared and was pregnant (12:1–2). 2. A dragon appeared. With his tail, he swept down 1/3 of the stars of heaven and threw them to the earth (12:3). 3. The dragon waited in front of the woman in order to devour the child at birth (12:4). 4. A male child was born (12:5a).	
5. The child was snatched up to heaven and to God's throne (12:5b).	1. War broke out in heaven. Michael and his angels fought against the dragon, and the dragon and his angels fought back (12:7). 2. The dragon and his angels were defeated. They were thrown down to the earth (12:8–9). 3. A voice proclaimed that the devil had been cast to the earth and the brethren had conquered the devil. The earth and the sea were then warned that the devil had come down to them with great wrath because he knows that his time is short (12:10–12). 4. When the dragon saw that he had been thrown down to the earth, he pursued the woman who had given birth to the male child (12:13).
The woman fled into the wilderness where she was nourished for 1,260 days (12:6).	The woman was given the two wings of an eagle so she could fly from the serpent into the wilderness for a time, and times, and half a time (12:14).

As to the question of precisely when the war will begin in relation to "the child being snatched up to heaven," that answer will have to wait.

For now, we will have to be content knowing the war between Michael and Satan will start at some point after the birth of the child but before the woman escapes into the wilderness.

The Dragon's Flood and Satan's Armies

After the dragon was cast to the earth by Michael, John saw the dragon, i.e., Satan, gather himself and pursue the woman who had given birth to the child. John then said out of the mouth of the serpent came water like a river in order to sweep the inhabitants away with a flood:

> Then from his mouth the serpent poured water like a river after the woman, to sweep her away with the flood. (Rev 12:15)

If not careful, one may get the impression that Satan is a super reptilian-like sea-monster flying through the air, spewing water out of his mouth similar to a fire-breathing dragon, with the intentions of actually trying to drown the inhabitants of Jerusalem as they attempt to escape the city. But that's not the case. The symbolic meaning of "poured water like a river" does not represent water. *In fact, a good first guess for the meaning of any symbol employed by God in his visions is anything other than the symbol itself.* So, as an example, in this case one should understand that the symbol of a flood represents anything other than a flood of water. Likewise, the dragon doesn't represent a real dragon and the woman doesn't represent a real woman, etc. Also, one must understand that unless otherwise permitted by God, Satan cannot directly attack humans, but rather must carry out his dastardly deeds against them by influencing other humans. One might ask, What about Satan's attacks against Job? But that is a perfect example of when Satan received permission from the Lord to directly attack an individual (compare Job 1:12 and 2:6). However, in most circumstances Satan must employ a "Haman" against Mordechai, a "Delilah" against Samson, a "Pharaoh's army" against Israel, or a "Judas" against Jesus. In the vision in question, the flood out of Satan's mouth simply represents the surrounding armies of Jerusalem that Satan will incite to invade Jerusalem. The following OT passage contains the identical symbolism:

"Thus says the Lord: See, waters are rising out of the north and shall become an overflowing torrent; they shall overflow the land and all that fills it, the city and those who live in it. People shall cry out, and all the inhabitants of the land shall wail" (Jer 47:2).

Here, the Lord wasn't foretelling a great water event. Rather, he was simply foretelling that the armies of Pharaoh were soon to invade the Philistines.

Jesus References the Same Invading Armies

In a passage cited earlier during our study of the Olivet Discourse, one sees Jesus referencing the same hostile armies symbolized by the flood out of the mouth of the dragon (Rev 12:15), but not at the time they chased the woman into the wilderness. Rather he references them at an earlier point in the sequence, when they had initially surrounded Jerusalem and were on the verge of invading the city:

"When you see Jerusalem surrounded by armies, then know that its desolation has come near. Then those in Judea must flee to the mountains, and those inside the city must leave it, and those out in the country must not enter it; for these are days of vengeance, as a fulfillment of all that is written. Woe to those who are pregnant and to those who are nursing infants in those days! For there will be great distress on the earth and wrath against this people; they will fall by the edge of the sword and be taken away as captives among all nations; and Jerusalem will be trampled on by the Gentiles, until the times of the Gentiles are fulfilled" (Luke 21:20–24).

Whereas Luke points to the appearance of the surrounding armies as triggering the time for the Jewish remnant to escape Jerusalem, if you recall, Matthew and Mark cite the appearance of the abomination of desolation as the time to flee (Matt 24:15 and Mark 13:14). Nonetheless, from these three accounts, one understands that the abomination of desolation as well as the appearance of the surrounding armies are the two milestone events that will trigger the remnant's escape.

The Earthquake

Restless with anxious anticipation, the armies surrounding Jerusalem will eventually come to the moment when they immediately converge upon the city. As dire as the circumstances appear to be, the entire 144,000 Jewish remnant will successfully escape the flood from the mouth of the dragon. But how? Though the passage appears to credit the earth, one knows that it is actually the hand of the Lord that will come to the rescue:

> But the earth came to the help of the woman; it opened its mouth and swallowed the river that the dragon had poured from his mouth. (Rev 12:16)

Here, the Lord personifies the earth with the following description: "it opened its mouth and swallowed the river." At the risk of sounding redundant, just as Satan is not a fire-breathing dragon, or in this case, a water-spouting dragon, the earth doesn't have a mouth with which to swallow anything. Again, one must interpret the Lord's symbols. However, in this case, the meaning of the symbolism poses no challenge, thanks to a parallel personification of the earth in the Old Testament. Recall when Korah, Dathan, and Abiram revolted against Moses in the wilderness, saying that all the people were just as holy as Moses and Aaron, and therefore anyone should be permitted to approach the Lord. And then recall how the Lord called those men out, including all of their families, and commanded them to stand outside of their tents on the following day so that he might judge between them and Moses. The next day, the men and their families did indeed step out of their tents. That's where we pick up:

"As soon as he [Moses] finished speaking all these words, the ground under them was split apart. The earth opened its mouth and swallowed them up, along with their households—everyone who belonged to Korah and all their goods. So they with all that belonged to them went down alive into Sheol; the earth closed over them, and they perished from the midst of the assembly" (Num 16:31–33).

In Scripture, when the earth is said to swallow something, it is simply a reference to an earthquake. Here, the earthquake "swallowed and engulfed" Korah and his family, just as an earthquake will one day swallow the flood (of armies) out of the dragon's mouth.

Zechariah Saw the Same Earthquake

John was not the only prophet to describe the Jewish remnant's escape from the pursuing armies in the last days. Zechariah spoke of the same event over five hundred years earlier:

"See, a day is coming for the Lord, when the plunder taken from you will be divided in your midst. For I will gather all the nations against Jerusalem to battle, and the city shall be taken and the houses looted and the women raped; half the city shall go into exile, but the rest of the people shall not be cut off from the city. Then the Lord will go forth and fight against those nations as when he fights on a day of battle" (Zech 14:1–3).

Zechariah's prophesied escape is the same escape symbolized by the dragon chasing the woman (Rev 12:13–15). But why did Zechariah say that only half of the inhabitants would go into exile and the other half wouldn't? Wouldn't it seem that every Jew living in Jerusalem at the time of the invasion would wish to escape? The explanation is found in the ethnic makeup of the city at the time of the invasion. Everyone in Jerusalem will not be Jewish. Even today, according to the most recent census, Jerusalem is composed of approximately 60 percent Jews and 40 percent Arabs.[3] As the trend of Arabs immigrating into Europe and Israel continues, a day will certainly come when the percentages of Jews and Arabs living in and around Jerusalem will reflect a fifty-fifty ratio. That's the simple explanation for Zechariah's prophecy: At the moment of the invasion, the Jewish half will flee, while the Arab half "shall not be cut off from the city."

The Common Misconception of Zechariah 14

Zechariah's narrative of the nations' invasion and remnant's escape brings us to a very popular misconception when interpreting Zech 14, and it concerns the splitting of the Mount of Olives. Here's the passage:

"On that day his feet shall stand on the Mount of Olives, which lies before Jerusalem on the east; and the Mount of Olives shall split in two from east to west by a very wide valley; so that one half of the Mount shall withdraw northward, and the other half southward. And you shall flee by the valley of the Lord's mountain, for the valley between the mountains shall reach to Azal; and you shall flee as you fled from the earthquake in the days of King Uzziah of Judah. Then the Lord my God will come, and all the holy ones with him" (Zech 14:4–5).

Many believe these two verses describe the Lord's appearance at the Battle of Armageddon, a battle that most are aware is the one where Jesus will return in the last days and fight against the nations who have gathered against him (Rev 19:11–21). Furthermore, the same believe that at his return, his feet shall stand on the Mount of Olives and when they do, the mountain will instantly split, creating a pathway of escape for the Jewish people.[4]

---

3. Jerusalem Post Staff, "Jerusalem Remains Israel's Biggest City."
4. Barker, *Zechariah*, 691.

It's quite certain that the Lord will one day split the Mount of Olives. But when? Did Zechariah truly say the Lord will split the mount at the second coming, as most believe, or did the prophet actually say something different? Before answering, let's examine the need for the Mount of Olives to be split in the first place. Zechariah said when the mountain splits from east to west, it will create a large valley, by which the remnant will be able to flee, as when the Jewish people fled from the earthquake in the days of King Uzziah (Amos 1:1). This brings up another question: In the end time, when might the Jewish remnant need a wide valley by which to escape the city? Is it when the Lord Jesus returns in all of his power and glory with his angels in flaming fire, ready to conquer everyone and everything that dares to oppose him, or is it on the day when the surrounding nations invade Jerusalem, taking the city, murdering the Jewish inhabitants, looting the houses, and raping the women? The answer is obvious, but let's continue. As Jesus descends to confront his enemies in the Valley of Armageddon, will he be contemplating, "I will avenge myself against the nations who have persecuted my people, but first I must provide them a way of escape from the vicinity of the battle so that they don't get harmed by the gathered armies, and I will do so by splitting the Mount of Olives, creating a valley through which they can escape?" The thought is almost too comical.

When will the remnant need to escape? Certainly not at the Lord's return! It is at the time that the nations invade Jerusalem at the abomination of desolation, and in order to facilitate the remnant's escape, the Lord (Hebrew: *Yahweh*) will cause an earthquake that splits the Mount of Olives (Zech 14:4), creating a path for their evacuation. This is the same earthquake that will swallow "the flood of armies" that comes from the mouth of the dragon (Rev 12:16). The remnant will flee through the valley caused by the earthquake, as they did in the days of Uzziah, and they will escape to a safe haven in the wilderness. Then, only well after the remnant's 1,260-day exile, will the Lord come and all the holy ones with him. When Christ finally does return and the Jewish remnant sees him in all of his glory, they will have no need to escape. At the Battle of Armageddon, the only ones looking for a way of escape will be God's enemies, not God's people.

An Actual Day vs. a Hypothetical Day

Since the interpretation of the passage seems so straightforward and logical, one might ask, Why do so many get it wrong? That answer is quite easy. The mistake is passed along from one theologian to another and from one commentator to the next because of a lack of understanding of Zechariah's grammatical usage of the word "day" in three places in the passage. Here are the three instances in the order of their appearance (italics used for emphasis):

1. "See, a *day* is coming for the Lord, when the plunder taken from you will be divided in your midst. For I will gather all the nations against Jerusalem to battle, and the city shall be taken and the houses looted and the women raped; half the city shall go into exile, but the rest of the people shall not be cut off from the city" (Zech 14:1–2).

2. "Then the Lord will go forth and fight against those nations as when he fights on a *day* of battle" (Zech 14:3).

3. "On that *day* his feet shall stand on the Mount of Olives, which lies before Jerusalem on the east; and the Mount of Olives shall split in two from east to west by a very wide valley; so that one half of the Mount shall withdraw northward, and the other half southward. And you shall flee by the valley of the Lord's mountain, for the valley between the mountains shall reach to Azal; and you shall flee as you fled from the earthquake in the days of King Uzziah of Judah. Then the Lord my God will come, and all the holy ones with him" (Zech 14:4–5).

It is mistakenly assumed that the *day* used in the third instance refers back to its use in the second instance. It does not. Rather, the third instance refers back to the first instance. How can one be sure? Although the day of the invasion and the day of the splitting of the Mount of Olives are *actual calendar days*, "the day of battle" is not. Instead, it is a *hypothetical day*, depicting how the Lord will fight against those nations once he returns, as he has always fought on any day of battle. Although Christ will indeed return on a certain day, i.e., the day of Armageddon, the phrase "as when he fights on a day of battle" is only a reference to a hypothetical day that doesn't actually exist. Here's the point: In a grammatically correct sentence, a hypothetical day can refer back to a hypothetical day and an actual day can refer back to an actual day, but an actual day can never refer back to a hypothetical day and visa versa. Therefore, the actual day of the splitting of the Mount of Olives can only be referring back to the actual day of the invasion, and not to a hypothetical day of battle. The grammar in the text will not allow for any other interpretation.

The following is a comparison of the correct and incorrect interpretations of Zech 14. Note that the correct sequence shows one escape, whereas the incorrect one shows two:

Table 6.6. Comparison of the Correct and Incorrect Sequences in Zechariah 14	
Correct Sequence (One escape)	**Incorrect Sequence** (Two escapes)
1. Nations invade Jerusalem (14:1–2a).	1. Nations invade Jerusalem (14:1–2a).
2. The Lord splits the Mount of Olives (14:4).	2. *The Jewish remnant escapes the nations to a safe exile (14:2b).*
3. *The remnant escapes the nations to a safe exile, through the valley created by the earthquake (14:2b, 5a).*	3. The Lord returns to fight the nations (14:3, 5b).
4. At some unknown point in time after the exile, the Lord will return and fight the nations as he has always fought on any given day of battle (14:3, 5b).	4. The Lord splits the Mount of Olives (14:4).
	5. *The remnant escapes a second time, through the valley created by the earthquake (14:5a).*

There aren't two escapes. There's just one, and that one is into the wilderness. If there were a second escape, to where would the remnant escape this time? Back to the wilderness, a second time?

Three Earthquakes

Up to this point, Revelation has referenced two earthquakes: The earthquake that splits the Mount of Olives at the abomination of desolation and the earthquake that will accompany the heavenly signs, as both the heavenly signs and earthquake usher in the Day of the Lord. Unlike the earthquake at the Mount of Olives, which is weaker and primarily centers around the city of Jerusalem, the earthquake at the Day of the Lord is global and is described as one that will shake every mountain and island from its place (Rev 6:14). However, later, Revelation will reference a third earthquake: This is the most powerful one and will occur at the seventh bowl judgment and will cause every mountain and island to completely disappear, as well as raze all the cities of the earth (Rev 16:20)! Here's the list:

1. Earthquake at the abomination of desolation (Rev 12:16).
2. Earthquake at the heavenly signs, which ushers in the Day of the Lord (Rev 6:12–14).
3. Earthquake at the seventh bowl of God's wrath (Rev 16:18–20).

Notice that Revelation doesn't record any earthquake at Christ's return, and why would it? After the earthquake at the seventh bowl judgment, which will be the most powerful one in the history of the world, any subsequent earthquake would be somewhat anticlimactic, wouldn't you agree? In reality, by the time Christ makes his appearance at the Battle of Armageddon, I'm pretty sure there will not be much of anything left of the Mount of Olives to split, since it will have been completely leveled by the seventh bowl earthquake, along with all the other mountains and islands of the earth.

Reconciliation of Four Accounts of the Remnant's Escape

As one has surely seen by now, the apocalyptic invasion of Jerusalem by the surrounding gentile nations followed by the subsequent escape of the 144,000 Jewish remnant at the time of the abomination of desolation is one of the most significant milestones in the sequence of end times, especially if multiple references are any indication. Here's an initial reconciliation of the four accounts we've looked at:[5]

---

[5]. When examining the chart, the reader will notice that many of the events within the Third and Fourth Sequences in Revelation are missing, namely, the events surrounding "the child" and "the war in heaven," respectively, and that is because these events are yet to be reconciled.

Table 6.7. Reconciliation of Four Sequences of the Remnant's Escape				
The Sequence	Seq. Olivet Discourse (Matt 24:15–20; Mark 13:14; Luke 21:20–24)	Seq. Zech 14 (14:2, 4–5)	3rd Seq. Rev: Woman, Child, and Dragon (12:6)	4th Seq. Rev: Heaven's War to Woman's Escape (12:14–16)
1. Abomination of Desolation.	The abomination of desolation occurs and the armies gather around Jerusalem. (Matt 24:15; Mark 13:14; Luke 21:20)	The nations are gathered around Jerusalem. (Zech 14:2a)		
2. Armies of the nations invade Jerusalem.	Armies invade Jerusalem. (Luke 21:21–24a)	Nations invade Jerusalem. (Zech 14:2b)		
3. The Lord splits the Mount of Olives and a large valley is created so that the Jewish inhabitants can escape the invading armies.		The Lord splits the Mount of Olives and a large valley is created. (Zech 14:4)		The woman was given the two wings of the great eagle, so that she could fly from the serpent into the wilderness, to her place where she will be nourished for a time, and times, and a half of time. (Rev 12:14)

The Sequence	Seq. Olivet Discourse (Matt 24:15–20; Mark 13:14; Luke 21:20–24)	Seq. Zech 14 (14:2, 4–5)	3rd Seq. Rev: Woman, Child, and Dragon (12:6)	4th Seq. Rev: Heaven's War to Woman's Escape (12:14–16)
4. The armies of Satan gave chase to the remnant, but the earthquake sent by God swallows some of the pursuing armies.				Then from the dragon's mouth poured water like a river after the woman, but the earth came to the aid of the woman by swallowing the river. (Rev 12:15–16)
5. Half of the inhabitants of Jerusalem escape into the wilderness. Within the survivors is the 144,000 Jewish remnant.	Many of the "readers" escape. (Matt 24:16–20)	Half of the inhabitants of Jerusalem escape and reach a safe exile. (Zech 14:2c, 5)	The woman escapes to the wilderness where she is nourished for 1,260 days. (Rev 12:6)	
6. After Jerusalem is left desolate, the gentile nations trample the city.	After Jerusalem is vacated she is left desolate, at which time the gentile nations trample the city. (Luke 21:24b)			

Table 6.7. Reconciliation of Four Sequences of the Remnant's Escape

A Fifth Account of the Remnant's Escape

Although two of the four accounts reference "the earthquake" and a third account references "the trampling of Jerusalem," does one recall reading a passage in Revelation that contained both the earthquake as well as the trampling of Jerusalem? It was the very brief Second Sequence from the third conversation, where the series of events surrounding the ministry of the two witnesses was given verbally to John by the angel and "the voice." Here are those references (italics used for emphasis):

1. "'Then I was given a measuring rod like a staff, and I was told, 'Come and measure the temple of God and the altar and those who worship there, but do not measure the court outside the temple; leave that out, *for it is given over to the nations, and they will trample over the holy city for forty-two months.* And I will grant my two witnesses authority to prophesy for one thousand two hundred sixty days, wearing sackcloth" (Rev 11:1–3).

2. "*At that moment there was a great earthquake, and a tenth of the city fell; seven thousand people were killed in the earthquake,* and the rest were terrified and gave glory to the God of heaven" (Rev 11:13).

Without specifically mentioning the invasion of Jerusalem by the nations nor the Jewish remnant's escape into the wilderness, one knows for certain that the narrative is a fifth account of the invasion because one knows the trampling of Jerusalem follows the invasion, and, secondly, of the three earthquakes referenced in Revelation, the only one that is centered around Jerusalem, as is this one, is the one that immediately follows the invasion. The other two earthquakes are global. And with these simple observations, here's the reconciliation of the five accounts:

Table 6.8. Reconciliation of Five Sequences of the Remnant's Escape					
The Sequence	Seq. Olivet Discourse (Matt 24:15–20; Mark 13:14; Luke 21:20–24)	Seq. Zech 14 (14:2, 4–5)	2nd Seq. Rev: 2 Witnesses (11:1–3, 13)	3rd Seq. Rev: Woman, Child, and Dragon (12:6)	4th Seq. Rev: Heaven's War to Woman's Escape (12:14–16)
1. Abomination of desolation.	The abomination of desolation occurs and the armies gather around Jerusalem. (Matt 24:15; Mark 13:14; Luke 21:20)	The nations are gathered around Jerusalem. (Zech 14:2a)			
2. Armies of the nations invade Jerusalem.	Armies invade Jerusalem. (Luke 21:21–24)	Nations invade Jerusalem. (Zech 14:2b)			
3. The Lord splits the Mount of Olives and a large valley is created so that the Jewish inhabitants can escape the invading armies.		The Lord splits the Mount of Olives and a large valley is created. (Zech 14:4)	God sends a great earthquake at the moment the 2 witnesses were taken back up to heaven. (Rev 11:13a)		The woman was given the 2 wings of the great eagle, so that she could fly from the serpent into the wilderness, to her place where she will be nourished for a time, and times, and a half of time. (Rev 12:14)

Table 6.8. Reconciliation of Five Sequences of the Remnant's Escape					
The Sequence	Seq. Olivet Discourse (Matt 24:15-20; Mark 13:14; Luke 21:20-24)	Seq. Zech 14 (14:2, 4-5)	2nd Seq. Rev: 2 Witnesses (11:1-3, 13)	3rd Seq. Rev: Woman, Child, and Dragon (12:6)	4th Seq. Rev: Heaven's War to Woman's Escape (12:14-16)
4. The armies of Satan gave chase to the remnant, but the earthquake sent by God swallows some of the pursuing armies.			The quake kills 7,000 people. (Rev 11:13b)		Then from the dragon's mouth poured water like a river after the woman, but the earth came to the aid of the woman by swallowing the river. (Rev 12:15-16)
5. Half of the inhabitants of Jerusalem escape into the wilderness. Within those inhabitants are the 144,000 Jewish remnant.	The "reader" escapes. (Matt 24:16-20)	Half of the inhabitants of Jerusalem escape into a safe exile. (Zech 14:2c,5)		The woman escapes to the wilderness where she is nourished for 1,260 days. (Rev 12:6)	
6. After Jerusalem is left desolate, the gentile nations trample the city for 42 months.	After Jerusalem is vacated she is left desolate, at which time the gentile nations trample the city. (Luke 21:24)		The court outside the temple was given over to the nations and they will trample the city for 42 months. (Rev 11:1-3)		

The Abomination of Desolation

Having now spent some time on the last-days invasion of Jerusalem by the nations, let's go back and recall exactly what two events prompt the Jewish inhabitants to escape the city. According to Luke's account of the Olivet Discourse, as well as Zech 14, one event will be the appearance of hostile armies:

1. "When you see Jerusalem surrounded by armies, then know that its desolation has come near. Then those in Judea must flee to the mountains, and those inside the city must leave it, and those out in the country must not enter it; for these are days of vengeance, as a fulfillment of all that is written" (Luke 21:20–22).

2. "See, a day is coming for the Lord when the plunder taken from you will be divided in your midst. For I will gather all the nations against Jerusalem to battle, and the city shall be taken . . ." (Zech 14:1–2a).

However, it is in Matthew and Mark where one sees the most infamous sign forewarning the inhabitants of Jerusalem to flee. Here's Matthew's account:

"So when you see the desolating sacrilege standing in the holy place, as was spoken by the prophet Daniel (let the reader understand), then those in Judea must flee to the mountains; the one on the housetop must not go down to take what is in the house; the one in the field must not turn back to get a coat. Woe to those who are pregnant and to those who are nursing infants in those days! Pray that your flight may not be in winter or on a sabbath" (Matt 24:15–20).

Despite the absence of a temple and despite the absence of a Holy of Holies, Jesus still warned the remnant that once you see "the desolating sacrilege standing in the holy place," flee as fast as you can. One must admit that the phrase "standing in the holy place" (Greek: *hesto en topō hagiō*) appears to initially indicate that the sacrilege will be placed inside a temple. Why would Jesus say that, especially since one now knows a temple will not be in existence? Answer: Recall, it was pointed out earlier that the phrase *hesto en topō hagiō* can also be translated "standing *on* the holy place" or "standing *at* the holy place."[6] Even without a temple, Jesus knew a desolating sacrilege would one day stand somewhere *on* or *at* the holy place, which in this instance was clearly a reference to the Temple Mount.

---

6. See p. 41.

Now, to the all important phrase in question: "the desolating sacrilege" (Greek: *tò bdelygma tēs erēmōseōs*). What will constitute this desolating sacrilege, often referred to as "the abomination of desolation"? Obviously, the word "desolating" means to cause a place to become desolate, or deserted. When the abomination causes the inhabitants of Jerusalem to flee, the city will become desolate—at least of the Jews. What about the word "sacrilege" or "abomination"? The word is generally defined as anything that causes hatred or disgust. In this case, it's something that will cause hatred or disgust in the eyes of God. The books of Proverbs and Jeremiah list several examples of acts that are abominable to God:

1. "There are six things that the Lord hates, seven that are an abomination to him: haughty eyes, a lying tongue, and hands that shed innocent blood, a heart that devises wicked plans, feet that hurry to run to evil, a lying witness who testifies falsely, and one who sows discord in a family" (Prov 6:16–19).

2. "Here you are, trusting in deceptive words to no avail. Will you steal, murder, commit adultery, swear falsely, make offerings to Baal, and go after other gods that you have not known, and then come and stand before me in this house, which is called by name, and say, 'We are safe!'—only to go on doing all these abominations?" (Jer 7:8–10).

As one can see, an abomination can be any number of sins, occurring anywhere and anytime. Therefore, this much is certain: An abomination of some kind, perhaps one of those listed above, will occur in the last days on the Temple Mount that will cause Jerusalem to become desolate, and this act, whatever it is, will cause hatred and disgust in the eyes of God.

The Identification of the Abomination of Desolation

Now to the follow-up, all important question: Does Scripture contain any account of a sinful and abominable act in the eyes of God that will cause the Jewish inhabitants to flee Jerusalem at the time of the future invasion of the city? And, of course, the answer is a resounding yes! It's in one of the five previously discussed accounts of the invasion. But which one? Well, it's not in the Olivet Discourse; there, Jesus only said there will be an abomination standing on the holy place. Neither does Zechariah reveal it, as the prophet only cites the invading armies that will trigger the remnant's escape. Lastly, the answer is not readily apparent in either of Rev 12's two narratives that record the woman's escape into the wilderness (12:1–6 and 12:7–14). That only leaves one account: the "Narrative of the Two Witnesses," found within the Second Sequence in Revelation:

"When they have finished their testimony, the beast that comes up from the bottomless pit will make war on them and conquer them and kill them, and their dead bodies will lie in the street of the great city that is prophetically called Sodom and Egypt, where also their Lord was crucified. For three and a half days members of the peoples and tribes and languages and nations will gaze at their bodies and refuse to let them be placed in a tomb; and the inhabitants of the earth will gloat over them and celebrate and exchange presents, because these two prophets had been a torment to the inhabitants of the earth.

"But after the three and a half days, the breath of life from God entered them, and they stood on their feet, and those who saw them were terrified. Then they heard a loud voice from heaven saying to them, 'Come up here!' And they went up to heaven in a cloud while their enemies watched them. At that moment there was a great earthquake, and a tenth of the city fell; seven thousand people were killed in the earthquake, and the rest were terrified and gave glory to the God of heaven" (Rev 11:7–13).

In the entire Bible, this is the only passage that reveals the mystery of the abomination of desolation: It is the murder of God's two witnesses and the subsequent desecration of their bodies for three and a half days on the Temple Mount. This abominable act—the shedding of innocent blood (Prov 6:17 and Jer 7:9)—will cause Jerusalem to become desolate in the end times. Here's the scenario:

After the completion of their 1,260-day ministry, the once invincible two witnesses will become vulnerable to the attack by the beast who comes up from the bottomless pit (Rev 11:7a). What Satan could not do in three and a half years, the beast will accomplish quickly. The beast will incite the inhabitants of the earth—the same inhabitants who had stood by helplessly, watching and seething at the two who had been a torment to them for 1,260 days—to now war against, conquer, and ultimately kill the two prophets (Rev 11:7b). After the murders, the dead bodies of the two will lie on a street on God's holy mountain for three and a half days, and will doubtless be desecrated with unspeakable acts by the deranged mob, thus fulfilling Christ's words in which he spoke of a desolating sacrilege that will be set up where it should not be (Matt 24:15 and Rev

11:8–10). In other words, the bodies will be set up in some type of public display on the Temple Mount for the sole purpose of publicly shaming the two prophets, disheartening God's people, and bringing a reproach against Jesus Christ and his name.

When the Jewish inhabitants see the abomination, some will immediately begin fleeing Jerusalem in order to save their lives—wisely heeding Christ's commandment given during the Olivet Discourse (Matt 24:15)—but others will inexplicably wait until the surrounding armies begin invading the city, not following the explicit warnings of Jesus to flee the city at the first sight of the abomination. But God is merciful; he will send an opportune earthquake that will enable the Jewish "remnant" to escape the clutches of the enemy, as the quake will kill seven thousand of the invading armies (Rev 11:13). It's the same earthquake that will swallow the flood that comes from the mouth of the dragon (Rev 12:16), and it's the same earthquake that will split the Mount of Olives from east to west, creating a large valley by which the remnant will escape into the wilderness where they will find a safe haven for 1,260 days (compare Zech 14:4–5 and Rev 12:6, 14).

The Identity of the Child

In the hours and days immediately following the murders, while the blood-stained bodies of the two witnesses are lying on a street commanding the world's attention, the inhabitants of the earth will be in a state of frenzy—mocking, exchanging gifts, and celebrating over the dead bodies of God's prophets—in one of the most despicable displays of human depravity ever witnessed (Rev 11:10). Although Scripture doesn't go into any specific detail about the desecration of the two nor the celebration over their deaths, one knows the celebration will quickly come to an abrupt halt, when, after three and a half days, God will bring the two witnesses back to life in the sight of the whole world. But he will not stop there. The Lord will then lift the two men bodily into the air and rapture them back to heaven and his throne! Now, where have we recently read of anyone being caught up to heaven like these two witnesses? Answer: In the "*Narrative of the Woman, the Child, and the Dragon*," which comprised the very brief Third Sequence in Revelation (italics used for emphasis):

"A great portent appeared in heaven: a woman clothed with the sun, with the moon under her feet, and on her head a crown of twelve stars.

She was pregnant and was crying out in birth pangs, in the agony of giving birth. Then another portent appeared in heaven: a great red dragon, with seven heads and ten horns, and seven diadems on his heads. His tail swept down a third of the stars of heaven and threw them to the earth. Then the dragon stood before the woman who was about to bear a child, so that he might devour her child as soon as it was born. And she gave birth to a son, a male child, who is to rule all the nations with a rod of iron. *But her child was snatched away and taken to God and to his throne; and the woman fled into the wilderness, where she had a place prepared by God, so that she can be nourished for one thousand two hundred sixty days"* (Rev 12:1–6).

The child was snatched up to heaven just as the two witnesses! And when was the child snatched up? Prior to the woman's escape from the dragon (Rev 12:5b), just as the two witnesses were caught up to heaven prior to the remnant's escape from Satan (Rev 11:12). And what happened the moment the child was raptured? The earth came to the aid of the woman and swallowed the flood that came from the mouth of the dragon (Rev 12:16), just as God sent an earthquake the moment the two witnesses were brought back up to heaven (Rev 11:13). It should be perfectly obvious to the reader that the "symbolic child" represents the two witnesses, or more precisely, "the two witnesses and their 1,260-day ministry." Observe (italics used for emphasis):

Table 6.9. The Child Represents the Two Witnesses and Their 1,260-Day Ministry		
The Sequence	2nd Seq. Rev: 2 Witnesses (11:3–13)	3rd Seq. Rev: Woman, Child, and Dragon (12:1–6)
1. The 2 witnesses are about to begin their 1,260-day ministry.		The woman was pregnant. (Rev 12:1–2)
2. Satan waits in Jerusalem, where the Jewish remnant lives, in an effort to stop the ministry of the 2 witnesses at its inception.		The dragon waited in front of the woman in order to devour the child once it was born. (Rev 12:3–4)
3. The 2 witnesses begin their 1,260-day ministry from atop the Temple Mount.	*The 2 witnesses begin their 1,260-day ministry from atop the Temple Mount.* (Rev 11:3)	A male child was born. (Rev 12:5a)

Table 6.9. The Child Represents the Two Witnesses and Their 1,260-Day Ministry		
The Sequence	**2nd Seq. Rev: 2 Witnesses (11:3–13)**	**3rd Seq. Rev: Woman, Child, and Dragon (12:1–6)**
4. The 2 witnesses minister the gospel with signs and wonders.	The 2 witnesses testify of Christ and have the authority to strike the earth with every kind of plague as often as they desire. (Rev 11:4–6)	
5. After the witnesses complete their 1,260-day ministry, the beast that comes up from the bottomless pit wars against, conquers, and kills the 2 witnesses.	After the witnesses complete their 1,260-day ministry, the beast that comes up from the bottomless pit wars against, conquers, and kills the 2 witnesses. (Rev 11:7)	
6. The bodies of the 2 witnesses will lie on the Temple Mount for 3 1/2 days. During this time the inhabitants of the world will celebrate and exchange gifts because the two prophets had been a torment to them.	The bodies of the 2 witnesses will lie on the Temple Mount for 3 1/2 days. During this time the inhabitants of the world will celebrate and exchange gifts because the two prophets had been a torment to them. (Rev 8–10)	
7. Three and a half days after the 2 witnesses are murdered, they are raised to life and snatched back up to heaven.	*Three and a half days after the 2 witnesses are murdered, they are raised to life and snatched back up to heaven. (Rev 11:11–12)*	*The child was snatched up to heaven and to God's throne. (Rev 12:5b)*
8. Within the hour that the 2 witnesses are taken back to heaven, God splits the Mount of Olives in order to help the 144,000 escape into the wilderness where they will be nourished for 1,260 days. The earthquake kills 7,000 people.	God sends a great earthquake within the hour that the 2 witnesses were taken back up to heaven. The quake kills 7,000 people. (Rev 11:13)	
9. The 144,000 Jewish remnant escapes to the wilderness where they are nourished for 1,260 days.		The woman escapes to the wilderness where she is nourished for 1,260 days. (Rev 12:6)

THE SEQUENCE

Although Christ will indeed rule all the nations with a rod of iron (compare Ps 2:9 and Rev 19:15), "the child" was never a reference to the Lord, but rather to the two witnesses whom the Lord will give that same authority to rule all the nations with a rod of iron along with everyone else who conquers and continues to do Christ's works:

"To everyone who conquers and continues to do my works to the end, I will give authority over the nations; to rule them with an iron rod, as when clay pots are shattered—even as I received authority from my Father. To the one who conquers I will also give the morning star. Let anyone who has an ear listen to what the Spirit is saying to the churches" (Rev 2:26–29).

And which "Christ's works" were the two witnesses going to continue to do? Preach the gospel to the whole world; Christ indicated as much in the Olivet Discourse, when he spoke about their world ministry immediately followed by their deaths (italics used for emphasis):

"And *this good news of the kingdom will be proclaimed throughout the world*, as a testimony to all the nations; and then the end will come . . . *So when you see the desolating sacrilege standing in the holy place*, as was spoken by the prophet Daniel (let the reader understand), then those in Judea must flee to the mountains; the one on the housetop must not go down to take what is in the house; the one in the field must not turn back to get a coat. Woe to those who are pregnant and to those who are nursing infants in those days! Pray that your flight may not be in winter or on a sabbath" (Matt 24:14–20).

Do you recall when the question was earlier posed, Why might the Lord consider the murder of the two witnesses as the beginning of the end?[7] Now, one knows the answer. Christ knew that after the two witnesses proclaimed the good news of the kingdom throughout the world as a testimony to all nations (24:14), they would then be murdered by the beast and for three and a half days their dead bodies would be displayed on the Temple Mount (24:15), and, furthermore, he knew this event constituted the abomination of desolation, and to Christ the abomination was the beginning of the end.

---

7. See p. 156.

FOURTH SEQUENCE IN REVELATION, PART 1

The Third and Final Reconciliation of the Child and the War

With our newfound knowledge that "the child" is representative of the two witnesses and their 1,260-day ministry, one is now almost able to properly reconcile the events surrounding "the child" and "the war." Here's where we left off:

Table 6.5. The Second Reconciliation of the Third and Fourth Sequences	
3rd Seq. Rev: Woman, Child, and Dragon **(12:1–6)**	**4th Seq. Rev: Heaven's War to Woman's Escape** **(12:7–14)**
1. The woman appeared and was pregnant (12:1–2). 2. A dragon appeared. With his tail, he swept down 1/3 of the stars of heaven and threw them to the earth (12:3). 3. The dragon waited in front of the woman in order to devour the child at birth (12:4). 4. A male child was born (12:5a).	
5. The child was snatched up to heaven and to God's throne (12:5b).	1. War broke out in heaven. Michael and his angels fought against the dragon, and the dragon and his angels fought back (12:7). 2. The dragon and his angels were defeated. They were thrown down to the earth (12:8–9). 3. A voice proclaimed that the devil had been cast to the earth and the brethren had conquered the devil. The earth and the sea were then warned that the devil had come down to them with great wrath because he knows that his time is short (12:10–12). 4. When the dragon saw that he had been thrown down to the earth, he pursued the woman who had given birth to the male child (12:13).

THE SEQUENCE

Table 6.5. The Second Reconciliation of the Third and Fourth Sequences	
3rd Seq. Rev: Woman, Child, and Dragon (12:1–6)	4th Seq. Rev: Heaven's War to Woman's Escape (12:7–14)
The woman fled into the wilderness where she was nourished for 1,260 days (12:6).	The woman was given the 2 wings of an eagle so she could fly from the serpent into the wilderness for a time, and times, and half a time (12:14).

As one again examines the chart, two previous conclusions are now better understood:

1. The fact that the war between Michael and Satan will start after the birth of the child simply means that the war will start after the two witnesses begin their ministry.
2. The fact that the child will be caught up to heaven before the woman flees to the wilderness means that the two witnesses will be caught up to heaven before the 144,000 Jewish remnant flees Jerusalem.

Although the above conclusions are invaluable, in order to completely understand the events surrounding the 1,260-day ministry of the two witnesses and the war in heaven between Michael and Satan, one must additionally reconcile the following three relationships:

1. The murder of the two witnesses and the end of the war.
2. The murder of the two witnesses and the start of the war.
3. The rapture of the two witnesses and the end of the war.

Let's examine:

First Additional Reconciliation: The Murder of the Two Witnesses and the End of the War

In order to reconcile the murders and the war's end, one must reexamine the voice's proclamation in heaven immediately after the war:

"Then I heard a loud voice in heaven, proclaiming, 'Now have come the salvation and the power and the kingdom of our God and the authority of his Messiah, for the accuser of our brothers has been thrown down, who accuses them day and night before our God. But they have conquered him by the blood of the Lamb and by the word of their testimony, for they did not cling to life even in the face of death. Rejoice then, you heavens and those who dwell in them! But woe to the earth and the sea, for the devil has come down to you with great wrath, because he knows that his time is short!'" Rev 12:10–12.

Who are "our brothers" (v. 10), Greek: *adelphōn hēmōn*, who conquered the devil by the blood of the Lamb and by the word of their testimony, and did not cling to life in the face of death? Since it is universally assumed that they are representative of "the saints" throughout history, then the reader might wonder how does the voice's proclamation concerning the faithfulness of the saints have anything to do with reconciling the murder of the two witnesses and the end of the war? And therein lies the point: The phrase "our brothers" is not representative of the saints throughout history; it specifically represents the two witnesses. And the proof? Although it is certainly true that all believers defeat the devil by the blood of the Lamb and, in some cases, by the word of their testimony, one must concede that few believers, in comparison to the total number of believers, have clung to life in the face of death for the cause of Christ. In other words, more saints have died to this point as non-martyrs than martyrs. But one might interject, "What about the last-days saints? Couldn't the 'brothers' represent the multiplied millions of saints who will be killed during the great tribulation, especially during its period of martyrdom? Surely they will not cling to life in the face of death!" That's absolutely true; the martyred, tribulation-saints won't cling to life. However, at the moment the voice proclaimed that the brothers "did not cling to life even in the face of death," the great tribulation with its period of martyrdom will not have occurred as of yet. Observe:

Table 6.10. The Two Witnesses Die as Martyrs before the Great Tribulation					
1,260-day ministry of the 2 witnesses	Abomination of Desolation (2 witnesses are martyred)	The voice proclaims the faithfulness of the "brothers"	The Great Tribulation		The Day of the Lord
			Nuclear war (Saints die during the war)	Nuclear aftermath (Saints die during the aftermath and . . . are killed during the period of martyrdom)	
	^ 2 Witnesses Martyred		^ Saints Martyred		

As one can see, "our brothers" cannot represent the tribulation-saints because at the time of the voice's proclamation the only ones who have died as martyrs since the beginning of the two witnesses' ministry are the two witnesses.[8] And the conclusion? The two witnesses are the subject of the voice's proclamation in heaven. They are . . .

1. the ones whom the devil will accuse day and night for 1,260 straight days.

2. the ones who will conquer the devil by the blood of the Lamb and by the word of their testimony on the Temple Mount for 1,260 straight days.

3. the ones who, after their 1,260-day ministry is fulfilled, will be mercilessly attacked and murdered by the beast prior to the voice's proclamation in heaven that Satan has been cast to the earth and that the two witnesses did not cling to life in the face of death.

Although the voice proclaimed that Satan had been cast down to the earth, as well as that the witnesses did not cling to life when martyred by

---

8. Even the vocabulary used during the voice's proclamation harkens back to the vocabulary used in the initial description of the two witnesses (italics used for emphasis): (1) "But they have conquered him by the blood of the Lamb and by the word of their *testimony* [Greek: *martyrias*], for they did not cling to life in the face of death" (Rev 12:11). (2) "And I will grant my two *witnesses* [Greek: *martysin*] authority to prophesy for one thousand two hundred sixty days, wearing sackcloth" (Rev 11:3).

the beast, still, it is obvious that this most recent development—Michael's casting down of Satan—is what prompted the proclamation. Observe:

"Then I heard a loud voice in heaven, proclaiming, 'Now have come the salvation and the power and the kingdom of our God and the authority of his Messiah, for the accuser of our brothers has been thrown down...'" (Rev 12:10a).

Since Satan has just "now" been cast down, it is certain that the witnesses were martyred prior to the end of the war.

Second Additional Reconciliation: The Murder of the Witnesses and the Start of the War

How does the murder of the two witnesses relate to the start of the war, i.e., when Michael attacked Satan? With the newfound knowledge that the two will be killed before the war's end, there are only two possibilities: they will be killed before the war starts or during the war. Observe:

	Table 6.11. The Relationship of the Murder of the Witnesses and the Start of the War
Option #1:	The beast kills the two witnesses before Michael attacks Satan. (This necessitates that Michael attacks Satan after the 1,260-day ministry of the witnesses.)
Option #2:	The beast kills the two witnesses after Michael attacks Satan. (This necessitates that Michael attacks Satan during the 1,260-day ministry of the two witnesses.)

As pointed out earlier, the fact that Michael and his angels fought against Satan, and Satan and his angels fought back, proves that Michael started the war, not Satan.[9] Since this is the case, one might now more easily determine which seems more likely: that God would commission Michael to attack Satan after the two witnesses were murdered by the beast (option #1), or during the 1,260-day ministry of the two witnesses (option #2)? Answer: There seems to be no conspicuous reason that God would commission Michael to attack Satan during the 1,260-day ministry of the two witnesses because the timing of that attack, which one now knows will result in a quick casting down of Satan to the earth, could only adversely affect the ministry of the witnesses. God has already

---

9. See p. 165.

preordained that the two witnesses will minister unimpeded during the full 1,260 days from the Temple Mount because the 144,000 Jewish remnant will need to hear the two's ministry, as well as the rest of the unconfessed elect around the world. On the other hand, there will be a very significant reason for God to commission Michael to attack and cast Satan to the earth immediately after the beast murders the two witnesses (option #1). How so? It will be time for the 144,000 Jewish remnant to get from point A to point B. With the greatest suffering in the history of mankind looming just around the corner, i.e., the nuclear war, the safety of the 144,000 Jewish remnant will theoretically be at stake. Because of this, God will proceed to move his "unconverted" Jewish remnant to a place of protection in the wilderness where they will be sheltered and nourished for 1,260 days. God knows that once Michael casts Satan to the ground, an angry and humiliated devil will pursue the 144,000, flushing the remnant out of the city and into the wilderness that God has prepared for them (Rev 12:13).[10] And to ensure that his remnant successfully reaches their destination, just for good measure, God will split the Mount of Olives to provide the remnant a pathway for escape. In the end, God has everything planned from the start: the 1,260-day ministry of the two witnesses, their deaths by the beast, the commissioning of Michael to attack Satan, the casting down of an angry and defeated devil to the earth, the chasing of the remnant into the wilderness, the 1,260-day Jewish exile, and, of course, prior to the end of that exile, the conversion of the 144,000 Jewish remnant at the appearance of the heavenly signs. God will leave nothing to chance.

Third Additional Reconciliation: The End of the War and the Rapture of the Witnesses

Knowing that Michael will attack Satan immediately after the beast murders the two witnesses, and yet the two will be raised to life and raptured back to heaven exactly three and a half days after their murders, how

---

10. The timeline of God's commission of Michael, which includes the archangel's rising to engage Satan, Satan's expulsion from heaven, and the Jewish remnant's deliverance into the wilderness, is clearly evidenced in the following:

"At that time Michael, the great prince, the protector of your people shall arise. There shall be a time of anguish, such as has never occurred since nations first came into existence. But at that time your people shall be delivered, everyone who is found written in the book." (Dan 12:1)

does the timing of Michael's casting down of Satan, i.e., the war's end, relate to the rapture of the two witnesses? Will Michael cast Satan to the earth before the two are raised to life or afterwards? In all likelihood, Michael will cast Satan to the earth after the rapture of the two witnesses and not before, for the simple reason that immediately prior to the two's rapture up to heaven, the Scripture clearly indicates that the inhabitants of the earth will be participating in a three-and-a-half-day state of frenzied celebration over their deaths (Rev 11:9–10), and since Scripture also indicates that when Michael casts Satan to the earth the devil will immediately pursue the Jewish remnant (Rev 12:13), it seems logical that the celebration by the inhabitants and the pursuit of the Jewish remnant by Satan will not overlap, thus ensuring that the three-and-a-half-day celebration remains uninterrupted. Observe:

Table 6.12. The Celebration Will Doubtless End before the Armies Pursue	
The 3 1/2 day celebration by the inhabitants ends with the rapture of the two witnesses.	Then Satan is cast down and his armies immediately pursue the Jewish remnant.

Although the above scenario might seem to allow for the possibility that the war between Michael and Satan could continue indefinitely after the rapture of the two witnesses, nothing could be further from the truth. Michael will make short work of the battle, bringing an end to it within an hour of the witnesses' rapture. How so? Once Satan is cast down and begins to pursue the remnant (Rev 12:13), God will send an earthquake "within the hour" of the witnesses' rapture in order to swallow part of the pursuing armies. Observe (italics used for emphasis):[11]

"But after the three and a half days, the breath of life from God entered them, and they stood on their feet, and those who saw them were terrified. Then they heard a loud voice from heaven saying to them, 'Come up here!' And they went up to heaven in a cloud while their enemies watched them. *At that moment* there was a great earthquake, and a tenth of the city fell; seven thousand people were killed in the earthquake, and the rest were terrified and gave glory to the God of heaven" (Rev 11:11–13).

Here's a schematic illustrating the timeline:

---

11. The Greek phrase *en ekeinē tē hōra*, here translated "At that moment" (v. 13), literally means "in that hour."

Table 6.13. The War in Heaven Will Last Less Than Three and a Half Days				
	<————The War in Heaven————> (Michael and Satan) (12:7–9)		Satan Pursues the Remnant (12:13)	The Remnant Escapes (12:6, 14)
	^ Michael Attacks Satan (12:7)		^ Michael Cast Satan to the Earth (12:9)	
1,260-Day Ministry of the 2 Witnesses (11:3)	<-Bodies of the 2 Witnesses-> Lie on the Temple Mount for 3 1/2 Days (Inhabitants of the Earth Celebrate) (11:8–10)		<—Within the Hour——> (11:13)	
^ The Beast Murders the 2 (11:7)		^ God Raptures the 2 (11:11–12, 12:5)		^ The Earthquake (11:13, 12:16)

And with the preceding discussion, the third of the three time-relationships has now been determined, enabling one to ascertain the final reconciliation of the third and fourth sequences:

Table 6.14. The Third and Final Reconciliation of the Third and Fourth Sequences	
3rd Seq. Rev: Woman, Child, and Dragon (12:1–6)	4th Seq. Rev: Heaven's War to Woman's Escape (12:7–16)
1. The woman appeared and was pregnant (12:1–2). 2. A dragon appeared. With his tail, he swept down 1/3 of the stars of heaven and threw them to the earth (12:3). 3. The dragon waited in front of the woman in order to devour the child at birth (12:4). 4. A male child was born (12:5a).	

Table 6.14. The Third and Final Reconciliation of the Third and Fourth Sequences	
3rd Seq. Rev: Woman, Child, and Dragon (12:1–6)	4th Seq. Rev: Heaven's War to Woman's Escape (12:7–16)
	5. War broke out in heaven. Michael and his angels fought against the dragon, and the dragon and his angels fought back (12:7).
6. The child was snatched up to heaven and to God's throne (12:5b).	
	7. The dragon and his angels were defeated. They were thrown down to the earth (12:8–9).
	8. A voice in heaven proclaimed that the devil had been cast to the earth and the brethren had conquered the devil. The earth and the sea were then warned that the devil had come down to them with great wrath because he knows that his time is short (12:10–12).
	9. When the dragon saw that he had been thrown down to the earth, he pursued the woman who had given birth to the male child (12:13).
	10. The woman was given the 2 wings of an eagle so she could fly from the serpent into the wilderness for a time, and times, and half a time (12:14).
	11. Out of the mouth of the dragon came water like a river to sweep the woman away, i.e., the armies of Satan chased the 144,000 Jewish remnant (12:15).
	12. The earth came to the aid of the woman and swallowed the flood, i.e., God sent an earthquake to swallow the armies of Satan (12:16).
13. The woman fled into the wilderness where she was nourished for 1,260 days (12:6).	

(Note: The reason "the woman's escape" in 12:14 has now been placed prior to "the woman's escape" in 12:6 is because 12:14 technically indicates that the woman is about to flee, whereas in 12:6, she has already fled.)

The Identity of the Woman: Our First Inclination Was Correct

After Satan fails to catch the woman by means of the pursuing armies, he will be frustrated, humiliated, and angry. Pondering his next move, he will then turn his attention to the rest of the woman's children:

> Then the dragon was angry with the woman, and went off to make war on the rest of her children, those who keep the commandments of God and hold the testimony of Jesus. (Rev 12:17)

As you recall, our first inclination was that the woman symbolized something closely related to the 144,000 Jewish remnant. This inclination has proven to be correct. When the woman fled Jerusalem, the 144,000 fled Jerusalem; when the woman was pursued by the dragon, the 144,000 was pursued by Satan; and when the woman reached the wilderness and was nourished for 1,260 days, so too the 144,000. It's abundantly clear that the woman symbolizes the 144,000 Jewish remnant.

Now one learns that not only has the woman given birth to "the child" but she has given birth to other children as well, to those who keep the commandments of God and hold the testimony of Jesus. In other words, not only has the woman given birth to the 1,260-day ministry of the two witnesses, but she has somehow given birth to other Christians as well! How can that be? Concerning the ministry of the two witnesses, because the unconverted 144,000 Jewish remnant will need to hear the gospel before they flee into the wilderness, God will send the ministry of Elijah and Enoch to Israel. In this sense, the 144,000 remnant will give birth to the ministry of the two witnesses. Recall the words of Malachi:

"Lo, I will send you the prophet Elijah before the great and terrible day of the Lord comes. He will turn the hearts of parents to their children and the hearts of children to their parents, so that I will not come and strike the land with a curse" (Mal 4:5–6).

In short, the spiritual need of the remnant will "birth" or "lead to" the appearance of the two witnesses, after their several-thousand-year hiatus. And although the 1,260-day ministry of the two will not result in the immediate conversion of the 144,000, it will certainly be the means by which God "calls" the 144,000.[12] After escaping Jerusalem at the abomination, the remnant will eventually see the appearance of the heavenly signs, and then, recalling the words spoken by the two and realizing that Christ is indeed the Messiah, they will promptly confess the name of Jesus Christ just before the arrival of the great and terrible Day of the Lord.

As to the next question: "How will the woman give birth to other Christians?" the answer is even easier than the first. It should go without saying that when the two prophets arrive and begin to preach Christ from high atop the Temple Mount every day for 1,260 days, and their ministry is viewed electronically by the entire world, that untold numbers of people will confess Christ and enter God's kingdom. In this sense the woman's need of salvation, which led to the arrival of the two witnesses' ministry, will also give birth to other Christians.

Concluding Thoughts: The Most Misunderstood Chapter in Revelation

Without a doubt, the chapter containing the portents of the woman, the child, and the dragon is the most misunderstood chapter in Revelation. By assuming the child represents Jesus and mistakenly believing that Rev 12 concerns the past events of the Lord's birth and ascension, regrettably, most have missed God's portrayal of the next major event on the apocalyptic calendar, which is the 1,260-day ministry of Elijah and Enoch. Rather than anticipating the appearance of the two witnesses of God on the Temple Mount, most in the church are either anticipating the sudden rapture of the saints or the sudden appearance of the man of lawlessness, both of which will come well after the ministry of the two witnesses. Nonetheless, one thing is certain: Satan is not anticipating wrongly. It is the looming appearance of the two witnesses that keeps him up at night, as it were. This explains the seemingly inexplicable reason that when the time comes, he and his angels will concentrate in and around Jerusalem, searching for any sign that the two witnesses have finally arrived (Rev 12:4). Satan knows that once they appear, the apocalyptic clock will start ticking, and that's why he will be frightened beyond all measure when he finally sees the faces of Elijah and Enoch a second time, having dreaded their return for millennia.

---

12. See table 2.2. "The Steps of Salvation." In the chart, God's "call" is listed as the third step, p. 49.

Not only is the appearance of the two witnesses on the Temple Mount the next great, supernatural event that will shock the world, but now one also knows that the murder of the two at the end of their 1,260-day ministry is what constitutes the abomination of desolation, which is yet another subject that has been abysmally misunderstood by theologians and commentators. Nevertheless, the correct interpretation of Rev 12 has been presented, and because of that, the reader is now in position to understand the period that will immediately follow the abomination of desolation, which is a time of unprecedented suffering that Jesus said will be "such as has not been from the beginning of the world until now, no, and never will be" (Matt 24:21).

∼

The following is the reconciliation of the six sequences from the beginning of the ministry of the two witnesses until the moment that Satan will go off to make war on the rest of the saints (the newly included events of Rev 12 are italicized):

FOURTH SEQUENCE IN REVELATION, PART 1

Table 6.15. Reconciliation of the Six Sequences from the Beginning of the Two Witnesses' 1,260-Day Ministry to the Moment Satan Will Go Off to Make War on the Rest of the Saints

The Sequence	Seq. 1 & 2 Thess	Seq. Olivet Discourse (Matt 24:15–20; Luke 21:21–24)	1st Seq. Rev, Part 1: Through 7 Trumpets	2nd Seq. Rev: 2 Witnesses (11:1–13)	3rd Seq. Rev: Woman, Child, and Dragon (12:1–6)	4th Seq. Rev: Heaven's War to Woman's Escape (12:7–17)
1. The 2 witnesses are about to begin their 1,260-day ministry.					A pregnant woman appeared. (Rev 12:1–2)	
2. Satan brings down 1/3 of the angels in an all-out effort to stop the ministry of the 2 witnesses at its inception.					The dragon swept down 1/3 of the stars of heaven and threw them to the earth. He waited before the woman in order to devour the child once it was born. (Rev 12:3–4)	
3. Despite Satan's efforts, the 2 witnesses begin their 1,260-day ministry from atop the Temple Mount.				The 2 witnesses begin their 1,260-day ministry from atop the Temple Mount. (Rev 11:3)	A male child was born. (Rev 12:5a)	

203

Table 6.15. Reconciliation of the Six Sequences from the Beginning of the Two Witnesses' 1,260-Day Ministry to the Moment Satan Will Go Off to Make War on the Rest of the Saints

The Sequence	Seq. 1 & 2 Thess	Seq. Olivet Discourse (Matt 24:15–20; Luke 21:21–24)	1st Seq. Rev, Part 1: Through 7 Trumpets	2nd Seq. Rev: 2 Witnesses (11:1–13)	3rd Seq. Rev: Woman, Child, and Dragon (12:1–6)	4th Seq. Rev: Heaven's War to Woman's Escape (12:7–17)
4. The 2 witnesses testify of Christ and have the authority to strike the earth with every kind of plague, as often as they desire.				The 2 witnesses testify of Christ and have the authority to strike the earth with every kind of plague, as often as they desire. (Rev 11:4–6)		
5. The abomination of desolation occurs when, after the witnesses have completed their 1,260-day ministry, the beast that comes up from the bottomless pit wars against, conquers, and kills the 2 witnesses.		Abomination of desolation. (Matt 24:15)		When the witnesses complete their 1,260-day ministry, the beast that comes up from the bottomless pit wars against, conquers, and kills the 2 witnesses. (Rev 11:7)		

Table 6.15. Reconciliation of the Six Sequences from the Beginning of the Two Witnesses' 1,260-Day Ministry to the Moment Satan Will Go Off to Make War on the Rest of the Saints

The Sequence	Seq. 1 & 2 Thess	Seq. Olivet Discourse (Matt 24:15–20; Luke 21:21–24)	1st Seq. Rev, Part 1: Through 7 Trumpets	2nd Seq. Rev: 2 Witnesses (11:1–13)	3rd Seq. Rev: Woman, Child, and Dragon (12:1–6)	4th Seq. Rev: Heaven's War to Woman's Escape (12:7–17)
6. Immediately after the beast kills the 2 witnesses and the inhabitants of the earth begin celebrating the deaths of the 2, the Lord commissions Michael and his angels to attack Satan and his angels in heaven.				The bodies of the 2 witnesses will lie on the Temple Mount for 3 1/2 days, as the inhabitants of the earth celebrate and exchange gifts because the 2 prophets had been a torment to them. (Rev 11:8–10)		War broke out in heaven. Michael and his angels fought against the dragon, and the dragon and his angels fought back. (Rev 12:7)
7. Three and a half days after the murder of the 2 witnesses, they are raised to life and snatched back up to heaven.				Three and a half days after the beast murders the 2 witnesses, they were raised to life and snatched back up to heaven. (Rev 11:11–12)	The child was snatched up to heaven and to God's throne. (Rev 12:5b)	

Table 6.15. Reconciliation of the Six Sequences from the Beginning of the Two Witnesses' 1,260-Day Ministry to the Moment Satan Will Go Off to Make War on the Rest of the Saints

The Sequence	Seq. 1 & 2 Thess	Seq. Olivet Discourse (Matt 24:15–20; Luke 21:21–24)	1st Seq. Rev, Part 1: Through 7 Trumpets	2nd Seq. Rev: 2 Witnesses (11:1–13)	3rd Seq. Rev: Woman, Child, and Dragon (12:1–6)	4th Seq. Rev: Heaven's War to Woman's Escape (12:7–17)
8. Michael and his angels defeat Satan and his angels and cast them out of heaven to the earth.						Michael and his angels defeated the dragon and his angels and cast them down to the earth. (Rev 12:8–9)
9. A voice in heaven proclaimed that the devil had been cast to the earth and that the 2 witnesses had defeated the devil by the blood of the Lamb and by the word of their testimony; the 2 witnesses did not cling to life even in the face of death.						A voice in heaven proclaimed that the devil had been cast to the earth and "the brethren" had defeated the devil by the blood of the Lamb and by the word of their testimony. They did not cling to life in the face of death. (Rev 12:10–12)

FOURTH SEQUENCE IN REVELATION, PART 1

Table 6.15. Reconciliation of the Six Sequences from the Beginning of the Two Witnesses' 1,260-Day Ministry to the Moment Satan Will Go Off to Make War on the Rest of the Saints

The Sequence	Seq. 1 & 2 Thess	Seq. Olivet Discourse (Matt 24:15-20; Luke 21:21-24)	1st Seq. Rev, Part 1: Through 7 Trumpets	2nd Seq. Rev: 2 Witnesses (11:1-13)	3rd Seq. Rev: Woman, Child, and Dragon (12:1-6)	4th Seq. Rev: Heaven's War to Woman's Escape (12:7-17)
10. When Satan saw that he has been cast down to the earth, he invades the city of Jerusalem with the armies of the surrounding nations and pursues the 144,000 Jewish remnant.		Armies invade Jerusalem. Many of the inhabitants of the city will fall by the edge of the sword and be taken away as captives among all nations. (Luke 21:21-24a)				When the dragon saw that he had been thrown down to the earth, he pursued the woman who had given birth to the male child. (Rev 12:13)

207

THE SEQUENCE

Table 6.15. Reconciliation of the Six Sequences from the Beginning of the Two Witnesses' 1,260-Day Ministry to the Moment Satan Will Go Off to Make War on the Rest of the Saints

The Sequence	Seq: 1 & 2 Thess	Seq. Olivet Discourse (Matt 24:15–20; Luke 21:21–24)	1st Seq. Rev, Part 1: Through 7 Trumpets	2nd Seq. Rev: 2 Witnesses (11:1–13)	3rd Seq. Rev: Woman, Child, and Dragon (12:1–6)	4th Seq. Rev: Heaven's War to Woman's Escape (12:7–17)
11. As the armies of Satan attack Jerusalem, the 144,000 Jewish remnant begins to flee into the wilderness, where she will be protected and nourished for 1,260 days.						*The woman was given the 2 wings of the great eagle, so that she could fly from the serpent into the wilderness, to her place where she will be nourished for a time, and times, and half a time. (Rev 12:14)*
12. Satan's armies give chase.						*From the dragon's mouth poured water like a river after the woman. (Rev 12:15)*

208

FOURTH SEQUENCE IN REVELATION, PART 1

Table 6.15. Reconciliation of the Six Sequences from the Beginning of the Two Witnesses' 1,260-Day Ministry to the Moment Satan Will Go Off to Make War on the Rest of the Saints

The Sequence	Seq. 1 & 2 Thess	Seq. Olivet Discourse (Matt 24:15–20; Luke 21:21–24)	1st Seq. Rev, Part 1: Through 7 Trumpets	2nd Seq. Rev: 2 Witnesses (11:1–13)	3rd Seq. Rev: Woman, Child, and Dragon (12:1–6)	4th Seq. Rev: Heaven's War to Woman's Escape (12:7–17)
						But the earth came to the aid of the woman by swallowing the river. (Rev 12:16)
				God sends a great earthquake at the very hour the 2 witnesses were taken back up to heaven. The quake kills 7,000 people. (Rev 11:13)		
					The woman escapes to the wilderness where she is nourished for 1,260 days. (Rev 12:6)	
		The "reader" escapes. (Matt 24:16–20)				
13. God splits the Mount of Olives in order to help the 144,000 Jewish remnant escape into the wilderness. The earthquake kills 7,000 people.						
14. With the aid of the earthquake, the 144,000 Jewish remnant escapes to the wilderness where she is nourished for 1,260 days.						

209

THE SEQUENCE

Table 6.15. Reconciliation of the Six Sequences from the Beginning of the Two Witnesses' 1,260-Day Ministry to the Moment Satan Will Go Off to Make War on the Rest of the Saints

The Sequence	Seq. 1 & 2 Thess	Seq. Olivet Discourse (Matt 24:15–20; Luke 21:21–24)	1st Seq. Rev, Part 1: Through 7 Trumpets	2nd Seq. Rev: 2 Witnesses (11:1–13)	3rd Seq. Rev: Woman, Child, and Dragon (12:1–6)	4th Seq. Rev: Heaven's War to Woman's Escape (12:7–17)
15. Having failed to catch the fleeing 144,000 Jewish remnant, Satan turns his attention to other Christians around the world.						*Angry with the woman, the dragon went off to make war on the rest of her children.* (12:17)

210

CHAPTER 7

Fourth Sequence, Part 2

The First and Second Beasts (12:18—13:18)

First Sequence	Second Sequence	Third Sequence	Fourth Sequence
		Chapter 6 3rd Seq.: The Woman, the Child, and the Dragon (12:1–6)	
			Chapter 6 (cont.) 4th Seq., Part 1: The War in Heaven to the Woman's Escape (12:7–17)
			Chapter 7* 4th Seq., Part 2: The 1st and 2nd Beasts (12:18—13:18)
			Chapter 8 4th Seq., Part 3: Mount Zion to the Worship around God's Throne (14:1—15:4)

THE SEQUENCE

AFTER FAILING TO CATCH the Jewish remnant as they miraculously escaped into the wilderness, Satan abandoned that lost cause and went off to make war on other Christians around the world, or as John put it, "the rest of her children, those who keep the commandments of God and hold the testimony of Jesus." Then John saw Satan take his stand on the sand of the seashore:

> Then the dragon took his stand on the sand of the seashore. And I saw a beast rising out of the sea, having ten horns and seven heads; and on its horns were ten diadems, and on its heads were blasphemous names. (Rev 12:18—13:1)

One knows definitively that the scene of the dragon standing on the seashore is a continuation of the Fourth Sequence in Revelation because this event immediately follows Satan's failure of catching the escaping 144,000 Jewish remnant into the wilderness (Rev 12:16–17), which, as you know, was the last event recorded in the Fourth Sequence to date.

Note that when John saw the beast "rising out of the sea" this could not have been the moment of the beast's release from the bottomless pit. By the time the dragon was seen taking his stand on the seashore, the following had already transpired: The beast had been released from the pit and killed the two witnesses, the witnesses had been caught back up to heaven, Michael had cast Satan to the earth, and the Jewish remnant had escaped the armies of Satan and found a safe haven in the wilderness. Here's the reconciled sequence from the beast's release out of the bottomless pit to his rendezvous with Satan at the seashore:

Table 7.1. Tracking the Beast: From the Bottomless Pit to the Seashore	
2nd Seq. Rev: 2 Witnesses (11:7, 11–12)	**4th Seq. Rev: Heaven's War to Appearance of Beast at Seashore (12:7–9, 13–18, 13:1)**
1. The beast comes up from the bottomless pit and kills the 2 witnesses. (11:7)	
2. The 2 witnesses are resurrected and taken up to heaven. (11:11–12)	
	3. Michael casts Satan to the earth. (12:7–9)

Table 7.1. Tracking the Beast: From the Bottomless Pit to the Seashore	
2nd Seq. Rev: 2 Witnesses (11:7, 11–12)	**4th Seq. Rev: Heaven's War to Appearance of Beast at Seashore (12:7–9, 13–18, 13:1)**
	4. The dragon pursues the 144,000. (12:13)
	5. The 144,000 was given the 2 wings of the great eagle, so that they could fly from Satan into the wilderness, where they will be protected and nourished for 1,260 days. Satan's armies pursue the 144,000. (12:14–15)
	6. The earthquake sent by God will swallow 7,000 people of the armies. (12:16)
	7. After Satan fails to catch the 144,000, he will turn his attention to other Christians. (12:17)
	8. Satan stands on the sand of the shore as the beast rises out of the sea. (12:18—13:1)

Since the beast's "rising out of the sea" cannot be representative of his "release from the bottomless pit," then what does it represent? The next verse reveals the answer:

> And the beast that I saw was like a leopard, its feet were like a bear's, and its mouth was like a lion's mouth. And the dragon gave it his power and his throne and great authority. (Rev 13:2)

In the meeting at the seashore, God was depicting the exact moment when Satan transferred all of "his power, his throne, and great authority" to the beast. What led Satan to such a drastic decision, whereby he was willing to give everything over to another angel, and to a rival, no less? Scripture doesn't say. Perhaps Satan will have no intention of transferring anything over to the beast early on, but because of two crushing defeats—first, his defeat by Michael in the war in heaven and, secondly, his failure to catch the fleeing 144,000 Jewish remnant—that might be all it takes for Satan to make the drastic and possibly reluctant decision to transfer everything over to the beast, including his power and his throne and his great authority. Whatever the reason, in that climatic moment at the seashore, for all intents and purposes, the beast will take the place of Satan. And just as Satan was forced to turn his attention away from the hidden Jewish remnant and toward the worldwide Christians (Rev 12:17), the beast will continue to focus on those same worldwide Christians.

Rider on the White Horse

Is the event of the transfer of Satan's authority to the beast (Rev 13:2), which is here reflected in the Fourth Sequence, possibly reflected in one of the other sequences of Revelation? Not exactly, but close. To illustrate, let's revisit the initial event of the First Sequence:

"Then I saw the Lamb open one of the seven seals, and I heard one of the four living creatures call out, as with a voice of thunder, 'Come!' I looked, and there was a white horse! Its rider had a bow; a crown was given to him, and he came out conquering and to conquer" (Rev 6:1–2).

The four angelic riders seen under the first four seals, often referred to as "the Four Horsemen of the Apocalypse," were determined to be the invisible forces behind the greatest suffering in history, a period of suffering that Christ prophesied as beginning immediately after the abomination of desolation (Matt 24:21–22 and Rev 6:1–8). Knowing that the four angelic spirits will appear together soon after the abomination, an event one now understands to consist of the murders of the two witnesses, it seems logical that the lead rider, the one on the white horse and the only one wearing a crown, is none other than the beast himself given the fact that the beast is the one who will personally perpetrate the abominable act that causes the desolation, paving the way for the global holocaust in the first place.

With the understanding that the rider wearing a crown is the beast, ask yourself the following: When might God's living creature command the beast "to go!" (Greek: *Erchou*, may be translated "Come!" or "Go!")? Will it be before or after the beast receives Satan's power, throne, and great authority at the seashore? Obviously, the answer is afterward. Had the living creature's command come before the transfer, the beast would have been ill-equipped for such a daunting commission. But with his newfound power, throne, and authority from Satan, the beast, along with his accompanying angelic riders on the red, black, and pale green horses, will be more than capable to instigate and lead the greatest and deadliest holocaust in world history, whereby a quarter of the earth's population will be killed by war, famine, pestilence, and wild animals, i.e., the nuclear war and its aftermath.

The Beast's Appearance

At the moment John describes Satan's transfer, he simultaneously describes the beast's strange appearance, which appears to be a hodgepodge of different characteristics from the animal kingdom:

"And I saw a beast rising out of the sea, having ten horns and seven heads; and on its horns were ten diadems, and on its heads were blasphemous names. And the beast that I saw was like a leopard, its feet were like a bear's, and its mouth was like a lion's mouth" (Rev 13:1–2a).

The beast looked like a composite drawing of a dragon, a leopard, a bear, and a lion. Nevertheless, and doubtless to John's surprise, parts of the image seemed familiar to the disciple because of an earlier vision of Satan:

"Then another portent appeared in heaven: a great red dragon, with seven heads and ten horns, and seven diadems on his heads" (Rev 12:3).

The seven-headed beast looked just like the seven-headed dragon ... almost. Whereas the dragon had seven crowns on his seven heads but no crowns on his ten horns, the beast had ten crowns on his ten horns but none on his seven heads. That's interesting. Of course, John had no idea as to the reason for the discrepancy. However one thing was certain: John knew the images were purely symbolic. John was seasoned enough in Scripture to know that neither Satan nor the beast had multiple heads or multiple horns. He knew that Satan and the beast were invisible angelic spirits just like millions of other angels. He also knew these images were just God's fantastic drawings, each with hidden meanings. Here's the comparison:

Table 7.2. Comparison of the Images of the Dragon and the Beast	
The Dragon (Rev 12:3)	**The Beast** (Rev 13:1)
Seven heads with seven crowns	Seven heads without crowns
Ten horns without crowns	Ten horns with ten crowns

What is God trying to convey to John with these visual monstrosities? At first glance, when looking at the dragon, his seven "crowned" heads could very well indicate seven heads with authority; and when looking at the beast, his ten "crowned" horns might indicate similarly. However, beyond that and until more information is gathered, one's guess is as good as another as to the meanings of the images.

Next, John saw one of the most curious as well as one of the most speculated-about verses in all of apocalyptic literature:

> "One of its heads seemed to have received a death blow, but its mortal wound had been healed. In amazement the whole earth followed the beast. They worshipped the dragon, for he had given his authority to the beast, and they worshipped the beast, saying, 'Who is like the beast, and who can fight against it?'" Rev 13:3–4.

Since John is already unsure of the symbolism of the heads, horns, and crowns, he's in certainly no position to hazard a guess as to the meaning of an apparent mortal wound on one of the beast's seven heads that had been healed. Of course, we know a genuine mortal wound implies that a man has received a wound that will ultimately lead to his death, but we also know that the beast is not a man. Instead, he is an angel who will be released out of the bottomless pit after the two witnesses complete their ministry (Rev 11:7). With this in mind, we are prompted to take a closer look at the above translation of the Greek phrase *hē plēgē tou thanatou autou* as "its mortal wound." Rather than the current translation, one should be aware that the phrase literally means "its wound of death," which, in contrast to "its mortal wound," indicates a deadly wound that could apply to any living creature, human or nonhuman. One might ask, What's the significance? In this instance, perhaps a lot. If the seven heads of the beast represent men, then the translation is proper, but if the heads represent angels, as are the beast and Satan, then the translation "mortal wound" is misleading. Again, we must wait for more information.

The Time Frame of the Beast's Reign

With the understanding that one of God's living creatures commanded the beast to go forth in order that he might begin causing chaos and destruction upon the earth, one now learns that with the command the beast will be harnessed with a certain time restraint:

> The beast was given a mouth uttering haughty and blasphemous words, and it was allowed to exercise authority for forty-two months. (Rev 13:5)

Forty-two months. That's it. And when will the clock start ticking on the forty-two months? Don't make the easy mistake of thinking it will start when Satan transfers his power, authority, and throne to the beast (Rev 13:2). It won't. That's merely a transaction between two fallen angels. The "forty-two month reign" of the beast will only start when God says so, and that permission officially starts with the living creature's command "to go" (Rev 6:1). In the following, note the difference between the two milestones:

Table 7.3. Tracking the Beast: From the Bottomless Pit to the Moment His 42-Month Reign Begins		
1st Seq. Rev: Through 7 Trumpets (6:1)	2nd Seq. Rev: 2 Witnesses (11:7, 11–12)	4th Seq. Rev: Heaven's War to Beast's Appearance at Seashore (12:7, 9, 13–18, 13:1–2)
	1. The beast comes up from the bottomless pit and kills the 2 witnesses. (11:7)	
		2. Michael attacks Satan. (12:7)
	3. Three and a half days after the murder of the 2 witnesses, the 2 are resurrected and taken up to heaven. (11:11–12)	
		4. Michael cast Satan to the earth. (12:9)
		5. Satan pursues the woman. (12:13)
		6. The woman is given the 2 wings of the great eagle, so that she can fly from the serpent into the wilderness, to her place where she will be nourished for a time, and times, and half a time. Satan then sends a flood (of armies) after the woman (the Jewish remnant). (12:14–15)

Table 7.3. Tracking the Beast: From the Bottomless Pit to the Moment His 42-Month Reign Begins		
1st Seq. Rev: Through 7 Trumpets (6:1)	2nd Seq. Rev: 2 Witnesses (11:7, 11–12)	4th Seq. Rev: Heaven's War to Beast's Appearance at Seashore (12:7, 9, 13–18, 13:1–2)
		7. The earth comes to the aid of the woman and swallows the flood. (12:16)
		8. After Satan fails to catch the Jewish remnant, he turns his attention to other Christians. (12:17)
		9. Satan stands on the sand of the shore as the beast rises out of the sea. Satan then gives the beast his power, his throne, and his authority. (12:18—13:2)
10. The living creature commands the beast on the white horse "to go." (6:1)		

Since the forty-two-month reign will begin with the living creature's command, is it also possible to determine when it will end? Absolutely. In order to determine, let's revisit John's vision of the seventh trumpet:

"Then the seventh angel blew his trumpet, and there were loud voices in heaven, saying, 'The kingdom of the world has become the kingdom of our Lord and of his Messiah, and he will reign forever and ever'" (Rev 11:15).

This is the same kingdom of the world that Satan has controlled since the fall of Adam and the same kingdom of the world that Satan relinquished to the beast in their meeting at the seashore (Rev 13:2b). Nevertheless, one might ask, How can one be truly sure that the seventh trumpet marks the end of the beast's forty-two-month reign over the world? Simply because it would be nonsensical and inexplicable that those in heaven would celebrate so exuberantly that the kingdom of the world had become the kingdom of God and his Messiah if the beast were still in the midst of his forty-two-month reign of terror over the earth, and especially over God's people. Therefore, it is certain that the beast's reign will end promptly at the seventh trumpet, and the celebration in heaven is indisputable proof of that conclusion. Here's the illustration:

Table 7.4. The Beast's 42-Month Reign Begins at the Living Creature's Command "To Go" and Ends at the Seventh Trumpet					
1,260-Day Ministry of the 2 Witnesses	Unknown Time Frame	The Great Tribulation of the Saints			Day of the Lord	
		Nuclear War	1. Nuclear Aftermath	7 Trumpets	The Day Continues
			2. Deception of the Unrighteous		
			3. Martyrdom of the Saints		
		Beast's 42-Month Reign				
^	^	^		^	^
Abomination	Command to the Beast "to Go"			1st Trumpet	7th Trumpet

Additionally, since the 1,260-day exile of the 144,000 Jewish remnant and the forty-two-month trampling of Jerusalem by the invading nations start soon after the abomination of desolation, then it is obvious that the forty-two-month reign of the beast is approximately parallel with those two time frames. (This is not to say that the exile and trampling have the exact same start-finish dates as the beast's reign; nevertheless, the three periods are essentially congruent.) Observe:

Table 7.5. The 42-Month Trampling of Jerusalem and the 1,260-Day Exile of the 144,000 Jewish Remnant Have Approximately the Same Parameters as the 42-Month Reign of the Beast

		The Great Tribulation of the Saints		Day of the Lord	
1,260-Day Ministry of the 2 Witnesses	Unknown Time Frame	Nuclear War	1. Nuclear Aftermath	7 Trumpets	The Day Continues
			2. Deception of the Unrighteous		
			3. Martyrdom of the Saints		
		Beast's 42-Month Reign			
		1,260-Day Exile of the 144,000 Jewish Remnant			
		42-Month Trampling of Jerusalem by the Gentile Nations			
^	^			^	^
Abomination	Command to the Beast "to Go"			1st Trumpet	7th Trumpet

Now that the parameters of the beast have been set, one may have just now realized that the reign of the beast actually extends well into the Day of the Lord. Although one might have initially thought, and understandably so, that the reign of the beast would end at the conclusion of "the great tribulation of the saints," just as God begins to unleash his mighty wrath at the arrival of the judgments of the Day of the Lord, i.e., with the first trumpet, this is not the case. Because the beast's reign doesn't end until the seventh trumpet, then naturally his reign extends throughout each of the six trumpet plagues.

The Great Tribulation of the Saints vs. the Lesser Tribulation

After disclosing the length of the beast's reign as forty-two months, John describes its worldwide effect upon the unrighteous inhabitants of the earth as well as the saints:

> It opened its mouth to utter blasphemies against God, blaspheming his name and his dwelling, that is, those who dwell in heaven. Also it was allowed to make war on the saints and to conquer them. It was given authority over every tribe and

people and language and nation, and all the inhabitants of the earth will worship it, everyone whose name has not been written from the foundation of the world in the book of life of the Lamb that was slaughtered. (Rev 13:6–8)

After suffering worldwide death and destruction during the nuclear war and the ensuing nuclear aftermath, the inhabitants of the earth will at some point be deceived into worshiping the beast during the aftermath. Then, at some unknown point in time, the judgments of the Day of the Lord will arrive with its four trumpet plagues directed against the earth, followed by the unprecedented torture and death brought by the fifth and sixth trumpet plagues. In short, the inhabitants' destiny is bleak. The saints, on the other hand, will experience a different journey during the forty-two-month reign of the beast. After similarly suffering the same deadly effects of the nuclear war and its aftermath, the saints will never cave to worshiping the beast, but instead will remain true to Christ. For this faithfulness, the beast will be allowed to make war on them and to conquer them (Rev 13:7). Don't let John's statement alarm you. The beast will only conquer the saints physically, not spiritually. Recall the same description was used in the narrative of the two witnesses:

"When they have finished their testimony, the beast that comes up from the bottomless pit will make war on them and conquer them and kill them . . ." (Rev 11:7).

That's all the beast can do. He can only kill the saints, physically. And remember, even his authority to kill the saints will be stripped away once the full number of the martyrs has been reached (Rev 6:11).[1] Once that number has been reached at some point prior to the heavenly signs, God will no longer allow his people to suffer martyrdom. Nevertheless, one now learns according to Rev 13:7 the saints will continue to suffer and be persecuted during the remainder of the beast's forty-two-month reign, but, of course, without the threat of martyrdom. For this reason, one could very well describe this latter period of suffering under the beast's reign—from the heavenly signs to the seventh trumpet—as "the lesser tribulation" of the saints. Observe:

---

1. See pp. 113–115.

THE SEQUENCE

Table 7.6. The Great and the Lesser Tribulation of the Saints

		The Great Tribulation of the Saints		Day of the Lord	
				7 Trumpets	
1,260-Day Ministry of the 2 Witnesses	Unknown Time Frame	Nuclear War	1. Nuclear Aftermath	Lesser Tribulation of the Saints	The Day Continues
			2. Deception of the Unrighteous	1. Cont. Nuclear Aftermath	
			3. Martyrdom of the Saints	2. Cont. Persecution (w/o martyrdom)	
		Beast's 42-Month Reign			
		1,260-Day Exile of the 144,000 Jewish Remnant			
		42-Month Trampling of Jerusalem by the Gentile Nations			

^ Abomination   ^ Command to the Beast "to Go"   ^ 1st Trumpet   ^ 7th Trumpet

As I'm sure the reader has noticed, instead of the common belief that the saints will suffer a lesser tribulation before suffering a greater tribulation, Scripture paints the opposite picture: The saints will suffer "the great tribulation," with its nuclear war, nuclear aftermath, and martyrdom, before suffering "the lesser tribulation," which will be without the nuclear war and without the threat of martyrdom. Nevertheless "the lesser tribulation" will continue with the suffering and death resulting from the lingering nuclear aftermath, as well as from any hardships and persecutions directly caused by the beast, short of martyrdom.[2]

---

2. The continued tribulation of the saints after the appearance of the heavenly signs is subtly indicated by Christ's words "immediately after the tribulation of those days the sun will be darkened," etc. (Matt 24:29). Had Christ wished to convey that the entire tribulation will end once and for all at the heavenly signs, as many mistakenly believe, he doubtless would have said "immediately after the tribulation, the sun will be darkened," etc. But he didn't say that; he added "of those days" indicating that there will be days of tribulation before the heavenly signs and there will be days of tribulation after the heavenly signs. It's obvious that Christ knew the saints would continue to suffer at the hands of the beast during his entire forty-two-month reign (Rev 13:5–7).

Call for the Endurance of the Saints

Finally, because of what John knew awaited the saints during the forty-two-month reign of the beast, the disciple called for the endurance and faith of the saints:

> Let anyone who has an ear listen: If you are to be taken captive, into captivity you go; if you kill with the sword, with the sword you must be killed. Here is a call for the endurance and faith of the saints. (Rev 13:9–10)

Not unlike Peter and Paul, John knew the generation of Christ's return would bring perilous times to the saints. In fact, Peter called the present sufferings of the saints "a fiery ordeal":

"Beloved, do not be surprised at the fiery ordeal that is taking place among you to test you, as though something strange were happening to you. But rejoice insofar as you are sharing Christ's sufferings, so that you may also be glad and shout for joy when his glory is revealed. If you are reviled for the name of Christ, you are blessed, because the spirit of glory, which is the Spirit of God, is resting on you" (1 Pet 4:12–14).

As one can see, Peter knew the church would continue to suffer up until the time of Christ's appearance. Instead of being surprised or shaken by these sufferings as well as the sufferings to come, the apostle told his recipients to embrace them. Similarly, when Paul wrote Timothy for the last time, instead of telling his young protégé that he was hoping that the apparently untested pastor might be spared suffering, the weathered and weary apostle told Timothy to join with him in suffering:

"Do not be ashamed, then, of the testimony about our Lord or of me his prisoner, but join with me in suffering for the gospel, relying on the power of God . . ." (2 Tim 1:8).

John, Peter, and Paul saw suffering for Christ differently than what is taught today. Whereas today it is taught that God expresses his blessings to the faithful by shielding them from persecutions, the apostles indicated the opposite: God actually blesses the faithful by allowing them to suffer for his Son. (Somebody's theology is wrong, and I don't think it's that of the apostles.)

The Second Beast

If the beast out of the bottomless pit is going to successfully orchestrate the many atrocities of his forty-two-month reign, i.e., the nuclear war, the nuclear aftermath, the deception of the unrighteous, and the targeted persecution of the righteous, he will need human assistance. Remember, as indicated in an earlier discussion, evil angels, including Satan and the beast, can't just cross over to the visible world and start indiscriminately killing and injuring unsuspecting human beings whenever and wherever they choose. Unless God permits, they are relegated to carrying out their heinous deeds through human vessels.[3] With that said, the following chart shows when the beast will doubtless need human assistance:

Table 7.7. The Two Time Periods the Beast Will Need Human Assistance					
1,260-Day Ministry of the 2 Witnesses	Unknown Time Frame	The Great Tribulation of the Saints			Day of the Lord	
^	^	Nuclear War Human Assist. Needed	1. Nuclear Aftermath 2. Deception of the Unrighteous 3. Martyrdom of the Saints	7 Trumpets	
^	^	^	^	Lesser Tribulation of the Saints 1. Cont. Nuclear Aftermath 2. Cont. Persecution (w/o martyrdom)	The Day Continues
^	^	Human Assistance Needed				
^	^	Beast's 42-Month Reign				
^	^	1,260-Day Exile of the 144,000 Jewish Remnant				
^	^	42-Month Trampling of Jerusalem by the Gentile Nations				
^	^	^		^	^
Abomination		Command to the Beast "to Go"		1st Trumpet	7th Trumpet

First, the angelic beast will need human assistance to orchestrate the nuclear war, and later he will need assistance during the nuclear aftermath,

3. See p. 171.

FOURTH SEQUENCE, PART 2

which includes the period of the martyrdom of the saints. In the following passage, John is introduced to a possible candidate. Whether this individual happens to be one of the human assistants remains to be seen. In the meantime, John curiously calls the individual "another beast":

> Then I saw another beast that rose out of the earth; it had two
> horns like a lamb and it spoke like a dragon. (Rev 13:11).

Rather than a beast with seven heads and ten horns, this one had just two horns like a lamb. What is the Lord attempting to convey by this more tamed and subdued-looking image as opposed to the fierce images of the first beast and the dragon? Well, first and foremost, the image of this one initially appears somewhat similar to the humble and vulnerable two-horned Lamb of God, first seen in Rev 5:6. But it is a deceptive facade because he "spoke like a dragon." Therefore, one knows that this humble-looking two-horned lamb is "a wolf in sheep's clothing."

Now one comes to a familiar question: Is this two-horned beast representative of an angel or a man? With an almost embarrassingly too easy of an answer, and unlike the first beast, one knows that God is portraying a man by this beast because in two upcoming passages, Rev 19:20 and 20:10, the second beast is referenced as "the false prophet." Angels are not prophets; only men are prophets, whether true or false.[4]

With the knowledge that the first beast is an angel and the second beast is a man, and that they appeared on different occasions, let's quickly review the timing of each appearance:

---

4. The realization that the second beast is a man is also confirmed by the fact that he is seen emerging from the earth, from where all men emerge, whereas the seven-headed beast was initially seen coming up from the bottomless pit (Rev 11:7), before later emerging from the sea (Rev 13:1). In Scripture, the sea is a common depiction by God of the underworld from where evil angels dwell. An example of this can be seen in one of Daniel's dreams where four of God's angels stir up the sea, causing four evil angels to emerge: "In the first year of King Belshazzar of Babylon, Daniel had a dream and visions of his head as he lay in bed. Then he wrote down the dream: I, Daniel, saw in my vision by night the four winds of heaven stirring up the great sea, and four great beasts came up out of the sea, different from one another" (Dan 7:1–3).

God's symbolism is unmistakable: Evil angels emerge from the sea and men emerge from the earth.

THE SEQUENCE

Table 7.8. The Two Appearances of the First Beast and the Appearance of the Second Beast		
1. The 1st Beast	**2. The 1st Beast**	**3. The 2nd Beast**
The beast will be released from the bottomless pit at the end of the 1,260-day ministry of the 2 witnesses, at which time he will then kill the 2 witnesses. (11:7)	Soon after the abomination, the beast will rise from the sea and meet Satan at the sand of the seashore, where he will receive the devil's power, throne, and authority. (13:1–2)	At some point after the transfer of power, the 2nd beast will rise from the earth. (13:11)

Why are the timings of the above three appearances significant? As you are probably aware, there are those who mistakenly think that the first beast is a man and will be active on the world stage three and a half years prior to the abomination of desolation, at which time he will sign a seven-year covenant with Israel, and then three and a half years later he will break that signed covenant at the abomination of desolation by desecrating a newly constructed temple. All of this conjecture is supposedly supported by a passage in Daniel where the Archangel Gabriel actually gives the prophet a glorious message of the coming Messiah and the new covenant, that is to be fulfilled within seventy weeks of years from a certain decree (Dan 9:20–27). Without going into any great detail at the present time, hopefully the reader is beginning to understand that nothing about the theory is possible, as seen in the following:

1. The first beast is an angel, and angels don't sign covenants.
2. Three and a half years prior to the actual abomination of desolation, i.e., the murder of the two witnesses, the angelic first beast will be imprisoned within the bottomless pit, where he resides to this day.
3. The second beast, who is indeed a man, also won't be signing any covenants. He will only rise from among men at some point in time, according to Rev 13:11, after the transfer of authority from Satan to the first beast, which is well after the murder of the two witnesses, i.e., the abomination.
4. Regarding the breaking of a signed covenant at its midway point by the offering of an unclean sacrifice in a newly constructed temple,

none of the three—a new temple, an unclean sacrifice, or a signed covenant—will ever materialize.

Suffice to say, the "Broken-Seven-Year-Treaty Theory" is fictional. (Note: In "Appendix B: Proof That Daniel's Seventieth Week Has Nothing to Do with End Times," one will be presented the correct interpretation of Gabriel's message of the seventy weeks as well as the interpretations of Daniel's two other referenced abominations of desolation; see pp. 460–484.)

One of the Beast's Human Assistants?

In order to determine whether the false prophet will assist the first beast during one of the two periods of suffering, let's closely examine John's descriptions of the false prophet's activities:

> It exercises all the authority of the first beast on its behalf, and it makes the earth and its inhabitants worship the first beast, whose plague of death had been healed. It performs great signs, even making fire come down from heaven to earth in the sight of all. (Rev 13:12–13)

The passage clearly indicates that the second beast is one of the human assistants needed by the first beast during his forty-two-month reign. He will exercise all of the first beast's authority and will make the earth and its inhabitants worship it and will perform great signs on its behalf. This new revelation explains an earlier text that was intentionally left unaddressed:

"The beast was given a mouth uttering haughty and blasphemous words, and it was allowed to exercise authority for forty-two months" (Rev 13:5).

This sentence is nonsensical if one attempts to interpret it as implying that the first beast was given his own mouth. Indeed, someone may be given a voice (Greek: *foni*), but no one is ever said to be given their own mouth (Greek: *stoma*), which is the word used in the text. When one understands the verse as indicating that the angelic first beast was given, as it were, the mouth of the human second beast, which is to say, a mouth in the visible realm, then the text makes perfect sense. And because this is the correct interpretation, one knows that John is indicating that it is the visible false prophet, not the invisible angel, who will be the one heard and seen by mankind, garnering all the world's attention and allegiance, while speaking on behalf of the first beast.

Which Period of Suffering Will the Second Beast Assist?

There still remains the matter of determining which period of suffering the man will serve: the first period of the nuclear explosions or the second period of the nuclear aftermath with its martyrdom of the saints? As you ponder the question, consider another question: Do the great signs and wonders by the false prophet remind you of anyone from an earlier study? They should. Recall the following passage in 2 Thessalonians:

"Let no one deceive you in any way; for that day will not come unless the rebellion comes first and the lawless one is revealed, the one destined for destruction. He opposes and exalts himself above every so-called god or object of worship, so that he takes his seat in the temple of God, declaring himself to be God . . . . And then the lawless one will be revealed, whom the Lord Jesus will destroy with the breath of his mouth, annihilating him by the manifestation of his coming. The coming of the lawless one is apparent in the working of Satan, who uses all power, signs, lying wonders, and every kind of wicked deception for those who are perishing, because they refuse to love the truth and so be saved. For this reason God sends them a powerful delusion, leading them to believe what is false, so that all who have not believed the truth but took pleasure in unrighteousness will be condemned" (2 Thess 2:3–4, 8–12).

According to Paul, the man of lawlessness will be revealed to the world in the last days (2 Thess 2:3), performing signs and wonders and deceiving the unrighteous (2 Thess 2:9), and will meet his demise at the *parousia* of Christ (2 Thess 2:8). Similarly, John said of the false prophet: He will arrive on the world stage at some point after the transfer of authority from Satan to the beast (Rev 13:11), performing signs and wonders that will deceive the inhabitants of the earth into worshiping the first beast (Rev 13:12–13), and will meet his demise at the *parousia* of Christ (Rev 19:20). Observe:

Table 7.9. Comparison of Paul's Man of Lawlessness and John's False Prophet

The Man of Lawlessness	The False Prophet
1. He will be revealed to the world in the last days. (2 Thess 2:3)	1. He will arrive on the world stage after the transfer of authority from Satan to the beast. (Rev 13:11)

Table 7.9. Comparison of Paul's Man of Lawlessness and John's False Prophet	
The Man of Lawlessness	**The False Prophet**
2. He will perform signs and wonders that will deceive the unrighteous. (2 Thess 2:9)	2. He will perform signs and wonders that will deceive the unrighteous into worshiping the beast. (Rev 13:12–13)
3. He will meet his demise at the *parousia* of Christ. (2 Thess 2:8)	3. He will meet his demise at the appearance of Christ at Armageddon. (Rev 19:20)

It's obvious: The false prophet and the man of lawlessness are one and the same. Since they are, what combined information can be gathered from Paul and John concerning how the man might be revealed? Unlike the common belief that the man of lawlessness will be revealed to the world by offering an unclean sacrifice upon the altar of a newly built temple—a temple which will never materialize—Paul simply said the man's coming will be apparent by signs, lying wonders, and every kind of wicked deception (2 Thess 2:9). In others words, the man will be revealed by spectacular miracles. But now John comes along and identifies the specific miracle that will reveal the man to the world:

"It performs great signs, even making fire come down from heaven to earth in the sight of all" (Rev 13:13).

He will make fire come down from heaven! The fact that John singled this miracle out from all of the man's other miracles undoubtedly infers that this is the miracle that will set the man apart from the other false messiahs and false prophets (Matt 24:24). Their signs and wonders will pale in comparison to this display of power. No one has seen this type of miracle since the days of Elijah (2 Kgs 1:10). The world will predictably be dumbfounded and mesmerized.

Now, back to the question of which period of suffering will the false prophet assist the beast? Of course, it's the period which has been determined to include the man of lawlessness. Since he will emerge from among the crowded field of false messiahs and false prophets during the nuclear aftermath—after God has miraculously shortened the days of the nuclear war for the sake of the elect—it is certain that the man will only assist the beast during the second period of suffering: the period of the nuclear aftermath with its martyrdom of the saints. Do you need further proof? The man could never have been revealed to the world during the first period of suffering, i.e., the nuclear explosions. Why not? For the simple reason that if the man called down fire from heaven during the nuclear explosions, no one would notice. As nuclear bombs are exploding everywhere and entire cities and countries are being leveled, everyone will be frantically running for their lives and doing anything within their power just to survive. The man could call down fire from heaven a hundred times over and no one would give his miracles a second glance. The conclusion is undeniable. And because of that, one knows the man of lawlessness will only make his debut onto the world stage at some point after the explosions end, during the quiet of the nuclear aftermath with its famine and pestilence. As the many false messiahs and false prophets are masquerading around the world, each trying to garner as much attention as possible, the period of the aftermath will be the perfect time for the man's appearance onto the world stage, as the inhabitants of the earth are looking to anyone who will promise them food, clean water, shelter, peace, and security. Observe:

Table 7.10. Man of Lawlessness Becomes the Beast's Human Assistant at Some Point during the Nuclear Aftermath and Remains So until the End

			The Great Tribulation of the Saints		Day of the Lord	
1,260-Day Ministry of the 2 Witnesses	Unknown Time Frame	Nuclear War Human Assist. Needed?	1. Nuclear Aftermath		7 Trumpets	The Day Continues
			2. Deception of the Unrighteous		Lesser Tribulation of the Saints Continues with the Man of Lawlessness (w/o martyrdom)	
			3. Martyrdom of the Saints Begins after the Revealing of the Man of Lawlessness			
			Human Assistance Needed: The Man of Lawlessness			
			Beast's 42-Month Reign			
			1,260-Day Exile of the 144,000 Jewish Remnant			
			42-Month Trampling of Jerusalem by the Gentile Nations			

^ Abomination   ^ Command to the Beast "to Go"   ^ 1st Trumpet   ^ 7th Trumpet

With the understanding that the man of lawlessness will be the beast's point man during the period of the nuclear aftermath and martyrdom, one can fully expect John to reveal somewhere along the way the circumstances surrounding the beast's institution of the martyrdom of the saints through the man. (And lest one forget, there still remains the task of determining who will assist the beast during the first period of suffering, i.e., the period of the nuclear explosions.)

The Image of the Beast

After emerging as the undisputed liaison between the beast and the inhabitants of the earth, the false prophet will follow up his miraculous debut onto the world stage by deceiving and convincing the inhabitants to construct an image of the invisible angel:

> And by the signs that it is allowed to perform on behalf of the beast, it deceives the inhabitants of earth, telling them to make an image for the beast that had received the plague of the sword and yet lived. (Rev 13:14)

The construction of an image of the first beast by the false prophet brings to light the very popular misconception circulating among today's church that has been referenced throughout this study: the belief that both the beast as well as the false prophet are men. The theory even includes assigned roles for each man: The first beast will be a worldwide political figure, bringing the inhabitants of the earth under a one-world government, while the second beast will be a worldwide religious leader, bringing those same inhabitants under a universal religious system. Although the notion of a one-world government and one-world religious system are scripturally correct (Rev 13:12), the thought that two men will accomplish the task is nevertheless unscriptural. How so? First and foremost, as you well know by now, there aren't two men; there are one angel and one man. In fact, the construction of the image confirms this truth. If the first beast were truly a man, why would the false prophet go to all the trouble of having an image constructed of the man rather than just pointing to the man himself? Why the image? The whole endeavor would be pointless. The angelic beast just wants to be worshiped and the world just wants to see what they are worshiping, and because that's initially impossible, the false prophet will accommodate the world by having a visible image constructed of the invisible beast.

In retrospect, one can be assured that if the first beast were a man, he'd rather be worshiped directly by his devoted followers rather than indirectly through some type of constructed image. One can be sure that the Dalai Lama, Sun Myung Moon, and Jim Jones relished and basked in the glow of direct homage from their brainwashed followers. They would have never been satisfied with some sort of inferior, indirect worship, whereby their cultists only gave praises and accolades to some carved-out statue of themselves.[5]

The Image Speaks

Next, John reveals the false prophet's second most notable miracle: He will cause the constructed image of the first beast to speak:

> And it was allowed to give breath to the image of the beast so that the image of the beast could even speak and cause those who would not worship the image of the beast to be killed. (Rev 13:15)

A statue that speaks will be more than the inhabitants of the earth can handle. While the inhabitants are stuck in the throes of the nuclear aftermath with its food shortages, inflation, scarcity of fresh drinking water, viral and bacterial pestilences, and lawlessness, the false prophet will promise them everything if only . . . and here's the catch . . . they submit and worship the newly constructed, talking image. And, of course, most will gladly oblige. And if there happen to be any holdouts, they will surely acquiesce when they run out of water and food!

What about the elect? Not one will give in. And the consequences? This is where John reveals the circumstances surrounding the beast's institution of the martyrdom of the saints through the man of lawlessness: The man will "cause those who would not worship the image of the beast to be killed" (Rev 13:15). This should come as no surprise to the reader, as we have already proposed this same scenario as far back as our study in 2 Thessalonians. At that time it was surmised that since Paul said that only the unrighteous would be deceived by the miracles of the man of lawlessness (2 Thess 2:9–12), then it stood to reason that the righteous would not be deceived by his miracles and instead would suffer whatever consequences

---

5. This entire scenario reminds one of the Second Commandment (Exod 20:4–6), where God forbids any graven image made of himself or anyone else to worship. Although the Lord knew that man will be tempted to construct a visible image of the invisible God, the Lord said don't! Why? Jesus said that God is spirit, and those who worship him must worship in spirit and truth (John 4:24).

that refusal might entail.[6] And now we know the consequences: If one does not worship the constructed image, they will be put to death. This also explains John's vision under the fifth seal (italics used for emphasis):

"When he opened the fifth seal, I saw under the altar the souls of those who had been slaughtered for the word of God and for the testimony they had given; they cried out with a loud voice, 'Sovereign Lord, holy and true, how long will it be before you judge and avenge our blood on the inhabitants of the earth?' They were each given a white robe and told to rest a little longer, until the number would be complete both of their fellow servants and of their brothers and sisters, *who were soon to be killed as they themselves had been killed*" (Rev 6:9–11).

Although doubtless millions of saints will die during the nuclear war as well as the nuclear aftermath, the above passage only references the ones "who had been slaughtered for the word of God and for the testimony they had given," which we now know will be the ones who are specifically slaughtered by the man of lawlessness because they will refuse to worship the "talking image" of the beast.

The Mark of the Beast

Just as God commissioned his angels to mark his people with an invisible mark on their foreheads that would protect them from his wrath (Rev 7:3), so now one reads that the beast will cause the man of lawlessness and his minions to mark his people with a visible mark across their foreheads that will protect them from his wrath:

> Also it causes all, both small and great, both rich and poor, both free and slave, to be marked on the right hand or the forehead, so that no one can buy or sell who does not have the mark, that is, the name of the beast or the number of its name. (Rev 13:16–17)

Few passages in Revelation have garnered as much attention as the one above. Even for those who couldn't care less about the things of God and his word (which is most of the world), the narrative surrounding the mark of the beast has commanded the imagination of the masses, generating seminars, magazine articles, books, TV programs, movies, etc., ranging from the scripturally well-meaning to the totally bizarre. According to John, the mark will be placed on someone's right hand or

---

6. See pp. 34, 91.

forehead, and will either display the name of the beast or the number of the beast. And what will the inhabitants receive in exchange for receiving the mark? They will be allowed to buy and sell food, water, shelter, clothing, medical services, and anything else that will obviously be in short supply because of the nuclear aftermath.

Having already said the mark will be the name of the beast or the number of its name (Rev 13:17), John now reveals that the number of its name is "the number of a person" (Greek: *arithmos gar anthrōpou*):

> This calls for wisdom: let anyone with understanding calculate the number of the beast, for it is the number of a person. Its number is six hundred sixty-six. (Rev 13:18)

Since the number of the beast is the number of a man and only the second beast is a man, then the number 666 is necessarily the number of the second beast, not the first beast.[7] Furthermore, it can be said that although God revealed the names of the first beast, i.e., *Abaddon* and *Apollyon*, he did not reveal his number, and, on the other hand, although God revealed the number of the second beast, i.e., 666, he did not reveal his name.[8]

Next question: How will the man of lawlessness distribute the mark of the beast? The consensus of many suggests that the mark will be distributed through some type of computer chip placed under one's skin. However, that scenario is virtually impossible. Anything of that nature would obviously require a significant electric power grid, complete with power plants, satellite towers, distribution centers, computers, and, last but not least, handheld scanners. With the understanding that the man of lawlessness won't even be revealed until sometime during the nuclear aftermath, the chances of these electric infrastructures surviving the devastation of the global nuclear war are slim to none. This brings us to the simplicity and practicality of the man having the inhabitants of the earth marked with just a simple tattoo of some sort, akin to the identifying tattoos used on Jewish prisoners in the concentration camps during WWII. Just as it was determined that those tattoos would be placed on the lower left arm, so too will the mark of the beast have designated areas for placement: an individual's right hand or forehead (Rev 13:16). The

---

7. Additionally, one knows the number in question is only the number of the second beast simply because when John said the number of the beast is the number of a man, the disciple was in the midst of the same ongoing discussion of the second beast, which started back in Rev 13:11.

8. Some scholars, because of certain manuscripts, have suggested that the number could possibly be 616 instead of 666; Metzger, *Breaking the Code*, 77.

easiest part of the body in which to quickly mark anyone is obviously the back of a person's hands. That's why one sees this practice used on millions of people annually as they enter amusement parks, national parks, county fairs, and even small places of business on a daily basis around the world. It's quick, painless, and most people readily comply with it. As the world will still be reeling from the worst global holocaust in human history, the man's choice of distributing the mark of the beast may be very limited—limited to something as primitive and simple as that used at an amusement park.

Closing Thoughts: The Antichrist

The beast, the first beast, another beast, the man of lawlessness, the false prophet, *Apollyon*, and *Abaddon* are all terms used by Paul and John at one time or another to identify the apocalyptic evil angel and his evil human assistant. But what about the term "antichrist"? Where does that fit in? The term is not found in 1 or 2 Thessalonians, the Olivet Discourse, or Revelation, yet it's without a doubt the most recognized identification for at least one of those individuals today. So where can the term be found? Translated from the Greek *antichristos*, it's only used by the apostle John in the letters of 1 and 2 John. Therefore, we are immediately faced with the following question: Does the apostle use it to reference the angelic first beast or the human second beast? Because most people today mistakenly think Revelation references two men instead of one angel and one man, it's understandable why most believe that the term *antichristos* is a reference to the leader of the two, the first beast. But now that one knows the two are one angel and one man, one must begin afresh in order to ascertain who the apostle John was referencing when he used the term. Was he referencing the man or the angel? or both? In order to determine, let's briefly examine the four passages that contain the term (italics used for emphasis):

1. "Children, it is the last hour! As you have heard that *antichrist* is coming, so now *many antichrists have come*. From this we know that it is the last hour. They went out from us, but they did not belong to us; for if they had belonged to us, they would have remained with us. But by going out they made it plain that none of them belongs to us" (1 John 2:18–19).

In this passage it's quite clear that when John used the phrase "many antichrists have come" (Greek: *antichristoi*), he was referencing men who were going in and out among the brethren. The idea of angels leaving the brethren, or not belonging to them, or not remaining with them, is the furthest thing from John's mind. However, when the apostle used the singular "antichrist" (Greek: *antichristos*) in the first part of the sentence: "As you have heard that antichrist is coming," one must concede that whether John was referencing the future beast or the future man of lawlessness is unclear.

2. "Who is the liar but the one who denies that Jesus is the Christ? This is the *antichrist*, the one who denies the Father and the Son. No one who denies the Son has the Father; everyone who confesses the Son has the Father also" (1 John 2:22–23).

Here, for the second time, John uses the singular *antichristos*, saying that he is the one who denies the Father and the Son. Rather than warning of the apocalyptic beast or the apocalyptic man of lawlessness, John again appears to be warning the churches of men who are presently denying Christ, as he did in 1 John 2:18.

3. "Beloved, do not believe every spirit, but test the spirits to see whether they are from God; for many false prophets have gone out into the world. By this you know the Spirit of God: every spirit that confesses that Jesus Christ has come in the flesh is from God, and every spirit that does not confess Jesus is not from God. And this is *the spirit of the antichrist*, of which you have heard that it is coming; and now it is already in the world. Little children, you are from God, and have conquered them; for the one who is in you is greater than the one who is in the world" (1 John 4:1–4).

For the first time, one can be certain that John is addressing the spirits behind the individuals who are coming in and out among the believers. John tells the believer to test those spirits. And how does one test a spirit? By listening to the words of the person who is under the influence of the spirit being tested. John said that every spirit that causes an individual to confess that Jesus Christ has come in the flesh is from God, and every spirit that causes an individual to not confess that Jesus Christ has come in the flesh is not from God. Here, John's words parallel Paul's in 1 Corinthians:

"Therefore I want you to understand that no one speaking by the Spirit of God ever says 'Let Jesus be cursed!' and no one can say 'Jesus is Lord' except by the Holy Spirit" (1 Cor 12:3).

John and Paul distinguish between those who are led by the Holy Spirit and those who are led by evil spirits. Those who are led by God's Spirit confess that Jesus Christ has come in the flesh and that he is Lord. Those who are led by evil spirits say "Let Jesus be cursed!" and that he has not come in the flesh. Furthermore, John indicated that these evil spirits are of the spirit of the antichrist who is coming, who is already in the world (1 John 4:3). Since the man of lawlessness had not been born at the time of John's letter, the only "spirit of the antichrist" that was technically in existence was the angelic first beast, who was presently residing in the bottomless pit.

Finally, 2 John:

4. "Many deceivers have gone out into the world, those who do not confess that Jesus Christ has come in the flesh; any such person is the deceiver and the *antichrist*! Be on your guard, so that you do not lose what we have worked for, but may receive a full reward. Everyone who does not abide in the teaching of Christ, but goes beyond it, does not have God; whoever abides in the teaching has both the Father and the Son. Do not receive into the house or welcome anyone who comes to you and does not bring this teaching; for to welcome is to participate in the evil deeds of such a person" (2 John 7–11).

Here, John clearly sets the thought of evil spirits aside for the moment and again references the person who does not confess that Jesus Christ has come in the flesh and calls that person a deceiver and the antichrist. John even goes so far as to say don't allow such a person into your house or else the believer could be said to participate in the evil deeds of that person!

In the end, the apostle John divulged that in his day evil spirits were causing evil men to say that Jesus Christ had not come in the flesh and was not from God. He indicated that both the spirits and the men were antichrists. However, he goes on to specifically reference a future evil man (1 John 2:18) and a future evil spirit (1 John 4:3), also calling them "the antichrist" and "the spirit of antichrist," respectively. Therefore, it seems safe to say that John used the term *antichristos* loosely, sometimes as a description of evil men and evil spirits in his day, and other times as a description of the coming man of lawlessness, and still other times as the coming angelic beast, depending on the context.

∼

The following is the reconciliation of the six sequences, beginning with Satan's transfer of his power, throne, and authority to the beast and continuing through the beast's forty-two-month reign (the newly included events of Rev 13 are italicized):

THE SEQUENCE

Table 7.11. Reconciliation of the Six Sequences Beginning with Satan's Transfer of His Power, Throne, and Authority to the Beast, and Continuing through the Beast's 42-Month Reign

The Sequence	Seq. 1 & 2 Thess (2 Thess 2:3, 9–12)	Seq. Olivet Discourse (Matt 24:21–29a)	1st Seq. Rev, Part 1: Through 7 Trumpets (6:1–8; 11:15)	2nd Seq. Rev: 2 Witnesses	3rd Seq. Rev: Woman, Child, and Dragon	4th Seq. Rev, Part 2: 1st and 2nd Beasts (12:18—13:18)
1. Perhaps because of 2 recent defeats—being cast out of heaven and failing to catch the fleeing 144,000—Satan decides to transfer his power, his throne, and his great authority to the beast.						*The dragon stood on the sand of the seashore as the beast rose out of the sea. The dragon then transferred his power, his throne, and his great authority to the beast. (Rev 12:18—13:4)*
2. One of God's living creatures commanded the beast "to go!" The beast was then allowed to rule over every nation of the earth for 42 months.			*Vision seen under the 1st seal: The rider on the white horse came out conquering and to conquer. He was commanded by one of the living creatures "to go!" (Rev 6:1–2)*			*The beast was allowed to make war on the saints and to conquer them, and to exercise authority over every tribe and people and language and nation for 42 months. (Rev 13:5–10)*

238

FOURTH SEQUENCE, PART 2

Table 7.11. Reconciliation of the Six Sequences Beginning with Satan's Transfer of His Power, Throne, and Authority to the Beast, and Continuing through the Beast's 42-Month Reign

The Sequence	Seq. 1 & 2 Thess (2 Thess 2:3, 9–12)	Seq. Olivet Discourse (Matt 24:21–29a)	1st Seq. Rev, Part 1: Through 7 Trumpets (6:1-8; 11:15)	2nd Seq. Rev: 2 Witnesses	3rd Seq. Rev: Woman, Child, and Dragon	4th Seq. Rev, Part 2: 1st and 2nd Beasts (12:18—13:18)
3. The 2nd angelic rider appears on a red horse and initiates nuclear war under the leadership of the beast.		Greatest suffering in the history of the world begins. (Matt 24:21)	Vision seen under the 2nd seal: The rider on the red horse caused the people on the earth to slaughter one another. (Rev 6:3-4)			
4. God ends the greatest suffering in history which is nuclear war. But then the rider on the black horse causes famine, which initiates the nuclear aftermath.		God ends the greatest suffering in world history. (Matt 24:22)	Vision seen under the 3rd seal: Rider on the black horse causes famine, which initiates the nuclear aftermath. (Rev 6:5–6)			

239

Table 7.11. Reconciliation of the Six Sequences Beginning with Satan's Transfer of His Power, Throne, and Authority to the Beast, and Continuing through the Beast's 42-Month Reign

The Sequence	Seq. 1 & 2 Thess (2 Thess 2:3, 9–12)	Seq. Olivet Discourse (Matt 24:21–29a)	1st Seq. Rev, Part 1: Through 7 Trumpets (6:1–8; 11:15)	2nd Seq. Rev: 2 Witnesses	3rd Seq. Rev: Woman, Child, and Dragon	4th Seq. Rev, Part 2: 1st and 2nd Beasts (12:18—13:18)
5. Death and Hades are given authority to kill 1/4 of the earth's population by the nuclear war as well as its aftermath: famine, pestilence, and death by wild animals.			Vision seen under the 4th seal: Rider on the pale green horse, who is Death, and his partner, Hades, were given authority to kill 1/4 of the earth by sword, famine, pestilence, and wild animals. (Rev 6:7–8)			

FOURTH SEQUENCE, PART 2

Table 7.11. Reconciliation of the Six Sequences Beginning with Satan's Transfer of His Power, Throne, and Authority to the Beast, and Continuing through the Beast's 42-Month Reign

The Sequence	Seq. 1 & 2 Thess (2 Thess 2:3, 9–12)	Seq. Olivet Discourse (Matt 24:21–29a)	1st Seq. Rev, Part 1: Through 7 Trumpets (6:1-8; 11:15)	2nd Seq. Rev: 2 Witnesses	3rd Seq. Rev: Woman, Child, and Dragon	4th Seq. Rev, Part 2: 1st and 2nd Beasts (12:18—13:18)
6. During the nuclear aftermath, false messiahs and false prophets appear and perform many signs and wonders, causing great deception. This deception plants the seeds for "the rebellion."		False messiahs and false prophets appear, causing great deception. (Matt 24:23–28)				

241

Table 7.11. Reconciliation of the Six Sequences Beginning with Satan's Transfer of His Power, Throne, and Authority to the Beast, and Continuing through the Beast's 42-Month Reign

The Sequence	Seq. 1 & 2 Thess (2 Thess 2:3, 9–12)	Seq. Olivet Discourse (Matt 24:21–29a)	1st Seq. Rev, Part 1: Through 7 Trumpets (6:1–8; 11:15)	2nd Seq. Rev: 2 Witnesses	3rd Seq. Rev: Woman, Child, and Dragon	4th Seq. Rev, Part 2: 1st and 2nd Beasts (12:18—13:18)
7. During the nuclear aftermath, the man of lawlessness emerges from all other false messiahs and false prophets when he is revealed to the world by calling down fire from heaven in the sight of all. He will then exercise all the authority and power of the beast.	The man of lawlessness is revealed. (2 Thess 2:3)					*A 2nd beast rose out of the earth and exercised all of the authority of the 1st beast. He performed great signs and wonders, even calling down fire from heaven. (Rev 13:11–13)*

Table 7.11. Reconciliation of the Six Sequences Beginning with Satan's Transfer of His Power, Throne, and Authority to the Beast, and Continuing through the Beast's 42-Month Reign

The Sequence	Seq. 1 & 2 Thess (2 Thess 2:3, 9–12)	Seq. Olivet Discourse (Matt 24:21–29a)	1st Seq. Rev, Part 1: Through 7 Trumpets (6:1-8; 11:15)	2nd Seq. Rev: 2 Witnesses	3rd Seq. Rev: Woman, Child, and Dragon	4th Seq. Rev, Part 2: 1st and 2nd Beasts (12:18—13:18)
8. The man of lawlessness deceives the inhabitants of the earth by telling them to make an image of the first beast.	The unrighteous will be deceived by the signs and wonders performed by the man of lawlessness. (2 Thess 2:9–12)					*The man of lawlessness deceived the inhabitants of the earth by telling them to make an image of the 1st beast. (Rev 13:14)*
9. The man of lawlessness is allowed to cause the image of the beast to speak. He causes those who do not worship the image to be killed.		A second period of suffering is in progress. (Matt 24:29a)				*The man was allowed to cause the image of the beast to speak. He then caused those who would not worship the image to be killed. (Rev 13:15)*

THE SEQUENCE

Table 7.11. Reconciliation of the Six Sequences Beginning with Satan's Transfer of His Power, Throne, and Authority to the Beast, and Continuing through the Beast's 42-Month Reign

The Sequence	Seq. 1 & 2 Thess (2 Thess 2:3, 9–12)	Seq. Olivet Discourse (Matt 24:21–29a)	1st Seq. Rev, Part 1: Through 7 Trumpets (6:1-8; 11:15)	2nd Seq. Rev: 2 Witnesses	3rd Seq. Rev: Woman, Child, and Dragon	4th Seq. Rev, Part 2: 1st and 2nd Beasts (12:18—13:18)
10. The man causes all who worship the image of the beast to be marked on the right hand or the forehead, so that no one is able to buy or sell who does not have the mark. The mark is the name of the 2nd beast or the number of his name, 666.			The 42-month reign of the beast ends at the 7th trumpet. (Rev 11:15)			*The man caused all to be marked on the right hand or the forehead, so that no one could buy or sell who does not have the mark. The mark is the name of the beast or the number of its name, 666. (Rev 13:16–18)*

244

CHAPTER 8

Fourth Sequence, Part 3

Mount Zion to the Worship around God's Throne (14:1—15:4)

First Sequence	Second Sequence	Third Sequence	Fourth Sequence
		Chapter 6 3rd Seq.: The Woman, the Child, and the Dragon (12:1–6)	
			Chapter 6 (cont.) 4th Seq., Part 1: The War in Heaven to the Woman's Escape (12:7-17)
			Chapter 7 4th Seq., Part 2: The 1st and 2nd Beasts (12:18—13:18)
			Chapter 8* 4th Seq., Part 3: Mount Zion to the Worship around God's Throne (14:1—15:4)

THE SEQUENCE

UNLIKE THE SIMPLE TRANSITION between Rev 12 and Rev 13, where in one moment Satan gives up on his failed attempt to catch the woman fleeing into the wilderness (Rev 12:17) and the next, he is transferring his power, throne, and great authority over to the beast at the seashore (Rev 13:1–4), the proper understanding of the transition between Rev 13 and Rev 14 will be a bit more challenging. Having addressed the forty-two-month reign of the beast and the later rise of his human cohort, the false prophet, also known as the man of lawlessness, one would expect the visions of Rev 14 to pick up seamlessly with the visions of Rev 13, that is, of course, if Rev 14 is a continuation of the Fourth Sequence, with its portent-visions of the woman, the dragon, and the two beasts. Whether that's the case or not remains to be seen, but this much is certain, the first vision of Rev 14 seemed to catch John completely off guard:

> Then I looked, and there was the Lamb, standing on Mount Zion! And with him were one hundred forty-four thousand who had his name and his Father's name written on their foreheads. (Rev 14:1)

For the first time John "sees" the 144,000. If you recall, he had only "heard" their number in the First Sequence in Revelation (italics used for emphasis):

"After this I saw four angels standing at the four corners of the earth, holding back the four winds of the earth so that no wind could blow on earth or sea or against any tree. I saw another angel ascending from the rising of the sun, having the seal of the living God, and he called with a loud voice to the four angels who had been given power to damage earth and sea, saying, 'Do not damage the earth or the sea or the trees, until we have marked the servants of our God with a seal on their foreheads.' *And I heard the number of those who were sealed*, one hundred forty-four thousand, sealed out of every tribe of the people of Israel" (Rev 7:1–4).

The fact that John has just seen the 144,000 with the mark of the names of the Father and Jesus on their foreheads—a mark which was applied to their foreheads by the four angels, recorded back in the First Sequence (Rev 7:3–4)—most certainly leaves open the possibility that Rev 14:1 ff. is a continuation of the First Sequence, with its heavenly signs and trumpets and its own account of the 144,000, rather than a continuation of the Fourth Sequence, as one might have originally assumed. Here are the two options:

Table 8.1. Options for Whether Rev 14 Is a Continuation of the Fourth Sequence or the First Sequence						
Option #1:	1st Seq. (cont.): The 144,000, Heavenly Signs, and Through 6 Trumpets (7:1—9:21)	2nd Seq.: 2 Witnesses (11:1–13)	1st Seq. (cont.): 7th Trumpet (11:15–19)	3rd Seq.: Woman, Child, and Dragon (12:1–6)	4th Seq.: Heaven's War through Reign of 2 Beasts (12:7—13:18)	4th Seq. (cont.): The 144,000 on Mt. Zion (14:1 ff.)
Option #2:	1st Seq. (cont.): The 144,000, Heavenly Signs, and Through 6 Trumpets (7:1—9:21)	2nd Seq.: 2 Witnesses (11:1–13)	1st Seq. (cont.): 7th Trumpet (11:15–19)	3rd Seq.: Woman, Child, and Dragon (12:1–6)	4th Seq.: Heaven's War through Reign of 2 Beasts (12:7—13:18)	1st Seq. (cont.): The 144,000 on Mt. Zion (14:1 ff.)

Perhaps, as we continue, the content of Rev 14 will reveal which of the two options is correct. In the meantime, let's review the circumstances surrounding the 144,000.

Revisiting the 144,000

Have you ever wondered why the 144,000 Jewish remnant will wait until the appearance of the heavenly signs before confessing Christ? Why not sooner? Prior to escaping Jerusalem, will they not be among the privileged few allowed to see and hear in person the ministry of the two witnesses on the Temple Mount for 1,260 straight days? How could they not be instantly persuaded to confess Christ once they hear the preaching and see the miracles by such men with the characteristics and anointings of Elijah and Enoch? Even in the book of Zechariah, the two are described as "the anointed ones" who stand by the Lord of the whole earth (Zech 4:14). It does seem curious, one must admit. And to compound the mystery, once the witnesses are killed and the remnant escapes into the wilderness, the 144,000 will remain unconverted from the time of the escape until the appearance of the heavenly signs. How can this be? Is there perhaps a hidden reason why they will not, or cannot, confess Christ in all that time? Paul comes to the rescue:

"I want you to understand this mystery: a hardening has come upon part of Israel, until the full number of the Gentiles has come in. And so all Israel will be saved" (Rom 11:25b–26a).

Despite the powerful ministry of Elijah and Enoch, Paul discloses that the hearts of the Jewish remnant will remain hardened until the last number of the gentiles confesses Christ, and then, when the Jewish remnant does eventually confess, all of "the true Israel" will be saved—Jew and gentile (compare Rom 9:6–8 and 11:25–26). And when will the full number of gentiles come into the kingdom? Answer: Since the 144,000 Jewish remnant will come into God's kingdom at the appearance of the heavenly signs (Joel 2:30–32), then obviously the last of the gentiles must come into the kingdom at some point prior to the heavenly signs, toward the end of the great tribulation. Once the full number of gentiles is complete, then, according to Paul, the hardened hearts of the Jewish remnant will be softened, as they will subsequently call on the Lord at the appearance of the heavenly signs.

Still, one might wonder "why" the remnant would choose to confess Christ at the moment of the heavenly signs. In other words, when the remnant sees the sun darken, the moon become like blood, and innumerable meteorites fall from the heavens, why will they immediately become convicted in their consciences enough to call on Christ? Because it's certain that throughout the 1,260-day ministry of the two witnesses, the prophets will continually preach about the crucifixion and resurrection of Jesus Christ, the approaching Day of the Lord, and the return of the Lord and the gathering of the saints. Doubtless, it is at the moment the remnant witnesses the supernatural heavenly signs that the 144,000 will recall all that was foretold by the two witnesses, especially the part about the heavenly signs and the looming great Day of the Lord. It is at the moment of the heavenly signs that they will become convinced in their minds and convicted in their hearts that everything the two prophesied was true, and that Jesus Christ was indeed the one and only Messiah.[1] They will then

---

1. The reaction to the heavenly signs by the 144,000 will be quite different than that of the unrighteous kings and generals, rich and poor, slave and free, who also will be privileged enough to hear the 1,260-day ministry of the two witnesses. However, when the inhabitants of the earth recall the two's warning concerning the heavenly signs and the coming of the Day of the Lord, instead of repenting and calling on the Lord, they

confess his name. And, of course, their confession will be the same as all confessions of Christ:

"Because if you confess with your lips that Jesus is Lord and believe in your heart that God raised him from the dead, you will be saved. For one believes with the heart and so is justified, and one confesses with the mouth and so is saved. The scripture says, 'No one who believes in him will be put to shame.' For there is no distinction between Jew and Greek; the same Lord is Lord of all and is generous to all who call on him. For, 'Everyone who calls on the name of the Lord shall be saved'" (Rom 10:9–13).

Despite the popular teaching that in the end times the last-generation Jews will be treated differently than gentiles in regards to their salvation, the teaching is woefully unscriptural.[2] The God of the Jews is no different than the God of the gentiles, and the God of the present is no different than the God of the future; his grace and justice do not vary from one to another. They are always expressed through the person and work of Jesus Christ (Gal 3:28–29). Whether that grace was provided for Isaac (an OT Jew) or Cornelius (a NT gentile), or that justice was meted out to Jezebel (an OT gentile) or Sapphira (a NT Jew), God doesn't change.[3] Therefore, if anyone, Jew or gentile, is to be reconciled to God, it will only be through the grace and righteousness provided through his Son, Jesus Christ. There is no plan B—even for the 144,000 Jewish remnant.

Heaven or Earth?

Many suppose that after John saw the 144,000 standing on Mount Zion with the Lamb in Jerusalem (Rev 14:1), he next heard the 144,000 singing a new song before the throne, the four living creatures, and the twenty-four elders. The next passage is from where they acquire this thought:

> And I heard a voice from heaven like the sound of many waters and like the sound of loud thunder; the voice I heard was like the sound of harpists playing on their harps, and they sing a

---

will scurry for cover, yelling, "Fall on us and hide us from the face of the one seated on the throne and from the wrath of the Lamb; for the great day of their wrath has come, and who is able to stand?" (Rev 6:16b–17). The only reason they will know to scream such phrases as "the one seated on the throne" and "from the wrath of the Lamb" and "the great day of their wrath has come" will be because they had heard those phrases articulated by the two witnesses.

2. Blaising et al., *Three Views on the Millennium*, 182–86.
3. Mal 3:6.

new song before the throne and before the four living creatures and before the elders. No one could learn that song except the one hundred forty-four thousand who have been redeemed from the earth. (Rev 14:2–3)

However, consider the following question: Did John actually say he heard "the 144,000" singing a new song in heaven, or did he say he heard "a sound like harpists" singing a new song in heaven? And moreover, if John did indeed see the 144,000 in heaven, how did they get there? And if they were there, did he see their bodies or their souls? Here are the options:

Table 8.2. Options for Whether the 144,000 Were Seen on Earth or in Heaven
Option #1: John saw the glorified bodies of the 144,000 in heaven.
Option #2: John saw the souls of the 144,000 in heaven.
Option #3: John only saw the 144,000 on the earth.

Let's examine:

Option #1: John saw the glorified bodies of the 144,000 Jewish remnant in heaven.

The only way John could have seen the glorified bodies of the 144,000 in heaven would have been if they had been resurrected or raptured along with all of the other saints in the first resurrection. But despite teaching to the contrary, the first resurrection and rapture of the saints are yet to occur at this stage in the sequence (Rev 20:5).

Option #2: John saw the souls of the 144,000 in heaven.

The only way John could have seen the souls of the 144,000 as one unit in heaven immediately after seeing them as one unit standing on Mount Zion is if they had all been killed together as martyrs on Mount Zion. However, this scenario is impossible because it has been proven that the martyrdom of the saints will be complete prior to the appearance of the heavenly signs (Rev 6:9–13),[4] and yet, according to Joel 2:32, the 144,000 will confess Christ at the heavenly signs, after which they will be marked with the seal of God for protection against the upcoming Day of the Lord and its first trumpet judgment. Suffice to say, the 144,000 Jewish remnant will not be martyred on Mount Zion while standing next to Christ.

Option #3: John saw the 144,000 on the earth.

---

4. See pp. 113–115.

Since John did not see the glorified bodies of the 144,000 in heaven because the resurrection and rapture of the saints were yet to occur, and since he did not see the souls of the 144,000 in heaven because they had not died as martyrs, then it is unequivocally proven that John only saw the 144,000 standing on Mount Zion with Christ on the earth—just as the text states.

How Did the 144,000 End Up on Mount Zion?

Since the 144,000 will stay in the wilderness for 1,260 days (compare Rev 12:6 and 12:14), and yet John now sees them standing on Mount Zion with Christ, then it is obvious that the 1,260 days have ended, allowing the remnant to return home. And what event will officially signal that the 1,260 days are over? The blast of the seventh trumpet. How can one be sure? Although it's still to be determined whether Rev 14:1 is a continuation of Rev 13:18 (a continuation of the Fourth Sequence), or a continuation of Rev 11:19 (a continuation of the First Sequence), both passages end with the seventh trumpet.[5] And why is this significant? As you are sure to remember, the forty-two month reign of the beast, the forty-two month trampling of Jerusalem, and the 1,260-day exile of the 144,000 were each determined to end at the seventh trumpet. Therefore, it is certain that when the seventh trumpet is finally blown, the Holy Spirit will begin leading the newly converted 144,000 out of the wilderness and back to Jerusalem. In the next verses, John describes the results of their conversion:

> It is these who have not defiled themselves with women, for they are virgins; these follow the Lamb wherever he goes. They have been redeemed from humankind as first fruits for God and the Lamb, and in their mouth no lie was found; they are blameless. (Rev 14:4–5)

Notice the phrase "these follow the Lamb wherever he goes." To follow Jesus is simply to be led by the Holy Spirit. Just as the sons of God are led by the Spirit of God (Rom 8:14), in the last days the Holy Spirit will lead the 144,000 in triumphal procession back to the very spot from where they had once fled, which was where Elijah and Enoch were

---

5. Rev 11:15–19 is a narrative of the seventh trumpet and Rev 13 describes the forty-two-month reign of the beast, which ends at the seventh trumpet. In other words, both Rev 11 and Rev 13 end at the seventh trumpet, however as part of different sequences.

murdered three and a half years earlier. And the gentiles, who had been trampling Jerusalem for forty-two months since that abominable act, will have already vacated the premises prior to the remnant's return. As Jesus stated in Luke 21:24, the gentile nations will trample Jerusalem "until the times of the Gentiles are fulfilled." At the seventh trumpet, their time is up. In fact, the next time one sees this same gentile horde similarly gathered in one spot will be in a large valley just east of Jerusalem.[6] In the meantime, the 144,000 Jewish remnant will finally be able to enjoy the presence of Christ on the Temple Mount without fear of reprisal. Their days of worshiping Christ underground are over.

Not Evangelists

It's no secret that there is a certain belief that says the 144,000 Jewish remnant will be Jewish evangelists who will spread the gospel during the great tribulation of the saints, filling a void left by a supposedly vacated church. Putting the mistaken thought of the vacated church aside for the moment, let's only address the belief that the 144,000 will be evangelists. Here's a snapshot of their spiritual progression:

Table 8.3. The Spiritual Progression of the 144,000 Jewish Remnant			
1. Unconverted ... during the 1,260-day ministry of the 2 witnesses.	2. Unconverted ... when they flee Jerusalem to the safety of the wilderness, at the abomination of desolation.	3. Converted ... after the appearance of the heavenly signs, just before the 1st trumpet.	4. Converted ... when they return home at the 7th trumpet.

As one can see, despite common belief, the 144,000 will never evangelize the world. Instead, they are the ones who will need evangelization—from the two witnesses, no less! And even after they confess Christ at the appearance of the heavenly signs, they will remain hidden in seclusion until the entire 1,260-day exile has come to an end. Then, at the blast of the seventh trumpet, they will finally return to Jerusalem but there will still not be an opportunity to witness to anyone because the gentiles who had trampled Jerusalem for forty-two months will have evacuated the city at the same blast of the seventh trumpet, leaving the city empty.

6. The "Valley of Harmagedon" (Rev 16:16).

Rather than through the 144,000 Jewish remnant, the ministry of the gospel will come by other means in the last days: First, the "heavy lifting" will come from the two witnesses. They will single-handedly preach Christ to the entire world from atop the Temple Mount for 1,260 straight days, accompanied by signs and wonders. It is certain that their ministry will be broadcast worldwide by every means available. Secondly, whomever among the elect are not brought into the kingdom prior to the murder of the two witnesses will be brought in through the preaching and testimony by the saints scattered around the world—just as it is today. One can rest assured that by these two means—the two witnesses and the saints scattered around the world—the Holy Spirit will bring in all the remaining elect of the last generation into God's kingdom.

In a way, the 144,000 will be like one of the two thieves who died next to Jesus on the cross. After finally realizing that Jesus was the Son of God, he asked Christ to remember him when he entered his kingdom. Jesus then turned and said to him, "Truly I tell you, today you will be with me in Paradise." The thief was always part of the elect from the foundation of the world, but during his entire life he remained unconverted. He never told anyone about Christ; he couldn't give what he didn't have. He only confessed Christ at the very last hour, of the very last day. In a sense, the 144,000 Jewish remnant will only confess Christ at the very last hour, of the very last day.

The Three Angelic Announcements

After John heard the sound of harpists singing a new song in heaven, he then looked between heaven and earth and saw three angels flying in the midheaven, each with a certain announcement. Here's the first angel:

> Then I saw another angel flying in midheaven, with an eternal gospel to proclaim to those who live on the earth—to every nation and tribe and language and people. He said in a loud voice, "Fear God and give him glory, for the hour of his judgment has come; and worship him who made heaven and earth, the sea and the springs of water." (Rev 14:6–7)

The first angel admonished everyone, everywhere, to fear God and give him glory because the hour of his judgment had come. The announcement of the impending judgment reminds one of the song sung by the twenty-four elders during the seventh trumpet celebration, which, at that time, warned of God's impending destruction of those who destroy the earth (italics used for emphasis):

"We give you thinks, Lord God Almighty, who are and who were, for you have taken your great power and begun to reign. The nations raged, but your wrath has come, and the time for judging the dead, for rewarding your servants, the prophets and saints and all who fear your name, both small and great, *and for destroying those who destroy the earth*" (Rev 11:17b–18).

But which judgment and destruction? Since one knows the seventh trumpet has sounded because of the fact that the 144,000 have returned home from the wilderness, the angel must be referencing a certain judgment that follows the seven trumpet judgments. Anyone who has previously read Revelation will know that the narrative of the seven bowl judgments is recorded in Rev 16, and for that reason many think the angel's reference to God's upcoming judgment must be a reference to those seven bowls. But let's not jump to that conclusion just yet. In the meantime, here's the second announcement:

> Then another angel, a second, followed, saying, "Fallen, fallen is Babylon the great! She has made all nations drink of the wine of the wrath of her fornication." (Rev 14:8)

The second angel announced that Babylon the great has fallen. Before one can rightly assess the significance of this announcement, again, one must wait until Scripture reveals the identity of Babylon. Lastly, here's the third announcement:

> Then another angel, a third, followed them, crying with a loud voice, "Those who worship the beast and its image, and receive a mark on their foreheads or on their hands, they will also drink the wine of God's wrath, poured unmixed into the cup of his anger, and they will be tormented with fire and sulfur in the presence of the holy angels and in the presence of the Lamb. And the smoke of their torment goes up forever and ever. There is no rest day or night for those who worship the beast and its image and for anyone who receives the mark of its name." (Rev 14:9–11)

Those who worship the beast and receive the mark will drink the wine of God's wrath. Although the warning should cause fear and dread to all who reject God and live unrighteously, unfortunately, the announcement has the reputation of striking fear in the righteous, as well as the unrighteous. Why? There are believers who worry about receiving the mark of the beast accidentally. But the scenario is impossible. Those who receive the mark will willingly and gladly worship the beast, as well as rebelliously and adamantly reject Christ. In actuality, "the mark" is not what dooms the unrighteous; it is "the heart" that chooses the mark, chooses to worship the beast, and chooses to reject Christ, that will be one's undoing. The righteous, on the other hand, will never receive the mark, purposely or accidentally.

The First or the Fourth Sequence?

The question still remains as to whether Rev 14:1 and the verses following are a continuation of the Fourth Sequence or the First Sequence. What makes the determination somewhat difficult, as indicated earlier, is that both sequences have paused at the seventh trumpet. Notwithstanding this obstacle, one now has conclusive evidence for what has been suspected all along: Rev 14:1 and the verses following are a continuation of Rev 13:18 and the Fourth Sequence. How can one be certain? One can easily see that the third angel's announcement was in direct response to the circumstances described in the latter part of Rev 13, even using much of the same vocabulary. The following juxtaposition of the end of Rev 13 and the third angel's announcement in Rev 14 demonstrates this fact (italics used for emphasis):

". . . and it was allowed to give breath to the *image of the beast* so that the *image of the beast* could even speak and cause those who would not *worship the image of the beast* to be killed. Also it causes all, both small and great, both rich and poor, both free and slave, to be *marked on the right hand or the forehead*, so that no one can buy or sell who does not have the mark, that is, *the name of the beast or the number of its name*. This calls for wisdom: let anyone with understanding calculate the number of the beast, for it is the number of a person. Its number is six hundred sixty-six" (Rev 13:15–18).

"Then another angel, a third, followed them, crying with a loud voice, 'Those who *worship the beast and its image*, and receive a *mark on their foreheads or on their hands*, they will also drink the wine of God's wrath, poured unmixed into the cup of his anger, and they will be tormented with fire and sulfur in the presence of the holy angels and in the presence of the Lamb. And the smoke of their torment goes up forever and ever. There is no rest day or night for those who *worship the beast and its image* and for anyone who receives *the mark of its name*'" (Rev 14:9–11).

As one can readily see, the themes and vocabulary of Rev 13 and 14, i.e., the beast, the image of the beast, the mark of the beast, and the future placement of the mark on the hands or forehead, are the same. To date, those themes and vocabulary are completely absent from the First Sequence, which has paused at Rev 11:19. And that's why one can be quite confident that Rev 14:1 and the verses following, at least to this point, are a continuation of Rev 13 and the Fourth Sequence.[7]

Next, John takes the occasion of the vision of the three angelic announcements to again call for the endurance of the saints:

> Here is a call for the endurance of the saints, those who keep the commandments of God and hold fast to the faith of Jesus. (Rev 14:12)

I say "again" because this call is reminiscent of John's earlier call for the endurance of the saints (in the same Fourth Sequence, mind you), after the disciple had described the future sufferings and persecutions of the saints during the forty-two-month reign of the beast (italics used for emphasis):

"Let anyone who has an ear listen: If you are to be taken captive, into captivity you go; if you kill with the sword, with the sword you must be killed. *Here is a call for the endurance and faith of the saints*" (Rev 13:9–10).

Fourth Conversation: "Blessed Are the Dead Who Die in the Lord"

Immediately after the vision of the three announcements, John heard a voice from heaven:

> And I heard a voice from heaven saying, "Write this: Blessed are the dead who from now on die in the Lord." "Yes," says the Spirit, "they will rest from their labors, for their deeds follow them." (Rev 14:13)

---

7. Although it is true that sequences can sometimes be distinguished from one another by certain themes and vocabulary such as is the case presented here, the more objective means of distinguishing between sequences will always be by identifying the presence of the same event more than once in any series of events.

The above statements directed to the disciple from "the voice" and "the Spirit" comprise the fourth conversation. The fact that "the voice" was distinguished from "the Spirit" indicates that the source of "the voice" was either the Son or the Father. (Perhaps later, the identity of the personality behind the voice will be revealed.) The "voice" told John to write that blessed are the dead who from now on die in the Lord. Since the "voice" directly engaged John, then one knows for certain that these words were spoken in John's presence two thousand years ago, which, in turn, proves that the blessing was actually pronounced upon all who were to die in the Lord—from the days of John until Christ's return.

The Son of Man Seated on a White Cloud

Next, John sees a vision of Jesus as one "like the Son of Man" rather than the frequently seen heretofore image of the Lamb:[8]

> Then I looked, and there was a white cloud, and seated on the cloud was one like the Son of Man, with a golden crown on his head, and a sharp sickle in his hand! (Rev 14:14)

As the Son of Man, Jesus is here revealed to John as One seated on a white cloud, with a golden crown on his head and a sharp sickle in his hand. Without any time to marvel at the vision, John immediately sees an angel exit the temple, telling Jesus the time to reap has come:

> Another angel came out of the temple, calling with a loud voice to the one who sat on the cloud, "Use your sickle and reap, for the hour to reap has come, because the harvest of the earth is fully ripe." So the one who sat on the cloud swung his sickle over the earth, and the earth was reaped. (Rev 14:15-16)

Of course, even with Jesus' realistic appearance as the Son of Man, John knows full well that Jesus is not actually sitting on a cloud and holding a metal sickle with a wooden handle, with the intention of swinging it over the earth like someone treading down a row of fully ripened wheat. John, like anyone familiar with Scripture's analogy of "gathering the harvest" as "gathering the elect," understood the symbolism of the sickle and the harvest:

---

8. From Rev 5:6 to 14:10 the image of the Lamb has been seen or mentioned seventeen times.

"Then he said to his disciples, 'The harvest is plentiful, but the laborers are few; therefore ask the Lord of the harvest to send out laborers into his harvest'" (Matt 9:37–38).

Jesus told the disciples that the harvest (of souls) is plentiful, but the laborers are few. Now, contrast that with what John heard in his vision: "The harvest of the earth is fully ripe." Although the full number of gentiles will come into the kingdom at some unknown point prior to the appearance of the heavenly signs (Rom 11:25), and then, at their appearance, the 144,000 Jewish remnant will begin calling on the Lord and confessing that Jesus is truly the Messiah (Joel 2:30–32), Rev 14:15 seems to suggest that there will still be some remaining Jews scattered around the world who will also confess Christ at some point after the heavenly signs but before the Lord's return, thus prompting the angel out of the temple to only now proclaim "The harvest of the earth is fully ripe."

The Great Wine Press of the Wrath of God

If one is to understand that the "harvest of the wheat" is representative of the "harvest of the elect," then the reader is sure to see the stark contrast between the righteous harvest and the gathering of the unrighteous "clusters of the vine of the earth":

> Then another angel came out of the temple in heaven, and he too had a sharp sickle. Then another angel came out from the altar, the angel who has authority over fire, and he called with a loud voice to him who had the sharp sickle, "Use your sharp sickle and gather the clusters of the vine of the earth, for its grapes are ripe." So the angel swung his sickle over the earth and gathered the vintage of the earth, and he threw it into the great wine press of the wrath of God. And the wine press was trodden outside the city, and blood flowed from the wine press, as high as a horse's bridle, for a distance of about two hundred miles. (Rev 14:17–20)

Again, the angel is not actually holding a metal sickle with a wooden handle. Nevertheless, the vision of an angel holding a sharp sickle in his hand, followed by another angel "who has authority over fire," surely indicated to John that something ominous was about to happen—at least to the unrighteous. The disciple certainly understood the apocalyptic symbolism of grapes being thrown into "the great wine press of the wrath of God" and that was that in the last days, God will gather his enemies to one location in order to bring vengeance upon them because they have opposed him, his Son, and his people. In the following passage, Joel uses this same language to describe the end-time fate of the gathered nations in the Valley of Jehoshaphat:

"Come quickly, all you nations all around, gather yourselves there. Bring down your warriors, O Lord. Let the nations rouse themselves, and come to the valley of Jehoshaphat; for there I will sit to judge all the neighboring nations. Put in the sickle, for the harvest is ripe. Go in, tread, for the wine press is full. The vats overflow, for their wickedness is great" (Joel 3:11–13).

Joel describes the battle in the Valley of Jehoshaphat with the same terms found in John's vision of the great wine press: the gathered nations, the valley, the sickle, the vats, the great wine press, and the treading of grapes. These are all symbolic images describing the climax of the Day of the Lord when Jesus will appear and enter into judgment with the armies of the nations and repay them for all of the sins and iniquities they have committed against God and his people. In the following passage, Isaiah sees the same climatic event, but with an added detail:

"Who is this that comes from Edom, from Bozrah in garments stained crimson? Who is this so splendidly robed, marching in his great might?

'It is I, announcing vindication, mighty to save.'

"Why are your robes red, and your garments like theirs who tread the wine press?

'I have trodden the wine press alone, and from the peoples no one was with me; I trod them in my anger and trampled them in my wrath; their juice spattered on my garments, and stained all my robes. For the day of vengeance was in my heart, and the year for my redeeming work had come. I looked, but there was no helper; I stared, but there was no one to sustain me; so my own arm brought me victory, and my wrath sustained me. I trampled down peoples in my anger, I crushed them in my wrath, and I poured out their lifeblood on the earth'" (Isa 63:1–6).

Unlike Joel and John, Isaiah saw the garments of Christ spattered with the blood of the unrighteous as a result of the battle. Of course, the most familiar text describing the great end-time wine press of the wrath of God did come from John:

"Then I saw heaven opened, and there was a white horse! Its rider is called Faithful and True, and in righteousness he judges and makes war ... He is clothed in a robe dipped in blood, and his name is called The Word of God.... From his mouth comes a sharp sword with which to strike down the nations, and he will rule them with a rod of iron; he will tread the wine press of the fury of the wrath of God the Almighty" (Rev 19:11, 13, 15).

John's two visions of the great wine press of God, Joel's description of the nations being gathered to the Valley of Jehoshaphat, and Isaiah's description of the Lord wearing juice-spattered garments as he marches through the great wine press alone all speak of Christ's second coming and his appearance at the apocalyptic Battle of Armageddon.

Another Portent

After John saw the Son of Man and an angel on the verge of gathering the ripened harvest of the earth and the clusters of the vine of the earth, respectively, the disciple then said he saw "another portent," which was a scene of seven angels with seven plagues, standing with the martyred souls who had conquered "the beast and its image and the number of its name." Observe:

> Then I saw another portent in heaven, great and amazing: seven angels with seven plagues, which are the last, for with them the wrath of God is ended.
> And I saw what appeared to be a sea of glass mixed with fire, and those who had conquered the beast and its image and the number of its name, standing beside the sea of glass with harps of God in their hands. And they sing the song of Moses, the servant of God, and the song of the Lamb:
> "Great and amazing are your deeds, Lord God the Almighty!
> Just and true are your ways, King of the nations!
> Lord, who will not fear and glorify your name?
> For you alone are holy.
> All nations will come and worship before you,
> for your judgments have been revealed." (Rev 15:1–4)

The last time John introduced any vision by calling them a "portent" (Greek: *sēmeion*) was back at the opening of Rev 12 and the Third Sequence. If one is counting, Rev 15:1 is the third time John has used the term; here were the first two instances (italics used for emphasis):

"A great *portent* appeared in heaven: a woman clothed with the sun, with the moon under her feet, and on her head a crown of twelve stars. She was pregnant and was crying out in birth pangs, in the agony of giving birth. Then another *portent* appeared in heaven: a great red dragon, with seven heads and ten horns, and seven diadems on his heads. His tail swept down a third of the stars of heaven and threw them to the earth. Then the dragon stood before the woman who was about to bear a child, so that he might devour her child as soon as it was born" (Rev 12:1–4).

Although Rev 15:1 is the third time the term has been mentioned, clearly, the scene of the seven angels with the seven plagues and the martyrs standing beside a sea of glass mixed with fire isn't the third portent. From John's perspective, the disciple has seen a string of portents beginning with the Third Sequence (the "Narrative of the Woman, the Child, and the Dragon") and continuing through the Fourth Sequence, up to this particular portent of angels and martyrs around God's throne. How can one be sure? If the reader recalls, when John first introduced us to the word *sēmeion*, which means "a sign" or "an omen," we were initially somewhat at a loss as to why he chose to distinguish the visions of the pregnant woman and the dragon as signs or omens to come, as opposed to the previous visions which were also events slated for the future, other than the fact that the visions of the woman and the dragon seemed extraordinarily fantastic and surreal. However, now that we have been thoroughly immersed into the portents throughout chapters 12–14, we are in a better position to make a more accurate assessment of what John was thinking. Unlike the various "live-action visions" of people running to hide in caves and under rocks, or visions of real earthquakes and volcanoes, or of a darkened sun and moon, the "portents" can be described as fantastic, animated, almost cartoonish-type images drawn by God for the express purpose of representing a reality of some sort. And why would God in some circumstances choose to present to John a drawn image rather than the real thing? Because, as the reader can readily attest, having come to understand such symbolism as that of the pregnant woman (the 144,000 Jewish remnant) and the male child (the 1,260-day ministry of the two witnesses), the Lord can often impart more information in a single portent than in several live-action visions. With that in mind, the following is a list of the portents seen in Rev 12–15, some of which John identified as portents and some he didn't:

Table 8.4. Examples of Portents Seen in Rev 12, 13, 14, and 15	
Images That John Identified as Portents	Images That John Neglected to Identify as Portents
1. The pregnant woman (12:1)	

Table 8.4. Examples of Portents Seen in Rev 12, 13, 14, and 15

Images That John Identified as Portents	Images That John Neglected to Identify as Portents
2. The red 7-headed dragon with 10 horns (12:3)	
	3. The male child (12:5)
	4. The 7-headed beast with 10 horns and a healed, wounded head (13:1)
	5. The 2-horned beast that spoke like a dragon (13:11)
	6. One like the Son of Man seated on a white cloud, wearing a golden crown and holding a sharp sickle in his hand (14:14)
	7. An angel holding a sharp sickle in his hand (14:17)
8. Seven angels with 7 plagues gathered with martyrs who appeared to be standing beside a sea of glass mixed with fire around the throne of God (15:1–2)	

Looking at the above examples, one might ask if John did indeed consider each of the above images "portents," why didn't he say so? In other words, just as he identified the pregnant woman and the seven-headed dragon as portents, why didn't he identify the child, the seven-headed beast, and the two-horned second beast as such? But why would he? His continual use of the word *sēmeion* in front of every new portent would have been superfluous, and, not to mention, grammatically monotonous. Somewhere along the way, John surely expected his readers to begin to understand which visions were real and which weren't, i.e., which were live-action and which were portents.

In retrospect, had one been privileged enough to have accompanied John to heaven on the day the visions were revealed, one would have had no problem distinguishing a live-action vision from a portent, just as one knows today when they are watching a live-action movie as opposed to an animated film. But since that wasn't the case, one must become adept at distinguishing the two types of visions solely from John's written account.

Which Sequence?

Although the portents of Rev 12, 13, and 14 have certainly spilled over into the fifteenth chapter, has the Fourth Sequence, with its uniquely characteristic themes of the beast, the image of the beast, the mark of the beast, etc., also spilled over into the fifteenth chapter? Let's look again at an excerpt from Rev 15:1-4 (italics used for emphasis):

"And I saw what appeared to be a sea of glass mixed with fire, and *those who had conquered the beast and its image and the number of its name*, standing beside the sea of glass with harps of God in their hands" (Rev 15:2).

At first glance, it initially appears that the themes and vocabulary of the Fourth Sequence, i.e., the beast, the image of the beast, its mark, and its number, have carried over from Rev 14 to Rev 15:1-4, supporting the fact that perhaps the passage is a continuation of the Fourth Sequence. But what about the next passage, Rev 15:5-8? I ask that because it is universally assumed that Rev 15:1-4 and Rev 15:5-8 comprise one series of events. In other words, it is assumed that the scene of the seven angels standing around God's throne with the martyrs is a direct precursor to the scene of those same seven angels exiting the temple doorway, as they are about to receive the seven golden bowls of God's wrath from one of God's living creatures. Here's the subsequent text:

> After this I looked, and the temple of the tent of witness in heaven was opened, and out of the temple came the seven angels with the seven plagues, robed in pure bright linen, with golden sashes across their chests. Then one of the four living creatures gave the seven angels seven golden bowls full of the wrath of God, who lives forever and ever; and the temple was filled with smoke from the glory of God and from his power, and no one could enter the temple until the seven plagues of the seven angels were ended. (Rev 15:5-8)

In order to determine the true relationship between Rev 15:1-4 and 15:5-8, let's first step back and examine the larger series of events that encompasses both texts—the series between Rev 14:1 and 19:21 (italics used for emphasis):

Table 8.5. A Sequence with One Too Many Battles of Armageddon

1. The 144,000 are seen on Mount Zion after the 7th trumpet (14:1-5).

THE SEQUENCE

Table 8.5. A Sequence with One Too Many Battles of Armageddon
2. Three angels make 3 announcements (14:6–11).
3. *The great wine press of God's wrath, a.k.a. the Battle of Armageddon, occurs (14:17–20).*
4. Seven angels with the 7 plagues are seen with the martyrs who are gathered before the throne, singing: "Your judgments have been revealed" (Rev 15:1-4).
5. The 7 angels exit the temple in anticipation of pouring the 7 golden bowls of wrath (15:5—16:21).
6. *The Battle of Armageddon follows the 7th bowl (19:11–21).*

As one can see, there's a problem. The Battle of Armageddon appears twice. And as one well knows by now, *the same event can never appear more than once in any one sequence. If the same event does appear twice in a series, then two sequences are necessarily present.* As has been the pattern, one's next step is to determine where one sequence ends and the next one starts.

As the reader will soon learn, unless he or she knows already, the scene whereby the seven angels receive the seven golden bowls from one of the living creatures (15:5-8), followed by the pouring of those bowls (16:1-21), most certainly precedes the Battle of Armageddon, which is recorded in 19:11-21. How can one be sure? Because the pouring of the sixth bowl (16:12-16), whereby the armies of the nations are gathered to the place called Armageddon, is a direct precursor to the battle. Therefore, since one knows that Rev 15:5-8 is part of the sequence that includes the Battle of Armageddon recorded in Rev 19:11-21, one must now definitively determine whether Rev 15:1-4 should also be placed with that same sequence, or with the earlier sequence that includes "the Battle of Armageddon" recorded in Rev 14:17-20. One thing is certain: It can't be with both. Here are the options (italics used for emphasis):

Table 8.6. The Correct Sequence Placement of Rev 15:1-4	
Option #1 Rev 15:1-4 Is a Continuation of the 4th Sequence	Option #2 Rev 15:1-4 Is Part of the Next Sequence
1. The 144,000 are seen on Mount Zion after the 7th trumpet (14:1–5).	

FOURTH SEQUENCE, PART 3

Option #1 Rev 15:1–4 Is a Continuation of the 4th Sequence	Option #2 Rev 15:1–4 Is Part of the Next Sequence
2. Three angels make 3 announcements (14:6–11).	
3. The great wine press of God's wrath, a.k.a. the Battle of Armageddon, occurs (14:17–20).	
Seven angels with the 7 plagues are seen with the martyrs who are gathered before the throne, singing: "Your judgments have been revealed" (15:1–4).	*Seven angels with the 7 plagues are seen with the martyrs who are gathered before the throne, singing: "Your judgments have been revealed" (15:1–4).*
	2. The 7 angels exit the temple in anticipation of pouring the 7 golden bowls of wrath (15:5—16:21).
	3. The Battle of Armageddon occurs (19:11–21).

Table 8.6. The Correct Sequence Placement of Rev 15:1–4

So which is it? Is the scene of the seven angels standing with the martyrs around the throne of God, singing the song of Moses and the song of the Lamb, a scene that takes place after the Battle of Armageddon (option #1) or before the battle (option #2)? The answer is found in one of the songs:

"Great and amazing are your deeds, Lord God the Almighty!
Just and true are your ways, King of the nations!
Lord, who will not fear and glorify your name?
For you alone are holy.
All nations will come and worship before you,
for your judgments have been revealed" (Rev 15:3b–4).

Notice the last line of the song: "for your judgments have been revealed." It's nonsensical to think that the martyrs would sing that song prior to the pouring of the seven bowls of wrath and prior to the Battle of Armageddon, when God's judgments have not been revealed (option #2). The martyrs could only have sung that song after the pouring of the seven bowls and after Armageddon (option #1).

The scenario is quite simple: Rev 15:1–4 is a continuation of the Fourth Sequence and shows the seven angels of God standing with the martyrs in heaven, as they are singing and worshiping around God's throne because they have defeated the beast and its image, and because of Christ's recent victory at the Battle of Armageddon.[9] On the other hand, Rev 15:5–8 is part of a different sequence, describing an earlier scene in which those same seven angels of God are on the verge of receiving the seven bowls of God's wrath from one of the living creatures, after which the angels will then pour the bowls upon the inhabitants of the earth.

Closing Thoughts: A Misplaced Chapter Heading

The placement of the chapter headings and verses, which, as most know, was not inspired by God,[10] did not show the true transition from the Fourth Sequence ending at Rev 15:4 to the next sequence beginning with Rev 15:5–8, and therefore, that misplacement worked to our detriment. Had the end of Rev 14 been placed at 15:4 instead of 14:20, and the beginning of Rev 15 been placed at 15:5 instead of 15:1, then the confusion surrounding the two appearances of the seven angels might have been avoided, or at least lessened. The following shows the juxtaposition of the current placement of chapters and verses with the better placement:

Table 8.7. The Juxtaposition of the Current Placement of Chapters and Verses Surrounding Rev 15 with the Better Placement			
Current Placement:	Rev 14:1–20	Rev 15:1–8	Rev 16:1–21
Better Placement:	Rev 14:1–24	Rev 15:1–25	

The better arrangement would have eliminated the awkward grouping of the eight verses comprising the fifteenth chapter (15:1–8), which, as one might not be aware, is the shortest chapter in Revelation. As stated above, if Rev 15:1–4 had been left with Rev 14 where it belonged, one might not have so quickly assumed that the scene of the seven angels and martyrs around God's throne preceded the scene of those same seven angels exiting the temple in order to receive the golden bowls. Nevertheless, the error of the chapter placement was not insurmountable. As demonstrated, the internal evidence of the text revealed the true relationship between the two sequences and because of that, one can now confidently

---

9. Although not cited in Rev 14 and the Fourth Sequence, it is to be understood that the seven bowls of wrath have already been dispersed prior to the Battle of Armageddon, recorded in Rev 14:17–20.

10. Metzger, *Bible in Translation*, 65.

proceed with the narrative of the pouring of the seven golden bowls of wrath, knowing that the Fourth Sequence ended at Rev 15:4 and another sequence has begun at Rev 15:5.

The following is the reconciliation of the six sequences, beginning with the 144,000 Jewish remnant standing on Mount Zion with the Lamb and continuing to the worship around God's throne that celebrated Christ's victory at Armageddon. (Note: The recently addressed events of Rev 14:1—15:4 are italicized):

THE SEQUENCE

Table 8.8. Reconciliation of the Six Sequences Beginning with the 144,000 Jewish Remnant Standing on Mount Zion with the Lamb and Continuing to the Worship around God's Throne

The Sequence	Seq. 1 & 2 Thess (2 Thess 1:6–10)	Seq. Olivet Discourse (Matt 24:30)	1st Seq. Rev, Part 1: Through 7 Trumpets	2nd Seq. Rev: 2 Witnesses	3rd Seq. Rev: Woman, Child, and Dragon	4th Seq. Rev, Part 3: Mt. Zion to God's Throne (14:1–15:4)
1. After the blowing of the 7th trumpet, the 144,000 Jewish remnant returns to Jerusalem from their 1,260-day exile in the wilderness, where they are seen standing on Mount Zion with Christ.						*The 144,000 Jewish remnant were seen standing on Mount Zion with the Lamb, and a voice was heard from heaven that sounded like harpists playing and singing a new song before the throne, and the 4 living creatures and the elders. (Rev 14:1–5)*

FOURTH SEQUENCE, PART 3

Table 8.8. Reconciliation of the Six Sequences Beginning with the 144,000 Jewish Remnant Standing on Mount Zion with the Lamb and Continuing to the Worship around God's Throne

The Sequence	Seq. 1 & 2 Thess (2 Thess 1:6–10)	Seq. Olivet Discourse (Matt 24:30)	1st Seq. Rev, Part 1: Through 7 Trumpets	2nd Seq. Rev: 2 Witnesses	3rd Seq. Rev: Woman, Child, and Dragon	4th Seq. Rev, Part 3: Mt. Zion to God's Throne (14:1—15:4)
2. Three angels appear in the midheaven and the 1st angel announces that the hour of God's judgment has come, which is a reference to the upcoming great wine press of God's wrath, i.e., the Battle of Armageddon.						*Three angels appeared in the midheaven. The 1st angel announced that the hour of God's judgment had come. (Rev 14:6–7)*
3. The 2nd angel announces that Babylon the great has fallen.						*The 2nd angel announced that Babylon the great has fallen! (Rev 14:8)*

269

THE SEQUENCE

Table 8.8. Reconciliation of the Six Sequences Beginning with the 144,000 Jewish Remnant Standing on Mount Zion with the Lamb and Continuing to the Worship around God's Throne

The Sequence	Seq. 1 & 2 Thess (2 Thess 1:6–10)	Seq. Olivet Discourse (Matt 24:30)	1st Seq. Rev, Part 1: Through 7 Trumpets	2nd Seq. Rev: 2 Witnesses	3rd Seq. Rev: Woman, Child, and Dragon	4th Seq. Rev, Part 3: Mt. Zion to God's Throne (14:1–15:4)
4. The 3rd angel announces that those who worship the beast will drink the wine of God's wrath as well as suffer eternal punishment.						*The 3rd angel announced that those who worship the beast will drink the wine of God's wrath as well as suffer eternal punishment. (Rev 14:9–11)*

270

FOURTH SEQUENCE, PART 3

Table 8.8. Reconciliation of the Six Sequences Beginning with the 144,000 Jewish Remnant Standing on Mount Zion with the Lamb and Continuing to the Worship around God's Throne

The Sequence	Seq. 1 & 2 Thess (2 Thess 1:6–10)	Seq. Olivet Discourse (Matt 24:30)	1st Seq. Rev, Part 1: Through 7 Trumpets	2nd Seq. Rev: 2 Witnesses	3rd Seq. Rev: Woman, Child, and Dragon	4th Seq. Rev, Part 3: Mt. Zion to God's Throne (14:1—15:4)
5. Jesus is seen seated on a white cloud just before he descends for the great wine press of the wrath of God, which represents the Battle of Armageddon.						*The Son of Man was seen seated on a white cloud, wearing a golden crown on his head and holding a sharp sickle in his hand. He was told to use his sickle for the hour to reap has come because the harvest of the earth was fully ripe.* (Rev 14:14–16)
6. The Lord appears and descends to the Battle of Armageddon.	The Lord returns. (2 Thess 1:6–10)	The Son of Man appears. (Matt 24:30)				*The great wine press of the wrath of God occurred.* (Rev 14:17–20)

THE SEQUENCE

Table 8.8. Reconciliation of the Six Sequences Beginning with the 144,000 Jewish Remnant Standing on Mount Zion with the Lamb and Continuing to the Worship around God's Throne

The Sequence	Seq. 1 & 2 Thess (2 Thess 1:6–10)	Seq. Olivet Discourse (Matt 24:30)	1st Seq. Rev, Part 1: Through 7 Trumpets	2nd Seq. Rev: 2 Witnesses	3rd Seq. Rev: Woman, Child, and Dragon	4th Seq. Rev, Part 3: Mt. Zion to God's Throne (14:1–15:4)
7. After Christ's victory at Armageddon, the 7 angels who had poured the 7 bowls of God's wrath appear with the martyrs who are seen worshiping and singing around God's throne because they have conquered the beast and its image and the number of its name, and because of Christ's victory at the Battle of Armageddon.						*The 7 angels with the 7 plagues appeared with the martyrs who were standing on a sea of glass mixed with fire. They were seen worshiping and singing before God's throne because they had conquered the beast and its image and the number of its name. (Rev 15:1–4)*

272

CHAPTER 9

First Sequence, Part 2
The Seven Bowls (15:5—19:10)

First Sequence	Second Sequence	Third Sequence	Fourth Sequence
			Chapter 8 4th Seq., Part 3: Mount Zion to the Worship around God's Throne (14:1—15:4)
Chapter 9* 1st Seq., Part 2: The 7 Bowls (15:5—19:10)			
Chapter 10 1st Seq., Part 3: The Lord's Return and the 1st Resurrection (19:11—20:6a)			
Chapter 11 1st Seq., Part 4: The Millennium and the Final Judgment (20:6b–15)			

THE SEQUENCE

With the knowledge that Rev 12:7—15:4 contained a rather lengthy series of "portents" that comprised the Fourth Sequence, beginning with the war in heaven between Michael and Satan, and continuing to the gathering of the seven angels and martyrs around God's throne in celebratory worship because of Christ's victory at the Battle of Armageddon, one must now again address the second appearance of those same seven angels exiting the temple doorway with the determined mindset of carrying out God's final wrath upon the inhabitants of the earth:

> After this I looked, and the temple of the tent of witness in heaven was opened, and out of the temple came the seven angels with the seven plagues, robed in pure bright linen, with golden sashes across their chests. Then one of the four living creatures gave the seven angels seven golden bowls full of the wrath of God, who lives forever and ever; and the temple was filled with smoke from the glory of God and from his power, and no one could enter the temple until the seven plagues of the seven angels were ended. (Rev 15:5-8)

Since it has already been established that Rev 15:1-4 is a continuation of the Fourth Sequence, one is now faced with whether Rev 15:5—16:21 is a continuation of the First Sequence, or, perhaps, starts a new sequence.[1] If a new sequence, then that necessarily indicates that a Fifth Sequence of Revelation has begun with the seven angels exiting the temple. Considering the early start-dates of the previous four sequences in Revelation (two began near the start of the two witnesses' ministry while two began near the end of their ministry), the late start of a potential Fifth Sequence at the pouring of the seven golden bowls of God's wrath might seem a little strange; however, it's not entirely impossible. In order to determine, let's compare the two hypotheticals (italics used for emphasis):

Table 9.1. The Correct Sequence of Rev 15:5—16:21	
Option #1 Rev 15:5—16:21 Is a Continuation of the 1st Sequence	Option #2 Rev 15:5—16:21 Begins a New, 5th Sequence
1. The great tribulation (6:1-11)	
2. The heavenly signs (6:12-17)	

---

1. Rev 15:5—16:21 cannot be a continuation of the Second or Third Sequence simply because those sequences have already ended.

Table 9.1. The Correct Sequence of Rev 15:5—16:21	
Option #1 Rev 15:5—16:21 Is a Continuation of the 1st Sequence	**Option #2** Rev 15:5—16:21 Begins a New, 5th Sequence
3. The 7 trumpets (8:6–21 and 11:15–19)	
4. The 7 angels exit the temple and prepare to pour the 7 bowls of God's wrath (15:5–8).	1. The 7 angels exit the temple and prepare to pour the 7 bowls of God's wrath (15:5–8).
5. The 7 angels pour the 7 bowls (16:1–21).	2. The 7 angels pour the 7 bowls (16:1–21).
1st Sequence continues . . .	5th Sequence continues . . .

In order to determine the correct option, the first question one must ask is whether Rev 15:5—16:21 is even a candidate as a continuation of the First Sequence, which left off at the seventh trumpet. And the answer is absolutely! What happens after the seventh trumpet? The pouring of the seven bowls. (So far, so good.) Now, let's take a closer look and examine the compatibility of the two passages in question: Rev 11:15–19 and Rev 15:5–8. Notice that the former ends with "the open temple" and the latter begins with "the open temple" (italics used for emphasis):

1. "Then *God's temple in heaven was opened*, and the ark of the covenant was seen within his temple; and there were flashes of lightning, rumblings, peals of thunder, an earthquake, and heavy hail" (Rev 11:19).

2. "After this I looked, and *the temple of the tent of witness in heaven was opened*, and out of the temple came the seven angels with the seven plagues, robed in pure bright linen, with golden sashes across their chests" (Rev 15:5–6).

What more needs to be said? Revelation 15:5–8 is unquestionably a continuation of Rev 11:15–19 and the First Sequence. While the disciple was in the midst of seeing the vision of the celebration caused by the seventh trumpet, he saw the ark of the covenant inside the open temple doorway (Rev 11:19). Then, after being shown a lengthy series of portent-visions (Rev 12:1—15:4), John is brought back to the same vision of the open temple doorway (Rev 15:5), but this time, instead of only seeing the ark of the covenant within the doorway, he now sees seven angels exiting that doorway, just as they are about to receive the golden bowls of God's wrath from one of the living creatures (Rev 15:6–7).[2]

What do you think went through John's mind when he initially saw the seven angels receive the seven golden bowls? Do you suppose that, as John now stood in the throne room seeing the vision, he believed that one day seven angels would actually pour seven golden bowls upon the inhabitants of the earth, dispersing plagues out of those bowls? Certainly not. Although John knew that God will certainly dispense real, terrifying judgments upon the last-generation inhabitants of the earth by means of powerful and obedient angels, he also knew that the bowls were simply "drawn" images by God, just as were the four colored horses seen under the first four seals, the locust-looking demons of the fifth and sixth trumpets, and the various "portents" of Rev 12:1—15:4. By now, John was becoming quite accustomed to seeing both the live-action visions as well as God's exquisite handiwork of drawn images.

The First Bowl

As John saw the seven angels holding the seven bowls, he next heard a loud voice from heaven instructing the seven to pour out the bowls upon the earth. Having received the mark of the beast and worshiped its image, and having eagerly thrown their lot in with the man of lawlessness, certain inhabitants of the earth now begin to reap in earnest what they have sown:

> Then I heard a loud voice from the temple telling the seven angels, "Go and pour out on the earth the seven bowls of the wrath of God."
> So the first angel went and poured his bowl on the earth, and a foul and painful sore came on those who had the mark of the beast and who worshiped its image. (Rev 16:1–2)

For the inhabitants of the earth who chose to worship the beast, the end did not justify the means. In the short term, the mark gifted them with the ability to purchase staples such as water, food, clothing, and shelter, but now the mark has turned out to be very costly; the inhabitants are suddenly struck with a foul and excruciatingly painful sore. Little do they know that the odorous and oozing lesion will be a precursor to long-term

---

2. A second proof that the two passages are connected concerns the flashes of lightning, rumblings, peals of thunder, an earthquake, and heavy hail. Just as those occurrences preceded the trumpet plagues (8:5), they now precede the bowl plagues (11:19).

spiritual repercussions. Recall the third angelic announcement (italics used for emphasis):

"Then another angel, a third, followed them, crying with a loud voice, 'Those who worship the beast and its image, and receive a mark on their foreheads or on their hands, they will also drink the wine of God's wrath, poured unmixed into the cup of his anger, *and they will be tormented with fire and sulfur in the presence of the holy angels and in the presence of the Lamb. And the smoke of their torment goes up forever and ever.* There is no rest day or night for those who worship the beast and its image and for anyone who receives the mark of its name'" (Rev 14:9–11).

In short, the mark will be costly for those inhabitants in this age and the age to come.

Second, Third, and Fourth Bowls

The next three bowl-plagues are similar to their corresponding trumpet-plagues, howbeit more severe. Instead of one third of the earth's saltwater being contaminated, all saltwater will be affected; instead of one third of freshwater contaminated, all freshwater will be contaminated; and instead of one third of the sun being darkened doubtless from cloud cover, the sun will now radiate unfiltered scorching heat upon the earth and its inhabitants. Observe:

> The second angel poured his bowl into the sea, and it became like the blood of a corpse, and every living thing in the sea died. The third angel poured his bowl into the rivers and the springs of water, and they became blood. And I heard the angel of the waters say,
>
> "You are just, O Holy One, who are and were, for you have judged these things; because they shed the blood of saints and prophets, you have given them blood to drink. It is what they deserve!"
>
> And I heard the altar respond, "Yes, O Lord God, the Almighty, your judgments are true and just!"
>
> The fourth angel poured his bowl on the sun, and it was allowed to scorch them with fire; they were scorched by the fierce heat, but they cursed the name of God, who had authority over these plagues, and they did not repent and give him glory. (Rev 16:3–9)

After the sun was allowed to scorch the inhabitants with fire, the Scripture recorded a familiar response by the unrighteous: "and they did not repent and give him glory" (compare Rev 9:21, 16:9, 11, and 21). Compare their response with those from "the angel of the waters" and the altar: "You are just, O Holy One, who are and were, for you have judged these things; because they shed the blood of saints and prophets, you have given them blood to drink. It is what they deserve!" and "Yes, O Lord God, the Almighty, your judgments are true and just!"

Fifth Bowl

When the fifth angel poured his bowl upon the earth, John said the sores caused by the first bowl were still causing unrelenting pain on the inhabitants, as the throne of the beast was plunged into darkness. Predictably, still no one repented:

> The fifth angel poured his bowl on the throne of the beast, and its kingdom was plunged into darkness; people gnawed their tongues in agony, and cursed the God of heaven because of their pains and sores, and they did not repent of their deeds. (Rev 16:10–11)

One might question, How could the beast's throne and kingdom be plunged into darkness at the fifth bowl if his forty-two-month rule over the earth ended at the seventh trumpet? The question is astute; however the answer is quite simple. Although the beast will receive all of Satan's power, throne, and great authority at their rendezvous on the sand of the seashore (Rev 12:18—13:2), remember, it is God who determines the parameters of the beast's forty-two-month reign, not Satan. According to God's decree, the reign will only begin at the moment one of the living creatures commands the beast-rider on the white horse to go forth (Rev 6:1), and it will end precisely at the blast of the seventh trumpet (Rev 11:15).[3] Those parameters are etched in stone. However, that's not to say that the beast won't possess Satan's transferred power, throne, and authority immediately prior to the living creature's command to go forth, as well as continue to possess it immediately after the blast of the seventh trumpet. It is this residual throne and kingdom of the beast that will be plunged into darkness at the fifth bowl, not the forty-two-month kingdom over the world that was stripped away by God at the seventh

3. See pp. 216–219.

trumpet. Case in point: The scenario reminds one of King Saul's judgment, when he disobeyed God concerning the battle with the Amalekites. If you recall, Saul had disobeyed God by sparing King Agag, as well as some of the choicest of sheep and cattle after the battle. In the following passage, which came immediately after Saul pleaded for forgiveness, one sees the fateful exchange between Saul and Samuel (italics used for emphasis):

"As Samuel turned to go away, Saul caught hold of the hem of his robe, and it tore. And Samuel said to him, 'The Lord has torn the kingdom of Israel from you *this very day*, and given it to a neighbor of yours, who is better than you'" (1 Sam 15:27–28).

Even after the kingdom of Israel was torn from Saul on the day that Samuel pronounced the Lord's judgment, Saul still sat on his throne and exercised his authority for several years over those who were unaware that the kingdom over Israel had already been stripped away from their fallen leader. Similarly, even after "the forty-two-month kingdom of the world" is torn away from the beast at the seventh trumpet, the beast will still exercise what's left of his throne and whatever semblance of authority he can muster over the inhabitants of the earth, until the day that even that is completely plunged into darkness at the fifth bowl.

Sixth Bowl

When the sixth angel poured his bowl of wrath, the water of the Euphrates River was dried up in order to prepare the way for the kings of the east. Next, three demons came from the mouths of Satan, the beast, and the false prophet, and they incited the kings and leaders of the whole world to send their military leaders and troops to the large plain that is located between the city of Jerusalem and the Mediterranean Sea, known as the valley or place of Harmagedon, also known as Armageddon:

> The sixth angel poured his bowl on the great river Euphrates, and its water was dried up in order to prepare the way for the kings from the east. And I saw three foul spirits like frogs coming from the mouth of the dragon, from the mouth of the beast, and from the mouth of the false prophet. These are demonic spirits, performing signs, who go abroad to the kings of the whole world, to assemble them for battle on the great day of God the Almighty. ("See, I am coming like a thief! Blessed is the one who stays awake and is clothed, not going about naked and

exposed to shame.") And they assembled them at the place that in Hebrew is called Harmagedon. (Rev 16:12–16)

This is the first time that one has seen or heard of Satan since he transferred his power and authority to the beast back on the sand of the seashore. If calculating the timeline, it's been slightly over three and a half years since the moment of the transfer. What's the significance? Although Satan will surely be up to no good during the beast's forty-two-month reign (2 Thess 2:9–12), it is the beast who will stand at the forefront during the reign, and this is clearly confirmed by Satan's absence from the pages of Scripture from the transfer until now. Nonetheless, now that both the beast and Satan find themselves without a kingdom, the two will unite one last time as they see the development of the dried-up Euphrates River as their last, best chance to retake control of the world's inhabitants. And how will they propose to accomplish this delusional feat? By bringing as much firepower to the table as possible. This is where the three foul spirits come in: The spirits will go abroad to the leaders of the world, assembling them and their armies to the plains of Armageddon by performing spectacular signs and wonders. No doubt, there will be hundreds of millions of willing volunteers, who are more than eager to act out their frustration and anger toward God, his Son, and his church, for all the torment they think they have unduly suffered: torment from the two witnesses, torment from the trumpet judgments, and, now, torment from the bowl judgments. Once these hard-hearted, obstinate, and blasphemous rebels assemble at Armageddon, it is unknown how long the Lord will make them wait before his next manifestation, but eventually God will make his mighty presence known one last time before the greatest event in the history of the world, which is the appearance of his Son, Jesus Christ.

Fifth Conversation: "I am coming like a thief!"

Notice at the end of the sixth-bowl narrative, the disciple unexpectedly hears a proclamation from the Lord:

"See, I am coming like a thief! Blessed is the one who stays awake and is clothed, not going about naked and exposed to shame" (Rev 16:15).

Why did the Lord choose now of all times to say that he was "coming like a thief"? Because by the time John saw the sixth bowl, the disciple had seen almost the entire set of visions revealing the great Day of the Lord, which began with all the plagues of the trumpets and bowls, and will culminate with the mighty judgment displayed at the glorious manifestation of Christ at Armageddon. Therefore it's important to understand that when the Lord said he was "coming like a thief" this was only a reference to the Day's unexpected arrival, with its heavenly signs and beginning plagues against the earth, not to Christ's manifestation at the end of the Day of the Lord. Observe:

Table 9.2. The Day of the Lord Will Come Like a Thief in the Night		
<————————————Day of the Lord———————————————>		
Heavenly Signs (arrives like a thief)	7 Trumpets and 7 Bowls	The Lord's Return (doesn't arrive like a thief)

If you recall, God's declaration that he is coming like a thief followed by his promise of a blessing to those who stay awake and are clothed (Rev 16:15) echo what Paul earlier said in his first letter to the Thessalonians (italics used for emphasis):

"For you yourselves know very well that the day of the Lord will come *like a thief in the night*. When they say, '*There is peace and security*,' then sudden destruction will come upon them, as labor pains come upon a pregnant woman, and there will be no escape! But you, beloved, are not in darkness, for that day to surprise you like a thief; for you are all children of light and children of the day; we are not of the night or of darkness. *So then let us not fall asleep as others do, but let us keep awake and be sober; for those who sleep sleep at night, and those who are drunk get drunk at night*" (1 Thess 5:2–7).

In the epistle, Paul's additional revelation stating that they will be saying "There is peace and security" at the Day's arrival makes it quite easy to prove that God and the apostle were not speaking about Christ's manifestation at Armageddon at the end of the Day of the Lord, but rather to the heavenly signs at the beginning of the Day. How so? When Christ finally does appear at Armageddon, absolutely no one among the unrighteous will be saying "there is peace and security," having just suffered through all the terrible trumpet plagues and bowl plagues of the Day of the Lord, which will include five months of demonic torture, a death toll of approximately two billion, and an excruciating sore appearing on all who have worshiped the beast and his image. I'm sure the unrighteous will be saying something at the Lord's return, but it won't be "there is peace and security."

Unless one grasps the fact that the arrival of the Day of the Lord with its heavenly signs and initial trumpet plagues is not synonymous with the very end of the Day with the appearance of Christ at Armageddon, then the correct interpretation of all New Testament passages that include the phrase "coming like a thief" will remain difficult to achieve. As an illustration, look at a very familiar text in 2 Peter:

"But the day of the Lord will come like a thief, and then the heavens will pass away with a loud noise, and the elements will be dissolved with fire, and the earth and everything that is done on it will be disclosed. Since all these things are to be dissolved in this way, what sort of persons ought you to be in leading lives of holiness and godliness, waiting for and hastening the coming of the day of God, because of which the heavens will be set ablaze and dissolved, and the elements will melt with fire?" (2 Pet 3:10–12).

Instead of correctly understanding Peter's description of the unexpected arrival of the Day of the Lord as the unexpected arrival of the heavenly signs and the Day of God—when the heavens will pass away with a loud noise, the elements will be dissolved with fire, and everything that has been done on the earth will be disclosed, as God begins to relentlessly shake the powers of heaven and the earth during each of the trumpet and bowl plagues—most mistakenly believe the apostle was only describing what will happen at the moment of Christ's appearance at Armageddon, which, of course, could not be further from the truth.

Seventh Bowl

At some point, while the world's armies are impatiently waiting on the plains of Armageddon, certainly in a state of confusion, suddenly and unexpectedly, the ground will begin to shake, initiating the greatest earthquake the world has ever seen:

> The seventh angel poured his bowl into the air, and a loud voice came out of the temple, from the throne, saying, "It is done!" And there came flashes of lightning, rumblings, peals of thunder, and a violent earthquake, such as had not occurred since people were upon the earth, so violent was that earthquake. The great city was split into three parts, and the cities of the nations fell. God remembered great Babylon and gave her the wine-cup

of the fury of his wrath. And every island fled away, and no mountains were to be found. (Rev 16:17–20)

As stated earlier in the study, Revelation speaks of three earthquakes; this is the latest and greatest. Again, here are the three:

Table 9.3. The Three Earthquakes in Revelation			
	1st Earthquake (Rev 11:13, 12:16)	2nd Earthquake (Rev 6:12)	3rd Earthquake (Rev 16:18)
When:	Abomination of Desolation	Along with the heavenly signs, the earthquake ushers in the Day of the Lord	7th Bowl
Where:	Jerusalem	Global	Global
What:	Mount of Olives is split, creating a very wide valley for the 144,000 Jewish remnant's escape	Every mountain and island is removed from its place at the coming of the Day of the Lord	Every mountain and island disappears prior to the Lord's return

Even after the seventh bowl earthquake, God still has another judgment in store for the rebellious inhabitants of the earth. With the aftershocks of the earthquake still reverberating, John saw people everywhere begin to fall lifeless to the ground as gigantic boulders of ice pounded the earth, destroying everything, everywhere:

> ... and huge hailstones, each weighing about a hundred pounds, dropped from heaven on people, until they cursed God for the plague of the hail, so fearful was that plague. (Rev 16:21)

The sights and sounds of one hundred-pound hail falling upon people must have pushed John's audio and visual perceptions to the limit. Just when the disciple may have thought he couldn't withstand any more visage of God's devastating power and destruction, the vision ended. Then, a familiar face was seen.

Sixth Conversation, First of Eight Subjects: Babylon the Great

The face belonged to one of the seven angels whom John had just seen in one of the visions of the seven bowls. The angel approached John from within the throne room and spoke with him concerning the mysterious, heretofore unknown "Babylon the great" and its end-time demise at the hands of the beast. As you know, John had already become quite familiar with the beast from the earlier portents and information found in Rev 13, which described the beast's forty-two-month reign over the inhabitants of the earth and how he would be allowed to conquer the saints using his human liaison, the man of lawlessness. As far as Babylon the great was concerned, that name had only been seen twice: first, in the second of the three angelic announcements, when an angel proclaimed "Fallen, fallen, is Babylon the great" (Rev 14:8), and just recently when John said during his description of the seventh-bowl plague that "God remembered great Babylon and gave her the wine-cup of the fury of his wrath." With that backdrop, here are John's introductory remarks describing the mystery of Babylon:

> Then one of the seven angels who had the seven bowls came and said to me, "Come, I will show you the judgment of the great whore who is seated on many waters, with whom the kings of the earth have committed fornication, and with the wine of whose fornication the inhabitants of the earth have become drunk." So he carried me away in the spirit into a wilderness, and I saw a woman sitting on a scarlet beast that was full of blasphemous names, and it had seven heads and ten horns. The woman was clothed in purple and scarlet, and adorned with gold and jewels and pearls, holding in her hand a golden cup full of abominations and the impurities of her fornication; and on her forehead was written a name, a mystery: "Babylon the great, mother of whores and of earth's abominations." And I saw that the woman was drunk with the blood of the saints and the blood of the witnesses to Jesus. When I saw her, I was greatly amazed. But the angel said to me, "Why are you so amazed? I will tell you the mystery of the woman, and of the beast with seven heads and ten horns that carries her." (Rev 17:1–7)

The circumstances surrounding the sixth conversation covered new territory for John: Instead of only verbal commentary given by God's representative (the pattern of the previous five conversations), this encounter included John being carried away in the spirit and shown a new vision. And make no mistake, the vision of the woman was startling! Obviously, this is another one of God's portents. The gaudily clad harlot sitting atop the scarlet-colored seven-headed beast symbolized something, and, thankfully, God's angel was about to reveal what that something was. Next is a list of some of the details of the portent. Let's see what can be gathered by an initial perusal.

Table 9.4. Vision of Babylon the Great	
1. Details	She was seated on many waters (17:1).
Comment	Whoever or whatever the woman represents, she appears to be global.
2. Details	She sits on the beast . . . (17:3a).
Comment	There's some sort of symbiotic relationship between the woman and the beast.
3. Details	The beast that she sat on had seven heads and ten horns (17:3b).
Comment	Let's wait for help from the angel!
4. Details	The woman was clothed with purple and scarlet and adorned with gold and jewels and pearls (17:4a).
Comment	She considers herself royalty, which explains her garb. Even if she's not royalty, she will feign royalty, and her enormous wealth will be very convincing to her subjects. Just as true royalty demands adoration and homage, she will expect likewise.
5. Details	She was holding in her hand a golden cup full of abominations and the impurities of her fornication. On her forehead was written, "Babylon the great, mother of whores and earth's abominations" (17:4b–5).
Comment	Not only has the woman committed multiple abominations against God, but in some way idolatry is among them. She has either been guilty of worshiping idols herself or has facilitated the sin of idolatry by her very existence, both of which rob God of worship due only to him.
6. Details	The woman was drunk with the blood of the saints and the blood of the witnesses to Jesus (17:6).
Comment	She has either directly killed the saints or has been complicit in their murders.

In short, Babylon the great is global, rich, and evil.

Sixth Conversation, Second of Eight Subjects: The Beast's Wounded Head

When John saw the portent of the woman for the first time, he was understandably greatly amazed (Rev 17:6). But that wasn't the case with the image of the scarlet beast and its seven heads and ten horns; he had previously seen that portent (Rev 13:1–3). However, if you recall, at the time there was something peculiar in the vision that had left the disciple as well as us quite perplexed:

"One of its heads seemed to have received a death blow, but its mortal wound had been healed" (Rev 13:3).

Finally, after several visions seen by John (not to mention four chapters read by us), the angel brings the mystery of the wounded head to the forefront:

> The beast that you saw was, and is not, and is about to ascend from the bottomless pit and go to destruction. And the inhabitants of the earth, whose names have not been written in the book of life from the foundation of the world, will be amazed when they see the beast, because it was and is not and is to come. This calls for a mind that has wisdom: the seven heads are seven mountains on which the woman is seated; also, they are seven kings, of whom five have fallen, one is living, and the other has not yet come; and when he comes, he must remain only a little while. (Rev 17:8–10)

According to the angel, not only do the seven heads of the beast represent the seven hills of Rome but they also represent seven kings. (Note: One knows that the angel could only have been referencing the city of Rome, i.e., the city of seven hills, because at the time of the conversation between the angel and John, the Roman Empire was ruling the nations of the earth; compare Rev 17:9a and 17:18). Notice that the angel was very specific: The heads do not represent seven kingdoms (Greek: *basileias*), but they represent seven kings (Greek: *basileis*). Next, the angel gave John a quick history of the seven kings:

1. Five have fallen.
2. One is living.
3. The other has not yet come.

The statements are quite simple: Five of the kings have been defeated; one is presently ruling, i.e., the Roman king, and the seventh is yet to rule. However, we still have a question: Are these kings human or angelic? Thankfully, something the angel said next reveals the answer. Since it has already been determined that the beast is an evil angel who will one day rise out of the bottomless pit (Rev 11:7), a fact again confirmed here (Rev 17:8),[4] the seven kings must also be angels because it was said that the beast "belongs to the seven":

> As for the beast that was and is not, it is an eighth but it belongs to the seven, and it goes to destruction. (Rev 17:11)

Since the beast is an angel and yet he's one of the seven heads, then by necessity, the other six heads must also represent angels, correct? But no sooner is that elementary question solved, that another one surfaces because of the little phrase "it is an eighth." Where did the number eight come from? The portent only showed seven heads. Nevertheless, the angel gave an explanation: The beast "was" and "is not" and "is an eighth." In other words, the beast was a ruler over one of the seven kingdoms; he's not presently ruling the sixth, Roman kingdom; but he will later rule a kingdom after the seven kingdoms, which, obviously, is the eighth kingdom.

In surprisingly short order, the angel has unlocked the mystery of the wounded head on the seven-headed beast. Recall at the time we initially addressed Rev 13:3 (chapter 7), we said that if the seven heads of the beast represented seven men, then the translation of one of the heads having "a mortal wound" would be acceptable, but if the seven heads represented angels, then the translation would be misleading. Since we now know the seven heads are indeed seven angels, then the translation should have more closely reflected the original text: "a plague of its death" (Greek: *hē plēgē tou thanatou autou*). And the meaning? The angel was wounded by a plague of death in a way that only an angel can suffer a deadly wound: by God casting him into the bottomless pit, where he has remained to this day. In most cases that would certainly be the death knell for any angel, wouldn't you agree? But not for the beast. According to the words of the angel, the beast will be released from the bottomless pit in the last days in order to rule a second time over what we now know

---

4. Rev 17:8 not only states that the beast will ascend from the bottomless pit, but that he will go to "destruction," which is quite prophetic since his Hebrew and Greek names, *Abaddon* and *Apollyon*, both mean "destruction," and his human liaison, the man of lawlessness, is called "the son of destruction" by the apostle Paul (Greek: *huios tēs apōleias*; see 2 Thess 2:3).

will be the eighth kingdom. It is with this understanding that one knows the "beast's future release from the bottomless pit," whereby the beast is in a sense coming back from the dead, is symbolized by the "healed" plague of death on one of the heads.

The angel's simple revelation is unprecedented, stupendous, and, regrettably, misunderstood. Since most have no comprehension that the beast is an angel but instead mistakenly believe him to be a man, many either predict that Satan is going to actually raise a man from the dead or at least deceive the inhabitants of the earth into thinking that he has raised a man from the dead, both of which are incorrect.[5] In no way has Scripture ever insinuated that Satan was going to raise some evil reprobate back from the dead in the last days because Scripture has always been abundantly clear that God alone possesses the power of life:

"Very truly, I tell you, the hour is coming, and is now here, when the dead will hear the voice of the Son of God, and those who hear will live. For just as the Father has life in himself, so he has granted the Son also to have life in himself" (John 5:25–26).

Only the Father, the Son, and the Holy Spirit have the power to raise the dead; angels do not; and, most certainly, men do not.

With the mystery of the wounded head solved, one should now understand that one of the major themes of Revelation is the chronicling of the beast's activities during the future forty-two-month eighth kingdom. And yet, theologians and commentators alike continue to propagate the idea that Revelation only concerned the first-century church and her persecution by Rome, which, as one now knows, was during the sixth kingdom.[6]

Sixth Conversation, Third of Eight Subjects: The Eight Empires

Now that one knows the seven heads on the scarlet beast represent seven angels who have ruled in the past or will rule in the future, what more

---

5. Rhodes, *End Times in Chronological Order*, 134.

6. The all too common sentiment expressed today by theologians and commentators goes something like this: Revelation is not a roadmap for the future but rather a letter written for the comfort of the first-century Christians. The sentiment is unfortunate, but predictable. Because most are unaware that the angel specifically revealed to John that the time of the beast pertains to the future eighth kingdom rather than the past sixth kingdom, i.e., the Roman Empire, it's natural to dismiss what one does not understand. Granted, although the letter doubtless encouraged the first-century saints, still, according to the angel, the vision spoke of future events.

can be known about them? With the help of the Old Testament, and especially the book of Daniel, the eight empires of the seven kings will be identified. And in so doing, one will learn that each empire had a common trait: Somewhere along the way, someone within the empire tried to destroy the nation of Israel. Beginning with the Egyptian Empire and Israel's birth as a nation in the land of Goshen, the following is a list of the eight empires plus a brief statement concerning the attempted destruction of God's people:

Table 9.5. The Eight Empires and Their Attempted Destruction of Israel	
The 8 Empires	**The Attempted Destruction of Israel**
1. Egyptian Empire	The last pharaoh during Israel's 400-year captivity attempted to kill every newborn male in order to weaken the nation so that it would remain in captivity (Exod 1).
2. Assyrian Empire	The armies of the empire conquered and kidnapped Israel's 10 northern tribes in 722 BC (2 Kgs 17).
3. Babylonian Empire	The armies of the empire conquered and kidnapped Israel's 2 southern tribes in 586 BC (2 Kgs 25).
4. Medes/Persian Empire	The principal minister of the empire, Haman, attempted to have all of the Jews killed (Esth 3).
5. Grecian Empire	One of the Seleucid kings, Antiochus Epiphanies, attempted to destroy Judaism and the people of Israel (Dan 11).
6. Roman Empire	The empire conquered and persecuted Israel through the likes of men such as Tiberius, Caligula, and Nero, before Jerusalem finally fell to Titus in AD 70 (the entire NT).
7. Seventh Empire	This empire will attempt, if it hasn't already, to destroy Israel at some point between the Roman Empire and the 8th empire (Rev 17:10).
8. Eighth Empire	Under the rule of the beast, the man of lawlessness will attempt to destroy all of God's people, Jew and gentile (Rev 13).

In addition to Rev 17, several of the seven angelic kings and/or their respective kingdoms are referenced in the book of Daniel. In the second chapter, Daniel records Nebuchadnezzar's dream of a large metallic statue. When the king sought the interpretation of the dream, all of the magicians, enchanters, and sorcerers were unable to do so; it was at this time Daniel was summoned and asked to interpret the dream:

"You were looking, O king, and lo! there was a great statue. This statue was huge, its brilliance extraordinary; it was standing before you, and its appearance was frightening. The head of that statue was of fine gold, its chest and arms of silver, its middle and thighs of bronze, its legs of iron, its feet partly of iron and partly of clay" (Dan 2:31–33).

Daniel identified the head of gold as representing Nebuchadnezzar's present Babylonian Empire, which one now knows from the above list was the third empire (italics used for emphasis):

"You, O king, the king of kings—to whom the God of heaven has given the kingdom, the power, the might, and the glory, into whose hand he has given human beings, wherever they live, the wild animals of the field, and the birds of the air, and whom he has established as ruler over them all—*you are the head of gold*" (Dan 2:37–38).

Since Daniel identified Babylon as the kingdom symbolized by the head of gold, the meaning of the other three sections of the statue are quite easy to determine when reconciling them to the eight rulers of Rev 17. Observe (italics used for emphasis):

Table 9.6. Reconciliation of the Eight Rulers of Rev 17 and the Four Empires of Dan 2	
8 Rulers in Rev 17	4 Empires in Dan 2
1. Egyptian Prince	
2. Assyrian Prince	
3. *Babylonian Prince*	*Head of Gold*
4. Medes and Persian Prince	Chest and Arms of Silver
5. Grecian Prince	Middle and Thighs of Bronze
6. Roman Prince	Legs of Iron, Feet and Toes Are Part Iron, Part Clay
7. The 7th Prince	
8. The Beast	

As one can see, the four sections of the statue correspond to the Babylonian Empire, the Medes and Persian Empire, the Grecian Empire, and the Roman Empire.[7]

---

7. The angelic princes of two of the four empires, the prince of Persia and the prince

Next, we turn to Daniel's dream of the four beasts in Dan 7:

"I, Daniel, saw in my vision by night the four winds of heaven stirring up the great sea, and four great beasts came up out of the sea, different from one another. The first one was like a lion and had eagles' wings. Then, as watched, its wings were plucked off, and it was lifted up from the ground and made to stand on two feet like a human being; and a human mind was given to it. Another beast appeared, a second one, that looked like a bear. It was raised up on one side, had three tusks in its mouth among its teeth and was told, 'Arise, devour many bodies!' After this, as I watched, another appeared, like a leopard. The beast had four wings of a bird on its back and four heads; and dominion was given to it. After this I saw in the visions by night a fourth beast, terrifying and dreadful and exceedingly strong. It had great iron teeth and was devouring, breaking in pieces, and stamping what was left with its feet. It was different from all the beasts that preceded it, and it had ten horns. I was considering the horns, when another horn appeared, a little one coming up among them; to make room for it, three of the earlier horns were plucked up by the roots. There were eyes like human eyes in this horn, and a mouth speaking arrogantly" (Dan 7:2-8).

Unlike the four empires in Dan 2, Dan 7 speaks of four angelic princes and their rule over a slightly different set of empires. These princes were drawn by God as four beasts in Daniel's dream. As the prophet was considering the fourth beast, which had ten horns, three horns were brought down to make room for an eleventh, little horn. Daniel later saw this same fourth beast, with his little horn, brought before the throne of God in heaven. And as Daniel describes the scene, the prophet was flabbergasted when he heard the little horn speaking arrogantly in front of the Father:

"I watched then because of the noise of the arrogant words that the horn was speaking. And as I watched, the beast was put to death, and its body destroyed and given over to be burned with fire. As for the rest of the beasts, their dominion was taken away, but their lives were prolonged for a season and a time" (Dan 7:11-12).

Later in Revelation, that scenario will be repeated again following the vision of the Battle of Armageddon, as the seven-headed beast and the false prophet are captured, judged, and thrown into the lake of fire. As stated in chapter 1 of this study, there are only two personalities in the

---

of Greece, are referenced in Dan 10:12-21.

world that will be cast into the lake of fire one thousand years prior to anyone else, and they are the beast and the false prophet. Therefore, the beast and false prophet of Revelation and the beast and the little horn of Dan 7 are one and the same. Now, with the knowledge that the fourth beast with ten horns in Dan 7 is the same beast with ten horns that will rule the eighth kingdom in Rev 17, the four beasts in Dan 7 can be identified as follows (italics used for emphasis):

Table 9.7. Reconciliation of Rev 17 and Dan 7	
Princes in Rev 17	**The 4 Evil Princes in Dan 7**
1. Angel over the Egyptian Empire	
2. Angel over the Assyrian Empire	
3. Angel over the Babylonian Empire	
4. Angel over the Medes and Persian Empire	
5. Angel over the Grecian Empire	1. The Lion-beast
6. Angel over the Roman Empire	2. The Bear-beast
7. Angel over the 7th Empire	3. The Leopard-beast
8. *Angel over the 8th Empire*	4. *The terrifying beast with 10 horns*

Next, by reconciling Rev 17, Dan 2, and Dan 7, one has the following:

Table 9.8. Reconciliation of Rev 17, Dan 2, and Dan 7		
Rev 17	**Dan 2**	**Dan 7**
1. Angel over the Egyptian Empire		
2. Angel over the Assyrian Empire		
3. Angel over the Babylonian Empire	1. Head of Gold	
4. Angel over the Medes and Persian Empire	2. Chest and Arms of Silver	
5. Angel over the Grecian Empire	3. Middle and Thighs of Bronze	1. Lion-beast
6. Angel over the Roman Empire	4. Legs, Feet of Iron and Clay	2. Bear-beast

Table 9.8. Reconciliation of Rev 17, Dan 2, and Dan 7		
Rev 17	**Dan 2**	**Dan 7**
7. Angel over the 7th Empire		3. Leopard-beast
8. Angel over the 8th Empire		4. Terrifying beast with 10 horns

While examining the chart, perhaps the reader has already detected a common mistake made by many commentators of Dan 2 and 7: They believe the four empires of Dan 2 correlate with the four angelic princes of Dan 7. As one can see, they do not. And what's the unfortunate result of this miscalculation? Many anticipate that the Roman Empire, the sixth empire, will return in the last days, rather than recognizing that a new, eighth empire will arise—the worldwide empire of the beast.[8]

Sixth Conversation, Fourth of Eight Subjects: The Seventh King

Prior to the above reconciliation of the three passages, the following is all we knew concerning the seventh king (italics used for emphasis):

"This calls for a mind that has wisdom: the seven heads are seven mountains on which the woman is seated; also, they are seven kings, of whom five have fallen, one is living, *and the other has not yet come; and when he comes, he must remain only a little while*" (Rev 17:9–10).

God's angel, who addressed John during the sixth empire, indicated that at some unknown point in time before the future arrival of the beast and the eighth kingdom that the seventh king will arrive and "remain only a little while." Granted, that's not much to go on, but at least one knows that the seventh king is distinguished from the beast, the eighth

---

8. While clinging to the belief of the Roman Empire's return, some might interject, "What about 'the ten toes' of the statue? Surely they must align with 'the ten horns' of Daniel's vision in chapter 7." However, as many are doubtless unaware, Scripture never once mentions the phrase "ten toes" in Dan 2; it only mentions "toes" as being part of the feet (Dan 2:41–42). The fact that two feet usually have ten toes is no more relevant to Nebuchadnezzar's dream and its meaning than the fact that, had Nebuchadnezzar somehow been able to count the fingers on the hands of the statue, he probably would have seen ten fingers. Here's the point: Assuming the statue had ten fingers and ten toes, those twenty appendages have nothing to do with the dream's meaning.

king. Furthermore, because of our most recent reconciliation, one knows the seventh king is identified with the leopard-beast:

"After this, as I watched, another appeared, like a leopard. The beast had four wings of a bird on its back and four heads; and dominion was given to it" (Dan 7:6).

As many may or may not be aware, the leopard has often been associated with Germany. The possibility of Germany being in some way connected to the seventh empire raises an interesting prospect: Could Hitler's persecution and attempted destruction of the nation of Israel during WWII have been under the direction of the seventh angelic king? It's highly probable. It is certain that Hitler's reign and the Third Reich were indeed short-lived in relation to the six other empires, only lasting approximately twelve years (1933–45). This brevity would fulfill the angel's comment in Rev 17:10 about the seventh king. However, the primary reason that the German Empire of the thirties and forties might indeed have been the seventh empire is because of the unprecedented persecution and genocide committed during the empire against the Jewish people, which, as one knows, was the predominant characteristic of each of the first six angelic rulers and their earthly empires. Although Israel constantly suffered at the hands of the six angelic rulers, her suffering under Adolf Hitler and the Third Reich during WWII not only matched their cruelty, but far surpassed it.[9] Unless Israel will somehow suffer another equivalent holocaust prior to the arrival of the beast and the eighth kingdom, then the evidence is overwhelming that the German Empire under the reign of Hitler was indeed the seventh empire. (Note: If the German Empire in WWII was the seventh kingdom, then that would make Rev 17:10 one of the earliest fulfilled prophecies given during John's visit to heaven, proving that, unbeknownst to all the naysayers, God's calendar of apocalyptic events has been silently marching closer and closer down through the centuries to the inevitable realization of the eighth kingdom—the kingdom of the beast.)

---

9. As noted earlier, approximately six million Jewish people were killed during WWII.

FIRST SEQUENCE, PART 2

Sixth Conversation, Fifth of Eight Subjects: The Beast's First Kingdom

Since the angel revealed that the beast is one of the seven kings and yet will return a second time in order to rule the eighth kingdom, which one of the seven kings might he be? We already know the beast was not the sixth angel, because God's angel said the beast "is not" during the time that the sixth angel was presently in power. Likewise, it was determined that the beast cannot be the seventh angel because God's angel distinguished the seventh angel from the beast (17:10). Therefore, it is certain that the beast was one of the first five kings. Here are the options:

Table 9.9. Five Options for the Beast's First Empire		
1. Egyptian Empire	3. Babylonian Empire	5. Grecian Empire
2. Assyrian Empire	4. Medes and Persian Empire	

Of the five empires, the third one—the Babylonian Empire—immediately jumps to the forefront because of two passages in the Old Testament. In the first passage, notice a unique characteristic shared by "the angel over the Babylonian Empire" and the beast:

"King Nebuchadnezzar made a golden statue whose height was sixty cubits and whose width was six cubits; he set it up on the plain of Dura in the province of Babylon. Then King Nebuchadnezzar sent for the satraps, the prefects, and the governors, the counselors, the treasurers, the justices, the magistrates, and all the officials of the provinces to assemble and come to the dedication of the statue that King Nebuchadnezzar had set up. So the satraps, the prefects, and the governors, the counselors, the treasurers, the justices, the magistrates, and all the officials of the provinces, assembled for the dedication of the statute that King Nebuchadnezzar had set up. When they were standing before the statute that Nebuchadnezzar had set up, the herald proclaimed aloud, 'You are commanded, O peoples, nations, and languages, that when you hear the sound of the horn, pipe, lyre, trigon, harp, drum, and entire musical ensemble, you are to fall down and worship the golden statute that King Nebuchadnezzar has set up. Whoever does not fall down and worship shall immediately be thrown into a furnace of blazing fire'" (Dan 3:1–6).

What's familiar? Of course, it's the statue. The beast will direct the man of lawlessness to cause the inhabitants of the earth to construct an image so that people from every nation and language are forced to fall down and worship the image (Rev 13:14–18), just as the angelic prince of the Babylonian Empire caused King Nebuchadnezzar to have a sixty-cubit golden statue built in order that all peoples and nations of every language would fall down and worship that image. And if they refused, a fiery furnace awaited them, just as a beheading will await those during the beast's empire.

If the third and eighth angelic princes are one and the same, the future saints have already been given a blueprint of how to respond to the threat of death. Of course, I am alluding to the three Hebrew young men, Shadrach, Meshach, and Abednego, who refused to bow down and worship anyone other than one true God.[10] As most know, the three were delivered unscathed out of the fiery furnace (Dan 3:19–30). However, at the time they made their stand, they did not know for certain that God was going to deliver them. What they did know was that they would rather die than bow down to anyone other than God. The Lord will expect nothing less from those who are confronted with the same threat in the future.

The second passage from the Old Testament suggesting that the beast may have been the angelic King of Babylon is found in Isa 14. Although the text is universally thought to be a reference to Satan, there's evidence that says otherwise. This much is certain: What began as a taunt by Isaiah directed to the "human" King of Babylon (Isa 14:4) soon turned into a taunt by the prophet directed to the "angelic" King of Babylon (Isa 14:12). Here's the taunt to the "angelic" king:

"How you are fallen from heaven, O Day Star, son of Dawn! How you are cut down to the ground, you who laid the nations low! You said in your heart, 'I will ascend to heaven; I will raise my throne above the stars of God; I will sit on the mount of assembly on the heights of Zaphon; I will ascend to the tops of the clouds, I will make myself like the Most High.' But you are brought down to Sheol, to the depths of the Pit. Those who see you will stare at you, and ponder over you: 'Is this the man who made the earth tremble, who shook kingdoms, who made the world like a desert and overthrew its cities, who would not let his prisoners go home?'" (Isa 14:12–17).

The primary reason that theologians and commentators believe the above passage is a description of Satan is because in their eyes there are no other candidates. And then, when that assumption is coupled with

---

10. The Hebrew names of the young men were Hananiah, Mishael, and Azariah, respectively (Dan 1:19).

the KJV's translation of the Hebrew word *hêlêl* in Isa 14:12, the result is another name for Satan:

"How art thou fallen from heaven, O *Lucifer*, son of the morning!"

For four hundred years and counting (since the KJV translation), everyone has accepted without question that one of Satan's names is Lucifer, and that acceptance, in turn, has solidified the notion that the angelic king of Babylon referenced in Isa 14:12–17 must be Satan. But is it? Admittedly, disputing the name of Lucifer as one of Satan's names may be an uphill battle; however, the foregone conclusion that the king of Babylon referenced in Isa 14:12–17 is Satan should certainly be up for debate. Of course, one knows where this is headed: Now that one knows the beast is also an angel, is it possible that Isaiah was actually taunting the beast, and not Satan? The question has merit. In order to examine, let's look again at Isaiah's taunt of the "angelic" king of Babylon, whoever he might be:

Table 9.10. Characteristics of the Angelic King of Babylon
1. You are fallen from heaven (14:12).
2. You are cut down to the ground and have laid the nations low (14:12).
3. You said "I will raise my throne above the stars of God; and I will sit on the mount of assembly on the heights of Zaphon" (14:13).
4. You said "I will ascend to the tops of the clouds, I will make myself like the Most High" (14:14).
5. You are brought down to Sheol, to the depths of the pit (14:15).
6. You caused curiosity and perplexity from the occupants of the bottomless pit (14:16).
7. You made the earth tremble, shook kingdoms, overthrew cities, and made the world like a desert (14:16–17).
8. You would not let your prisoners go home (14:17).

One must admit, this king doesn't seem human. He had fallen from heaven and wanted to raise his throne above the stars of God, to ascend to the tops of the clouds, and to make himself like the Most High (Isa 14:12–14). These descriptions sound more like that of a fallen angel rather than a fallen man. Nevertheless, if indeed he is an angel, was he Satan, or the beast, or perhaps just the unnamed angel over the Babylonian Empire? Let's determine:

THE SEQUENCE

Note that Isaiah said once the king of Babylon is brought down to the bottomless pit that those who are already confined to the pit will stare at him and ponder over him out of curiosity and perplexity as to his identity (Isa 14:16). Doesn't it seem strange that if the king were indeed Satan, the occupants of the bottomless pit would be so astounded and perplexed the moment they laid eyes on Satan that they would stare at him and ponder over him, and then question whether or not he was the one who made the earth tremble, shook the kingdoms, and made the world like a desert, overthrowing its cities? Wouldn't those who had previously been thrown in the bottomless pit be familiar with Satan and his atrocities against the earth, especially since he had doubtless been their leader since his primeval rebellion against God? If the occupants of the pit did not think Satan was the one who made the earth tremble and shook the kingdoms, then who did they expect? Furthermore, if the occupants were indeed expressing perplexity toward Satan as he entered the bottomless pit, then that particular event is yet to be fulfilled! Why you ask? Satan has never been brought down to the bottomless pit to date and will never darken its gates until the end of the Battle of Armageddon, at which time only then will he be bound and thrown into the pit (Rev 20:2–3). Therefore, if Isaiah was truly taunting Satan, he could only have been taunting him with an event, as it stands now, that was almost three thousand years in the future from the time Isaiah spoke those words! One would think that Isaiah's taunting of the individual in question would lose some of its effectiveness if the threatened event was over three thousand years in the individual's future, correct? Besides, if Satan was the one being taunted, that would necessarily mean that after at least three thousand years—when Satan is finally cast into the pit—the occupants of the bottomless pit still don't recognize him! The implications are inexplicable.

Next, there's the issue of the following statement: "who would not let his prisoners go home" (Isa 14:17). When did Satan not let his prisoners go home? I'm well aware of the concept of one being imprisoned by Satan while one remains captive to sin, and that Jesus was sent to set the captive free (Luke 4:18), but Isa 14:17 specifically states that the king of Babylon would not let his prisoners "go home." Although the metaphor of Jesus setting the captive free from the bondage of Satan certainly carries with it the thought of "freedom in Christ" it doesn't carry with it the thought of the new convert's "freedom to return home" because before Christ set the captive free, the captive's home would have been with Satan in sin (Acts 26:18). In other words, when one is set free from sin, one doesn't return "home" to a life of sin, but instead one has become a new creature in Christ (2 Cor 5:17). Something continues to seem amiss.

As one can see, the assumption that Satan is the king of Babylon is fraught with difficulties. Therefore, if one will momentarily suspend that assumption, and, instead, entertain the thought that the "king of Babylon" represents the beast, then one will see that each of the difficulties suddenly disappear. Observe the following explanations:

1. If the king of Babylon was the beast, then Isaiah's taunt to him has left us this scenario: Immediately after the beast's reign over the Babylonian Empire (ca. 539 BC), he was caught and cast into the bottomless pit, at which time the occupants of the pit understandably did not recognize him, as they immediately questioned his identity and whether he was the one behind the reputation that preceded him, which was that this powerful prince, whoever he was, had wreaked unprecedented havoc all over the known world, shaking kingdoms, and making the world like a desert.

2. If Isaiah, who prophesied approximately 740 BC, was indeed taunting the beast about his upcoming future, then the taunted event of "being cast into the bottomless pit" would only have been two hundred years from being fulfilled (ca. 539 BC), rather than three thousand years and counting, had the taunt truly applied to Satan.

3. If the king of Babylon was the beast, the phrase "who would not let his prisoners go home" could easily be explained as follows: Once the human king of Babylon, Nabonidus, who was under the influence of the beast, refused to allow the Jewish prisoners to return home after their seventy-year captivity imposed by God, the Lord then caused Cyrus the Great, the human king over the next empire, i.e., the Persian Empire, to facilitate their release in order that they might finally return to their homeland (Ezra 1:1–11).

The above remarks perfectly support the scenario that Isaiah was sent by God to taunt the beast two hundred years prior to the end of his reign over the Babylonian Empire, at which time he was then accosted and cast into the bottomless pit. And speaking of the pit, if the beast was unrecognizable when he entered, he certainly isn't now. By the time of the first century, which was when John penned the following words concerning the demons that will be released out of the pit at the fifth trumpet, the beast had already gained quite the reputation, to the point that he was simply known as "the angel of the bottomless pit":

"They have as king over them the angel of the bottomless pit; his name in Hebrew is *Abaddon*, and in Greek he is called *Apollyon*" (Rev 9:11).

Assuming the preceding postulations are correct, not only is the beast known as "the angel of the bottomless pit," *Abaddon*, and *Apollyon*, but now, one more name can be added to his repertoire of identifications, and that is the name "Lucifer."

Sixth Conversation, Sixth of Eight Subjects: The Beast's Ten Horns

After revealing to John the mystery of the wounded head on the seven-headed beast, the angel turned the disciple's attention to the meaning of the beast's ten horns:

> And the ten horns that you saw are ten kings who have not yet received a kingdom, but they are to receive authority as kings for one hour, together with the beast. These are united in yielding their power and authority to the beast. (Rev 17:12–13)

The angel said the ten horns are ten kings. Again, the same question: Are the ten kings angels or humans? Let's return to Dan 7 for help:

"After this I saw in the visions by night a fourth beast, terrifying and dreadful and exceedingly strong. It had great iron teeth and was devouring, breaking in pieces, and stamping what was left with its feet. It was different from all the beasts that preceded it, and it had ten horns. I was considering the horns, when another horn appeared, a little one coming up among them; to make room for it, three of the earlier horns were plucked up by the roots. There were eyes like human eyes in this horn, and a mouth speaking arrogantly" (Dan 7:7–8).

The prophet said the eleventh, little horn had eyes like "a human" and a mouth speaking arrogantly. And just a little later, Daniel again spoke about the little horn's arrogant words:

"I watched then because of the noise of the arrogant words that the horn was speaking. And as I watched, the beast was put to death, and its body destroyed and given over to be burned with fire" (Dan 7:11).

Since this scene was shown earlier to be the moment when God will judge the beast and the false prophet just before having them cast into the lake of fire (Rev 19:20), which proved that the little horn was the human false prophet, it stands to reason that if God's "symbolism of the ten horns" is to remain consistent with "the symbolism of the eleventh horn," then each of the ten horns must also represent men, just as the little horn represents a man.

Now, with that deduction, one can easily understand the reason why the angel told John the ten kings had not yet received a kingdom (Rev 17:12a): Since the ten kings will only receive authority to rule together with the beast after his future release from the bottomless pit (Rev 17:12b), and since at the time of the conversation between the angel and John—which was two thousand years ago—the beast was still confined to the pit (Rev 17:11), then one knows for certain that the ten human kings were not born at the time of the conversation. Furthermore, these determinations now explain the presence of the ten diadems on the ten horns in John's first vision of the seven-headed beast (italics used for emphasis):

"And I saw a beast rising out of the sea, having ten horns and seven heads; and *on its horns were ten diadems*, and on its heads were blasphemous names . . . . One of its heads seemed to have a deathblow, but its plague of death had been healed" (Rev 13:1, 3a).

Since the ten kings will only rule together with the beast after his future release from the bottomless pit, which, as explained earlier, is signified by one of the seven heads appearing as wounded and healed, then naturally God will only show an image of the wounded and healed head along with the ten horns wearing ten crowns as he does here in Rev 13:1–3; if, on the other hand, hypothetically speaking, God were to draw an image of the beast without a wounded and healed head, then by necessity, the ten horns could only be depicted without the ten crowns, signifying that the ten human kings are not yet in existence and the beast is still confined to the bottomless pit.

Question: Do you recall our earlier discussion where it was pointed out that the beast will require human assistance in order to carry out the many atrocities during his forty-two-month reign (Rev 13)?[11] In that discussion it was eventually determined that the man of lawlessness is the human who will assist the beast during the second period of the great tribulation of the saints, i.e., during the nuclear aftermath of pestilence, famine, and death by wild animals, at which time he will then begin to deceive the unrighteous into building an image to the beast as well as target the righteous with beheadings because they refuse to worship that image. At the time of the discussion, it was also revealed that the man will continue to exercise the authority of the beast for the remainder of the beast's forty-two-month reign. But we were still at a loss as to who

11. See p. 224.

was going to assist the beast during the first period of the great tribulation, when the angel will need someone or some group to carry out the nuclear war itself.[12] Since it was proven that the man of lawlessness will not be revealed until the nuclear aftermath, one knew that the beast's human assistance during the first period of suffering had to come from elsewhere. But where? Daniel comes to our rescue:

"I was considering the [ten] horns, when another horn appeared, a little one coming up among them; to make room for it, three of the earlier horns were plucked up by the roots" (Dan 7:8a).

Since it's apparent that "when another horn appeared, a little one coming up among them" depicts the precise moment when the man of lawlessness will be revealed to the world by calling down fire from heaven (Rev 13:13), then it doesn't require much discernment to recognize that the ten kings, who will already be on the scene prior to the revealing of the man, are doubtless the human assistants the beast will incite to initiate the nuclear war. Observe:

Table 9.11. The Ten-Nation Confederation Carries Out the Nuclear War					
1,260-Day Ministry of the 2 Witnesses	Unknown Time Frame	Nuclear War Human Assist. Needed: The 10 Kings	The Great Tribulation of the Saints || Day of the Lord	
^	^	^	1. Nuclear Aftermath	7 Trumpets	The Day Continues
^	^	^	2. Deception of the Unrighteous	Lesser Tribulation of the Saints from the Man of Lawlessness (w/o martyrdom)	^
^	^	^	3. Martyrdom of the Saints after the Revealing of the Man of Lawlessness	^	^
^	^	Human Assistance Needed: The Man of Lawlessness				^
^	^	Beast's 42-Month Reign				^
^	^	1,260-Day Exile of the 144,000 Jewish Remnant				^
^	^	42-Month Trampling of Jerusalem by the Gentile Nations				^
^	^	^	^	^	^
Abomination	Command to the Beast "to Go"			1st Trumpet	7th Trumpet

12. See pp. 224–231.

And from where did the ten kings come? All or part of these ten kings will doubtless come from the same nations that will initially invade Israel at the time of the abomination of desolation. Recall Zechariah's description of the event:

"For I will gather all the nations against Jerusalem to battle, and the city shall be taken and the houses looted and the women raped; half the city shall go into exile, but the rest of the people shall not be cut off from the city" (Zech 14:2).

At the time the nations invade Jerusalem they will still be under the dominion of Satan. Although one does not know exactly how many nations will invade Jerusalem, it is certain that after Satan transfers his power, throne, and great authority to the beast (Rev 13:2), ten of the nations will soon form a confederation under the new leadership of the beast (Rev 17:12–13). And what will be their first assignment? To assist the beast in his quest to conquer the world by the most efficient means possible: a global, nuclear holocaust. Thankfully, as the reader well knows by now, God will stop the nuclear war for the sake of the elect (Matt 24:22), but even after the bombings have stopped, the world will continue to be ravaged by the ensuing nuclear aftermath: pestilence, famine, and death by wild animals (Rev 6:8). As per John, the death count will continue to escalate until a quarter of the earth's population has died. These insufferable conditions will set the stage for the revealing of the man of lawlessness and all of his empty promises.

Sixth Conversation, Seventh of Eight Subjects: The Demise of the Ten Kings

After God shortens the days of the nuclear war and thereby simultaneously shortens the leash of the ten kings, the man of lawlessness will emerge at some point during the nuclear aftermath. The conditions surrounding the man's revealing could easily be described as "the perfect storm." As the inhabitants of the earth are hopelessly floundering in the war's aftermath, the man will emerge from among the many false messiahs and false prophets by calling down fire from heaven (Rev 13:13). He will then proceed to tell the inhabitants all the things that they want to hear, including the bold promise that he will supply all of their needs. It is somewhere around this time, soon after his revealing, that the man will conquer three kings of the recently formed ten-nation confederation in order to make room for himself:

> "As for the ten horns, out of this kingdom ten kings shall arise, and another shall arise after them. This one shall be different from the former ones, and shall put down three kings" (Dan 7:24).

After the three kings are conquered, one would naturally assume that would only leave the man and the remaining seven kings standing; however, God's angel clearly indicates that even after the three kings are subdued, the ten-nation confederation will remain intact, as they are later seen together once again, making war on the Lamb:

> . . . they [the ten kings] will make war on the Lamb, and the Lamb will conquer them, for he is Lord of lords and King of kings, and those with him are called and chosen and faithful. (Rev 17:14)

The fact that the angel continues to refer to the ten kings as "they" until the time they are conquered by the Lamb (which is an obvious reference to Armageddon) confirms that the ten-nation confederation won't dissipate just because the man subdues three of the ten at his revealing to the world.

Sixth Conversation, Eighth of Eight Subjects: The Ten Kings and Babylon the Great

Just as God's angel began the sixth conversation with the subject of Babylon the great, saying that she was seated on many waters, he now ends the conversation with the same subject, revealing that the many waters represented peoples, multitudes, nations, and languages around the globe. Then the angel proceeded to add one additional piece of information: The ten kings in the confederation and the beast will hate Babylon the great and destroy her with fire! Observe:

> And he said to me, "The waters that you saw, where the whore is seated, are peoples and multitudes and nations and languages. And the ten horns that you saw, they and the beast will hate the whore; they will make her desolate and naked; they will devour her flesh and burn her up with fire. For God has put it into their hearts to carry out his purpose by agreeing to give their kingdom to the beast, until the words of God will be fulfilled. The

FIRST SEQUENCE, PART 2

woman you saw is the great city that rules over the kings of the earth." (Rev 17:15–18)

After having seen the woman sitting on top of the beast (Rev 17:3), which, as stated earlier, seemed to imply some sort of symbiotic relationship between the two, one could hardly have anticipated the following: The beast, with the help of his ten-nation confederation, will hate the woman and will devour her flesh and burn her up with fire. Apparently, whatever goodwill he and the woman will have with each other in the beginning won't last too long.[13]

Have you noticed something glaringly absent in the angel's description of Babylon's destruction? There's no mention of the man of lawlessness. True, the beast and the ten kings will hate the woman and destroy her with fire, but what about the man? What's the explanation for his absence? The answer is simple: The beast and the ten kings will destroy Babylon the great before the man of lawlessness is ever revealed to the world.

Fallen, Fallen Is Babylon the Great!

Immediately after the encounter with the angel and the sixth conversation, John resumes seeing the future events of the First Sequence that had temporarily paused after the vision of the seventh bowl. John then saw a vision of an angel proclaiming that "Fallen, fallen is Babylon the great!"

> After this I saw another angel coming down from heaven, having great authority; and the earth was made bright with his splendor. He cried out with a mighty voice, "Fallen, fallen is Babylon the great! It has become a dwelling place of demons, a haunt of every foul spirit, a haunt of every foul bird, a haunt of every foul and hateful beast. For all the nations have drunk of the wine of the wrath of her fornication, and the kings of the earth have committed fornication with her, and the merchants of the earth have grown rich from the power of her luxury." (Rev 18:1–3)

---

13. Concerning the future relationship between the beast and Babylon the great, what might be the impetus behind it? The answer might be found in what each will have to offer one another. From our study it is certain that the beast will be powerful (Rev 13:4) and Babylon will be rich (Rev 17:4). With that said, one possible scenario is that the beast and his ten kings will need the wealth of Babylon to fund the nuclear war, and she will no doubt readily comply to their demands in order to ensure her own safety. Nevertheless, when the nuclear explosions have come and gone, and the beast and the ten kings no longer need Babylon or her wealth, they will "hate the whore; they will make her desolate and naked; they will devour her flesh and burn her up with fire" (Rev 17:16b).

Having just seen the visions of the bowls, the disciple knew this proclamation was in direct response to the catastrophic earthquake of the seventh bowl (italics used for emphasis):

"The seventh angel poured his bowl into the air, and a loud voice came out of the temple, from the throne, saying, 'It is done!' And there came flashes of lightning, rumblings, peals of thunder, and a violent earthquake, such as had not occurred since people were upon the earth, so violent was that earthquake. The great city was split into three parts, and the cities of the nations fell. *God remembered great Babylon and gave her the wine-cup of the fury of his wrath.* And every island fled away, and no mountains were to be found; and huge hailstones, each weighing about a hundred pounds, dropped from heaven on people, until they cursed God for the plague of the hail, so fearful was that plague" (Rev 16:17–21).

At the exact moment of the great earthquake, John said, "God remembered great Babylon and gave her the wine-cup of the fury of his wrath." In other words, as all the cities of the nations around the globe were simultaneously crumbling to the ground (Rev 16:19), it's as if God's eyes glanced in the direction of Rome, the seat of Babylon the great, and watched her as she fell headlong into the Mediterranean Sea, never to be seen or heard from again. But, as you are well aware, this wasn't the first time John heard the announcement. Here's the earlier account recorded back in Rev 14:

"Then another angel, a second, followed, saying, 'Fallen, fallen is Babylon the great! She has made all nations drink of the wine of the wrath of her fornication'" (Rev 14:8).

It's the same announcement made by the same angel at the same moment in time, but in a different sequence. But one might ask, Why is it shorter? As stated in Chapter 3, in Rev 14:8 John only heard part of the announcement; in Rev 18:1–3, he heard the full content.

The fact that we are seeing this announcement a second time is just the latest confirmation of the cardinal rule in the study of sequences: *If the same event is seen twice in a series of events, then two sequences are necessarily present.* In this case, the event of "the fall-of-Babylon announcement" is seen in the Fourth Sequence as well as the First Sequence. Observe:

Table 9.12. The Angelic Announcement "Fallen, Fallen Is Babylon the Great" Appears Twice	
4th Sequence of Revelation	**1st Sequence of Revelation**
1. The 144,000 Jewish remnant are seen standing on Mount Zion with the Lamb (14:1–5).	
2. The 7 angels pour the 7 bowls (implied).	The 7 angels exit the temple and pour the 7 bowls of God's wrath upon the earth (15:5—16:21).
3. 1st angelic announcement (14:6–7).	
4. Second angelic announcement: "Fallen, fallen is Babylon the great!" (14:8).	Second angelic announcement: "Fallen, fallen is Babylon the great! It has become a dwelling place of demons, a haunt of every foul spirit, a haunt of every foul bird, a haunt of every foul and hateful beast. For all nations have drunk of the wine of the wrath of her fornication, and the kings of the earth have committed fornication with her, and the merchants of the earth have grown rich from the power of her luxury" (18:1–3).
5. Third angelic announcement (14:9–11).	
6. The Son of Man is seen seated on a white cloud (14:14–16).	
7. The vintage of the earth is gathered and thrown into the great wine press of God (14:17–20).	
8. After Christ's victory at Armageddon, the 7 angels who had poured the 7 bowls of God's wrath appear with the martyrs who are seen standing and worshiping around God's throne (15:1–4).	

If the reader is keeping tabs, one has learned that Babylon the great will suffer two judgments:

1. First, she will be devoured and burned by the beast and the ten-nation confederation prior to the revealing of the man of lawlessness (Rev 17:16).

2. And, secondly, she will fall headlong into the Mediterranean Sea during the greatest earthquake in history at the pouring of the seventh bowl of God's final wrath (Rev 16:19–20).

The first judgment will destroy Babylon and make her desolate, and the second, for all intents and purposes, will erase all traces of her from having ever existed.

Seventh Conversation: "Come out of her, my people"

Next, John heard another voice from heaven telling "my people" to come out of Babylon:

> Then I heard another voice from heaven saying, "Come out of her, my people, so that you do not take part in her sins, and so that you do not share in her plagues; for her sins are heaped high as heaven, and God has remembered her iniquities. Render to her as she herself has rendered, and repay her double for her deeds; mix a double draught for her in the cup she mixed. As she glorified herself and lived luxuriously, so give her a like measure of torment and grief. Since in heart she says, 'I rule as a queen; I am no widow, and I will never see grief,' therefore her plagues will come in a single day—pestilence and mourning and famine—and she will be burned with fire; for mighty is the Lord God who judges her." (Rev 18:4–8)

Because of the phrase "Come out of her, my people" one knows that the voice is from one of the following: the Father or the Son or the Holy Spirit. Let's determine: Because "the voice" was distinguished from the Holy Spirit in Rev 14:13, one knows that the voice only belongs to the Father or the Son; and because "the voice" specifically makes reference to God (Rev 18:5), then one can be quite certain that the voice belongs to Christ.

Next, a slightly more difficult question is, When did Christ say the phrase "Come out of her, my people"? Did the Lord give the warning two thousand years ago while John was still in the midst of seeing the vision of "the angel making the announcement that Babylon had fallen," or did John hear the Lord's warning "within the vision," placing the timing of the Lord's command alongside the angel's pronouncement in the future? The answer is quite easy: If the Lord's words were truly part of the vision, then the vision records the Lord's command as coming after the angelic announcement, correct? In that scenario, Christ would be telling his people to come out of Babylon after Babylon had already fallen! Obviously, that scenario is nonsensical, which proves that the Lord's warning was not part of the vision, and, instead, was spoken in John's presence two thousand years ago. This fact leads one to a follow-up question: Why would Christ tell his people "to come out" of Babylon two thousand years ago? Was he indicating by this stern warning that the entity of Babylon the great, whatever it is, will eventually deceive the saints into thinking that it was the true church and therefore make them susceptible into joining something that is false? Can there be any other explanation? But if that's true, Babylon the great would have to be a master of disguise, especially since John attributed to her so many overt iniquities: She's filled with pride; she's committed innumerable abominations, including idolatry and the murder of the saints. How could something so evil deceive so many into thinking that she's the true church? Although it seems impossible, obviously it's not or else Christ wouldn't have given the command to come out of her.

A Confirmation of an Earlier Determination

Did you notice the last verse of the above passage, which described the conditions surrounding Babylon's burning at the hands of the ten-nation confederation? Here again is the verse:

"... therefore her plagues will come in a single day—pestilence and mourning and famine—and she will be burned with fire; for mighty is the Lord God who judges her" (Rev 18:8).

According to the Lord's statement, Babylon's burning at the hands of the ten-nation confederacy will occur in the midst of pestilence, mourning, and famine. From this statement alone, one knows that Babylon will be destroyed by the confederation during the nuclear aftermath, which aligns with our earlier determination that Babylon will be destroyed by the confederation prior to the revealing of the man of lawlessness.[14] Observe:

---

14. See p. 305.

Table 9.13. The Ten Kings Will Destroy Babylon during the Nuclear Aftermath, prior to the Revealing of the Man of Lawlessness

1. The Nuclear Aftermath Has Begun	2. 10 Kings Destroy Babylon during the Nuclear Aftermath	3. The Man Is Revealed during the Nuclear Aftermath
"I looked and there was a pale green horse! Its rider's name was Death, and Hades followed with him; they were given authority over a fourth of the earth, to kill with sword (nuclear war), *famine, pestilence, and by the wild animals of the earth*" (Rev 6:8).	". . . therefore her plagues will come in a single day—*pestilence and mourning and famine—and she will be burned with fire*; for mighty is the Lord God who judges her" (Rev 18:8).	"Then I saw another beast that rose out of the earth. . . .It exercises all the authority of the first beast on its behalf, and it makes the earth and its inhabitants worship the first beast. . ." (Rev 13:11a, 12a).

Have you ever wondered why the beast and the ten kings will so hate Babylon that they destroy her and burn her with fire? Doesn't it seem odd that one evil entity would so wish to destroy another evil entity, despite the fact that they are both opposed to God? Won't the confederation know that they and the woman are on the same side? Actually, they won't. And therein lies the rub. Just as Babylon will deceive many believers into thinking that she is the true church—so too will she deceive the ten-nation confederation into thinking the same thing. In the end, little will Babylon know that it was her great ability to deceive that led to her undoing.

Revelations of Babylon's Future Demise Continue

Next, Christ continues his dialogue by revealing the reactions to Babylon's destruction from her future admirers.[15] Not only does he reveal how future kings, merchants, shipmasters, and seafarers will react to the sight of Babylon's burning at the hands of the beast and the ten kings, but he also passes along some of the direct quotations from these admirers once they see the smoke of their beloved Babylon rising to the heavens. First, the kings:

15. As to whether Christ continues his dialogue begun in 18:4 or instead John now resumes his commentary in 18:9, the evidence seems to indicate the former, especially since 18:20, the last sentence of the section pertaining to the "future admirers" begun in 18:9, belongs to Christ; (compare Christ's reference to God's judgment in 18:20 with the same reference to God's judgment in 18:5, 8).

> And the kings of the earth, who committed fornication and lived in luxury with her, will weep and wail over her when they see the smoke of her burning; they will stand far off, in fear of her torment, and say,
> "Alas, alas, the great city, Babylon, the mighty city! For in one hour your judgment has come." (Rev 18:9–10)

Although one can see that the kings will truly love Babylon, as evidenced by their weeping and mourning, they will only mourn for her at a distance. Why? Because they will fear the same fate from the ten-nation confederation as the fate they dealt Babylon. Also notice that the kings revealed a new detail concerning Babylon's destruction: She will be burned within one hour (Rev 18:10).

Next, the merchants of the earth:

> And the merchants of the earth weep and mourn for her, since no one buys their cargo any more, cargo of gold, silver, jewels and pearls, fine linen, purple, silk and scarlet, all kinds of scented wood, all articles of ivory, all articles of costly wood, bronze, iron, and marble, cinnamon, spice, incense, myrrh, frankincense, wine, olive oil, choice flour and wheat, cattle and sheep, horses and chariots, slaves—and human lives.
> "The fruit for which your soul longed has gone from you, and all your dainties and your splendor are lost to you, never to be found again!"
> The merchants of these wares, who gained wealth from her, will stand far off, in fear of her torment, weeping and mourning aloud,
> "Alas, alas, the great city, clothed in fine linen, in purple and scarlet, adorned with gold, with jewels, and with pearls! For in one hour all this wealth has been laid waste!" (Rev 18:11–17a)

Just as the kings, the merchants will keep their distance from the city of Rome while she is burning because they too will fear the ten-nation confederacy.[16] Nonetheless, they will weep and mourn for Babylon, just as the kings.

---

16. If the reader is still not quite sure whether "the burning of Babylon" at the hands of the ten-nation confederation is indeed different than "the fall of Babylon" during the seventh bowl, consider the following: One can be sure that the demeanor of the kings and merchants at the time of Babylon's burning during the nuclear aftermath—which is characterized by their weeping and mourning for the city of Rome as they simultaneously tremble with fear because of the threat from the ten-nation confederacy—will not be their demeanor during the seventh bowl of God's wrath. By the time the seven trumpets and seven bowls have run their course, with their earthquakes, demonic torture

Finally, the shipmasters and seafarers:

> And all shipmasters and seafarers, sailors and all whose trade is on the sea, stood far off and cried out as they saw the smoke of her burning,
> "What city was like the great city?"
> And they threw dust on their heads, as they wept and mourned, crying out,
> "Alas, alas, the great city, where all who had ships at sea grew rich by her wealth! For in one hour she has been laid waste." (Rev 18:17b–19)

For the third time, her future admirers said that Babylon will be destroyed within one hour. By this triple testimony, it is certain that the overwhelming display of power by the ten-nation confederacy will leave an indelible mark upon the minds of the kings, merchants, and seafarers.

Finally, after revealing the reactions from kings, merchants, shipmasters, and seafarers to Babylon's future burning at the hands of the ten-nation confederacy (Rev 18:9–19), as well as some of their direct quotations, Christ gives a most assuring promise:

> Rejoice over her, O heaven, you saints and apostles and prophets! For God has given judgment for you against her. (Rev 18:20)

Although he has already warned his people to come out of Babylon so as not to participate in any of her sins and therefore share in her plagues, Christ now tells all the saints and apostles and prophets to rejoice over her because God the Father has already pronounced judgment for them against her.

Eighth Conversation: An Angel Illustrates Babylon's Fall

After the Lord's revelations, a mighty angel unexpectedly appeared and gave a visual illustration of Babylon's disappearance by taking a large millstone and throwing it into the sea:

> Then a mighty angel took a stone like a great millstone and threw it into the sea, saying, "With such violence Babylon the

---

and slaughter, excruciating sores, and hundred-pound hail falling from the skies, one can be sure that no one will be standing in the distance, weeping for a city because they can no longer trade for her exquisite wares (Rev 18:11–17a). To be sure, many of the inhabitants of the earth will be weeping, but they will be weeping for themselves, not for the city of Rome.

great city will be thrown down, and will be found no more; and the sound of harpists and minstrels and of flutists and trumpeters will be heard in you no more; and an artisan of any trade will be found in you no more; and the sound of the millstone will be heard in you no more; and the light of a lamp will shine in you no more; and the voice of bridegroom and bride will be heard in you no more; for your merchants were the magnates of the earth, and all nations were deceived by your sorcery. And in you was found the blood of prophets and of saints, and of all who have been slaughtered on earth." (Rev 18:21–24)

When the angel threw the millstone into the sea was he illustrating the future burning of Babylon at the hands of the beast and the ten kings, or the future disappearance of Babylon into the Mediterranean Sea during the seventh-bowl earthquake? The answer is the latter. Although for the better part of Rev 18, the focus has been on the destruction of Babylon at the hands of the ten-nation confederation, the mighty angel now brings attention to Babylon's ultimate disgrace and downfall, before listing some of her past sights and sounds, including those from harpists, minstrels, flutists, trumpeters, trade of artisans, and even weddings, saying that those activities will never return again, once the Lord causes the city to fall off into the Mediterranean Sea during the great and terrible Day of the Lord. Although the city of Rome may be known as the eternal city, her "eternity" will end at the seventh bowl earthquake.

Celebration in Heaven

After the prophecy by Christ concerning the judgment of Babylon at the hands of the beast and the ten-nation confederacy (Rev 18:4–20), and the subsequent illustration by the mighty angel concerning her final judgment during the seventh bowl earthquake (Rev 18:21), both of which were given in the presence of John two thousand years ago, the disciple next sees the result of the fulfillment of the Lord's prophecy and the angel's illustration in the very next vision, which was a celebration around heaven's throne:

> After this I heard what seemed to be the loud voice of a great multitude in heaven, saying, "Hallelujah! Salvation and glory and power to our God, for his judgments are true and just; he has judged the great whore who corrupted the earth with her fornication, and he has avenged on her the blood of his servants."

> Once more they said, "Hallelujah! The smoke goes up from her forever and ever."
> And the twenty-four elders and the four living creatures fell down and worshiped God who is seated on the throne, saying, "Amen. Hallelujah!"
> And from the throne came a voice, saying, "Praise our God, all you his servants, and all who fear him, small and great."
> Then I heard what seemed to be the voice of a great multitude, like the sound of many waters and like the sound of mighty thunderpeals, crying out, "Hallelujah! For the Lord our God the Almighty reigns. Let us rejoice and exult and give him the glory, for the marriage of the Lamb has come, and his bride has made herself ready; to her it has been granted to be clothed with fine linen, bright and pure"—for the linen is the righteous deeds of the saints. (Rev 19:1–8)

John heard the multitude celebrating and worshiping God because of two facts: First, Babylon the great had received God's final judgment at the seventh bowl, and secondly, after the completion of the trumpet and bowl judgments, the marriage of the Lamb was finally at hand. It was a joyous announcement because many of the righteous souls in heaven had been waiting patiently for the marriage of the Lamb for millennia! And what is the marriage of the Lamb? Of course, it's a metaphor for the full spiritual communion between Christ and His Bride at the resurrection and rapture of the saints.[17] When addressing the Corinthians and Ephesians, Paul put it like this:

1. "I feel a divine jealousy for you, for I promised you in marriage to one husband, to present you as a chaste virgin to Christ" (2 Cor 11:2).
2. "Husbands, love your wives, just as Christ loved the church and gave himself up for her, in order to make her holy by cleansing her with the washing of water by the word, so as to present the church to himself in splendor, without a spot or wrinkle or anything of the kind—yes, so that she may be holy and without blemish" (Eph 5:25–27).

At the marriage of the Lamb, i.e., the resurrection and rapture of the church, the bride will be without spot or wrinkle and will be holy

---

17. Only after seeing the visions of the pouring of the seven bowls did John see a vision of heaven celebrating the upcoming resurrection and rapture of the saints. And the significance? Even after the seven bowls of wrath are poured, the resurrection and rapture are yet to occur.

and without blemish (Eph 5:27). In other words, she will be a virgin (2 Cor 11:2). This last statement will hopefully help one's understanding of a comment made by John following an earlier scene during the Fourth Sequence when the disciple saw the 144,000 Jewish remnant standing on Mount Zion with the Lamb. Just as Paul called the church a virgin in 2 Corinthians, John described the 144,000 likewise (italics used for emphasis):

"It is these who have not defiled themselves with women, for they are *virgins*; these follow the Lamb wherever he goes. They have been redeemed from humankind as first fruits for God and the Lamb, and in their mouth no lie was found; they are blameless" (Rev 14:4–5).

The 144,000 Jewish remnant, who will escape Jerusalem at the time of the abomination, find refuge in a 1,260-day exile in the wilderness, confess Christ at the appearance of the heavenly signs, and return to Jerusalem and Mount Zion at the blast of the seventh trumpet, are no more actual virgins than the majority of the church. The church, which will eventually include the 144,000 Jewish remnant, is only a virgin spiritually because of the imputed righteousness of Christ. The metaphor has nothing to do with being an actual virgin. To prove this, look again at the words of Christ to "the reader" in the Olivet Discourse (italics used for emphasis):

"So when you see the desolating sacrilege standing in the holy place, as was spoken of by the prophet Daniel (let the reader understand), then those in Judea must flee to the mountains; the one on the housetop must not go down to take what is in the house; the one in the field must not turn back to get a coat. *Woe to those who are pregnant and to those who are nursing infants in those days*! Pray that your flight may not be in winter or on a sabbath" (Matt 24:15–20).

In the Olivet Discourse, Christ gave a warning to the future reader (which included his target audience of the 144,000 Jewish remnant), when he said, "Woe to those who are pregnant and to those who are nursing infants in those days!" And what's the implication? Some of the last-generation, 144,000 Jewish remnant might very well be pregnant and nursing at the time of the abomination! In other words, the 144,000 Jewish remnant will be composed of men and women, who are obviously not virgins, physically speaking—just like the majority of the rest of the church. Again, to think that the 144,000 Jewish remnant will only be composed of men who are virgins is to completely miss the point that God is making, and that is that all of the saints are viewed by God as perfectly holy and virtuous, spiritually speaking, because of the imputed righteousness of his Son.

Ninth Conversation: The Marriage Supper

With the celebratory sounds still ringing in his ears, John receives instructions to write the following message from the same mighty angel who had just illustrated the fall of Babylon:

> And the angel said to me, "Write this: Blessed are those who are invited to the marriage supper of the Lamb." And he said to me, "These are true words of God." Then I fell down at his feet to worship him, but he said to me, "You must not do that! I am a fellow servant with you and your comrades who hold the testimony of Jesus. Worship God! For the testimony of Jesus is the spirit of prophecy." (Rev 19:9–10)

When the angel told John that blessed are they who are invited to "the marriage supper of the Lamb,"[18] he was saying in essence if you are invited to the marriage supper, you are "blessed" because it is certain that you are part of God's family and you will dwell with the Father, the Son, and the Holy Spirit forever. No wonder John was overcome with emotion and had to be restrained from bowing down to the angel.[19]

---

18. Curiously, instead of the angel directly commenting on the marriage of the Lamb—the resurrection and the rapture of the saints—he directed John's attention to what will follow the marriage: the marriage supper of the Lamb. Nevertheless, the reader has been given a preview of a developing sequence: The pouring of the seven bowls will precede the marriage of the Lamb, and the marriage, in turn, will obviously precede the marriage supper.

19. Because most do not understand that the mighty angel spoke with John two thousand years ago in what has been labeled "the ninth conversation," and that he was only commenting on the marriage supper because John had just seen a vision of a multitude around the throne celebrating the fact that the marriage of the Lamb was about to occur, most unfortunately think the event of the marriage supper will occur between the celebration in heaven (Rev 19:1–8) and the Lord's second coming at Armageddon (Rev 19:11–21), which is incorrect. The only connection between the multitude's celebration, the marriage supper, and Armageddon is that the angel spoke to John about the marriage supper in between the vision of the celebration and the vision of Armageddon.

Closing Thoughts: Interpreting the Meanings of Various Hypothetical Drawings

Having now been thoroughly initiated into the symbolism of the seven heads and the ten horns, let's go back and review the visions of the seven-headed dragon and the seven-headed beast while applying our newfound ability to some hypothetical images that God didn't draw:

1. We begin our review with the seven-headed dragon.

"Then another portent appeared in heaven: a great red dragon, with seven heads and ten horns, and seven diadems on his heads. His tail swept down a third of the stars of heaven and threw them to the earth. Then the dragon stood before the woman who was about to bear a child, so that he might devour her child as soon as it was born" (Rev 12:3-4).

Here, God portrayed the moment Satan was impatiently waiting for the appearance of the two witnesses, in order that he might squash their 1,260-day ministry at its inception. And what was the significance of the seven crowns on top of the heads? That at the time Satan was seen waiting for the arrival of the two, each of the seven angelic princes had already reigned over their respective empires under the direction of Satan. Therefore, had God depicted the dragon with only four crowns on seven heads or five crowns on seven heads, then that would have necessarily indicated that only four or five angelic princes, respectively, had ruled their empires by the time Satan was seen waiting for the arrival of the two witnesses. Since this is the case, how would God have depicted the seven-headed dragon had he actually been waiting for the birth of Jesus, as most everyone mistakenly believes? God would have drawn the seven-headed dragon wearing only six crowns, since Jesus' birth occurred during the reign of the sixth angel, which was the angel over the Roman Empire. But since God represented all seven heads as wearing crowns, that meant that at the time John saw Satan waiting for the birth of the child, the seventh angel had already ruled the seventh empire, thereby proving that the child could not have represented Jesus. The following chart illustrates this truth:

Table 9.14. Six Hypothetical Drawings and One Real Drawing by God Depicting the Exact Empire After Which the Dragon Was Seen Waiting for the Pregnant Woman to Give Birth to the Child

The 7 Empires of the 7 Angelic Princes	6 Hypothetical Drawings and 1 Real Drawing
1. Egyptian Empire	One of the 7 heads would be wearing a crown.
2. Assyrian Empire	Two of the 7 heads would be wearing crowns.
3. Babylonian Empire	Three of the 7 heads would be wearing crowns.
4. Medes and Persian Empire	Four of the 7 heads would be wearing crowns.
5. Grecian Empire	Five of the 7 heads would be wearing crowns.
6. Roman Empire	Six of the 7 heads would be wearing crowns. (This would have been the drawing had the child truly represented Christ since Christ was born during the Roman Empire.)
7. 7th Empire	Seven of the 7 heads are wearing crowns. (This was the only real drawing; see Rev 12:3.)

2. Next, we come to John's first vision of the beast.

"And I saw a beast rising out of the sea, having ten horns and seven heads; and on its horns were ten diadems, and on its heads were blasphemous names.... One of its heads seemed to have received a death blow, but its mortal wound had been healed" (Rev 13:1, 3a).

Although God portrayed both the dragon and the beast with seven heads and ten horns, he never portrayed the beast with seven "crowned" heads because the seven angelic kings, whom the heads represent and to whom the beast belongs, never serve the beast; they only serve Satan. Similarly, God never portrayed the dragon with ten "crowned" horns because the ten human kings, whom the horns represent, will never serve under Satan; the ten-nation confederation will only serve the beast. Furthermore, when God did happen to portray the beast with ten crowned horns, as he does here in Rev 13:1, he only showed the ten crowned horns together with the healed, wounded head. And why is that? As you know, the "healed, wounded head" represents the beast after he has been released out of the bottomless pit in order to rule a second time, and it is only after that release that the ten human kings will become a confederation and yield their power and authority to the beast:

"And the ten horns that you saw are ten kings who have not yet received a kingdom, but they are to receive authority as kings for one hour, together with the beast. These are united in yielding their power and authority to the beast" (Rev 17:12–13).

Has the reader ever wondered how the images of the ten horns are positioned in relation to the seven heads, whether seen on the dragon or the beast? As you know, John never indicated that particular detail. Nevertheless, it's easily determined: If the beast was indeed the king of the Babylonian Empire, as we have strongly suggested,[20] it would be certain that John saw all ten horns positioned on the third head of the dragon as well as the third head of the beast.

3. Finally, we come to John's second vision of the beast, which was given at the beginning of the sixth conversation.

"So he carried me away in the spirit into a wilderness, and I saw a woman sitting on a scarlet beast that was full of blasphemous names, and it had seven heads and ten horns" (Rev 17:3).

For the first time, it initially appears that God depicted the beast without ten crowns on the ten horns, which would necessarily imply that the beast was still confined to the bottomless pit. But is this what John actually saw? Not at all. The fact that John simultaneously saw the harlot sitting atop the beast indicated that the beast had already been released out of the pit, which, in turn, indicated that the ten kings had to be wearing the ten crowns and that one of the seven heads had to have appeared wounded and healed, neither of which John mentioned. And what's the explanation? The image of the beast seen by John in Rev 17:3 is the same image he saw earlier in Rev 13:1–3, and the only reason the disciple didn't mention the ten crowns on the ten horns or the healed, wounded head the second time was because it would have been superfluous. Instead,

---

20. See pp. 295–300.

John only added the one new detail: This time, a woman, called Babylon the great, was sitting atop the seven-headed, ten-horned beast.

∼

The following is the reconciliation of the six sequences beginning with the seven angels exiting the temple just prior to receiving the seven golden bowls of God's wrath, and continuing until the celebration in heaven because of two events: Babylon the great had fallen and the marriage of the Lamb was soon to occur (the newly added events found within Rev 15:5 to Rev 19:8 are italicized):

FIRST SEQUENCE, PART 2

Table 9.15. The Reconciliation of the Six Sequences Beginning with the Seven Angels Exiting the Temple and Continuing to the Celebration in Heaven

The Sequence	Seq. 1 & 2 Thess	Seq. Olivet Discourse	1st Seq. Rev, Part 2: 7 Bowls (15:5—16:21, 18:1–3, 19:1–8)	2nd Seq. Rev: 2 Witnesses	3rd Seq. Rev: Woman, Child, and Dragon	4th Seq. Rev, Part 3: Mt. Zion to God's Throne (14:6–11)
1. The angels exit the temple doorway and are each given a golden bowl full of the wrath of God by 1 of the living creatures.			The angels exited the temple doorway and were each given a golden bowl full of the wrath of God by 1 of the living creatures. (Rev 15:5–8)			
2. The angels are told to pour the 7 bowls. 1st Bowl: A painful sore appears on those who have the mark of the beast and who worshiped its image.			The angels are told to pour the 7 bowls. 1st Bowl: A painful sore appears on those who have the mark of the beast and who worshiped its image. (Rev 16:1–2)			

321

Table 9.15. The Reconciliation of the Six Sequences Beginning with the Seven Angels Exiting the Temple and Continuing to the Celebration in Heaven

The Sequence	Seq. 1 & 2 Thess	Seq. Olivet Discourse	1st Seq. Rev, Part 2: 7 Bowls (15:5—16:21, 18:1–3, 19:1–8)	2nd Seq. Rev: 2 Witnesses	3rd Seq. Rev: Woman, Child, and Dragon	4th Seq. Rev, Part 3: Mt. Zion to God's Throne (14:6–11)
3. 2nd Bowl: The sea becomes like the blood of a corpse and every living thing in the sea dies.			2nd Bowl: The sea became like the blood of a corpse and every living thing in the sea died. (16:3)			
4. 3rd Bowl: The rivers and the springs of water become like blood.			3rd Bowl: The rivers and the springs of water became like blood. (16:4–7)			
5. 4th Bowl: The sun's heat is allowed to scorch the inhabitants of the earth with fire.			4th Bowl: The sun's heat was allowed to scorch the inhabitants of the earth with fire. (16:8–9)			

Table 9.15. The Reconciliation of the Six Sequences Beginning with the Seven Angels Exiting the Temple and Continuing to the Celebration in Heaven

The Sequence	Seq. 1 & 2 Thess	Seq. Olivet Discourse	1st Seq. Rev, Part 2: 7 Bowls (15:5—16:21, 18:1–3, 19:1–8)	2nd Seq. Rev: 2 Witnesses	3rd Seq. Rev: Woman, Child, and Dragon	4th Seq. Rev, Part 3: Mt. Zion to God's Throne (14:6–11)
6. 5th Bowl: Although the 42-month reign of the beast ended at the 7th trumpet, the residual throne and kingdom of the beast that were received from Satan are now plunged into darkness.			5th Bowl: The throne of the beast and its kingdom were plunged into darkness. (16:10–11)			

Table 9.15. The Reconciliation of the Six Sequences Beginning with the Seven Angels Exiting the Temple and Continuing to the Celebration in Heaven

The Sequence	Seq. 1 & 2 Thess	Seq. Olivet Discourse	1st Seq. Rev, Part 2: 7 Bowls (15:5—16:21, 18:1–3, 19:1–8)	2nd Seq. Rev: 2 Witnesses	3rd Seq. Rev: Woman, Child, and Dragon	4th Seq. Rev, Part 3: Mt. Zion to God's Throne (14:6–11)
7. 6th Bowl: The River Euphrates is dried up in order to prepare the way for the kings from the east to assemble for the battle against Christ on the plains of Armageddon.			6th Bowl: The River Euphrates was dried up in order to prepare the way for the kings from the east to assemble for the battle against Christ on the plains of Armageddon. (16:12–16)			

FIRST SEQUENCE, PART 2

Table 9.15. The Reconciliation of the Six Sequences Beginning with the Seven Angels Exiting the Temple and Continuing to the Celebration in Heaven

The Sequence	Seq. 1 & 2 Thess	Seq. Olivet Discourse	1st Seq. Rev, Part 2: 7 Bowls (15:5—16:21, 18:1–3, 19:1–8)	2nd Seq. Rev: 2 Witnesses	3rd Seq. Rev: Woman, Child, and Dragon	4th Seq. Rev, Part 3: Mt. Zion to God's Throne (14:6–11)
8. 7th Bowl: The greatest earthquake in the history of the world destroys all cities, and every island and mountain on the earth disappear, as 100 lb. hailstones fall upon the inhabitants of the earth.			*7th Bowl: The greatest earthquake in the history of the world destroyed all cities, and every island and mountain on the earth disappeared, as 100 lb. hailstones fell upon the inhabitants of the earth. (16:17–21)*			

THE SEQUENCE

Table 9.15. The Reconciliation of the Six Sequences Beginning with the Seven Angels Exiting the Temple and Continuing to the Celebration in Heaven

The Sequence	Seq. 1 & 2 Thess	Seq. Olivet Discourse	1st Seq. Rev, Part 2: 7 Bowls (15:5—16:21, 18:1–3, 19:1–8)	2nd Seq. Rev: 2 Witnesses	3rd Seq. Rev: Woman, Child, and Dragon	4th Seq. Rev, Part 3: Mt. Zion to God's Throne (14:6–11)
9. Three angels appear in the midheaven with 3 announcements. The 1st angel announces that the hour of God's judgment has come. This is a reference to the upcoming Battle of Armageddon.						Three angels appeared in the midheaven. The 1st angel announced that the hour of God's judgment has come. (14:6-7)
10. A 2nd angel announces that Babylon the great has fallen, which is a result of the earthquake of the 7th bowl.			*An angel announced that Babylon the great has fallen!* (18:1–3)			A 2nd angel was seen flying in the midheaven with the announcement that Babylon the great has fallen! (14:8)

326

Table 9.15. The Reconciliation of the Six Sequences Beginning with the Seven Angels Exiting the Temple and Continuing to the Celebration in Heaven

The Sequence	Seq. 1 & 2 Thess	Seq. Olivet Discourse	1st Seq. Rev, Part 2: 7 Bowls (15:5—16:21, 18:1–3, 19:1–8)	2nd Seq. Rev: 2 Witnesses	3rd Seq. Rev: Woman, Child, and Dragon	4th Seq. Rev, Part 3: Mt. Zion to God's Throne (14:6–11)
11. A 3rd angel announces that those who worship the beast and receive its mark will suffer eternal punishment.						A 3rd angel was seen flying in the midheaven with the announcement that those who worship the beast and receive its mark will suffer eternal punishment.(14:9–11)
12. Heaven celebrates the fact that Babylon the great has fallen and that the marriage of the Lamb is soon to come, which is a reference to the upcoming resurrection and rapture of the saints.			*Heaven celebrated the fact that Babylon the great had fallen and that the marriage of the Lamb was soon to come. (19:1–8)*			

CHAPTER 10

First Sequence, Part 3

The Lord's Return and the First Resurrection (19:11—20:6a)

First Sequence	Second Sequence	Third Sequence	Fourth Sequence
			Chapter 8 4th Seq., Part 3: Mount Zion to the Worship around God's Throne (14:1—15:4)
Chapter 9 1st Seq., Part 2: The 7 Bowls (15:5—19:10)			
Chapter 10* 1st Seq., Part 3: The Lord's Return and the 1st Resurrection (19:11—20:6a)			
Chapter 11 1st Seq., Part 4: The Millennium and the Final Judgment (20:6b–15)			

FIRST SEQUENCE, PART 3

EVER SINCE CHRIST WAS crucified on the cross at Golgotha two thousand years ago and resurrected from the grave three days later, and then ascended from the Mount of Olives forty days after that, the church has been patiently waiting for his return. And just as she has been waiting, John had to patiently wait, albeit on a much smaller scale, for a vision of Christ's return. But the wait is finally over. Nevertheless, instead of God choosing to reveal a clear, live-action vision of his Son's manifestation, one that would have revealed something akin to a video of the actual appearance of Christ to the world, the Lord chose to reveal a vision of Christ's return steeped in symbolism, thus keeping the manifestation of Christ hidden to all eyes until the actual event takes place. Although God had allowed John to see many live-action visions to this point, the manifestation of Christ was not going to be one of them. Instead, here's what John saw:

> Then I saw heaven opened, and there was a white horse! Its rider is called Faithful and True, and in righteousness he judges and makes war. His eyes are like a flame of fire, and on his head are many diadems; and he has a name inscribed that no one knows but himself. He is clothed in a robe dipped in blood, and his name is called The Word of God. And the armies of heaven, wearing fine linen, white and pure, were following him on white horses. From his mouth comes a sharp sword with which to strike down the nations, and he will rule them with a rod of iron; he will tread the wine press of the fury of the wrath of God the Almighty. On his robe and on his thigh he has a name inscribed, "King of kings and Lord of lords." (Rev 19:11–16)

Regrettably, because many do not understand God's alternating use of live-action visions and drawn images, they naively believe that when Christ returns he will be riding a white horse in the sky, wearing many crowns on his head, wearing a robe dipped in blood, and having two flames of fire in the place of his two eyes and a sharp sword protruding from his mouth. But however disappointing this may sound to some, Christ will not return this way. And, furthermore, the Father never intended the saints to believe such a thing. When compared to his earlier drawn image of the beast also riding a white horse, wearing a crown, and carrying a bow (Rev 6:1–2), God simply wanted John as well as the church to know that, when Christ returns, pictured with his sword, his many crowns, and also riding a white horse, he will come with greater power and greater authority than anyone else in the world, and this includes Satan and the beast.[1] Therefore, since the drawing of Christ's return is indeed symbolic, one might be tempted to ask, What will Jesus look like when he returns? Well, if it's any consolation to the reader, no one knows for sure. At least, John and Paul didn't know:

1. "Beloved, we are God's children now; what we will be has not yet been revealed. What we do know is this: when he is revealed, we will be like him, for we will see him as he is" (1 John 3:2).

2. "I consider that the sufferings of this present time are not worth comparing with the glory about to be revealed to us" (Rom 8:18).

If the apostles didn't know, I don't think there's any chance that you and I know. Even the next to last scene in the Fourth Sequence, which depicted Christ just prior to his descent to the great wine press of the wrath of God, i.e., the Battle of Armageddon, was a portent that was masked in elaborate symbolism:

"Then I looked, and there was a white cloud, and seated on the cloud was one like the Son of Man, with a golden crown on his head, and a sharp sickle in his hand! Another angel came out of the temple, calling with a loud voice to the one who sat on the cloud, 'Use your sickle and reap, for the hour to reap has come, because the harvest of the earth is fully ripe.' So the one who sat on the cloud swung his sickle over the earth, and the earth was reaped'" (Rev 14:14–16).

Whether Christ is depicted as seated on a white cloud wearing a golden crown on his head and holding a sharp sickle in his hand "before His appearance," or riding a white horse wearing many crowns on his head with a sword coming out of his mouth "at His appearance," God expects the saints, somewhere along the way, to recognize if a vision is symbolic or not. And in the case of the Rider returning on a white horse, the depiction is obviously symbolic.

Two Different Receptions

Although Christ's return will certainly be met with wonder and marvel by the saints (2 Thess 1:10), the same cannot be said about the reaction from the inhabitants of the earth. John continues the Armageddon narrative:

---

1. As one is sure to realize, both riders on a white horse happen to be part of the First Sequence (compare Rev 6:2 and 19:11).

> Then I saw an angel standing in the sun, and with a loud voice he called to all the birds that fly in midheaven, "Come, gather for the great supper of God, to eat the flesh of kings, the flesh of captains, the flesh of the mighty, the flesh of horses and their riders—flesh of all, both free and slave, both small and great." Then I saw the beast and the kings of the earth with their armies gathered to make war against the rider on the horse and against his army. (Rev 19:17–19)

The armies from around the earth who will be gathered by the three demons during the plague of the sixth bowl surely will not expect this outcome. Had they known the overwhelming power of Christ, they doubtless would have stayed home. The so-called battle will be swift and decisive. Note that the angel called for the birds to gather even before the battle began. Just as were the battles of David and Goliath, and Joshua and Jericho, the outcome will be a foregone conclusion. Jesus will mete out a very swift judgment of physical death to those who have defiantly and rebelliously gathered in the valley with the pitifully preconceived notion of somehow conquering the Creator of the universe. All those who will one day assemble on the plains of Armageddon with the intention of harming the Lord Jesus will reap what they have sown. Because they have already sown to please their flesh by worshiping the image of the beast, receiving its mark, afflicting and killing the saints, and now, audaciously, choosing to confront Christ, they will reap a special and dreadful physical death. This is how Zechariah describes it:

> "... their flesh shall rot while they are still on their feet; their eyes shall rot in their sockets, and their tongues shall rot in their mouths. On that day a great panic from the Lord shall fall on them, so that each will seize the hand of a neighbor, and the hand of one will be raised against the hand of another" (Zech 14:12b–13).

It's not a pretty sight. Although only a percentage of the inhabitants of the earth will journey to the valley, the Lord will see to it those who have made the special effort to act so brazenly as to conspire to actually fight Christ will suffer the above fate during the so-called battle on the plains of Armageddon—all except two.

The Beast and False Prophet Are Captured

At some point during the battle, the beast and the false prophet will draw the undivided attention of Christ. One can almost imagine Christ in swift flight, grabbing them both by the nape of the neck as they squirm like caught vermin and bringing them to justice:

> And the beast was captured, and with it the false prophet who had performed in its presence the signs by which he deceived those who had received the mark of the beast and those who worshiped its image. These two were thrown alive into the lake of fire that burns with sulfur. And the rest were killed by the sword of the rider on the horse, the sword that came from his mouth; and all the birds were gorged with their flesh. (Rev 19:20–21)

Rather than the two being killed as were the other accomplices at the battle (19:21a), John said the beast and false prophet were captured alive before being brought to justice.[2] And what was their judgment? They were "thrown alive" into the lake of fire that burns with sulfur.

The Martyrs around the Throne

After the capture of the beast and the false prophet, John can barely catch his breath before he sees a vision of a third capture:

> Then I saw an angel coming down from heaven, holding in his hand the key to the bottomless pit and a great chain. He seized the dragon, that ancient serpent, who is the Devil and Satan, and bound him for a thousand years, and threw him into the

---

2. Recall the words of Paul concerning the Lord's initial encounter with the man of lawlessness, also known as the false prophet: "For the mystery of lawlessness is already at work, but only until the one who now restrains it is removed. And then the lawless one will be revealed, whom the Lord Jesus will destroy with the breath of his mouth, annihilating him by the manifestation of his coming" (2 Thess 2:7–8).

As was noted earlier, the NRSV's translations "destroy" and "annihilate" certainly give one the impression that at the manifestation of Christ the man of lawlessness will be utterly destroyed on the spot. But that translation appears to be in conflict with John's vision indicating that the man, as well as the angelic beast, will not be destroyed on the spot, but, rather, captured alive before being brought into the presence of the Father in order to face his judgment. So who's correct? Of course both are, but the translation of Paul's words in 2 Thessalonians leaves a lot to be desired. When reviewing the phrase "will destroy with the breath of his mouth, annihilating him by the manifestation of his coming," the Greek word *anelie*, translated "will destroy," is better translated "will take up" or "will take away." Likewise, the Greek word *katargēsei*, translated "annihilating," is better translated with the meanings "nullifying," "doing away with," "bringing to nought," or "rendering inoperative." Rather than destroy the man of lawlessness at the *parousia*, Jesus will take him out of the way, rendering him inoperative by the manifestation of his coming. In other words, the beast and the false prophet will be captured.

> pit, and locked and sealed it over him, so that he would deceive the nations no more, until the thousand years were ended. After that he must be let out for a little while. (Rev 20:1–3)

John identifies the dragon as that ancient serpent, the devil, and Satan, just as he did earlier when describing Michael's victory over Satan:

"The great dragon was thrown down, that ancient serpent, who is called the Devil and Satan, the deceiver of the whole world—he was thrown down to the earth, and his angels were thrown down with him" (Rev 12:9).

At the beginning of the Fourth Sequence, one saw Michael cast the dragon down from heaven to earth, but now, toward the end of the First Sequence, one sees the dragon cast down even further—from the surface of the earth to the bottomless pit.

Next, God takes John's attention away from his adversaries, i.e., the beast, the false prophet, and Satan, and shows the disciple visions of those who love and obey him. Standing around the thrones were the souls of the martyrs who had died at the hands of the beast and the false prophet:

> Then I saw thrones, and those seated on them were given authority to judge. I also saw the souls of those who had been beheaded for their testimony to Jesus and for the word of God. They had not worshiped the beast or its image and had not received its mark on their foreheads or their hands. (Rev 20:4a)

This is the fourth time that John has seen a vision of the souls of the martyrs. Observe:

Table 10.1. Tracing the Martyrs in Heaven: Before the Heavenly Signs, before the First Trumpet, and after Armageddon

	1. Before the Heavenly Signs	2. Before the 1st Trumpet	3. After Armageddon
1st Sequence	"When he opened the fifth seal, I saw under the altar the souls of those who had been slaughtered for the word of God and for the testimony they had given.... They were each given a white robe and told to rest a little longer, until the number would be complete both of their fellow servants and of their brothers and sisters, who were soon to be killed as they themselves had been killed" (Rev 6:9, 11).	"After this I looked and there was a great multitude that no one could count, from every nation, from all tribes and peoples and languages, standing before the throne and before the Lamb, robed in white, with palm branches in their hands.... These are they who have come out of the great ordeal; they have washed their robes and made them white in the blood of the Lamb" (Rev 7:9, 14b).	"I also saw the souls of those who had been beheaded for their testimony to Jesus and for the word of God. They had not worshiped the beast or its image and had not received its mark on their foreheads or their hands" (Rev 20:4a).
4th Sequence			"Then I saw another portent in heaven, great and amazing: seven angels with seven plagues, which are the last, for with them the wrath of God is ended. And I saw what appeared to be a sea of glass mixed with fire, and those who had conquered the beast and its image and the number of its name, standing beside the sea of glass with harps of God in their hands" (Rev 15:1–2).

Did you notice anything that stood out in the above chart? The martyrs are seen around God's throne after Armageddon twice, which necessarily indicates that two sequences are present, which, in this case, are the First and the Fourth Sequences.

The First Resurrection

After reminding the reader that the martyrs had died because they had not worshiped the beast or its image, John said they came to life and reigned with Christ a thousand years. He also said that this was the first resurrection. The words are simple and direct. Apparently for most, they are too simple and too direct. Here's the text:

> They came to life and reigned with Christ a thousand years. (The rest of the dead did not come to life until the thousand years were ended.) This is the first resurrection. Blessed and holy are those who share in the first resurrection. Over these the second death has no power, but they will be priests of God and of Christ, and they will reign with him a thousand years. (Rev 20:4b–6)

Although the subject of the resurrection is referenced only occasionally in the Old Testament, the event is referenced throughout the New Testament. Paul spoke of the resurrection and the gathering of the saints in almost every epistle, while Jesus' teaching on the subject is recorded in each of the four Gospels. But surprisingly, this is the only reference in Revelation. Yet the reference wasn't without its bombshell: There will be two resurrections! The first resurrection will occur prior to Christ's reign of one thousand years (Rev 20:4), and the second resurrection will take place after the thousand years (Rev 20:5a). Concerning the first one, John did not see that resurrection occurring at the beginning of the 1,260-day ministry of the two witnesses nor at the end of it; he didn't see it taking place before the great tribulation of the saints nor before the Day of the Lord. The disciple only saw the first resurrection occur at this point in the sequence—after the Battle of Armageddon. Period. And because of that, no one, as tempting as it may be, can haphazardly pencil it in whenever they think best suits their worldview. Had John actually seen a vision of the resurrection as having occurred during any of the aforementioned events, the church would gladly rejoice along with the disciple and wait patiently for that moment in the sequence to arrive, resting assured that

that was God's will. But the Lord didn't choose another time for the resurrection; he chose this one: after the Battle of Armageddon.

Why the scarcity on the subject of the resurrection among the visions? No one can be certain; but perhaps it seemed to the Lord that his previous revelations on the subject were sufficient, especially the ones given to Paul. In any case, despite its one reference here in Revelation, it is the church's responsibility to embrace the timing of the resurrection exactly as John revealed it, and that is that the martyred tribulation saints came to life at some point after their souls were seen gathered around the throne in heaven, which in turn, was after the Battle of Armageddon.

Notice that John did not say that he actually saw the martyrs come to life; he simply said that they did and that they will reign with Christ for a thousand years. The fact is, unless the settings of John's visions immediately changed from heaven to earth, from the souls of the martyrs around the thrones in heaven to their dead, headless bodies lying on the earth, it would have been impossible for him to see them come back to life. And the simple reason is the fact that the bodily resurrection of the saints, including the tribulation saints, occurs on earth, not in heaven. There are no dead bodies in heaven waiting to be resurrected. As the author of Hebrews put it, in heaven there are only "the spirits" of the righteous made perfect (Heb 12:23). Similarly, Paul indicated when Jesus descends from heaven, he will bring with him those same spirits back from heaven to the earth for the resurrection. Again, the words of the apostle:

"For since we believe that Jesus died and rose again, even so, through Jesus, God will bring with him those who have died. For this we declare to you by the word of the Lord, that we who are alive, who are left until the coming of the Lord, will by no means precede those who have died. For the Lord himself, with a cry of command, with the archangel's call and with the sound of God's trumpet, will descend from heaven, and the dead in Christ will rise first. Then we who are alive, who are left, will be caught up in the clouds together with them to meet the Lord in the air; and so we will be with the Lord forever. Therefore encourage one another with these words" (1 Thess 4:14–18).

One knows for a fact that Paul was speaking about the first resurrection because he later told Timothy that Hymenaeus and Philetus had swerved from the truth by claiming that the resurrection had already taken place (2 Tim 2:18). Knowing that the resurrection had not previously taken place, Paul could only have been describing to the Thessalonians what he understood to be the first resurrection. So much for Paul.

John was even more emphatic. As clearly as one can state a fact, John said when the tribulation martyrs come to life, that will be the first resurrection. And then he wonderfully added, "blessed and holy are those who share in the first resurrection." By this last comment, John was pronouncing a blessing upon all of the saints in every generation leading up to the first resurrection, including himself!

Upon reflection, the moment one reads that John saw just the souls of the martyred saints around God's throne, one should instinctively know that the first resurrection has not taken place because their souls have yet to be united with their glorified bodies. And for that to happen, Paul told the Thessalonians that Jesus must first accompany the souls from heaven, including those of the tribulation martyrs, back to earth so they can receive their glorified bodies. Naturally, for Jesus to descend from heaven to earth with the souls, he must first be in heaven in order to descend to the earth. And not just at any time. He must be in heaven at some point after the Battle of Armageddon because that is when John said the tribulation saints came to life. Therefore, the obvious question is whether there is a place in Scripture that reveals that Jesus will be in heaven immediately after the Battle of Armageddon, yet prior to the first resurrection. There is one place.

Daniel Sees the Throne Room

John was not the only one blessed with the privilege of witnessing heaven's throne room immediately after the Battle of Armageddon; Daniel also saw the scene:

"As I watched, thrones were set in place, and an Ancient of Days took his throne, his clothing was white as snow, and the hair of his head like pure wool; his throne was fiery flames, and its wheels were burning fire. A stream of fire issued and flowed out from his presence. A thousand thousands served him, and ten thousand times ten thousand stood attending him. The court sat in judgment, and the books were opened" (Dan 7:9–10).

After the thrones were set in place, the Father entered and took his seat on his throne, as millions and millions of angels simultaneously enveloped, worshiped, and waited eagerly to serve the Ancient of Days. And why were the thrones set in place? One reason appears to be because the two reprobates, the beast and the false prophet, were about to be judged. Recall that John earlier reported that the two were captured in battle and subsequently thrown into the lake of fire (Rev 19:20), but he made no reference as to what actually transpired between the capture and the two being cast into the lake of fire. Thankfully, Daniel does. What stands out in the scene is the bizarre conduct of the false prophet as he is brought before the Ancient of Days:

"I watched then because of the noise of the arrogant words that the horn was speaking. And as I watched, the beast was put to death, and its body destroyed and given over to be burned with fire. As for the rest of the beasts, their dominion was taken away, but their lives were prolonged for a season and a time" (Dan 7:11–12).

As was earlier indicated in chapter 1 of this study, "the beast and the little horn" in Daniel's dream and "the beast and the false prophet" in John's visions are one and the same.[3] How can one be sure? Only two individuals will be captured, judged, and thrown into the lake of fire immediately after the Battle of Armageddon, and these are the two. Furthermore, this is the exact scene that Paul referenced in 2 Thessalonians (italics used for emphasis):

"He opposes and exalts himself above every so-called god or object of worship, *so that he takes his seat in the temple of God, declaring himself to be God*. Do you not remember that I told you these things when I was still with you?" (2 Thess 2:4–5).

Most mistakenly believe that Paul is here describing how the man of lawlessness will be revealed to the world. But as painstakingly proven, Paul was simply recalling what was written in Dan 7:11–12, which described the scene immediately following the man's capture at the Battle of Armageddon. It is then that he will be brought into the temple of God in heaven and made "to sit down" (Greek: *kathisai*; "to sit down") in front of the Ancient of Days.[4] Once seated, the man of lawlessness will inexplicably speak arrogantly in front of the Father and claim to be God! As to the reason why the man will act so deranged and foolishly, speaking words of blasphemy while seated directly in front of the Ancient of Days, while the beast apparently stands by submissively and silently, it can only be attributed to the man's pure ignorance of the gravity of the situation, coupled with his psychotic delusions of grandeur. Although the beast and false

---

3. See pp. 27–28.

4. Many translations read "take his seat" as if the man will sit down of his own volition, which, in this instance, reflect certain translators' misconceived notion that the man will voluntarily sit down in a future rebuilt temple.

prophet will be equally guilty in their iniquities and crimes against God and the saints, as attested by their equal punishment, at least to some degree the beast will have a concept of the greatness and holiness of the Father, whereas, the false prophet will be apparently devoid of any such knowledge. The reader may recall our earlier discussion on the subject, when Peter's words were cited concerning certain ignorant men, who were bold and willful and were not afraid to slander the glorious ones in heaven, whereas often in the same circumstance, angels, who are greater in intellect and power, would not dare do such a thing.[5] In the following, Jude echoed the same sentiment as Peter:

"Yet in the same way these dreamers also defile the flesh, reject authority, and slander the glorious ones. But when the archangel Michael contended with the devil and disputed about the body of Moses, he did not dare to bring a condemnation of slander against him, but said, 'The Lord rebuke you!' But these people slander whatever they do not understand, and they are destroyed by those things that, like irrational animals, they know by instinct" (Jude 8–10).

Just as these past dreamers had no understanding of heavenly things, the future man of lawlessness will also have no understanding of heavenly things, which explains his bizarre behavior.

After the beast and false prophet are judged and sentenced to the lake of fire, the two will be led away, never to be heard from or seen again. One might think their exit would end the drama, and if Daniel expected that, he was wonderfully mistaken:

"As I watched in the night visions, I saw one like a Son of Man, coming with the clouds of heaven. And he came to the Ancient of Days and was presented before him. To him was given dominion and glory and kingship, that all peoples, nations, and languages should serve him. His dominion is an everlasting dominion that shall not pass away, and his kingship is one that shall never be destroyed" (Dan 7:13–14).

Here, Daniel saw something that even John didn't see: the Son of Man being presented to the Ancient of Days after the judgment of the beast and the false prophet! This scene is the missing piece of the puzzle that completes all of the pertinent events between the return of the Lord at Armageddon and the resurrection and rapture of the saints. Since Paul said the Lord will descend from heaven to earth for the resurrection, one needed this revelation that placed Jesus back up in heaven after the

---

5. See p. 28.

Battle of Armageddon, alongside the souls of the martyred tribulation saints. After the beast and the false prophet are led away to the lake of fire, Daniel saw the Son of Man enter into the spotlight of one of the most fabulous scenes in all of Scripture! Just imagine the Father seated on his throne as the Son is ushered in before him, having returned from his glorious manifestation to the world and his magnificent victory over all of his adversaries at the Battle of Armageddon. As the Son approaches the Father, the two persons of the Trinity are surrounded by innumerable angels and a great multitude of the souls of the saints, all watching every movement and listening to every word spoken by the two. It is only at the end of this otherworldly, almost surreal encounter that Daniel saw the Ancient of Days formally bestow upon his Son all the dominions of the earth, after which, according to Paul, Jesus will descend from heaven with the spirits of the saints, with a cry of command, with the archangel's call, and with the sound of God's trumpet, for the long-awaited resurrection and rapture of the church.

The following is the reconciliation of the events between the Battle of Armageddon and the resurrection of the saints, given by Jesus, Paul, John, and Daniel:

Table 10.2. Reconciliation of the Events between Armageddon and the Resurrection					
The Sequence	Seq. Olivet Discourse (Matt 24:30-31)	Seq. 1 & 2 Thess (1 Thess 4:16-17; 2 Thess 1:6-10, 2:4, 8)	1st Seq. Rev, Part 3: Lord's Return and 1st Resurrection (Rev 19:11—20:6)	4th Seq. Rev, Part 3: Mt. Zion to God's Throne (Rev 14:17—15:4)	Seq. Dan 7 (Dan 7:9-14)
1. Battle of Armageddon.	The sign of the Son of Man will appear in heaven. (Matt 24:30)	The Lord returns. (2 Thess 1:6-10)	Battle of Armageddon (Rev 19:11-19)	The vintage of the earth is gathered and thrown into the great wine press of God. (Rev 14:17-20)	

Table 10.2. Reconciliation of the Events between Armageddon and the Resurrection

The Sequence	Seq. Olivet Discourse (Matt 24:30–31)	Seq. 1 & 2 Thess (1 Thess 4:16–17; 2 Thess 1:6–10, 2:4, 8)	1st Seq. Rev, Part 3: Lord's Return and 1st Resurrection (Rev 19:11—20:6)	4th Seq. Rev, Part 3: Mt. Zion to God's Throne (Rev 14:17—15:4)	Seq. Dan 7 (Dan 7:9–14)
2. Beast and the false prophet are captured.		The man of lawlessness is taken away at Christ's manifestation. (2 Thess 2:8)	Beast and false prophet are captured. (Rev 19:20a)		
3. Thrones are set in place in heaven.					Daniel saw thrones set in place. (Dan 7:9)
4. Innumerable angels are gathered around the Father.					Ten thousand times 10,000 angels stood attending the Ancient of Days. (Dan 7:10)
5. The beast and the false prophet are brought before the Father for judgment, and the false prophet is heard speaking arrogantly.		The man of lawlessness is brought into the temple of God and is made to sit, where he then declares himself to be God. (2 Thess 2:4)			The little horn was heard speaking arrogantly in front of the Ancient of Days. (Dan 7:11a)

Table 10.2. Reconciliation of the Events between Armageddon and the Resurrection

The Sequence	Seq. Olivet Discourse (Matt 24:30-31)	Seq. 1 & 2 Thess (1 Thess 4:16-17; 2 Thess 1:6-10, 2:4, 8)	1st Seq. Rev, Part 3: Lord's Return and 1st Resurrection (Rev 19:11—20:6)	4th Seq. Rev, Part 3: Mt. Zion to God's Throne (Rev 14:17—15:4)	Seq. Dan 7 (Dan 7:9-14)
6. The beast and the false prophet are judged and cast into the lake of fire.			The beast and the false prophet were cast into the lake of fire. (Rev 19:20b)		The beast and the little horn were cast into the fire. (Dan 7:11b)
7. The dominion of the 5th, 6th, and 7th angelic princes are taken away but their lives are prolonged for a season and a time.					As for the rest of the beasts, their dominion was taken away, but their lives were prolonged for a season and a time. (Dan 7:12)
8. Satan is seized and thrown into the bottomless pit.			Satan was seized and thrown into the bottomless pit. (Rev 20:1-3)		
9. John sees the same thrones that Daniel had seen set in place.			John saw thrones that had been set in place. (Rev 20:4a)		

Table 10.2. Reconciliation of the Events between Armageddon and the Resurrection

The Sequence	Seq. Olivet Discourse (Matt 24:30–31)	Seq. 1 & 2 Thess (1 Thess 4:16–17; 2 Thess 1:6–10, 2:4, 8)	1st Seq. Rev, Part 3: Lord's Return and 1st Resurrection (Rev 19:11—20:6)	4th Seq. Rev, Part 3: Mt. Zion to God's Throne (Rev 14:17—15:4)	Seq. Dan 7 (Dan 7:9–14)
10. The 7 angels and the martyred souls from the tribulation are seen standing around God's throne, as the martyrs sing the Song of Moses and the Song of the Lamb.			The souls of those who had been beheaded during the tribulation, who had not worshiped the beast or its image or had received its mark, are seen standing around the thrones in heaven and worshiping the Lord. (Rev 20:4b)	The 7 angels appeared with the martyrs who had conquered the beast, its image, and the number of its name. The martyrs were seen standing around God's throne, as they sang the Song of Moses and the Song of the Lamb. (Rev 15:1–4)	
11. After his victory at the Battle of Armageddon Jesus is ushered in before the Father.					The Son of Man was ushered in before the Ancient of Days. (Dan 7:13)

THE SEQUENCE

Table 10.2. Reconciliation of the Events between Armageddon and the Resurrection

The Sequence	Seq. Olivet Discourse (Matt 24:30–31)	Seq. 1 & 2 Thess (1 Thess 4:16–17; 2 Thess 1:6–10, 2:4, 8)	1st Seq. Rev, Part 3: Lord's Return and 1st Resurrection (Rev 19:11—20:6)	4th Seq. Rev, Part 3: Mt. Zion to God's Throne (Rev 14:17—15:4)	Seq. Dan 7 (Dan 7:9–14)
12. The Father gives Jesus the dominion of the earth.					The Son of Man was given the dominion of the earth by the Ancient of Days. (Dan 7:14a)
13. Jesus descends for the 1st resurrection and rapture of the saints.	Jesus will send out his angels with a loud trumpet call, and they will gather his elect from the 4 winds, from one end of heaven to the other. (Matt 24:31)	With a cry of command, the archangel's call, and the sound of God's trumpet, Christ descends with the souls of all the righteous, and the dead in Christ rise first. Then, those who are alive and left on the earth are caught up together with those who were resurrected to meet the Lord in the air. (1 Thess 4:16–17a)	The martyrs came to life in the 1st resurrection. (Rev 20:4c–6a)		

344

Table 10.2. Reconciliation of the Events between Armageddon and the Resurrection

The Sequence	Seq. Olivet Discourse (Matt 24:30-31)	Seq. 1 & 2 Thess (1 Thess 4:16-17; 2 Thess 1:6-10, 2:4, 8)	1st Seq. Rev, Part 3: Lord's Return and 1st Resurrection (Rev 19:11—20:6)	4th Seq. Rev, Part 3: Mt. Zion to God's Throne (Rev 14:17—15:4)	Seq. Dan 7 (Dan 7:9-14)
14. Christ begins his millennial kingdom; he is assisted by the resurrected and raptured saints.		Saints are with the Lord forever. (1 Thess 4:17b)	They will be priests of God and Jesus, and they will reign with him 1,000 years. (Rev 20:6b)		The Son of Man reigns over an everlasting kingdom. (Dan 7:14b)

The Post-Armageddon, Premillennial Resurrection and Rapture of the Saints

Not only do Jesus, Paul, and John agree that the resurrection of the saints will follow Christ's appearance at Armageddon, but, as one can see, since John added that Christ's millennial kingdom will follow the first resurrection (Rev 20:6b), one can now see why the *Post-Armageddon, Premillennial Resurrection* is the only correct description of the timing of the resurrection in the sequence of end times.

Now (and finally!), with the knowledge that Christ's return and the resurrection of the saints are indeed separate events, let's look at several passages in the epistles that include both events. As one can readily see, the coming of Christ is always mentioned before the resurrection:

Table 10.3. Passages That Cite Both the Coming of Christ and the Resurrection and Rapture of the Saints

Passages	Christ's Appearance at Armageddon	Resurrection and Rapture
2 Thess 2:1a	"As to the coming of our Lord Jesus Christ . . .	and our being gathered together to him . . ."
1 Cor 15:21–23	"For since death came through a human being, the resurrection of the dead has also come through a human being; for as all die in Adam, so all will be made alive in Christ. But each in his own order: Christ the first fruits, then at his coming . . .	those who belong to Christ."
Phil 3:20–21	"But our citizenship is in heaven, and it is from there that we are expecting a Savior, the Lord Jesus Christ . . .	He will transform the body of our humiliation that it may be conformed to the body of his glory, by the power that also enables him to make all things subject to himself."
Col 3:4	"When Christ who is your life is revealed . . .	then you also will be revealed with him in glory."
1 Pet 5:4	"And when the chief shepherd appears . . .	you will win the crown of glory that never fades away."
1 John 3:2	"Beloved, we are God's children now; what we will be has not yet been revealed. What we do know is this: when he is revealed . . .	we will be like him, for we will see him as he is."

Table 10.3. Passages That Cite Both the Coming of Christ and the Resurrection and Rapture of the Saints

Passages	Christ's Appearance at Armageddon	Resurrection and Rapture
1 Thess 4:15–18	"For this we declare to you by the word of the Lord, that we who are alive, who are left until the coming of the Lord . . .	will by no means precede those who have died. For the Lord himself, with a cry of command, with the archangel's call and with the sound of God's trumpet, will descend from heaven, and the dead in Christ will rise first. Then we who are alive, who are left, will be caught up in the clouds together with them to meet the Lord in the air; and so we will be with the Lord forever. Therefore encourage one another with these words."

As one might expect, each of the above passages are usually misinterpreted. They are either thought to refer to a pretribulational or pre-wrath rapture prior to Christ's appearance at Armageddon, or they are thought to reference the appearance of Christ at Armageddon with a simultaneous resurrection and rapture of the saints.[6] Each view is incorrect. Rather, the passages only reflect the *Post-Armageddon, Premillennial Resurrection*. To illustrate, let's take a closer look at the last passage, 1 Thess 4:15–18, which is arguably the most familiar resurrection and rapture passage in Scripture. Although most understand that the phrase "who are left until the coming of the Lord" certainly refers to the *parousia* of Christ at Armageddon, one now knows that the subsequent phrase, "For the Lord, himself, with a cry of command, with the archangel's call and with the sound of God's trumpet, will descend from heaven, and the dead in Christ will rise first," does not refer to a pretribulational or pre-wrath resurrection/rapture, nor to a resurrection/rapture simultaneous with the *parousia*, but rather, to the *post-Armageddon, premillennial* resurrection/rapture of the saints.

---

6. The beliefs are Pretribulationism, Pre-wrath, and Historic Premillennialism, respectively.

Martha and the Last Day

As one is well aware by now, it has been the author's contention all along that the Lord never intended for the sequence of the return of Christ and the resurrection of the saints to be shrouded in mystery and confusion. To further illustrate this fact, look at Martha's response to a statement from Jesus concerning Lazarus's resurrection, which confirmed her basic knowledge of the timing of the resurrection (italics used for emphasis):

"When Martha heard that Jesus was coming, she went and met him, while Mary stayed home. Martha said to Jesus, 'Lord, if you had been here, my brother would not have died. But even now I know that God will give you whatever you ask of him.' Jesus said to her, 'Your brother will rise again.' Martha said to him, 'I know that he will rise again in the resurrection *on the last day*'" (John 11:20–24).

Martha knew not only that Lazarus would be resurrected, but that he would be resurrected "on the last day." One might suppose that Martha's response was generic in nature and therefore she may not have been as knowledgeable on the subject as here proposed. But I beg to differ. She among others had repeatedly heard Christ teach that the resurrection will specifically occur "on the last day":

1. "And this is the will of him who sent me, that I should lose nothing of all that he has given me, but raise it up *on the last day*. This is indeed the will of my Father, that all who see the Son and believe in him may have eternal life; and I will raise them up *on the last day*" (John 6:39–40).

2. "No one can come to me unless drawn by the Father who sent me; and I will raise that person up *on the last day*" (John 6:44).

3. "Those who eat my flesh and drink my blood have eternal life, and I will raise them up *on the last day*" (John 6:54).

It's quite apparent that Martha knew there's more to the phrase "on the last day" than meets the eye. But do we? Let's turn to Paul for help:

"But each in his own order: Christ the first fruits, then at his coming those who belong to Christ. Then comes the end, when he hands over the kingdom to God the Father, after he has destroyed every ruler and every authority and power. For he must reign until he has put all his enemies under his feet. The last enemy to be destroyed is death. For 'God has put all things in subjection under this feet.' But when it says, 'All things are put in subjection,' it is plain that this does not include the one who put all things in subjection under him. When all things are subjected to him, then the Son himself will also be subjected to the one who put all things in subjection under him, so that God may be all in all" (1 Cor 15:23–28).

When Paul taught the sequence of events surrounding the first resurrection of the saints to the Corinthians, he placed the event among three consecutive periods:

Table 10.4. The Three Time Periods Taught by Paul in 1 Cor 15:20–28	
1st Period (1 Cor 15:20–23)	The First Period Ends at the Resurrection of the Saints
2nd Period (1 Cor 15:24b–27)	The Second Period Comprises the Millennium
3rd Period (1 Cor 15:24a, 28)	The Third Period Comprises the Father's Eternal Kingdom

It's clear that when Jesus taught Martha that the resurrection will take place "on the last day" he was specifically referencing the last day of the first period. The second period begins immediately after the resurrection and comprises Christ's millennial kingdom. The third period begins immediately after the millennial kingdom, and extends throughout eternity. Here's the point: If Martha knew this much about the timing of the resurrection prior to Christ's discourse on the Mount of Olives, and prior to Paul's epistles, and prior to John's visions, then shouldn't the church, who has access to all three of these sources, not to mention the rest of Scripture, have much more understanding on the subject than did Martha?

The Days of Noah

Now, let's go back and address a section of the Lord's Olivet Discourse that we intentionally neglected back in chapter 2 of our study. After Jesus gave the chronology of end-time events, beginning with the abomination of desolation and continuing through the gathering of the saints (Matt 24:15–31), he eventually said the following:

> But about that day and hour no one knows, neither the angels of heaven, nor the Son, but only the Father. For as the days of Noah were, so will be the coming of the Son of Man. For as in those days before the flood they were eating and drinking, marrying and giving in marriage, until the day Noah entered

the ark, and they knew nothing until the flood came and swept them all away, so too will be the coming of the Son of Man. (Matt 24:36–39)

When Jesus said the above words, it's often assumed that the Lord was either referring to a pretribulation resurrection/rapture of the saints, or the post-tribulation manifestation of Christ at Armageddon. But in reality, Christ was referencing neither his manifestation nor the gathering of the saints. To prove that statement, ask yourself this question: Will the days just prior to Armageddon or the days just prior to the resurrection and rapture of the saints be like the days of Noah? Will the wicked be eating and drinking, marrying and giving in marriage up until either of those events? Absolutely not! First, let's review the days prior to Armageddon:

With the remaining unrighteous having somehow survived the trumpet plagues and the bowl plagues, which included five months of global demonic torture, the killing of one-third of the unrighteous, and many of the remaining two-thirds receiving an excruciating sore on their bodies because they had worshiped the beast and received its mark, I think it's safe to say none of the surviving unrighteous will be reveling in a merry time of eating, drinking, marrying, and giving in marriage in the midst of the seventh bowl plague—with its greatest earthquake in the history of the world that causes every mountain, every island, and every city to disappear, coupled with the onslaught of hundred-pound hail—just prior to Christ's appearance at Armageddon.

What about the days preceding the resurrection/rapture of the saints? Now that one knows that the gathering of the saints will follow Christ's victory at the Battle of Armageddon, then it should go without saying, if the unrighteous will not be in a joyful and lighthearted mood prior to Christ's appearance at Armageddon, they certainly will not have recovered from all of their mental anguish and near-death experiences by the time of the upcoming gathering of the saints.

So, what are we left with? There's only one future period of days similar to the days of Noah, when the unrighteous will be carrying on as if all is well, and that is the period of days prior to the appearance of the heavenly signs which ushers in the Day of the Lord. It is then that the inhabitants of the earth will be eating, drinking, and having a merry time—just like the days of Noah. Here's the scenario:

Once the man of lawlessness is revealed by calling down fire from heaven during the nuclear aftermath, he will promptly have the image of the beast constructed, in order that he may cause the world to worship the image. However, the saints will steadfastly refuse to worship the image, which will lead to their beheading. On the other hand, the unrighteous will gladly worship the image, and for this obedience, the man will spare their lives and place a mark on their right hand or forehead, by which, according to Rev 13:17, they will be provided the privilege to buy and sell, eat and drink, and seemingly return to a somewhat normal way of life. It is during this period that Paul revealed that "they" will begin proclaiming "there is peace and security!" Although an innumerable number of righteous around the world will be murdered during this period, the unrighteous will act as if all is well until the moment—the moment that no one knows, neither the angels of heaven, nor the Son, but only the Father—when God unexpectedly shakes the earth with a devastating earthquake that will move every mountain and island out of their place, and shakes the heavens by blackening the sun, darkening the moon, and causing an unprecedented meteoric shower to fall upon the earth (Rev 6:12–14). According to Jesus, this is the moment that the inhabitants of the earth will begin to faint from fear and foreboding of what is coming upon the world (Luke 21:26). One moment the unrighteous are fawning over the man of lawlessness and enjoying how good life has become, and the next, they are fainting from fear because their world has been turned upside down. No wonder Paul, Peter, and God himself said the Day of the Lord will come like a thief (compare 1 Thess 5:2; 2 Pet 3:10; and Rev 16:15).

One Final Objection?

But still one might counter and say that Christ had to be comparing the days of Noah to the days leading up to his manifestation at Armageddon rather than to the days leading up to the Day of the Lord because of the phrase "so will be the coming of the Son of Man" (Matt 24:37). Granted, although Jesus did say these words, nonetheless, in this context he was still comparing the naïveté of the unrighteous during "the days of Noah" to the naïveté of the unrighteous during "the days of the Son of Man." And the proof? Here's Luke's account (italics used for emphasis):

"Just as it was in the *days of Noah*, so too will it be in the *days of the Son of Man*. They were eating and drinking, and marrying and being given in marriage, until the day Noah entered the ark, and the flood came and destroyed all of them" (Luke 17:26–27).

And the conclusion? When Jesus said, "For as the days of Noah were, so will be the coming of the Son of Man" (Matt 24:37), he actually meant, in context, with some clarity provided by Luke, "Just as it was in the days of Noah—leading up to the flood, so will it be in the days of the Son of Man—leading up to the Day of the Lord."

One Taken and One Left

Since the message of Christ's words in Matt 24:36–39 has been universally misunderstood, then one should not be surprised that Christ's next two sentences are misunderstood as well:

> Then two will be in the field; one will be taken and one will be left. Two women will be grinding meal together; one will be taken and one will be left. (Matt 24:40–41)

Here, Jesus is simply describing what will happen to the righteous who have survived the nightmare caused by the beast and his man of lawlessness, who have witnessed Christ's manifestation, and who are now anticipating the long-awaited gathering of the saints. Obviously the "one taken" represents the righteous taken up to meet the Lord in the air, while the "one left" in the field or grinding meal represents the surviving unrighteous.[7] How can one be sure? Because of the disciples' follow-up question (italics used for emphasis):

"I tell you, on that night there will be two in one bed; one will be taken and the other left. There will be two women grinding meal together; one will be taken and the other left. Two will be in the field, one will be taken and the other left. *Then they asked him, 'Where, Lord?' He said to them, 'Where the corpse is, there the vultures will gather'*" (Luke 17:34–37).

Notice the order of exchange between Jesus and the disciples: Jesus first said "one will be taken" and then he said "and the other left,"

---

7. Just as not all of the unrighteous around the world will journey to the plains of Armageddon in order to war against Christ, so too many of the same will not worship the beast nor receive its mark. Nevertheless these people have not been imputed the righteousness of Christ and for that, they remain unrighteous.

which was immediately followed by the disciples' query "Where, Lord?" Grammatically, one knows the disciples' question could only have been in response to the Lord's last phrase: "and the other left." Had the disciples' question pertained to the first phrase "one will be taken" then the disciples would have needed to qualify their question in a way similar to the following: "Where, Lord, will one be taken?" But since they did not qualify their question as such, the disciples could only have been responding to the last phrase of Christ, with the following result:

Table 10.5. The Righteous Are Taken and the Unrighteous Are Left		
Jesus:	"One will be taken . . .	and the other left."
The disciples:		"Where, Lord?"
Jesus:		"Where the corpse is, there the vultures will gather."

What did Christ mean by this mysterious response? One moment, Christ is foretelling the rapture of the saints who are still living, and the next, he is saying something about the unrighteous being left among corpses and vultures! But no worries; Christ's response is not as mysterious as it first appears. As the saints are caught up in the clouds to meet the Lord in the air, the remaining unrighteous will be left on the earth, where, as the reader well knows, a battle has just been fought—where the vultures of the air will still be gathered, feasting upon the scattered corpses from the battle. Here again is the description of the grisly scene:

"Then I saw an angel standing in the sun, and with a loud voice he called to all the birds that fly in midheaven, 'Come, gather for the great supper of God, to eat the flesh of kings, the flesh of captains, the flesh of the mighty, the flesh of horses and their riders—flesh of all, both free and slave, both small and great'" (Rev 19:17–18).

It's quite apparent that when Jesus responded to the disciples, he had in mind the wake of frenzied vultures blanketed upon the war-torn battlefields of the earth, especially the fields of Armageddon.

Closing Thoughts: Dinner Reservations and Army Recruits

Once the dead in Christ are resurrected, they will be joined in the clouds by those who are alive and left, where together they will meet the Lord in the air (italics used for emphasis):

"Then we who are alive, who are left, will be caught up in the clouds together with them to *meet* the Lord in the air; and so we will be with the Lord forever" (1 Thess 4:17).

The word "meet" has a unique connotation (Greek: *apantēsin*). It's often translated "to greet" rather than "to meet," as when the townspeople and a mayor of a community go out "to greet" a king upon his arrival and then accompany the king back into the city. The word is also used in the parable of the ten virgins when the five wise virgins went out "to greet" the bridegroom upon his arrival. After greeting the bridegroom, the virgins would then naturally accompany the groom back into the city for the wedding ceremony. Therefore, with that backdrop, Paul's words could easily be translated as:

"Then we who are alive, who are left, will be caught up in the clouds together with them to *greet* the Lord in the air; and so we will be with the Lord forever."

As the narrative implies, after greeting the Lord the glorified saints will return with their King back to the earth, where they will all gather and celebrate the marriage supper, just before reigning with Christ during the millennial kingdom. One cannot help but be reminded of the angel's words to John:

"Blessed are those who are invited to the marriage supper of the Lamb" (Rev 19:9b).

The marriage supper will be the setting for the greatest of celebrations: The enemies of God have been defeated at Armageddon; the beast and the false prophet have been cast into the lake of fire; Satan has been bound for a thousand years; the saints of God have just received their glorified bodies, and the Son of God is about to reign from Jerusalem for a thousand years! Could there be a greater time for celebration! And although there will still be enemies left to conquer at the end of the millennium, i.e., the rebellious nations, Satan, Death, Hades, etc., those battles are left for another day. At the marriage supper all is well. Each of the elect who share in the first resurrection will now begin a fellowship and a communion with God and the other saints that will last for eternity. Jesus will be at the head of the marriage supper table and will then be showered with glory and honor from the saints of every generation. The sequence of events ordained by God is sublime. However, when that sequence is misunderstood, not only do misconceptions and errors arise, but some of the errors that surface are quite bizarre, to put it mildly. One such idea goes as follows:

After the church is whisked away to heaven before the great tribulation begins on the earth, the newly raptured saints will soon begin to celebrate the marriage supper in heaven, while their less fortunate brothers and sisters back on the earth must face the great tribulation perpetrated by the beast and the man of lawlessness.

Reflect on that scenario for just a moment. To believe that one could engage in a celebration in heaven while, at the same time, there are hundreds of thousands or perhaps millions of brothers and sisters down on the earth, immersed in the blood, sweat, and tears of the battle for the cause of Christ, with its untold atrocities and beheadings caused by the beast and his false prophet, is frankly grotesque. And as if the error couldn't get any more unseemly, that same belief places Christ in the midst of the celebration! Of course, the teaching is false. The imaginary marriage supper for "early arrivals" will never materialize. There will be no celebration until all the saints, including the tribulation saints, are seated at the table. (And yes, the marriage supper will take place on the earth, not in heaven.)

A second far-fetched idea concerns the armies of heaven. Many think that when the Lord appears at the Battle of Armageddon after a supposed pretribulation rapture, he will be accompanied by a great army of saints. If I've heard it once, I've heard it a thousand times: First the Lord comes for his saints, then he comes with his saints. Here's the passage in question:

"Then I saw heaven opened, and there was a white horse! Its rider is called Faithful and True, and in righteousness he judges and makes war. His eyes are like a flame of fire, and on his head are many diadems; and he has a name inscribed that no one knows but himself. He is clothed in a robe dipped in blood, and his name is called The Word of God. And the armies of heaven, wearing fine linen, white and pure, were following him on white horses" (Rev 19:11–14).

With the knowledge that the resurrection and rapture will occur after Armageddon, then obviously the armies seen here are not the saints.

That shouldn't come as a surprise to anyone since Paul has already identified the recruits in 2 Thessalonians (italics used for emphasis):

"For it is indeed just of God to repay with affliction those who afflict you, and to give relief to the afflicted as well as to us, *when the Lord Jesus is revealed from heaven with his mighty angels in flaming fire*, inflicting vengeance on those who do not know God and on those who do not obey the gospel of our Lord Jesus. These will suffer the punishment of eternal destruction, separated from the presence of the Lord and from the glory of his might, when he comes to be glorified by his saints and to be marveled at on that day among all who have believed, because our testimony to you was believed" (2 Thess 1:6–10).

Paul said that when Jesus is revealed he will be accompanied by "angels" in flaming fire (Greek: *angelōn*). Matthew and Mark agree:

1. "For the Son of Man is to come with his *angels* in the glory of his Father, and then he will repay everyone for what has been done" (Matt 16:27).

2. "Those who are ashamed of me and of my words in this adulterous and sinful generation, of them the Son of Man will also be ashamed when he comes in the glory of his Father with the holy *angels*" (Mark 8:38).

As did Paul in 2 Thessalonians, both Matthew and Mark employed the Greek word *angelōn*, which is from where the word "angels" derives. But despite the Scripture's clarity on who will, and who will not, accompany Christ at his revelation, many become needlessly confused when the New Testament writers happen to employ a second, frequently used term (italics used for emphasis):

"See, the Lord is coming with ten thousands of his *holy ones*, to execute judgment on all, and to convict everyone of all the deeds of ungodliness that they have committed in such an ungodly way, and of all the harsh things that ungodly sinners have spoken against him" (Jude 14b–15).

Instead of ten thousands of his *angelōn*, Jude simply said the Lord will be accompanied by ten thousands of his *hagiais* (Greek: "holy ones"). However, even with the change in vocabulary, all should know that in this context, the holy ones are angels. Paul himself used both terms interchangeably. Before using *angelōn* in 2 Thessalonians, the apostle used *hagiais* in the first letter:

"And may he so strengthen your hearts in holiness that you may be blameless before our God and Father at the coming of our Lord Jesus with all his holy ones" (1 Thess 3:13).

Paul was referencing the same angels in both instances. Despite wishful thinking, Christ's army will not be composed of grandparents and grandchildren, aunts and uncles, or moms and dads, for the simple reason that the resurrection and rapture haven't yet occurred. In the end, Christ's armies will be composed of warring and powerful angels in flaming fire, just as the Scripture indicates.

Upon reflection, isn't it ironic that those who embrace this mistaken belief are quite eager to enlist in the armies of Christ, as he is about to descend and confront the opposing nations at the Battle of Armageddon, but with one caveat: They must be already equipped with a glorified, imperishable, immortal, and indestructible body. That way, no one gets hurt. However, if these same proponents ever come to realize that at the time of Christ's appearance at Armageddon, the transformation of the saints' bodies still lies in the future, they might not be so eager to join the fray.

∼

Here's the reconciliation of the six sequences from the return of the Lord to the first resurrection of the saints (the newly added events from Rev 19:11—20:6a are italicized):

Table 10.6. Reconciliation of the Six Sequences from the Return of the Lord to the First Resurrection

The Sequence	Seq. 1 & 2 Thess (1 Thess 4:13–17a; 2 Thess 1:6–10, 2:4, 8)	Seq. Olivet Discourse (Matt 24:30–31)	1st Seq. Rev, Part 3: Lord's Return and 1st Resurrection (19:11—20:6a)	2nd Seq. Rev: 2 Witnesses	3rd Seq. Rev: Woman, Child, and Dragon	4th Seq. Rev, Part 3: Mt. Zion to God's Throne (14:17—15:4)
1. The Lord returns and engages the hostile armies of the earth at the Battle of Armageddon.	The Lord returns. (2 Thess 1:6–10)	The Son of Man appears. (Matt 24:30)	*The rider on a white horse descended from heaven and fought the armies of the earth at the Battle of Armageddon. (Rev 19:11–19)*			The great wine press of the wrath of God occurs. (Rev 14:17–20)
2. The beast and the false prophet are captured alive.	The man of lawlessness is taken away at Christ's appearance. (2 Thess 2:8)		The beast and the false prophet were captured alive. (Rev 19:20a)			

FIRST SEQUENCE, PART 3

Table 10.6. Reconciliation of the Six Sequences from the Return of the Lord to the First Resurrection

The Sequence	Seq. 1 & 2 Thess (1 Thess 4:13–17a; 2 Thess 1:6–10, 2:4, 8)	Seq. Olivet Discourse (Matt 24:30–31)	1st Seq. Rev, Part 3: Lord's Return and 1st Resurrection (19:11—20:6a)	2nd Seq. Rev: 2 Witnesses	3rd Seq. Rev: Woman, Child, and Dragon	4th Seq. Rev, Part 3: Mt. Zion to God's Throne (14:17—15:4)
3. The beast and the man of lawlessness are brought before the Father for judgment. The man is made to sit, at which time he then begins to speak arrogantly, declaring himself to be God.	The man of lawlessness enters the temple of God where he is made to sit. He then declares himself to be God. (2 Thess 2:4)					
4. The beast and the false prophet are judged and thrown into the lake of fire. The rest of those at the Battle of Armageddon had already been killed.			The beast and the false prophet were thrown into the lake of fire. The rest of those at the battle had already been killed. (Rev 19:20b–21)			

359

Table 10.6. Reconciliation of the Six Sequences from the Return of the Lord to the First Resurrection

The Sequence	Seq. 1 & 2 Thess (1 Thess 4:13–17a; 2 Thess 1:6–10, 2:4, 8)	Seq. Olivet Discourse (Matt 24:30–31)	1st Seq. Rev, Part 3: Lord's Return and 1st Resurrection (19:11—20:6a)	2nd Seq. Rev: 2 Witnesses	3rd Seq. Rev: Woman, Child, and Dragon	4th Seq. Rev, Part 3: Mt. Zion to God's Throne (14:17–15:4)
5. Satan is seized and cast into the bottomless pit for 1,000 years.			*Satan was seized and cast into the bottomless pit for 1,000 years. (Rev 20:1–3)*			
6. Those who were seated on the thrones are given authority to judge.			*Those who were seated on the thrones were given authority to judge. (Rev 20:4a)*			

FIRST SEQUENCE, PART 3

Table 10.6. Reconciliation of the Six Sequences from the Return of the Lord to the First Resurrection

The Sequence	Seq. 1 & 2 Thess (1 Thess 4:13–17a; 2 Thess 1:6–10, 2:4, 8)	Seq. Olivet Discourse (Matt 24:30–31)	1st Seq. Rev, Part 3: Lord's Return and 1st Resurrection (19:11—20:6a)	2nd Seq. Rev: 2 Witnesses	3rd Seq. Rev: Woman, Child, and Dragon	4th Seq. Rev, Part 3: Mt. Zion to God's Throne (14:17—15:4)
7. The 7 angels appeared in heaven with the martyrs who had conquered the beast, its image, and the number of its name. The martyrs were singing the Song of Moses and the Song of the Lamb.			*The souls of those who had been beheaded during the tribulation, who had not worshiped the beast or its image or received its mark, are seen standing around the thrones in heaven and worshiping the Lord. (Rev 20:4b)*			The 7 angels appeared in heaven with the martyrs who had conquered the beast, its image, and the number of its name. The martyrs were singing the Song of Moses and the Song of the Lamb.(Rev 15:1–4)

Table 10.6. Reconciliation of the Six Sequences from the Return of the Lord to the First Resurrection

The Sequence	Seq. 1 & 2 Thess (1 Thess 4:13–17a; 2 Thess 1:6–10, 2:4, 8)	Seq. Olivet Discourse (Matt 24:30–31)	1st Seq. Rev, Part 3: Lord's Return and 1st Resurrection (19:11—20:6a)	2nd Seq. Rev: 2 Witnesses	3rd Seq. Rev: Woman, Child, and Dragon	4th Seq. Rev, Part 3: Mt. Zion to God's Throne (14:17—15:4)
8. After the Father bestows upon Jesus the dominion of the world, Jesus descends with the souls of all the saints who have died in Christ for the 1st resurrection and rapture of the saints.	With a cry of command, the archangel's call, and the sound of God's trumpet, the saints are resurrected and raptured. (1 Thess 4:13–17a)	Jesus sends out his angels with a loud trumpet call, and they gather his elect from the 4 winds, from one end of heaven to the other. (Matt 24:31)	*The martyrs came to life in the 1st resurrection. (Rev 20:4c–6a)*			

362

CHAPTER 11

First Sequence, Part 4

The Millennium and the Final Judgment (20:6b–15)

First Sequence	Second Sequence	Third Sequence	Fourth Sequence
Chapter 9 1st Seq., Part 2: The 7 Bowls (15:5—19:10)			
Chapter 10 1st Seq., Part 3: The Lord's Return and the 1st Resurrection (19:11—20:6a)			
Chapter 11* 1st Seq., Part 4: The Millennium and the Final Judgment (20:6b–15)			
Chapter 12 1st Seq., Part 5: The 2nd Resurrection and the New Jerusalem (21:1—22:5)			

THE SEQUENCE

WHEN SOME IN THE Corinthian church expressed doubt as to whether there was actually going to be a future resurrection, Paul listed many witnesses of Christ's resurrection, including the twelve disciples, a group of over five hundred believers at one time, James (the brother of Christ), all the apostles, and last but not least, Paul himself. The apostle then said if there isn't any future resurrection of the saints, then Christ hasn't been raised from the dead; and if Christ hasn't been raised from the dead, their faith was futile, and they were still in their sins and have no hope. But since he has been raised, they can rest assured that there will be a resurrection of the saints. Paul then shares with them the sequence surrounding the resurrection:

"But each in his own order: Christ the first fruits, then at his coming those who belong to Christ. Then comes the end, when he hands over the kingdom to God the Father, after he has destroyed every ruler and every authority and power. For he must reign until he has put all his enemies under his feet. The last enemy to be destroyed is death. For 'God has put all things in subjection under his feet.' But when it says, 'All things are put in subjection,' it is plain that this does not include the one who put all things in subjection under him. When all things are subjected to him, then the Son himself will also be subjected to the one who put all things in subjection under him, so that God may be all in all" (1 Cor 15:23–28).

Having recently addressed this passage, it is at the following sentence that we now find ourselves: "For he must reign until he has put all his enemies under his feet." Immediately after Christ is formally given all the kingdoms of the world by the Father (Dan 7:14), Christ will descend and gather all of the elect in the first resurrection and rapture of the saints from the four corners of the earth, at which time he will begin his millennial reign with assistance from the saints:

> Blessed and holy are those who share in the first resurrection. Over these the second death has no power, but they will be priests of God and of Christ, and they will reign with him a thousand years. (Rev 20:6)

After Christ has destroyed every ruler and every authority and power during the millennium, he will then return the kingdom of the earth to the Father. Only after the kingdom has been completely purged of all evil, including death, will the Son present the kingdom back to the Father, because only that which is perfect and holy is acceptable to the Father.

The Millennium

One might assume that, after the destruction of the armies of the hostile nations in the Battle of Armageddon, as well as the capture and disposal of the beast, the false prophet, and Satan, the Lord's thousand-year kingdom will be a utopia on earth, filled with universal peace and bliss. Not so. Granted, although many of the earth's unrighteous population, i.e., those who survive the nuclear global holocaust as well as the fourteen trumpets and bowls, will be more than willing to submit and serve Christ as they enter his millennial reign, others, even with Satan locked up, will enter the millennium resenting Christ, his authority, and his people. These are those whom the Lord must rule with a rod of iron (Rev 19:15). And do so he will. Christ will promptly begin to test those who are obstinate from the start:

"Then all who survive of the nations that have come against Jerusalem shall go up year after year to worship the King, the Lord of Hosts, and to keep the festival of booths. If any of the families of the earth do not go up to Jerusalem to worship the King, the Lord of hosts, there will be no rain upon them. And if the family of Egypt do not go up and present themselves, then on them shall come the plague that the Lord inflicts on the nations that do not go up to keep the festival of booths. Such shall be the punishment of Egypt and the punishment of all the nations that do not go up to keep the festival of booths" (Zech 14:16-19).

This may not sound like the utopia taught in churches across the nation on any given Sunday, but to those who choose to follow the Lord wholeheartedly, it will indeed be like heaven on earth. The glory, holiness, and justice emanating from Jerusalem, as Jesus reigns from his throne in the city, will be as the balm of Gilead to a world that has sorely needed his rule and will be a welcome reprieve from what Christians are subjected to presently. Today, evil is not only tolerated, but it is condoned and openly applauded. Compare today's lawlessness to that of Paul's day:

"They were filled with every kind of wickedness, evil, covetousness, malice. Full of envy, murder, strife, deceit, craftiness, they are gossips, slanderers, God-haters, insolent, haughty, boastful, inventors of evil, rebellious toward parents, foolish, faithless, heartless, ruthless. They know God's decree, that those who practice such things deserve to die—yet they not only do them but even applaud others who practice them" (Rom 1:29-32).

The sins of this present generation are no less than the one Paul described in Romans. In fact, this generation is probably worse. Thankfully, Jesus will not tolerate this kind of behavior during the millennium. And not only will that behavior not be allowed, but the reprobates of the world will no longer be permitted to impose their mores upon society. No longer will there be wicked kings, dictators, presidents, governors, or mayors in positions of power. Rather, Jesus will be the one in power. Imagine having a ruler who can actually control the weather by stopping the rain, as a way of keeping the rebellious in check (Zech 14:17). But for the individuals who submit, who choose to become obedient to the Lord and go up year after year to Jerusalem and worship the Lord, their obedience will lead to eternal life. These are the people who will desire to know Christ and his ways:

"In days to come the mountain of the Lord's house shall be established as the highest of the mountains, and shall be raised above the hills; all the nations shall stream to it. Many peoples shall come and say, 'Come, let us go up to the mountain of the Lord, to the house of the God of Jacob; that he may teach us his ways and that we may walk in his paths.' For out of Zion shall go forth instruction, and the word of the Lord from Jerusalem. He shall judge between the nations, and shall arbitrate for many peoples; they shall beat their swords into plowshares, and their spears into pruning hooks; nation shall not lift up sword against nation, neither shall they learn war any more" (Isa 2:2–4).

Although the devotion to love and honor Christ among the gentile nations will vary from nation to nation and from person to person during the millennium, it's hard to conceive of any Jewish residents choosing not to love and adore their Messiah during the thousand years. With the understanding that the surviving unrepentant Jews of the last generation had seen Christ's glorious return and will then witness his holiness and justice up close as he rules all the nations of the earth literally from their doorsteps, one can hopefully envision how the trend of countless past generations will be completely reversed during the millennial reign as the children of Israel now choose to fully give their hearts to him during the entire millennium, generation after generation. This willingness to follow Christ by the Jews throughout the thousand years explains the perplexing phrase that we came across in Rev 14, describing the 144,000 Jewish remnant who, as you remember, were seen standing with the Lamb on Mount Zion (italics used for emphasis):

"They have been redeemed from humankind *as first fruits* for God and the Lamb" (Rev 14:4b).

Notice that John said the 144,000 Jewish remnant, who had wonderfully confessed Christ at the sight of the heavenly signs (Joel 2:32), which qualified them to share in the first resurrection and receive their glorified bodies along with the rest of the saints, were called "first fruits" for God and the Lamb. How can that be? The statement sounds inexplicable especially when compared to all of the saints who shared in the first resurrection. After all, when compared to them, the 144,000 did not come into the fold first, but rather, last. In other words, not only did the 144,000 come into God's kingdom in the last generation, but they came in at the last minute in the last generation, just before the Day of the Lord. That certainly doesn't sound like first fruits by any stretch of the imagination, does it? However, there is an explanation: The 144,000 Jewish remnant are not considered "first fruits" when compared to others who will share in the first resurrection, but rather, they are "first fruits" compared to the millions and millions of their Jewish brothers and sisters who will convert to Christ during the millennium. In one of the most familiar millennial passages in the OT, see how Isaiah describes the great influx of Jews into God's kingdom during Christ's millennial reign (italics used for emphasis):

"The wolf shall live with the lamb, the leopard shall lie down with the kid, the calf and the lion and the fatling together, and the little child shall lead them. The cow and the bear shall graze, their young shall lie down together; and the lion shall eat straw like the ox. The nursing child shall play over the hole of the asp, and the weaned child shall put its hand on the adder's den. They will not hurt or destroy on all my holy mountain; for the earth will be full of the knowledge of the Lord as the waters cover the sea.

"On that day the root of Jesse shall stand as a signal to the peoples; the nations shall inquire of him, and his dwelling shall be glorious. *On that day the Lord will extend his hand yet a second time to recover the remnant that is left of his people, from Assyria, from Egypt, from Pathros, from Ethiopia, from Elam, from Shinar, from Hamath, and from the coastlands of the sea. He will raise a signal for the nations, and will assemble the outcasts of Israel, and gather the dispersed of Judah from the four corners of the earth*" (Isa 11:6–12).

At the appearance of the heavenly signs, the 144,000 Jewish remnant will be recovered from Jerusalem and the surrounding areas, but during the millennium, the Jewish remnant will be recovered from all the nations of the earth. It is because of this second recovery—this great conversion of the Jews during Christ's millennial kingdom—that one might speculate that just as the gentiles have comprised the overwhelming majority of those who have entered the kingdom of God during the past two thousand years, perhaps the Jewish people might "catch up" during the millennium, causing God's eternal kingdom to be composed equally of Jews and gentiles. Who knows?

The Millennial Temple

After the greatest earthquake in the history of the world occurs during the seventh bowl of God's wrath, resulting in the disappearance of every mountain and island on earth, the following passage, one we have just cited, will then be fulfilled (italics used for emphasis):

"*In days to come the mountain of the Lord's house shall be established as the highest of the mountains*, and shall be raised above the hills; all the nations shall stream to it. Many peoples shall come and say, 'Come, let us go up to the mountain of the Lord, to the house of the God of Jacob; that he may teach us his ways and that we may walk in his paths.' For out of Zion shall go forth instruction, and the word of the Lord from Jerusalem" (Isa 2:2–3).

Of course, the mountain referenced is none other than Mount Zion. But which house is Isaiah referencing? It is certainly the millennial temple prophesied by Zechariah:

"Thus says the Lord of hosts: Here is a man whose name is Branch: for he shall branch out in his place, and he shall build the temple of the Lord. It is he that shall build the temple of the Lord; he shall bear royal honor, and shall sit and rule on his throne" (Zech 6:12b–13a).

The Branch is Jesus Christ. The Lord himself will commission the building of the house of God from where he will rule all the nations of the earth during his thousand-year kingdom. Although many OT prophets spoke of the millennial temple, it was only the prophet Ezekiel who was given the architectural plans of the structure. In the following, Ezekiel sees a vision of the structure perched atop Mount Zion in the distant future:

"In the twenty-fifth year of our exile, at the beginning of the year, on the tenth day of the month, in the fourteenth year after the city was struck down, on that very day, the hand of the Lord was upon me, and he brought me there. He brought me, in visions of God, to the land of Israel, and set me down upon a very high mountain, on which was a structure like a city to the south. When he brought me there, a man was there, whose appearance shone like bronze, with a linen cord and a measuring reed in his hand; and he was standing in the gateway. The man said to me, 'Mortal, look closely and listen attentively, and set your mind upon all that I shall show you, for you were brought here in order that I might show it to you; declare all that you see to the house of Israel'" (Ezek 40:1–4).

Just as an angel instructed John to measure the land where Herod's temple was located in preparation for the future ministry of the two witnesses (Rev 11:1–2), the angel accompanying Ezekiel had already measured a larger area on the mount in preparation for the building of Christ's grandiose temple during the millennial kingdom (Ezek 45:1–8). Accompanying the measurements for the area are hundreds and hundreds of intricate details describing the structure, the courtyard, and the daily activities of the priests and the Prince (Jesus). It should go without saying that the details surrounding the millennial temple are not symbolic. Ezekiel's visions were visions of a real, future temple, surrounded by real, future activities. And the proof? Consider the following:

1. When the Lord said concerning the attending levitical priests of the temple that only the descendants of Zadok could enter the sanctuary of the temple (Ezek 44:15), what possibly could the Lord have been attempting to symbolize by citing "the descendants of Zadok"? Nothing comes to mind.

2. How about when the Lord said the priests of the temple shall only wear linen vestments, and nothing of wool, so as not to bind themselves with anything that causes sweat (Ezek 44:15–18)? Is there any symbolic significance of certain fabrics preventing sweat? None, whatsoever.

3. Next, look at just one example of the extraordinary details of the architecture itself: "There were three recesses on either side of the east gate; the three were of the same size; and the pilasters on either side were of the same size. Then he measured the width of the opening of the gateway, ten cubits; and the width of the gateway, thirteen cubits. There was a barrier before the recesses, one cubit on either side; and the recesses were six cubits on either side. Then he measured the gate from the back of the one recess to the back of the other, a width of

twenty-five cubits, from wall to wall. He measured also the vestibule, twenty cubits, and the gate next to the pilaster on every side of the court. From the front of the gate at the entrance to the end of the inner vestibule of the gate was fifty cubits. The recesses and their pilasters had windows, with shutters on the inside of the gateway all around, and the vestibules also had windows on the inside all around; and on the pilasters were palm trees" (Ezek 40:10–16). Where's the symbolism in one cubit, six cubits, ten cubits, thirteen cubits, twenty cubits, twenty-five cubits, and fifty cubits? There isn't any.

One can be certain that Ezekiel saw a real, future temple, complete with real priests and real activities, from where Jesus will rule during his millennial kingdom. For those who willingly submit to the Lord, the many generations living throughout the millennium will have the opportunity and privilege to travel to Jerusalem and see the glory of the house, but more importantly, to see the glory of the Master of the house. Once there, they will be able to see and worship him in person! But for those who do not submit, life will be tough. In the end, the Lord will prove to the unrighteous of the earth that even with Satan confined, the depravity of the unrighteous is present in every generation and the inclination of their hearts is on evil continually, with or without the prodding of the enemy. This depravity will be on full display when, toward the end of the millennium, Satan will be released one more time and will incite those who continually choose to walk in the flesh, bringing the evil that is festering within their hearts to the surface, and the result will be war.

The Battle of Gog and Magog

Devoting only four sentences to the next subject, John identifies the war at the end of the millennium as one that will be instigated by Satan after his release from the bottomless pit, and it will include nations from every quadrant of the earth as they march against "the beloved city." Unlike the Battle of Armageddon, which doesn't start out as an invasion of Jerusalem, per se (Rev 16:12–16), John said the number of those joining in the effort to invade the city at the end of the millennium will be as numerous as the sands of the seas:

> When the thousand years are ended, Satan will be released from his prison and will come out to deceive the nations at the four corners of the earth, Gog and Magog, in order to gather them

for battle; they are as numerous as the sands of the sea. They marched up over the breadth of the earth and surrounded the camp of the saints and the beloved city. And fire came down from heaven and consumed them. (Rev 20:7–9)

Even to the most cynical of observers, the fact that after Jesus returns to the earth in all of his glory and splendor, and then begins to reign in perfect righteousness and holiness, that a possible majority of mankind would still choose to reject him seems incomprehensible. But reject they will. Whereas John only identified the end-time revolt as Gog and Magog, Ezekiel, who received a much more comprehensive revelation on the subject than did John, identified the meaning of the two terms comprising the battle's title: Gog will be the antagonist at the center of the future revolt and Magog will be the land from whence he will come (Ezek 38:2). Furthermore, one knows that Gog will be a human prince just as was the man of lawlessness a thousand years earlier:

"On that day I will give to Gog a place for burial in Israel, the Valley of the Travelers east of the sea; it shall block the path of the travelers, for there Gog and all his horde will be buried; it shall be called the Valley of Hamon-gog. Seven months the house of Israel shall spend burying them, in order to cleanse the land. All the people of the land shall bury them; and it will bring them honor on the day that I show my glory, says the Lord God" (Ezek 39:11–13).

Angels are not buried; men are buried. Therefore "Gog and all his horde" are men. And although Gog and the man of lawlessness are both evil men who will militarily oppose God in the future, the similarity, for all intents and purposes, stops there. Gog will be buried at the end of Christ's millennial kingdom, and the man of lawlessness, along with his angelic leader, the beast, will be thrown alive into the lake of fire prior to it.

There's Only One Battle of Gog and Magog

Don't make the surprisingly common mistake of believing that the Battle of Gog and Magog referenced in Ezek 38 and 39 is somehow different than the Battle of Gog and Magog in Rev 20, and that the one in Ezekiel precedes not only the one in Revelation but also the Battle of Armageddon. There's only one Battle of Gog and Magog and it will occur at the end of the millennium. And the proof? Well, the uniqueness of the title of the battle should be proof enough, however, for some that's not enough. Therefore, let's add more proof:

First, note the timing of the battle; Gog will attempt to invade Israel when the people of Jerusalem are living in perfect safety:

"You will say, 'I will go up against the land of unwalled villages; I will fall upon the quiet people who live in safety, all of them living without walls, and having no bars or gates'" (Ezek 38:11).

Prior to the Battle of Gog and Magog, Israel will be living in safety; prior to the Battle of Armageddon, Israel will not be living in safety, just as she doesn't live in safety now. She will never live in peace and security until the Lord returns and sets up his millennial kingdom. Although today she has her walls, her gates, her nuclear weapons, and one of the most advanced militaries on earth, she continues to live in a constant state of readiness because of the daily threat to her very existence by the surrounding nations. Their stated mission is to eradicate Israel from the face of the earth, and anyone who doesn't realize that is hopelessly naive. Each night Jewish families go to bed, they are cognizant of the fact that it could be their last night on earth because those around them are burning the midnight oil, plotting ways to destroy them. However, that's not the scenario during the millennium. Unlike the constant dread and fear that the country experiences today, Israel will indeed be living in safety during that time. And why wouldn't she? The Lord Jesus will be dwelling in her city for the entirety of the millennium, from where he will be ruling the rebellious nations of the earth with a rod of iron (Rev 19:15). Nevertheless, despite the presence of Christ and in order that Scripture may be fulfilled, there will come a moment in time when Gog and the nations of the earth succumb to the proddings of Satan and converge upon the beautiful city. And how will Satan tempt Gog to entertain such a heinous and seemingly inexplicable act as to invade Jerusalem, even as Christ sits on his throne in the city? By one of the seven deadly sins: *greed*. During the Lord's thousand-year reign, Israel will become rich—very rich! In fact, just as the nation started out with riches during the Egyptian exodus (Exod 11:2-3 and 12:35-36), Israel will begin the millennium in similar fashion. In the following, Zechariah describes her financial windfall after the Battle of Armageddon:

"On that day living waters shall flow out from Jerusalem, half of them to the eastern sea and half of them to the western sea; it shall continue in summer as in winter. And the Lord will become king over all the earth; on that day the Lord will be one and his name one . . . . And the wealth of all the surrounding nations shall be collected—gold, silver, and garments in great abundance" (Zech 14:8–9, 14b).

After Jerusalem is invaded by the surrounding nations at the abomination of desolation—a time when her houses will be looted, her women raped, and many of her inhabitants killed or chased into the wilderness—the Lord will flip the script at the beginning of the millennium and bless Israel with the wealth of those same nations who had invaded and violated her at the abomination. And God will continue to bless Jerusalem with this abundance during the entire millennium. Whereas the nation of Israel is now looked down upon and despised by the nations, as evidenced by today's rampant anti-Semitism, the country will then exist as the crown jewel of all the nations of the earth. The nations who have always thought they were superior to Israel, who thought they were the head while she was the tail, will be brought down to size during the millennium, where, if anything, they will be the tail and she will be the head. And because of this providential turn of events, the nations' long-held sense of superiority will eventually give way to jealousy and covetousness during the thousand years. But because of the intimidating presence of Christ the nations will keep their distance and at least have the good sense not to act on their hidden thoughts—that is until Satan is released from the bottomless pit. And then, as is so often the case, the Deceiver will have success in tempting his victim to do something very irrational. In the following, God describes the satanic thoughts that will one day enter Gog's mind:

"Thus says the Lord God: On that day thoughts will come into your mind, and you will devise an evil scheme. You will say, 'I will go up against the land of unwalled villages; I will fall upon the quiet people who live in safety, all of them living without walls, and having no bars or gates'; to seize spoil and carry off plunder; to assail the waste places that are now inhabited, and the people who were gathered from the nations, who are acquiring cattle and goods, who live at the center of the earth. Sheba and Dedan and the merchants of Tarshish and all its young warriors will say to you, 'Have you come to seize spoil? Have you assembled your horde to carry off plunder, to carry away silver and gold, to take away cattle and goods, to seize a great amount of booty?'

"Therefore, mortal, prophesy, and say to Gog: Thus says the Lord God: On that day when my people are living securely, you will rouse yourself and come from your place out of the remotest parts of the north, you and many peoples with you, all of them riding on horses, a great horde, a mighty army; you will come up against my people Israel, like a cloud covering the earth. In the latter days I will bring you against my land, so that the nations may know me, when through you, O Gog, I display my holiness before their eyes" (Ezek 38:10–16).

Unlike the Battle of Armageddon, when three demons will proceed from the mouths of Satan, the beast, and the man of lawlessness, with the purpose of gathering the armies of the nations to the plains of Megiddo in order to confront Jesus Christ in battle and retake the world (Rev 16:12–16 and 17:13–14), the Battle of Gog and Magog will come about when Satan single-handedly imparts an evil scheme into the mind of Gog to go and pillage the people of Israel because of their wealth. But just as was the Battle of Armageddon, the Battle of Gog and Magog will end in God's victory. John simply said of the invading nations' demise, "fire will come down from heaven and consume them" (Rev 20:9). But Ezekiel was a little more graphic:[1]

"On that day, when Gog comes against the land of Israel, says the Lord God, my wrath shall be aroused. For in my jealousy and in my blazing wrath I declare: On that day there shall be a great shaking in the land of Israel; the fish of the sea, and the birds of the air, and the animals of the field, and all creeping things that creep on the ground, and all human beings that are on the face of the earth, shall quake at my presence, and the mountains shall be thrown down, and the cliffs shall fall, and every wall shall tumble to the ground. I will summon the sword against Gog in all my mountains, says the Lord God; the swords of all will be against their comrades. With pestilence and bloodshed I will enter into judgment with him; and I will pour out torrential rains and hailstones, fire and sulfur, upon him and his troops and the many peoples that are with him. So I will display my greatness and my holiness and make myself known in the eyes of many nations. Then they shall know that I am the Lord" (Ezek 38:18–23).

And with that predictable and almost anticlimactic outcome, the Battle of Gog and Magog will end as quickly as it began. Nonetheless, God's purposes will be fully accomplished through his instant defeat of Gog, which was to make his greatness and holiness known in the eyes of all the nations of the earth (Ezek 38:23).

---

1. Although the prophecies of Ezekiel may give many more details of the Battle of Gog and Magog, one must not forget that it is the smaller prophecy of John that reveals the timing of the battle: at the end of Christ's millennial kingdom.

Next, a final proof that the Battle of Gog and Magog in Ezekiel and the Battle of Gog and Magog in Revelation are one and the same is seen in how God uniquely describes the battle in Ezekiel:

"My holy name I will make known among my people Israel; and I will not let my holy name be profaned any more; and the nations shall know that I am the Lord, the Holy One in Israel. It has come! It has happened, says the Lord God. This is the day of which I have spoken" (Ezek 39:7–8).

Notice the Lord's description of the finality that the end of the war in Ezekiel brings: "It has happened," and "This is the day of which I have spoken," and "I will not let my holy name be profaned any more." I ask you, does this sound like something God would say after just any battle, or would he only say these words after the very last battle of all time?

The Seven-Year Interlude

As indicated previously, the loss of life will be so great among the followers of Gog that it will take seven months for the house of Israel to bury the dead:

"Seven months the house of Israel shall spend burying them, in order to cleanse the land. All the people of the land shall bury them; and it will bring them honor on the day that I show my glory, says the Lord God" (Ezek 39:12–13).

And why will the house of Israel be so eager to bury the bodies as quickly as possible? Because the day is soon coming when the Father himself will descend from heaven and dwell with his people for eternity. This explains the last phrase of the passage: "and it will bring them honor on the day that I show my glory, says the Lord God." One knows that this is a specific reference to the Father and not to the Son, since Christ's glory will have been on display to the world for the entirety of his millennial kingdom. However, the Father's glory will not be seen by the saints until the end of the millennium. Furthermore, the following passage reveals that the Father will not immediately descend even after the seven months (italics used for emphasis):

"Then those who live in the towns of Israel will go out and make fires of the weapons and burn them—bucklers and shields, bows and arrows, handpikes and spears—*and they will make fires of them for seven years.* They will not need to take wood out of the field or cut down any trees in the forests, for they will make their fires of the weapons; they will despoil those who despoiled them, and plunder those who plundered them, says the Lord God" (Ezek 39:9–10).

Question: Which of the following do you think accurately describes the above scenario:

1. After the Battle of Gog and Magog, the Father will wait seven years before descending because he is waiting until the people burn all of the leftover weaponry from the battle, or . . .

2. After the Battle of Gog and Magog, the Father will wait seven years before descending because that is the moment he has preordained as the time for his descent, regardless of how long the people have been burning the leftover weaponry.

Of course, the answer is the second one. The Father is not placing his descent on hold until a seven-year pile of wood is burned. For some reason God will wait seven years after the battle before descending. Why seven? The Scripture doesn't say.[2] Nevertheless, because of Ezek 39:9 it is certain that the Battle of Gog and Magog will end approximately seven years prior to the end of the millennium, and more specifically, seven years prior to the moment that the Son will transfer the millennial kingdom to the Father, at which time the Father will then descend to the earth (I Cor 15:24). But how can one be sure that the Father will not descend to the earth during those seven years? Because Ezekiel indicated that during the seven years, the burning of the weapons will supply "a need" for the people:

"They will not need to take wood out of the field or cut down any trees in the forests, for they will make their fires of the weapons; they will despoil those who despoiled them, and plunder those who plundered them, says the Lord God" (Ezek 39:10).

Only the righteous who are still in their natural bodies will "need" fuel and heat from a fire, and despoil and plunder the unrighteous, not the millennial saints who have already received their glorified, imperishable, immortal bodies, at the second resurrection. And why is that significant? The reader will soon learn, unless he or she knows already, God the Father will not descend to the earth and begin his eternal kingdom in the presence of the righteous in their natural bodies. Unlike the Son's

---

2. Perhaps God will impose a seven-year moratorium on the earth in order for the land to become ceremonially clean because of all the bloodshed that occurred during the Battle of Gog and Magog . . . or perhaps that's not the reason.

millennial kingdom, the Father's eternal kingdom will only be composed of saints with glorified bodies—no one will be burning wood for warmth in the Father's kingdom. Remember, Paul said "flesh and blood," i.e., people in natural bodies, cannot inherit the kingdom of God (1 Cor 15:50).

Finally, John ends his comments on the Battle of Gog and Magog by assuring the reader that the devil, who had lured the nations of the earth into their own death trap, was captured once again, but this time he wasn't tossed into the bottomless pit; instead he was cast into the lake of fire, joining the beast and false prophet who had been cast there a thousand years earlier:

> And the devil who had deceived them was thrown into the lake of fire and sulfur, where the beast and the false prophet were, and they will be tormented day and night forever and ever. (Rev 20:10)

For those who might believe the lake of fire is just a euphemism for the total annihilation of the unrighteous, this passage doesn't support that hypothesis. Rather, the text supports the thought that the same torment the beast and false prophet have endured for a thousand years now awaits Satan.

The Great White Throne Judgment

After giving a brief commentary on earth's final battle, John immediately describes a vision of a scene which has come to be known as "The Great White Throne Judgment." One learns that the judgment will include all of the unrighteous souls from the time of Adam to the last person who died during Christ's millennial reign, which one would assume to be the last person killed during the Battle of Gog and Magog. Whether history's dead bodies were buried, cremated, lost at sea, lost on land, or simply vaporized in a nuclear war, all unrighteous souls will be gathered at the judgment:

> Then I saw a great white throne and the one who sat on it; the earth and the heaven fled from his presence, and no place was found for them. And I saw the dead, great and small, standing before the throne, and books were opened. Also another book was opened, the book of life. And the dead were judged according to their works, as recorded in the books. And the sea gave up the dead that were in it. Death and Hades gave up the dead that were in them, and all were judged according to what they

had done. Then Death and Hades were thrown into the lake of fire. This is the second death, the lake of fire; and anyone whose name was not found written in the book of life was thrown into the lake of fire. (Rev 20:11–15)

Not only will the Father be sitting on his throne in judgment, but according to Paul, Christ will also be present:[3]

1. "Since we are God's offspring, we ought not to think that the deity is like gold, or silver, or stone, an image formed by the art and imagination of mortals. While God has overlooked the times of human ignorance, now he commands all people everywhere to repent, because he has fixed a day on which he will have the world judged in righteousness by a man whom he has appointed, and of this he has given assurance to all by raising him from the dead" (Acts 17:29–31).

2. "In the presence of God and of Christ Jesus, who is to judge the living and the dead, and in view of his appearing and his kingdom . . ." (2 Tim 4:1a).

The number of the dead at the judgment will seem infinite; it will be well into the billions, as far as the eye can see. To John, it must have seemed that the whole world stood trembling before the Father, whose Son they had always scoffed at, mocked, and rejected. The scene is surreal with its ear-piercing screams of terror, intermingled with faint sounds of weeping, but all inundated with unintelligible pleadings to God that are too little, too late. All eyes, human and angelic, are fixed upon the Father and his Son. The court comes to order. Just as in any courtroom scene, there is an anxiousness with the defendant, but unlike those courtrooms, the anxiousness here is not from the question of the outcome but rather from the fear of the unknown. The reputation of the lake of fire has no doubt dogged the unrighteous since the moment of their death, whether that death was thousands of years ago, as was the case of Cain, or, very recently, as will be the case of those who died in the Battle of Gog and Magog. Nonetheless, hopelessness and despair will rule the day, as the sentence of the second death echoes throughout the throne room. Anyone whose name is not found in the book of life will be thrown into the lake of fire (Rev 20:15).

3. Just as the riders Death and Hades were both introduced in the letter at the beginning of the First Sequence (Rev 6:8), they now exit together at the end of that same sequence (Rev 20:14).

FIRST SEQUENCE, PART 4

Judgment of the Living

Does something seem amiss? Didn't Paul say that Christ would judge not only the dead but the living as well (2 Tim 4:1)? Although John's account has carried the reader straight from the Battle of Gog and Magog to the Great White Throne Judgment, somewhere along the way there is the business of judging the living who are still on the earth at the end of the millennium. Fortunately for us, Jesus speaks of this judgment in two passages, both of which are found in Matthew: "the parable of the weeds and the wheat" (Matt 13:24–30, 37–43) and "the judgment of the nations" (Matt 25:31–46). Regrettably, most mistakenly think these two passages are references to the beginning of the millennium rather than to the end of it. How can one be certain that both narratives are references to the separation of the "living" unrighteous from the "living" righteous at the end of Christ's millennial reign, rather than the beginning of his reign? Two reasons:

1. First, it's nonsensical to think that the first thing on Christ's agenda when he sits down at the beginning of his millennial reign is to gather the people from all the nations of the earth in order to determine who's righteous and who's not, when literally, just hours or days before, all who were living on the earth at the time of the first resurrection/rapture of the saints were instantly judged according to their righteousness with the following results: Whoever was credited with the righteousness of Christ was raptured and received a glorified body, and whoever was not credited with Christ's righteousness was not raptured and remained in their natural bodies. That's about as plain as it gets. Had Jesus indeed separated the unrighteous from the righteous as portrayed in "the judgment of the nations" immediately after the first resurrection and rapture of the saints, this would be the scenario: At the moment of the first resurrection, those who were "in Christ" received glorified bodies, but those who were not "in Christ" did not receive glorified bodies. But then, as Christ takes his seat on his throne, he immediately gathers those same, previously deemed unrighteous individuals who had not been raptured and proceeds to divide them according to how they had treated their neighbors prior to the resurrection and rapture. Then, if anyone somehow managed to treat their neighbors

with love and kindness, now, for some inexplicable reason, they are suddenly declared righteous! The scenario is ridiculous.

2. Although no other illustration than the above is needed to prove that Christ's "judgment of the nations" and "the parable of the weeds and wheat" have nothing to do with a judgment at the beginning of the millennium, still, a second reason is available: At the end of each narrative, the "living" unrighteous are immediately cast into what is described as "the furnace of fire" (parable of the weeds and wheat) and "eternal punishment" (judgment of the nations). Because both of these phrases are designations for the lake of fire, and since no one other than the beast and the man of lawlessness will be cast into the lake until the end of the millennium, these phrases irrefutably prove that "the parable of the weeds and wheat" and "the judgment of the nations" describe the fate of the unrighteous who are living at the end of the millennium.

Now, with these introductory remarks, let's briefly address both narratives.

The First Narrative: Parable of the Weeds and the Wheat

In the form of a parable, Jesus describes in the presence of all who were listening, the crowd as well as the disciples, how the Son of Man will one day judge the living at the end of his earthly one-thousand-year kingdom. In the parable, Jesus spoke of a land owner sowing good seed in a field of his, but later, the slaves of the owner noticed weeds had come up in the field among the wheat. When the owner said an enemy had sown weeds in the field after everyone was asleep, the slaves offered to immediately go through the field and pull up the weeds. However, the owner dissuaded them from doing so and instead told them to wait until the harvest, letting both the wheat and weeds grow together (Matt 13:24–30). When Jesus had finished telling the parable, the disciples were bewildered as to its meaning. Once they and Jesus returned to the house, they immediately asked the Lord its meaning, and this was his reply:

> He answered, "The one who sows the seed is the Son of Man; the field is the world, and the good seed are the children of the kingdom; and the weeds are the children of the evil one, and the enemy who sowed them is the devil; the harvest is the end of the age, and the reapers are angels. Just as the weeds are collected

and burned up with fire, so will it be at the end of the age." (Matt 13:37–40)

Although the first generation of Christ's millennial kingdom will be populated by those who are not included in the first rapture of the living saints,[4] some of that initial population will repent and convert to Christ, but the remainder will not. This pattern of repentance and rebellion will continue throughout each successive generation of the millennium among the offspring: The rebellious among the offspring, i.e., "the weeds," as opposed to the repentant among the offspring, i.e., "the wheat," will soon begin to show their true colors by revealing the jealousy, hatred, and envy within their hearts. As the wicked and the rebellious begin to take root and spread throughout the kingdom, the angels of the Lord will be dumbfounded as to how anyone could act so brazenly and so unrighteously when none other than the Lord Jesus was their King (13:27). Nevertheless, Jesus said that Satan is the cause for the presence of unrighteousness in the kingdom (13:39). And just as one might expect, God's angels will eagerly volunteer to canvas the earth and forcibly remove the rebellious (13:28), but the Lord will dissuade such actions, telling them to wait until the end of the millennium because if they remove the unrighteous too soon, they might inadvertently disturb the righteous (13:29). However, at the end of Christ's millennial reign, the angels will certainly be permitted to fulfill their duties:

> The Son of Man will send his angels, and they will collect out of his kingdom all causes of sin and all evildoers, and they will throw them into the furnace of fire, where there will be weeping and gnashing of teeth. (Matt 13:41–42)

Note that at the end of the millennium the unrighteous will be taken from among the righteous, whereas, prior to the millennium, at the first resurrection, the righteous will be taken from among the unrighteous. Nevertheless, whether the righteous are taken away from the unrighteous or the unrighteous are removed from the righteous, one thing is certain: The righteous in both instances will receive a glorified body. This truth is expressed in the last phrase of Christ's explanation of the parable:

---

4. As you well recall, when Christ told the disciples that some would be taken and some would be left (Luke 17:34–37), it was determined that those who will be left will be the ones not included in the first resurrection, and, therefore, it is certain that they will necessarily be the ones who initially populate the first generation of Christ's millennial kingdom. See pp. 352–353.

> Then the righteous will shine like the sun in the kingdom of their Father. Let anyone with ears listen! (Matt 13:43)

The phrase is a subtle reference to the apparent illumination of the believer's glorified body. Similarly to that passage, Daniel revealed that same illumination concerning the saints in the first resurrection:

"Many of those who sleep in the dust of the earth shall awake, some to everlasting life, and some to shame and everlasting contempt. Those who are wise shall shine like the brightness of the sky, and those who lead many to righteousness, like the stars forever and ever" (Dan 12:2–3).

The Second Narrative: The Judgment of the Nations

The primary difference between "the parable of the weeds and the wheat" and the narrative of "the judgment of the nations" is that, whereas both give the result of the last-generation judgment of the living, "the judgment of the nations" additionally reveals the criteria by which the two groups will be judged:

> When the Son of Man comes in his glory, and all the angels with him, then he will sit on the throne of his glory. All the nations will be gathered before him, and he will separate people one from another as a shepherd separates the sheep from the goats, and he will put the sheep at his right hand and the goats at the left. Then the king will say to those at his right hand, "Come, you that are blessed by my Father, inherit the kingdom prepared for you from the foundation of the world; for I was hungry and you gave me food, I was thirsty and you gave me something to drink, I was a stranger and you welcomed me, I was naked and you gave me clothing, I was sick and you took care of me, I was in prison and you visited me." Then the righteous will answer him, "Lord, when was it that we saw you hungry and gave you food, or thirsty and gave you something to drink? And when was it that we saw you a stranger and welcomed you, or naked and gave you clothing? And when was it that we saw you sick or in prison and visited you?" And the king will answer them, "Truly I tell you, just as you did it to one of the least of these who are members of my family, you did it to me." Then he will say to those at his left hand, "You that are accursed, depart from me into the eternal fire prepared for the devil and his angels; for I was hungry and you gave me no food, I was thirsty and you gave me nothing to drink, I was a stranger and you did not welcome

me, naked and you did not give me clothing, sick and in prison and you did not visit me." Then they also will answer, "Lord, when was it that we saw you hungry or thirsty or a stranger or naked or sick or in prison, and did not take care of you?" Then he will answer them, "Truly I tell you, just as you did not do it to one of the least of these, you did not do it to me." And these will go away into eternal punishment, but the righteous into eternal life. (Matt 25:31–46)

Jesus indicates that after poverty, sickness, and crime have surfaced throughout the many generations of his millennial kingdom, he will then gather and address those who are living at the end of the last generation and direct certain individuals to his right side and others to his left. He will then tell those to his right that you fed me, clothed me, gave me something to drink, visited me in prison, and took care of me when I was sick, but will tell those to his left that you never fed me, never clothed me, never gave me something to drink, and never visited me when I was in prison. Neither side will understand the credit given or the accusation levied against one another because neither side will be able to recall such an instance as having ever occurred between them and the Lord. Jesus will then explain to them that he was not actually speaking about how they had treated him, but rather how they had treated one another. Then, those who have not acted in love and kindness and faith will immediately be carried away into "eternal punishment" while those who have acted in love, kindness, and faith will be the ones who enter into "eternal life."

Whether one realizes it or not, the identical response to Christ's words by both sides is actually a third proof that "the judgment of the nations" is a reference to the end of the millennium, rather than the beginning. How so? Had Jesus addressed the two groups at the beginning of the millennium, not only would both groups have been unable to recall the scenario that Jesus had described, but they would not have known what he was talking about whatsoever, since at the beginning of the millennium there had not been any interaction between them and the Lord, rendering the Lord's remarks nonsensical and baffling. Instead of saying "When did we treat you well?" or "When did we treat you badly?" they would have responded "What are you talking about?" But since Jesus will say these words at the end of the millennium—after which both sides will have served under Christ's reign their entire lives, as well as have had a chance to witness their neighbors suffer poverty, sickness, and crime, and would have responded according to whether they were led by the

Spirit of God or according to their own selfishness desires—both sides will know exactly what Christ is saying, once he clarifies himself. At that moment, "the sheep" on his right side will feel relief and joy, but "the goats" on his left will suddenly be overcome with fear and trepidation.

Judging by Works or Faith?

In the narrative, does Christ sound as if he is judging the millennial individuals by works rather than by faith? To some it might, but it shouldn't. Actually Christ is judging those individuals as he judges all individuals: by whether or not they truly have faith in God, which is a faith characterized by the imputed righteousness of Christ inwardly and love outwardly—love for God and love for one's neighbor. If you recall, when someone inquired of Jesus during his earthly ministry as to what they must do to inherit eternal life, Jesus always pointed to the following requirements in one way or the other: Love God, believe God, obey God, and love your neighbor as yourself. And here's the beauty of those requirements: You can't have one without the other. If you love God, you will believe him; if you believe him, you will obey him; and if you obey him, you will love your neighbor as yourself. The following are two examples that come to mind:

1. "Just then a lawyer stood up to test Jesus. 'Teacher,' he said, 'what must I do to inherit eternal life?' He said to him, 'What is written in the law? What do you read there?' He answered, 'You shall love the Lord your God with all your heart, and all your soul, and with all your strength, and with all your mind; and your neighbor as yourself.' And he said to him, 'You have given the right answer; do this, and you will live'" (Luke 10:25–28).

2. "As he was setting out on a journey, a man ran up and knelt before him, and asked him, 'Good Teacher, what must I do to inherit eternal life?' Jesus said to him, 'Why do you call me good? No one is good but God alone. You know the commandments: "You shall not murder; You shall not commit adultery; You shall not steal; You shall not bear false witness; You shall not defraud; Honor your father and mother."' He said to him, 'Teacher, I have kept all these since my youth.' Jesus, looking at him, loved him and said, 'You lack one thing; go, sell what you own, and give the money to the poor, and you will have treasure in heaven; then come, follow me.' When

he heard this, he was shocked and went away grieving, for he had many possessions" (Mark 10:17–22).

The criteria for eternal life that Christ gave to the lawyer and the rich man are exactly the same as that which will be required for those living during the millennium: Love God and love your neighbor as yourself. Still one might interject and say that's certainly not the way believers are qualified today. Actually it is. It's the same faith in God expressed in the same love. In the following, see how John and James both agree that the one who truly believes in and confesses Christ will necessarily walk in love. First, the words of John followed by those of James:

1. "Beloved, let us love one another, because love is from God; everyone who loves is born of God and knows God. Whoever does not love does not know God, for God is love. God's love was revealed among us in this way: God sent his only Son into the world so that we might live through him. In this is love, not that we loved God but that he loved us and sent his Son to be the atoning sacrifice for our sins. Beloved, since God loved us so much, we also ought to love one another. No one has ever seen God; if we love one another, God lives in us, and his love is perfected in us . . . . Those who say, 'I love God,' and hate their brothers or sisters, are liars; for those who do not love a brother or sister whom they have seen, cannot love God whom they have not seen. The commandment we have from him is this: those who love God must love their brothers and sisters also" (1 John 4:7–12, 20–21).

2. "What good is it, my brothers and sisters, if you say you have faith but do not have works? Can faith save you? If a brother or sister is naked and lacks daily food, and one of you says to them, 'Go in peace; keep warm and eat your fill,' and yet you do not supply their bodily needs, what is the good of that? So faith by itself, if it has no works, is dead. But someone will say, 'You have faith and I have works.' Show me your faith apart from your works, and I by my works will show you my faith" (Jas 2:14–18).

John and James agree: Faith and love for God will be seen in one's love for one another. Granted, although Paul pronounced that if today one confesses that Jesus is Lord and believes that God raised him from the dead, that person will be saved (Rom 10:9), still, the apostle agrees with John and James that faith in God is expressed through love:

1. "For in Christ Jesus neither circumcision nor uncircumcision counts for anything; the only thing that counts is faith working through love" (Gal 5:6).
2. "For the whole law is summed up in a single commandment, 'You shall love your neighbor as yourself'" (Gal 5:14).

Concerning Paul's pronouncement that a person will be saved if one confesses and believes that God raised Christ from the dead, God could not have required that same confession from the lawyer or the rich young man for the simple reason the crucifixion and resurrection hadn't taken place. Similarly, for those living during the millennium, confession and faith in the resurrection of Christ will be a moot point since the whole world will know that Christ has been resurrected from the dead because they will see him ruling from Jerusalem during the entire millennial kingdom. Nevertheless, had the lawyer or the rich young man truly loved and believed God, that belief would have indeed been expressed in their love for their neighbor. The same will hold true for anyone living during the millennium.

Closings Thoughts: The Timing of the Judgment of the Living

Since Ezekiel has revealed that a seven-year interim will exist between the end of the Battle of Gog and Magog, and the Father's descent to the earth, then it is certain that the judgments of the living and the dead must occur after this interlude. Therefore, we are confronted with the obvious question as to which occurs first, the judgment of the living or the dead. Here are the only options:

	Table 11.1. The Timing of the Judgment of the Living and the Judgment of the Dead		
Option #1	1. Gog and Magog.	2. After the 7-year interlude, the dead will be judged before the living.	3. The Father descends.
Option #2	1. Gog and Magog.	2. After the 7-year interlude, the living will be judged before the dead.	3. The Father descends.

So which is it? Without a doubt, it is option #2. The fact that the vision of "The Great White Throne Judgment" records the moment that Death was cast into the lake of fire (Rev 20:14), which according to Paul is the last enemy to be destroyed (1 Cor 15:26), inherently implies that no judgments remain, which necessarily implies that the judgment of the living has already been accomplished. A likely scenario might unfold as follows:

1. *"The Judgment of the Living"*: Once the seven-year interlude after the Battle of Gog and Magog has been completed, and while the righteous are still in the midst of burning the leftover weaponry for fuel, and despoiling the unrighteous who despoiled them (Ezek 39:9–10), Jesus will gather all "the living" and then proceed to separate the unrighteous from the righteous.

2. *"The Judgment of the Dead"*: Once the judgment of the living has been accomplished, Jesus will ascend to heaven, leaving the righteous on the earth, in order to assist the Father at "The Great White Throne Judgment."

3. *"The Father Descends to the Earth"*: Once the judgment of the dead has been completed, the Father and the Son will then descend together with the millennial souls of the righteous to the earth, at which time, they, together with the righteous men and women who had been left on the earth, will receive their glorified bodies in the second resurrection (Rev 20:5).

―

The following is the reconciliation of the six sequences from the beginning of the millennium to "The Great White Throne Judgment." (The most recently added events from Rev 20:6b–15 are italicized):

Table 11.2. Reconciliation of the Six Sequences from the Millennium through the Great White Throne Judgment

The Sequence	Seq. 1 & 2 Thess (1 Thess 4:17b)	Seq. Olivet Discourse	1st Seq. Rev, Part 4: Millennium and Final Judgment (Rev 20:6b–15)	2nd Seq. Rev: 2 Witnesses	3rd Seq. Rev: Woman, Child, and Dragon	4th Seq. Rev, Part 3: Mt. Zion to God's Throne
1. Jesus begins his millennial reign on the earth with the assistance of the glorified saints from the 1st resurrection/rapture.	Saints are with the Lord forever. (1 Thess 4:17b)		*Those who share in the 1st resurrection will be priests of God and Jesus, and they will reign with him 1,000 years. (Rev 20:6b)*			

Table 11.2. Reconciliation of the Six Sequences from the Millennium through the Great White Throne Judgment

The Sequence	Seq. 1 & 2 Thess (1 Thess 4:17b)	Seq. Olivet Discourse	1st Seq. Rev, Part 4: Millennium and Final Judgment (Rev 20:6b–15)	2nd Seq. Rev: 2 Witnesses	3rd Seq. Rev: Woman, Child, and Dragon	4th Seq. Rev, Part 3: Mt. Zion to God's Throne
2. At the end of the millennial reign, the rebellious and jealous nations of the earth, with the prodding of the just released Satan, come up against Jerusalem in order to plunder her, but God rains fire down from heaven and destroys those nations.			*The Battle of Gog and Magog* (Rev 20:7–10)			

THE SEQUENCE

Table 11.2. Reconciliation of the Six Sequences from the Millennium through the Great White Throne Judgment

The Sequence	Seq. 1 & 2 Thess (1 Thess 4:17b)	Seq. Olivet Discourse	1st Seq. Rev, Part 4: Millennium and Final Judgment (Rev 20:6b–15)	2nd Seq. Rev: 2 Witnesses	3rd Seq. Rev: Woman, Child, and Dragon	4th Seq. Rev, Part 3: Mt. Zion to God's Throne
3. God gathers all of the unrighteous who have died from the beginning of time up through the millennial reign of Christ. All are judged, sentenced, and cast into the lake of fire.			*The Great White Throne Judgment* (Rev 20:11–15)			

CHAPTER 12

First Sequence, Part 5

The Second Resurrection and the New Jerusalem (21:1—22:5)

First Sequence	Second Sequence	Third Sequence	Fourth Sequence
Chapter 9 1st Seq., Part 2: The 7 Bowls (15:5—19:10)			
Chapter 10 1st Seq., Part 3: The Lord's Return and the 1st Resurrection (19:11—20:6a)			
Chapter 11 1st Seq., Part 4: The Millennium and the Final Judgment (20:6b–15)			
Chapter 12* 1st Seq., Part 5: The 2nd Resurrection and the New Jerusalem (21:1—22:5)			

THE SEQUENCE

ACCORDING TO PAUL, JESUS will hand the earthly millennial kingdom back to God, once he has destroyed every ruler, every authority, and power. The last enemy to be destroyed is death (1 Cor 15:26), and that enemy will be officially destroyed once and for all, at "The Great White Throne Judgment" (Rev 20:14). Again, here's the earlier chart displaying the three time frames taught by Paul:

Table 10.4. The Three Time Periods Taught by Paul in 1 Cor 15:20–28	
1st Period (1 Cor 15:20–23)	*The First Period Ends at the Resurrection of the Saints*
2nd Period (1 Cor 15:24b–27)	The Second Period Comprises the Millennium
3rd Period (1 Cor 15:24a, 28)	The Third Period Comprises the Father's Eternal Kingdom

When attempting to reconcile the three time frames with the period immediately following "The Great White Throne Judgment," which is where we find ourselves in the sequence, it should be obvious to the reader that we are somewhere at the end of the second time frame or the beginning of the third. If the second resurrection of the saints has occurred, then one might assume that Christ has or is about to turn the kingdom over to the Father (1 Cor 15:24), placing us at the beginning of the third time frame. If the second resurrection has not taken place, we are still at the end of the second time frame. How will one know? If somehow the visions of Rev 21–22 reveal to us the whereabouts of the souls of the millennial saints, then we'll know for sure. Just as with the first resurrection and the souls of the premillennial saints, the second resurrection cannot take place until the souls of the millennial saints are escorted back to the earth. In order to determine their whereabouts, let's be on the lookout for any vision that might indicate one of the following three scenes:

1. The souls of the millennial saints are still in heaven.
2. The souls of the millennial saints are descending from heaven.
3. The millennial saints have received their glorified bodies and are on the earth.

FIRST SEQUENCE, PART 5

The Vision of the Rainbow-Colored Cube

After the vision of "The Great White Throne Judgment" had vanished, taking with it the final judgment of the dead, John sees a perplexing sight of an enormous and beautiful rainbow-colored cube, only identified as "the holy city, the New Jerusalem" descending from heaven:

> Then I saw a new heaven and a new earth; for the first heaven and the first earth had passed away, and the sea was no more.[1] And I saw the holy city, the new Jerusalem, coming down out of heaven from God, prepared as a bride adorned for her husband. (Rev 21:1–2)

In most cases, if someone today saw an enormous multicolored cubed structure floating down from the skies, one would either think they were dreaming or seeing an otherworldly, fantastic vision. John was no different. However, since the disciple had just seen upwards of fifty visions, some live-action and some drawn by God, he knew this was a vision of the latter because live-action structures, regardless of their size, are usually built from the ground up and are not assembled among the stars before being lowered to the earth. And just as the previous drawn images, including the seven-headed dragon, the seven-headed beast, the harlot woman adorned with jewels and pearls, and the pregnant woman adorned with the sun, moon, and stars, John knew that God was attempting to convey some type of message concerning a future entity, event, or personality by means of this drawn multicolored image. All John had to do was wait for it. But just as he began to wait, he suddenly heard a familiar voice from the throne.

---

1. The thought here is not that God is going to replace the earth with another planet, but rather that the earth, along with all other creation, will no longer be subjected to the ravages of sin and decay, once the children of God are revealed. In the following, Paul articulates the sentiment: "For the creation waits with eager longing for the revealing of the children of God; for the creation was subjected to futility, not of its own will but by the will of the one who subjected it, in hope that the creation itself will be set free from its bondage to decay and will obtain the freedom of the glory of the children of God. We know that the whole creation has been groaning in labor pains until now; and not only the creation, but we ourselves, who have the first fruits of the Spirit, groan inwardly while we wait for adoption, the redemption of our bodies" (Rom 8:19–23).

Tenth Conversation: A Voice Speaks about God's New Home

A loud voice from the throne suddenly commented on the vision, saying that the home of God is among mortals and that he will dwell with them as their God:

> And I heard a loud voice from the throne saying, "See, the home of God is among mortals. He will dwell with them as their God; they will be his peoples, and God himself will be with them; he will wipe every tear from their eyes. Death will be no more; mourning and crying and pain will be no more, for the first things have passed away." (Rev 21:3-4)

Whose voice was it? By a comparative study of Rev 14:13 (whereby "the voice" was distinguished from the Holy Spirit) and Rev 18:20 (whereby "the voice" spoke of God's judgment upon Babylon), the voice was determined to belong to Christ.[2]

The timing of Christ's interruption was surely deliberate. By choosing the exact moment during the vision of the descending image to announce that a day is coming when the Father will dwell with his people on earth, Christ seemed to be making a direct correlation between the descent of the multicolored-cube and the time when the Father will make his home among his people. If that's the case, is this the clue for which we've been looking? In other words, does the image of the descending multicolored-cube have anything to do with the status of the second resurrection of the saints? Perhaps. Let's continue in order to find out.

Among Mortals?

Notice the translation of Rev 21:3, "See, the home of God is among mortals," which gives the distinct impression that God will one day dwell among people in their natural bodies. Despite the fact that the text goes on to say that these "mortals" will not die, or mourn, or cry (Rev 21:4), the idea that God will live among mortals is in direct conflict with the words of Paul:

"What I am saying, brothers and sisters, is this: flesh and blood cannot inherit the kingdom of God, nor does the perishable inherit the imperishable. Listen, I will tell you a mystery! We will not all die, but

---

2. See p. 308.

we will all be changed, in a moment, in the twinkling of an eye, at the last trumpet. For the trumpet will sound, and the dead will be raised imperishable, and we will be changed. For this perishable body must put on imperishability, and this mortal body must put on immortality" (1 Cor 15:50–53).

Paul said that a natural, "mortal" person with flesh and blood will never enter God's eternal kingdom and therefore will never see God. In order to see the Lord, Paul indicated that one's body must go through a metamorphosis, implying that the natural, mortal body is not equipped to see God and survive. Recall the exchange between the Lord and Moses:

"Moses said, 'Show me your glory, I pray.' And he said, 'I will make all my goodness pass before you, and will proclaim before you the name, "The Lord"; and I will be gracious to whom I will be gracious, and will show mercy on whom I will show mercy. But,' he said, 'you cannot see my face; for no one shall see me and live.' And the Lord continued, 'See, there is a place by me where you shall stand on the rock; and while my glory passes by I will put you in a cleft of the rock, and I will cover you with my hand until I have passed by; then I will take away my hand, and you shall see my back; but my face shall not be seen'" (Exod 33:18–23).

In the natural, Moses was ill-equipped to glance at the full, unfiltered glory of God (Hebrew: *Yahweh*) even for a second, much less enter his kingdom and behold him for eternity. That's why anyone, without exception, must be clothed with a glorified body in order to enter the Father's eternal kingdom. The apostle John hinted at this newfound ability of the glorified body when he told the church that when they are like him, only then will they be able to see Christ "as he is" (italics used for emphasis):

"Beloved, we are God's children now; what we will be has not yet been revealed. What we do know is this: when he is revealed, we will be like him, *for we will see him as he is*" (1 John 3:2).

It stands to reason, if one can't truly behold and comprehend the glory of the risen Christ without having received a glorified body, then what chance does one have of beholding the glory of the Father without a glorified body? The answer is no chance. Therefore, what are we to make of the various translations reading that the home of God will be among "mortals"? The answer is simple: They could have simply translated the Greek word *anthrōpōn* as "men" instead of "mortals," with the following result: "See, the home of God is among men." Although all men and women are mortals now, not all men and women will be considered mortals in the future, when the righteous receive their glorified bodies and become immortal (1 Cor 15:53).

Eleventh Conversation: "It Is Done"

After John heard "a loud voice from the throne" saying, "See, the home of God is among mortals" (21:3), a voice which has been identified as belonging to Christ, the disciple then said, "And the one seated on the throne said, 'See, I am making all things new.'" Since John distinguishes "the loud voice from the throne" from "the One who is seated on the throne," then it is apparent that the One seated on the throne is the Father.[3] With that somewhat easy determination, one knows the following words came from the Father:

> And the one who was seated on the throne said, "See, I am making all things new." Also he said, "Write this, for these words are trustworthy and true." Then he said to me, "It is done! I am the Alpha and the Omega, the beginning and the end. To the thirsty I will give water as a gift from the spring of the water of life. Those who conquer will inherit these things, and I will be their God and they will be my children. But as for the cowardly, the faithless, the polluted, the murderers, the fornicators, the sorcerers, the idolaters, and all liars, their place will be in the lake that burns with fire and sulfur, which is the second death."
> (Rev 21:5–8)

God told John to write, "It is done!" What was done? Although most think that the Lord was indicating that all the events of Revelation had been accomplished—the 1,260-day ministry of the two witnesses, the forty-two-month reign of the beast, the fourteen trumpet and bowl judgments, the manifestation of Christ at Armageddon, the first resurrection, etc., in reality, none of those events had taken place. At the moment God made the statement two thousand years ago, the only thing that was "done" was that God had presented each of the visions to John.[4]

---

3. The identification of "the One who was seated on the throne" as being the Father is also confirmed by an earlier passage in the letter which concerned the onset of the Day of the Lord that included references both to the Father and the Son:
"Fall on us and hide us from the face of the one seated on the throne and from the wrath of the Lamb; for the great day of their wrath has come, and who is able to stand?" (Rev 6:16b–17).

4. The upcoming vision of the New Jerusalem, recorded in Rev 21:9–27, is actually an up-close look of the previously seen vision of the New Jerusalem in Rev 21:1–2.

Twelfth Conversation: The Mystery of the Image Is Finally Revealed

Having seen the vision of the multicolored, cube-shaped image called "the New Jerusalem" descend from the heavens, John was still waiting on someone in the throne room to provide him with the meaning of the image. The wait is over. An angel separated himself from the others and approached John:

> Then one of the seven angels who had the seven bowls full of the seven last plagues came and said to me, "Come, I will show you the bride, the wife of the Lamb." And in the spirit he carried me away to a great, high mountain and showed me the holy city Jerusalem coming down out of heaven from God. It has the glory of God and a radiance like a very rare jewel, like jasper, clear as crystal. (Rev 21:9–11)

Dispensing with any introductory remarks that might needlessly prolong the mystery, the angel simply told John the meaning (italics used for emphasis):

"Come, I will show you *the bride, the wife of the Lamb*" (21:9b).

There you have it. According to the angel, the image of the multicolored cube floating down from the sky represented the bride, the wife of the Lamb—the family of God. However, John may have already known that. If the disciple had been privy to any of Paul's letters to the churches, there was one circulating that contained a description of a structure built on the foundation of the apostles and the prophets, that seemed almost identical to the image of the New Jerusalem:

"So then you are no longer strangers and aliens, but you are citizens with the saints, and also members of the household of God, built upon the foundation of the apostles, and prophets, with Christ Jesus himself as the cornerstone. In him the whole structure is joined together and grows into a holy temple in the Lord; in whom you also are built together spiritually into a dwelling place for God" (Eph 2:19–22).

It's as if Paul saw the New Jerusalem before John did. Although Paul called the structure a temple and John described it as a city, both structures represented the elect of God. The only difference was that Paul's temple was still expanding and growing, whereas the New Jerusalem was completed and perfected. Other than that, the two structures are virtual images of each other: The temple's cornerstone is Jesus and its foundation was built on the ministry of the NT apostles and the OT prophets.

Similarly, the twelve gates of the city are inscribed with the names of the twelve OT tribes of Israel and the twelve foundations are inscribed with the names of the twelve NT apostles. And, of course, though not specifically mentioned, Jesus is the cornerstone. Yet, for reasons that can only be attributed to a poor understanding of God's frequent use of symbolism, while everyone knows Paul's temple was a metaphor, most believe John's city is a real, monolithic structure traveling through space. It's baffling to say the least.

The Status of the Second Resurrection Is Finally Revealed

At the start of this chapter, it was determined that in order to understand the status of the second resurrection, one simply had to discover the whereabouts of the souls of the millennial saints: If they were still in heaven, the second resurrection hadn't taken place; if the souls were descending from heaven, the second resurrection was about to take place; and if the glorified, millennial saints were standing on the earth, then the second resurrection had taken place. So, what's the verdict? It should be obvious to the reader that the vision of the "descending bride of Christ" metaphorically depicts the millennial souls' descent from heaven to the earth for the second resurrection. Although the cube-shaped image symbolizes the complete bride of Christ, still, the fact that the bride is seen "descending" from heaven to earth necessarily indicates that the millennial saints are yet to receive their glorified bodies, or else the city would have been depicted as firmly planted on the earth. Remember, the second resurrection, as the first, will only take place on the earth. It will not take place in heaven, nor in the midheaven, for that matter.

The Number Twelve and the Bride

With the knowledge that the "New Jerusalem" represents the elect of God, one is finally in position to analyze the numerous symbols accompanying the image; let's begin with the number twelve. After the angel brought John into close proximity to the multicolored, translucent image, he began to reveal certain measurements of the image. As the angel proceeded, John soon noticed that the measurements were multiples of twelve:

FIRST SEQUENCE, PART 5

"It has a great, high wall with twelve gates, and at the gates twelve angels, and on the gates are inscribed the names of the twelve tribes of the Israelites; on the east three gates, on the north three gates, on the south three gates, and on the west three gates. And the wall of the city has twelve foundations, and on them are the twelve names of the twelve apostles of the Lamb.

The angel who talked to me had a measuring rod of gold to measure the city and its gates and walls. The city lies foursquare, its length the same as its width; and he measured the city with his rod, twelve thousand stadia; its length and width and height are equal. He also measured its wall, one hundred forty-four cubits by human measurement, which the angel was using. (Rev 21:12–17)

Here's a breakdown of the measurements:

Table 12.1. The Multiple-of-Twelve Measurements of the New Jerusalem	
12 Gates	12 Apostles of the Lamb Written on the Foundations
12 Angels at the Gates	12,000 Stadia Equals the Length, Height, and Width of Each Wall
12 Tribes of Israel Written on the Gates	12 Times 12 Cubits Equals the Thickness of Each Wall
12 Foundations	

Since the number twelve in Scripture is often associated with the thought of "completeness" it's no wonder that the number is associated with the bride of Christ resulting in the clear message that, at the end of all things, God's people will be complete and whole. But one might ask, since it's readily admitted that the multiples of twelve obviously have symbolic meaning, could not the city of the New Jerusalem still be a real structure in addition to her measurements having symbolic significance? The answer is a resounding no. Not only has the angel just confirmed to John that the image wasn't real, but the measurements themselves prohibit the image from being real. For proof, consider the following:

1. Twelve thousand stadia equals about fifteen hundred miles. (Mount Everest is less than six miles high.) Imagine a gargantuan, fifteen-hundred-mile tall, fifteen-hundred-mile wide, cubed-shaped object—about the size of the moon—perched atop the surface of the earth. You must agree, it's not exactly aesthetically pleasing.

2. Next, imagine the sparsity of gates surrounding a structure that size. Hypothetically, if someone decided to exit one gate and enter another, one would have to travel about three hundred miles from one gate to the next.

3. And if the above isn't comical enough, because of the thicknesses of the walls, each gate would necessarily open up to a two-hundred-foot tunnel, i.e., two-thirds the length of a football field, extending from the outer surface of the wall to the inner surface. Surely, these nonsensical measurements, not to mention the angel's testimony, should prove to anyone that the image wasn't real.

The Twelve Jeweled Stones and the Bride

Not only are the bride's perfection and completeness symbolized by the multiple-of-twelve measurements of the image, but they are also symbolized by twelve jeweled stones comprising the image:

> The wall is built of jasper, while the city is pure gold, clear as glass. The foundations of the wall of the city are adorned with every jewel; the first was jasper, the second sapphire, the third agate, the fourth emerald, the fifth onyx, the sixth carnelian, the seventh chrysolite, the eighth beryl, the ninth topaz, the tenth chrysoprase, the eleventh jacinth, the twelfth amethyst. And the twelve gates are twelve pearls, each of the gates is a single pearl, and the street of the city is pure gold, transparent as glass. (Rev 21:18–21)

This is not the first time that God's people have been symbolized by twelve jeweled stones. Straightaway, John must have remembered the apparel of Aaron, as the high priest entered the Holy of Holies on the Day of Atonement, wearing a breastplate covered with essentially the same twelve precious stones as those comprising the image, each representing one of the twelve tribes of Israel (Exod 28:17–20). It was on that one day of the year that God's people entered into the Holy of Holies, as it were, carried on the shoulders of Aaron as he approached the Almighty with fear and trembling and offered up the required sacrifice of blood to atone for his as well as the people's sins, thus maintaining fellowship and communion with God for another year. The following shows the comparison of each set of jeweled stones:

Table 12.2. The Twelve Precious Stones of the New Jerusalem and Aaron's Breastplate	
The New Jerusalem	**Aaron's Breastplate**
jasper, sapphire, agate, emerald	jasper, sapphire, agate, emerald
onyx, carnelian, chrysolite, beryl	onyx, carnelian, chrysolite, beryl
topaz, chrysoprase, jacinth, amethyst	turquoise, moonstone, jacinth, amethyst

The similarities of the two sets are undeniable. It's as if Aaron carried an ephod covered with the stones of the New Jerusalem into the Holy of Holies, and John looked up and saw a city descending from heaven to earth, clad with the breastplate of Aaron.[5]

Living Waters and the Bride

After seeing the bride of Christ symbolized by the multiple-of-twelve measurements and the twelve jeweled stones adorning the outside of the image, John's spirit was then carried inside the image:

---

5. Besides Aaron's breastplate, there is yet another place in the OT where precious stones represented the people and family of God. It was the set of jeweled stones given to the king of Tyre: "You were the signet of perfection, full of wisdom and perfect in beauty. You were in Eden, the garden of God; every precious stone was your covering, carnelian, chrysolite, and moonstone, beryl, onyx, and jasper, sapphire, turquoise, and emerald, and worked in gold were your settings and your engravings. On the day that you were created they were prepared" (Ezek 28:12b–13).

Although the list contains only nine of the twelve stones seen by John and worn by Aaron, still, the nine stones represented the original people of God. Unfortunately, many are not aware of this truth because many have been mistakenly taught that the identity of the king of Tyre was Satan. It wasn't. While examining the above text, it is certainly true that both Adam and Satan were in the garden of Eden, and both were created beings; however Satan was just one of multiplied millions, or possibly billions, of angels created on the day of their creation, whereas Adam was the only one created in the image of God on the sixth day of creation. Does it seem logical that at the moment all the angels were created, God would pull aside one angel and give him a set of beautifully engraved jewels set in gold for no apparent reason? Furthermore, of what value are physical jewels and gold to an angelic spirit? On the other hand, it's perfectly reasonable to suppose that on the day Adam was created precious stones were engraved and worked in gold and were given to him as a symbolic representation of his offspring who were to be placed in his trust because, as the first man, the Lord deemed it fitting that he stand in a priestly function as the representative of the entire human race. Of course, because of his sins Adam forfeited that responsibility, paving the way for the "last Adam," i.e., Christ Jesus, to represent the elect of God (see 1 Cor 15:45–49).

> I saw no temple in the city, for its temple is the Lord God the Almighty and the Lamb. And the city has no need of sun or moon to shine on it, for the glory of God is its light, and its lamp is the Lamb. (Rev 21:22–23)

Once inside, John didn't see a temple in the city. And the implication? That in the Father's eternal kingdom, the millennial temple seen by Ezekiel and built by Christ will be done away with. For the very idea of a temple, even one as magnificent as the millennial temple, implies a type of separation between God and man: God dwells in the temple and man dwells outside the temple. But those are not the conditions during the eternal kingdom. In it God and his people will dwell together:

> The nations will walk by its light, and the kings of the earth will bring their glory into it. Its gates will never be shut by day—and there will be no night there. People will bring into it the glory and the honor of the nations. But nothing unclean will enter it, nor anyone who practices abomination or falsehood, but only those who are written in the Lamb's book of life. (Rev 21:24–27)

If one momentarily forgets that God's eternal kingdom is only inhabited by the glorified saints, then phrases such as "the honor of the nations," "the kings of the earth," "the glory and the honor of the nations," etc., might give one the impression that nations filled with natural, mortal men and women are on the outside of a walled city, and if they behave themselves, they will be allowed to bring their glory into the city where God and the saints dwell. However, nothing could be further from the truth. As most of you know by now, a distinguishing feature between Christ's millennial kingdom and the Father's eternal kingdom is that the millennial kingdom will be composed of natural people, some righteous, some unrighteous, whereas the eternal kingdom will only consist of the glorified saints from the first and second resurrections. Remember the words of Jesus to Nicodemus:

"Very truly, I tell you, no one can see the kingdom of God without being born from above" (John 3:3b).

According to Jesus, not only will natural, mortal men and women never enter the eternal kingdom of God, but they will never see it! In other words, the phrase "nothing unclean will enter it, nor anyone who practices abomination or falsehood" is not a reference to those on the outside of a walled city looking in, but rather, it is a reference to those who have been cast into the lake of fire.

FIRST SEQUENCE, PART 5

The tour of the inside of the image continues:

> Then the angel showed me the river of the water of life, bright as crystal, flowing from the throne of God and of the Lamb through the middle of the street of the city. On either side of the river is the tree of life with its twelve kinds of fruit, producing its fruit each month; and the leaves of the tree are for the healing of the nations. Nothing accursed will be found there any more. But the throne of God and of the Lamb will be in it, and his servants will worship him; they will see his face, and his name will be on their foreheads. And there will be no more night; they need no light of lamp or sun, for the Lord God will be their light, and they will reign forever and ever. (Rev 22:1–5)

Since most do not understand that John is still in the process of touring a symbolic image drawn by God, the same believe that there will be an actual river flowing from the throne of God as he sits inside a fifteen-hundred-mile tall, multicolored, cubed structure, forgetting the fact that, in Scripture, a flowing river often symbolized the Holy Spirit:

"On the last day of the festival, the great day, while Jesus was standing there, he cried out, 'Let anyone who is thirsty come to me, and let the one who believes in me drink. As the scripture has said, "Out of his belly shall flow rivers of living water."' Now he said this about the Spirit, which believers in him were to receive; for as yet the Spirit had not been given, because Jesus was not yet glorified" (John 7:37–39).

A river with healing powers that is flowing from the throne of the Father and the Son is symbolism in its purest form. Only the Lord has the power of life as well as the ability to heal. Remember the miracle at the Pool of Bethesda, where people thought that the waters of a pool contained healing powers. But they were wrong; the power resided within Christ:

"Now in Jerusalem by the Sheep Gate there is a pool, called in Hebrew Beth-zatha, by which has five porticoes. In these lay many invalids—blind, lame, and paralyzed. One man was there who had been ill for thirty-eight years. When Jesus saw him lying there and knew that he had been there a long time, he said to him, 'Do you want to be made well?' The sick man answered him, 'Sir, I have no one to put me into the pool when the water is stirred up; and while I am making my way, someone else steps down ahead of me.' Jesus said to him, 'Stand up, take your mat and walk.' At once the man was made well, and he took up his mat and began to walk" (John 5:2–9a).

The power to heal was no more in the water at the pool than it will be in a "river of life" in the future. The river is purely symbolic.

Predictably, those who believe in a real river also believe that there will be an actual tree standing on either side of the river, complete with brown bark, green leaves, and twelve kinds of fruit, whereby the leaves will be used to heal people, evidently people who actually will require healing from time to time for the rest of eternity. (Talk about high maintenance!) Think about that for a moment. Despite the fact that Paul said the glorified body will be immortal and imperishable (1 Cor 15:53), many continue to believe that natural, mortal, and perishable people will inherit the kingdom, while rivers, trees, fruits, and leaves sustain them. The misunderstanding is widespread. That's a pity. The church is missing God's glorious message: In eternity, the saints of God will never die and will never be sick—not because of rivers and trees and leaves, but because God, and God alone, will sustain them.

The Beauty of the City vs. the Beauty of the Bride

The image of the multicolored cube floating down from space was breathtakingly huge and stunningly beautiful, but it was still just an image. Nothing about it was real. God knew it because he's the one who drew it; John knew it because he saw it; but what about John's readers, two thousand years removed? It's a little more precarious for them to know one way or the other. Nevertheless, they should. That's why the angel was commissioned by God to quickly disclose the meaning of the image, so as to leave no misunderstanding: The image represented "the bride, the wife of the Lamb" (21:9). But regrettably, confusion still exists because many have ignored the angel's statement, and instead have been overly enamored with the spectacle of the vision. But if only they knew that God's sole purpose for the image was to somehow convey how beautiful his people are in his eyes; they are much more beautiful than the jeweled stones of Aaron's ephod or the multicolored image of the New Jerusalem. The multitude seen by John that no one could count, from every tribe and nation, standing before the throne and before the Lamb, robed in white with palm branches in their hands are much more beautiful than any vision of jaspers, sapphires, pearls, or streets of gold. And the sunburned and battle-scarred faces of David, Jeremiah, Stephen, and Paul, with the sweat from their brows intermingled with tears from their eyes and blood from their sufferings, are far more precious than any vision of the names of the apostles and the names of the tribes of Israel etched on twelve foundations, or any vision of a gate made from a single pearl. Indeed, the image was beautiful, but the bride is more beautiful.

Not only is the bride beautiful, but she is complete. Not one person throughout the generations, Jew or gentile, will be missing from God's elect. Whether it's the last of the premillennial gentiles (Rom 11), or the last of the 144,000 premillennial Jews (Rev 7), or the last of the millennial Jews (Isa 11), or the last of the martyrs (Rev 6), all will make it. The entire family of God will triumph and radiate the glory of God like the facets of an exquisitely crafted diamond engagement ring. Just as every facet is cut, shaped, and polished under the careful eye of the gemologist, so every man, woman, and child, who has been chosen in Christ before the foundation of the world, will be identified, preserved, and accounted for by the Holy Spirit. As Paul stated, these are they who have been predestined, called, justified, and glorified (Rom 8:30).

Speaking of the 144,000 Jewish remnant, which happens to be another example of a multiple of twelve, will the number of the Jewish remnant total exactly 144,000 individuals, 12,000 each from the twelve tribes of Israel? Technically it could, but it won't. But again one might interject, "Did not John say he heard the number 144,000 in Rev 7:4?" Absolutely, he did. But that doesn't mean the number was real. He also "saw" a red seven-headed, ten-horned dragon waiting before a pregnant woman clothed with the sun, with the moon under her feet, who gave birth to a male child, but none of those images were real. They symbolized something else. Similarly, "the number 144,000" symbolizes the wholeness and completeness of the last-generation Jewish elect. The bottom line is that if John can "see" a symbolic image, he can "hear" one as well. And if one doesn't realize this simple truth, and instead thinks that God must find exactly 12,000 believers from the great tribe of Judah, not one more or one less, and then 12,000 believers from the tiny tribe of Manasseh, not one more or one less, and 12,000 from the tribe of Zebulun, not one more or one less, etc., until the number of the last-generation Jewish remnant totals exactly 144,000, then again one has unfortunately become entangled and confused by God's exquisite use of metaphors and symbols, and missed the greater and more lofty message that he is attempting to convey to his people, which is that just as not one saint will be missing from the final number of the elect so too will not one Jewish saint be missing from the last-generation Jewish elect.

Eventually the tour of the image concluded. The angel then assured John that everything he had seen was trustworthy and true:

> And he said to me, "These words are trustworthy and true, for the Lord, the God of the spirits of the prophets, has sent his angel to show his servants what must soon take place." (Rev 22:6)

If John initially thought the angel's phrase "These words are trustworthy and true" was only a reference to the vision of "the New Jerusalem," he soon learned the angel was referencing every vision seen by the disciple that day. In essence, John's visit to heaven was quickly coming to an end.

Thirteenth Conversation: The Father, the Son, the Holy Spirit, and the Angel Speak

After the angel told John that he had been sent by God to tell the disciple what must soon take place, the Lord himself proclaimed that he was coming soon:

> See, I am coming soon! Blessed is the one who keeps the words of the prophecy of this book. (Rev 22:7)

Next, in what must have been an overwhelming moment of thanksgiving and ecstasy because of all of his experiences that day, John, for the second time, falls at the angel's feet:

> I, John, am the one who heard and saw these things. And when I heard and saw them, I fell down to worship at the feet of the angel who showed them to me. (Rev 22:8)

But before John could utter any words of gratitude, the angel almost seemed to reprimand John as he admonished the disciple with the following:

> ... but he said to me, "You must not do that! I am a fellow servant with you and your comrades the prophets, and with those who keep the words of this book. Worship God!" And he said to me, "Do not seal up the words of the prophecy of this book, for the time is near. Let the evildoer still do evil, and the filthy still be filthy, and the righteous still do right, and the holy still be holy." (Rev 22:9–11)

FIRST SEQUENCE, PART 5

After the angel spoke for the last time, the Lord again proclaims that he is coming soon:

> See, I am coming soon; my reward is with me, to repay according to everyone's work. I am the Alpha and the Omega, the first and the last, the beginning and the end. Blessed are those who wash their robes, so that they will have the right to the tree of life and may enter the city by the gates. Outside are the dogs and sorcerers and fornicators and murderers and idolaters, and everyone who loves and practices falsehood. (Rev 22:12–15)

Although it's universally assumed that the above words belong to Christ, with its introductory phrase "See, I am coming soon" seemingly referring to his manifestation at Armageddon, the words probably belong to the Father, with the introductory phrase instead referring to God's coming in judgment at the "Day of the Lord." And the proof? The words in the above dialogue are almost identical to the words spoken by "the One seated on the throne," recorded in Rev 21:5–8, who likewise stated that he was the Alpha and Omega before speaking of the future reward of the righteous and the fate of all fornicators, murderers, idolaters, and liars. And of course, as you well recall, "the One seated on the throne" was definitively determined to be the Father.[6]

After the Father finished speaking, Jesus told John that it was he who sent his angel to the disciple with this testimony for the churches:

> It is I, Jesus, who sent my angel to you with this testimony for the churches. I am the root and the descendant of David, the bright morning star. (Rev 22:16)

Before bringing the letter to an end, John records the words of the Holy Spirit and the bride:

> The Spirit and the bride say, "Come." And let everyone who hears say, "Come." And let everyone who is thirsty come. Let anyone who wishes take the water of life as a gift. (Rev 22:17)

John concludes by solemnly warning everyone who hears the words of the letter not to add anything or take anything away from it, before praying for the Lord's return:

> I warn everyone who hears the words of the prophecy of this book: if anyone adds to them, God will add to that person the plagues described in this book; if anyone takes away from the

---

6. See p. 396.

words of the book of this prophecy, God will take away that person's share in the tree of life and in the holy city, which are described in this book.

The one who testifies to these things says, "Surely I am coming soon."

Amen. Come, Lord Jesus!

The grace of the Lord Jesus be with all the saints. Amen. (Rev 22:18–21)

Closing Thoughts: Mansions and the Bride

When many reflect on John's vision of the New Jerusalem, not only do they anticipate streets of gold, gates of pearl, and a glistening, rainbow-colored city the size of the moon, but they also anticipate . . . mansions. Where did that thought come from, especially since there aren't any mentioned in Revelation? It's actually the result of a combination of miscues: First, there's the common assumption that the city is real. Secondly, when this error is coupled with a faulty translation of a particular passage in Matthew, then Revelation's "streets of gold" suddenly become blanketed with beautifully adorned "mansions." As I'm sure to no one's surprise, here's the passage in question:

"In my Father's house are many mansions: if it were not so, I would have told you. I go to prepare a place for you. And if I go and prepare a place for you, I will come again, and receive you unto myself; that where I am, there ye may be also" (John 14:2–3 KJV).

Unfortunately, many believe the above KJV translation of these verses indicate that Jesus told the disciples that he was going away to prepare mansions, apparently, to line those same streets of gold seen by John so that when the Lord returns the disciples will be able to accompany Jesus back to heaven and live in the most beautiful intergalactic neighborhood that one could imagine. But did Jesus actually say that he was going away to prepare mansions for the disciples? Let's examine:

First, a brief word study is in order: The Greek word *monai*, translated by the KJV as "mansions," is only used twice in the New Testament and both times were by Christ. After John 14:2, the second occurrence soon follows:

"Jesus answered and said unto him, 'If a man love me, he will keep my words: and my Father will love him, and we will come unto him, and make our abode with him'" (John 14:23 KJV).

Instead of "mansions" as in 14:2, the KJV translated the second occurrence of *monai* as "abode" in 14:23, which simply means a dwelling place or a place of abode. When translators of more recent Bible versions concurred that "abode" or "dwelling place" was a better translation for both instances, the resultant translation in the first instance now reads as the following:

"In my Father's house there are many dwelling places. If it were not so, would I have told you that I go to prepare a place for you?" (John 14:2 NRSV).

Granted, the newer translations of these verses are a welcomed change from the KJV's, but even with the more accurate translation, the majority's understanding of Christ's words is still lacking. Now, instead of many believing that there will be huge mansions lining streets of gold in a city that is a fifteen-hundred-mile cube, many believe that there will be smaller, more modest dwelling places lining the streets of gold. I'm afraid the second belief is not that much of an improvement over the first.

Just for a moment, think about the above scenario: Jesus is going away to heaven, at which time he will prepare mansions, or perhaps, if you prefer, smaller dwelling places, and when he returns, those places will then be ready for the believers' occupancy. Carrying the hypothetical scenario a step further, imagine if you will, once the believers return to their new addresses in heaven, if at any point they wish to have a time of seclusion or alone-time, they can then apparently retire to his or her own, particular, dwelling place. And how might those dwellings appear? Are some larger and nicer than others? Or do they all look the same? Furthermore, with what will the dwellings be equipped? Beds? No need. The glorified saint will never be tired. Restrooms? Again, no need. Perhaps some of the rooms will at least have some chairs and couches on which to sit. Will the mansions come with closets for a change of clothes? Will there be any cooking utensils? Will the mansions have refrigerators? Stoves? Running water? If no furnishings, are the dwelling places just large beautiful facades on the outside covering large empty boxes on the inside? I believe you get the point. The scenario is bizarre, even comical. And why is that? Because it's unscriptural. It has nothing to do with what Jesus told his disciples. When Jesus said he was going away to prepare a place, his words had nothing to do with floors, doors, windows, ceilings, or walls. To the contrary, the Holy Spirit gave the true meaning of what Christ meant through the writings of Paul:

THE SEQUENCE

"For we know that if the earthly tent we live in is destroyed, we have a building from God, a house not made with hands, eternal in the heavens. For in this tent we groan, longing to be clothed with our heavenly dwelling—if indeed, when we have taken it off we will not be found naked. For while we are still in this tent, we groan under our burden, because we wish not to be unclothed but to be further clothed, so that what is mortal may be swallowed up by life. He who has prepared us for this very thing is God, who has given us the Spirit as a guarantee" (2 Cor 5:1–5).

Paul likens our natural body to "a tent" that can be destroyed, but he calls the glorified body "a building" and "a house" that is eternal and is not made with human hands. When Jesus told the disciples that he was going away to prepare a place for them, he wasn't talking about houses or mansions, but rather he was speaking about the new, glorified body of the believer. And why was it imperative that Jesus prepare these "indestructible dwelling places"? Jesus gave the answer:

"... that where I am, there ye may be also" (John 14:3b KJV).

And where was Jesus going to be? Most think that Jesus was talking about heaven. He wasn't. He was talking about being with the Father. In order for the disciples to spend eternity where Jesus was going to be, which was with the Father, preparations would have to be made: The disciples would have to undergo a metamorphosis, in which the perishable body puts on imperishability and the mortal body puts on immortality (1 Cor 15:53). This is the house not made with hands that Jesus promised the disciples that he would go and prepare for them, and then later, return and receive them unto himself, so that where he was, there they may be also.

∼

The following reconciled sequence ends with the second resurrection and the eternal state (the last events of Rev 21:1—22:5 are italicized):

FIRST SEQUENCE, PART 5

Table 12.3. Reconciliation of the Six Sequences from the Great White Throne Judgment to the Second Resurrection and the Eternal State

The Sequence	Seq. 1 & 2 Thess	Seq. Olivet Discourse	1st Seq. Rev, Part 5: 2nd Resurrection and Eternal State (Rev 21:1—22:5)	2nd Seq. Rev: 2 Witnesses	3rd Seq. Rev: Woman, Child, and Dragon	4th Seq. Rev, Part 3: Mt. Zion to God's Throne
1. God gathers all of the unrighteous who have died from the beginning of time up through the millennial reign of Christ. All are judged, sentenced, and cast into the lake of fire.			The Great White Throne Judgment (Rev 20:11–15)			

Table 12.3. Reconciliation of the Six Sequences from the Great White Throne Judgment to the Second Resurrection and the Eternal State

The Sequence	Seq. 1 & 2 Thess	Seq. Olivet Discourse	1st Seq. Rev, Part 5: 2nd Resurrection and Eternal State (Rev 21:1—22:5)	2nd Seq. Rev: 2 Witnesses	3rd Seq. Rev: Woman, Child, and Dragon	4th Seq. Rev, Part 3: Mt. Zion to God's Throne
2. The millennial souls descend from heaven for the 2nd resurrection, accompanied by the Father and the Son. Then, the Father, the Son, and the Holy Spirit will dwell on earth with the bride of Christ for eternity.			John saw the holy city, the New Jerusalem, descending down from heaven toward the earth. (Rev 21:1—22:5)			

Conclusion
Truth and Error

Do you recall back in the introduction when I shared with you that a certain theologian made the comment that there was a crisis in eschatology? He made the statement because there were supposedly unaddressed questions posed by certain theologians of the nineteenth and twentieth centuries that surrounded Christ's words concerning his return. I assured the reader at the time there was no crisis, at least in that regard, although there was a very real crisis in eschatology because of the current lack of proper teaching on the subject from within the church. I went on to say that the improper teaching was evidenced by the many and varied opinions offered concerning the return of Christ and the resurrection and rapture of the saints, especially as they pertain to their placement in the sequence of end times. Now, however, I wish to bring your attention to another theologian who, unlike the first gentleman, unabashedly expressed his disdain for the field of eschatology because of that same plethora of opinions of which I have made reference. But rather than attributing the innumerable speculations to the current lack of knowledge and qualified teaching on the subject, which is the true cause, this theologian believes the reason that there isn't any consensus in eschatology is because Scripture is deliberately ambiguous on the subject of end times and that is because God considers our understanding of the subject not to be of the greatest importance! His reasoning is that had God considered our understanding of end times crucial, then he would have been less ambiguous in his word, resulting in a greater consensus on the subject. I must admit, the first time I heard this I was flabbergasted! I do regret this man's disillusionment, but blaming God for the pitiful state of affairs in eschatology is ludicrous. In reality, God considers our understanding

THE SEQUENCE

of every biblical truth to be of the utmost importance and he has proven this by his undeniable clarity and forthrightness in every doctrine of Scripture, including eschatology. To illustrate, look if you will at the one question that seems to be on everyone's mind, and that is When does Scripture say that the resurrection and rapture of the saints will occur? Recall how a passage in Rev 20 coupled with a passage in Dan 7 revealed the precise answer. There wasn't any ambiguity on God's part, was there? When the Holy Spirit said unequivocally that the first resurrection of the saints will occur after the beast, the false prophet, and Satan are properly disposed, the Lord didn't mince any words, did he? After seeing the souls of those who had been beheaded for their testimony of Jesus and for the word of God during the great tribulation standing amid the thrones that had been set in place, John succinctly said, "They came to life and reigned with Christ a thousand years." He then said, "This is the first resurrection." Daniel saw the same scene: After the beast and the false prophet were judged and thrown into the lake of fire, Daniel saw Christ waiting to be brought before the Ancient of Days and receive the kingdoms of the earth, at which time Christ would then descend with the same souls that John had seen standing around the thrones. What John didn't say was that the blood-stained, beheaded bodies of the martyrs were still lying on the earth where they had been slaughtered because they refused to worship the beast or its image. He also didn't say that before descending to recover those bodies, the Lord Jesus must first gather not only the souls of those who had been beheaded during the tribulation, but all of the righteous souls who have been patiently waiting for millennia in heaven because the first resurrection includes all of the dead in Christ from the beginning of time to his return. And why didn't the Holy Spirit inspire John to write these details? Perhaps because the Lord considered them superfluous. In the Olivet Discourse, Jesus had already revealed that it was only after his appearance to the world (which one knows to be the Armageddon event) that he would "send out his angels with a loud trumpet call, and they will gather his elect from the four winds, from one end of heaven to the other." Later, Paul said the gathering of the saints would only occur after Christ descended "from heaven" with the souls of those who had previously died in Christ, which is exactly where Daniel placed Jesus immediately after the judgment of the beast and the false prophet. In other words, the Holy Spirit didn't need John to disclose everything surrounding the first resurrection in Rev 20 because most of the details had already been revealed elsewhere by Jesus, Paul, and Daniel.

CONCLUSION

Although the details surrounding the first resurrection in Rev 20 my indeed seem sparse, the one revelation that the Holy Spirit did instruct John to write has been grossly misinterpreted, and of course I am speaking of the simple statement "This is the first resurrection." If there had been a previous resurrection before this one, then this one would not have been the first resurrection, correct? There is no way around this fact. No, the Holy Spirit did not say this was the first resurrection of the Jews, or the first resurrection of the martyrs, or the first spiritual resurrection of the martyrs; he simply said this was the first resurrection. The only reason theologians and commentators play havoc with the simplicity of the Holy Spirit's statement is because their preconceived ideas of the sequence of end times don't align with the words of the Holy Spirit.

Past Errors

Are the sundry misconceptions surrounding the timing of the resurrection a new phenomenon in the church? Not really. Confusion surrounding the resurrection has plagued the church since the beginning. Look at Paul's admonition to Timothy:

"Do your best to present yourself to God as one approved by him, a worker who has no need to be ashamed, rightly explaining the word of truth. Avoid profane chatter, for it will lead people into more and more impiety, and their talk will spread like gangrene. Among them are Hymenaeus and Philetus, who have swerved from the truth by claiming that the resurrection has already taken place. They are upsetting the faith of some. But God's firm foundation stands, bearing this inscription: 'The Lord knows those who are his,' and, 'Let everyone who calls on the name of the Lord turn away from wickedness'" (2 Tim 2:15–19).

Hymenaeus and Philetus claimed that the resurrection had already occurred. That might sound unbelievable, but it shouldn't. There is a large contingent today who espouse the same error. They are known as preterists.[1] In their minds, the resurrection as well as all other end-time events have already occurred. What did Paul think about the two's teaching back then? Probably the same as what he would think of the preterists' teaching today: not much. He said the pair's teaching has swerved from the truth and will spread like gangrene. And just as the apostle prophesied, the teachings of the preterists have indeed spread like gangrene. The

---

1. Preterism was briefly referenced earlier in chapter 2 (see pp. 44–45).

modus operandi of the group is to point to certain reported events of the past—some documented, but most undocumented—and then naively claim that these "historical events" fulfilled the Lord's prophecies catalogued in the Olivet Discourse. Of course, their explanations are rubbish and absurd, as none of the purported events in the past have anything to do with the Lord's prophesies of the future. Whether from the most infamous preterists, Hymenaeus and Philetus, or from the current crop of adherents, the teachings of the preterists are quite preposterous and are not to be taken seriously.

The two were not Paul's only headache concerning false teaching involving the resurrection. When attempting to correct the many problems of the Corinthians, Paul disclosed that some in the community were actually claiming that there will not even be a resurrection of the saints. In a sense, this was worse than the deception of Hymenaeus and Philetus. By saying the resurrection had passed, at least the two reprobates were acknowledging that the resurrection was real. Paul, never one to shy away from defending the truth, told the Corinthians if there wasn't a future resurrection of the saints, then Christ had not been resurrected, and if Christ has not been raised, then his preaching was in vain, as well as their faith. Here are his exact words:

"We are even found to be misrepresenting God, because we testified of God that he raised Christ—whom he did not raise if it is true that the dead are not raised. For if the dead are not raised, then Christ has not been raised. If Christ has not been raised, your faith is futile and you are still in your sins. Then those also who have died in Christ have perished. If for this life only we have hoped in Christ, we are of all people most to be pitied" (1 Cor 15:15-19).

By his answer, Paul in essence told the Corinthians that the hope of the resurrection of the saints was irreversibly intertwined with the resurrection of Christ himself, which of course, is the central tenet of the Christian faith. Therefore, without the resurrection of the saints, Christianity is meaningless. As stated in chapter 11 of this study, Paul then proceeded to prove the truth of the resurrection by listing those who had seen the risen Christ: Cephas, the twelve, the multitude of five hundred brethren at one time, James, then all of the apostles, and last of all, Paul, himself. After establishing the truth of Christ's resurrection and therefore the truth of the resurrection of the saints, Paul then gave the Corinthians the sequence surrounding the resurrection (1 Cor 15:20-28).

CONCLUSION

The next and last example of past false eschatological teachings, which came even before the Corinthians, was the dilemma stirring in Thessalonica. When comparing the questions of the two churches, it is quite apparent that the Thessalonians had a better grasp of the doctrine of the resurrection than the confused faction present within the Corinthian church. There are no indications that the Thessalonians ever lapsed into doubting the resurrection, and contrary to the opinion of most, the Thessalonians were much more cognizant of the sequence of end times than today's church. They knew that the Day of the Lord preceded the coming of the Lord, just as they knew the coming of the Lord preceded the gathering of the saints. Their only issue was that they had forgotten that the rebellion and the revealing of the man of lawlessness preceded the Day of the Lord, and by forgetting that all-important detail, they inevitably came to believe that the Day of the Lord had arrived. But when Paul responded with his second letter, reminding them of his previous teaching surrounding the rebellion and the revealing of the man, the problem was quickly abated.

Present Error

Although the Corinthians and Thessalonians may have had their share of difficulties when trying to understand the sequence of end times, they were not alone. Today's church is battling a similar error. Unfortunately, today's error just won't go away. One reason it is so tenacious is because, unlike the short-lived errors of the Corinthians and the Thessalonians, this one has been constantly promoted for almost two centuries. Of course, the error referenced and which has been frequently alluded to in our studies is the teaching that the first resurrection and rapture of the saints are imminent and will precede the great tribulation of the saints. By contrast, this is a far cry from the Thessalonians' minor error, who briefly thought the Day of the Lord was imminent. Although the Day will certainly fall upon the unrighteous unexpectedly, Paul had to remind the Thessalonians that since the Day must be preceded by the rebellion and the revealing of the man of lawlessness, then naturally it couldn't be considered imminent, as well as any event following the Day, including the return of Christ and the gathering of the saints. In fact, one now knows that even the rebellion and the revealing of the man of lawlessness are not technically imminent, since those events themselves must be preceded by the 1,260-day ministry of the two witnesses.

In retrospect, had someone told the Thessalonians that one day in the distant future a portion of the church would believe the resurrection of the saints will precede the tribulation of the saints, they probably would have found that difficult to comprehend. To them, no doubt, the error would have seemed too colossal. Nonetheless, in defense of those in the church today, since most have not been correctly taught the difference between the tribulation of the saints and the Day of the Lord, or the difference between the Day of the Lord and the return of the Lord, or the difference between the return of the Lord and the gathering of the saints, then any number of false doctrines are to be expected. It just so happens that pretribulationism happens to be "the latest and greatest" among the false teachings at this moment in eschatology. But by God's grace, the teaching will soon pass, as signs of its demise are already beginning to show. But be forewarned, once that teaching is tossed into the dump-heap of false doctrines, other more sinister teachings will be sure to follow. And when they do, it is imperative that there are those in the church ready to wage war against them as well. The words of Paul come to mind:

"Indeed, we live as human beings, but we do not wage war according to human standards; for the weapons of our warfare are not merely human, but they have divine power to destroy strongholds. We destroy arguments and every proud obstacle raised up against the knowledge of God, and we take every thought captive to obey Christ" (2 Cor 10:3–5).

Upsetting the Faith of Some

Finally, have you ever seen someone stand up just before a debate in eschatology and open with words similar to the following: "We want everyone to know beforehand that our subject matter has nothing to do with your salvation; my colleague and I are just going to engage in some friendly banter back and forth and discover where we agree and disagree concerning the details of Christ's return, the Day of the Lord, and the resurrection and rapture of the saints. But rest assured, one's understanding of end times has absolutely nothing to do with your salvation!" Although I know they mean well, they do not realize the gravity of their topic. One thing is certain: Paul would surely disagree with their disclaimer. Do you recall what the apostle said of Hymenaeus and Philetus? Their teaching was "upsetting the faith of some." Again, here's the text:

CONCLUSION

"They are upsetting the faith of some. But God's firm foundation stands, bearing this inscription: 'The Lord knows those who are his,' and, 'Let everyone who calls on the name of the Lord turn away from wickedness'" (2 Tim 2:18b–19).

Although the phrase "upsetting the faith of some" might sound somewhat innocuous, Paul was actually implying something quite serious. The Greek word *anatrepousin*, translated "upsetting" by the NRSV, is found only twice in the New Testament and more accurately means "to overthrow, or to subvert," which carries a much more severe connotation than just merely "upset." Paul was actually indicating that the false teaching by Hymenaeus and Philetus was "overthrowing and subverting" the Christian faith of some. (That's a far cry from having nothing to do with one's salvation.) But before allowing Timothy to become too worried or anxious that someone in his congregation might actually fall from the faith, Paul assured Timothy that the two's false teaching would not affect the elect, whether in his church or any church. The apostle did this by stating:

"But God's firm foundation stands, bearing this inscription: 'The Lord knows those who are his'" (2 Tim 2:19a).

In other words, "Pastor Timothy, although some in your church might indeed fall from the faith because of their teaching, rest assured that the elect in your church will never fall away." How could Paul be so confident? He knew that if certain individuals fell away for any reason, whether because of false teaching, or persecution, or just the cares of life, their falling away proved that they were never part of the elect. John confirms the sentiment:

"Children, it is the last hour! As you have heard that antichrist is coming, so now many antichrists have come. From this we know that it is the last hour. They went out from us, but they did not belong to us; for if they had belonged to us, they would have remained with us. But by going out they made it plain that none of them belongs to us" (1 John 2:18–19).

This is why Paul was constantly urging the saints, beginning with the new converts, to persevere and live holy and righteous lives so as to prevent them from falling away, which would necessarily disqualify them as being part of the elect. One sees this trait in Paul's ministry as early as his first missionary journey (italics used for emphasis):

"After they had proclaimed the good news to that city [Derbe] and had made many disciples, they returned to Lystra, then on to Iconium and Antioch. There they *strengthened the souls of the disciples and encouraged them to continue in the faith*, saying, 'It is through many persecutions that we must enter the kingdom of God'" (Acts 14:21–22).

Paul knew it was one thing to choose Christ, but it was entirely another to stay true to Christ. And because of this biblical truth, when Paul initially thought he was part of the last generation, he cautioned the recipients of his letters to prepare for "the evil day" that he thought was soon to arrive. And how were they to prepare? By preparing to stand their ground even in the face of death by putting on the armor of God:

"Therefore take up the whole armor of God, so that you may be able to withstand on that evil day, and having done everything, to stand firm" (Eph 6:13).

Believing that the rebellion and the revealing of the man of lawlessness were on the horizon, Paul encouraged the church—by way of letters to the Thessalonians, the Ephesians, and the Romans—to prepare for "that evil day" when the beast and the false prophet were going to attempt to force all mankind to bow their knees and worship the image of the beast under the threat of death. The apostle recognized that if his converts entered the tribulation unprepared to give up their life at the moment of testing, they might become panic-stricken and susceptible to recanting the faith and betraying Christ. Paul's concern was doubtless well placed; nevertheless, he and the first-century churches were not part of the last generation. They were never going to lay eyes on the man of lawlessness. But what about the churches of this generation? Should "that evil day" come sooner than later, how will we fare? Unfortunately, not only would countless believers be caught off-guard by what Jesus has called the time of the greatest suffering in the history of the world, but many would become doubly dumbfounded and shaken to the core because, unlike the converts established under Paul's ministry, many of today's believers have been promised that not only will they never have to endure any end-time suffering but they will be whisked away before it ever begins.

APPENDIX A

Chart Showing the Complete Reconciliation of the Six Sequences

APPENDIX A

Reconciliation of the Six Sequences

The Sequence	Seq. 1 & 2 Thess	Seq. Olivet Discourse	1st Seq. Rev: Abomination to Eternal State	2nd Seq. Rev: 2 Witnesses	3rd Seq. Rev: Woman, Child, and Dragon	4th Seq. Rev: Heaven's War to God's Throne
1. The 2 witnesses are about to begin their 1,260-day ministry.					A pregnant woman appeared. (Rev 12:1–2)	
2. Satan brings down 1/3 of the angels from heaven in an effort to stop the ministry of the 2 witnesses at its inception.					The dragon swept down 1/3 of the stars of heaven and waited in front of the pregnant woman in order to devour her child once it was born. (Rev 12:3–4)	
3. Despite Satan's efforts, the 2 witnesses begin their 1,260-day ministry from the Temple Mount.				The 2 witnesses will begin their 1,260-day ministry from the Temple Mount. (Rev 11:3)	A male child was born. (Rev 12:5a)	

422

CHART SHOWING THE COMPLETE RECONCILIATION OF THE SIX SEQUENCES

Reconciliation of the Six Sequences

The Sequence	Seq. 1 & 2 Thess	Seq. Olivet Discourse	1st Seq. Rev: Abomination to Eternal State	2nd Seq. Rev: 2 Witnesses	3rd Seq. Rev: Woman, Child, and Dragon	4th Seq. Rev: Heaven's War to God's Throne
4. The 2 witnesses testify of Christ and have the authority to strike the earth with every kind of plague.				The 2 witnesses will testify of Christ and have the authority to strike the earth with every kind of plague. (Rev 11:4–6)		
5. When the witnesses complete their 1,260-day ministry, the beast that comes up from the bottomless pit wars against, conquers, and kills the 2 witnesses. This is the abomination of desolation.		Abomination of desolation (Matt 24:15; Mark 13:14)		When the witnesses complete their 1,260-day ministry, the beast that comes up from the bottomless pit wars against, conquers, and kills the 2 witnesses. (Rev 11:7)		

APPENDIX A

Reconciliation of the Six Sequences

The Sequence	Seq. 1 & 2 Thess	Seq. Olivet Discourse	1st Seq. Rev: Abomination to Eternal State	2nd Seq. Rev: 2 Witnesses	3rd Seq. Rev: Woman, Child, and Dragon	4th Seq. Rev: Heaven's War to God's Throne
6. Immediately after the beast kills the 2 witnesses, the Lord commissions Michael and his angels to attack Satan and his angels in heaven as the inhabitants of the earth celebrate the deaths of the 2 prophets for 3 1/2 days.				The bodies of the 2 witnesses will lie on the Temple Mount for 3 1/2 days, as the inhabitants of the earth celebrate and exchange gifts because the 2 prophets had been a torment to them. (Rev 11:8–10)		War broke out in heaven. Michael and his angels fought against the dragon, and the dragon and his angels fought back. (Rev 12:7)
7. Three and a half days after the murder of the 2 witnesses, they are raised to life and snatched back up to heaven.				Three and a half days after the beast murders the 2 witnesses, they were raised to life and snatched back up to heaven. (Rev 11:11–12)	The child was snatched up to heaven and to God's throne. (Rev 12:5b)	

424

CHART SHOWING THE COMPLETE RECONCILIATION OF THE SIX SEQUENCES

Reconciliation of the Six Sequences

The Sequence	Seq. 1 & 2 Thess	Seq. Olivet Discourse	1st Seq. Rev: Abomination to Eternal State	2nd Seq. Rev: 2 Witnesses	3rd Seq. Rev: Woman, Child, and Dragon	4th Seq. Rev: Heaven's War to God's Throne
8. Michael and his angels defeat Satan and his angels and cast them out of heaven to the earth.						Michael and his angels defeated the dragon and his angels and cast them down to the earth. (Rev 12:8–9)
9. A voice in heaven proclaimed that the devil had been cast to the earth and that the 2 witnesses had defeated the devil by the blood of the Lamb and by the word of their testimony; the 2 witnesses did not cling to life even in the face of death.						A voice in heaven proclaimed that the devil had been cast to the earth and "the brethren" had defeated the devil by the blood of the Lamb and by the word of their testimony; they did not cling to life in the face of death. (Rev 12:10–12)

425

APPENDIX A

Reconciliation of the Six Sequences

The Sequence	Seq. 1 & 2 Thess	Seq. Olivet Discourse	1st Seq. Rev: Abomination to Eternal State	2nd Seq. Rev: 2 Witnesses	3rd Seq. Rev: Woman, Child, and Dragon	4th Seq. Rev: Heaven's War to God's Throne
10. When Satan sees that he has been cast down to the earth, he invades the city of Jerusalem with the armies of the surrounding nations and pursues the 144,000 Jewish remnant.		Armies invade Jerusalem. Many of the inhabitants of the city will fall by the edge of the sword and are taken away as captives among all nations. (Luke 21:21–24a)				When the dragon saw that he had been thrown down to the earth, he pursued the woman who had given birth to the male child. (Rev 12:13)
11. As the armies of Satan attack Jerusalem, the 144,000 Jewish remnant begins to flee into the wilderness.						The woman was given the 2 wings of the great eagle, so that she could fly from the serpent into the wilderness, to her place where she will be nourished for a time, and times, and a half of time. (Rev 12:14)

426

CHART SHOWING THE COMPLETE RECONCILIATION OF THE SIX SEQUENCES

Reconciliation of the Six Sequences

The Sequence	Seq. 1 & 2 Thess	Seq. Olivet Discourse	1st Seq. Rev: Abomination to Eternal State	2nd Seq. Rev: 2 Witnesses	3rd Seq. Rev: Woman, Child, and Dragon	4th Seq. Rev: Heaven's War to God's Throne
12. The armies of Satan give chase.						Then from the dragon's mouth poured water like a river after the woman. (Rev 12:15)
13. Within the hour of the 2 witnesses' rapture, God splits the Mount of Olives to help the 144,000 Jewish remnant escape into the wilderness, where she will be nourished for 1,260 days. The earthquake kills 7,000 people.				God sends a great earthquake within the very hour the 2 witnesses were taken back up to heaven. The earthquake kills 7,000 people. (Rev 11:13)		But the earth came to the aid of the woman by swallowing the river. (Rev 12:16)
14. Many Jewish inhabitants escape Jerusalem into the wilderness. Within the escapees is the 144,000 Jewish remnant, who is nourished for 1,260 days.		The "reader" escapes. (Matt 24:16–20)			The woman escapes to the wilderness where she is nourished for 1,260 days. (Rev 12:6)	

APPENDIX A

Reconciliation of the Six Sequences

The Sequence	Seq. 1 & 2 Thess	Seq. Olivet Discourse	1st Seq. Rev: Abomination to Eternal State	2nd Seq. Rev: 2 Witnesses	3rd Seq. Rev: Woman, Child, and Dragon	4th Seq. Rev: Heaven's War to God's Throne
15. Having failed to catch the fleeing 144,000 Jewish remnant, Satan turns his attention to other Christians around the world.						Angry with the woman, the dragon went off to make war on the rest of her children. (Rev 12:17)
16. After Jerusalem is left desolate, the gentile nations that had invaded the city now trample the city for 42 months.		After Jerusalem is vacated she is left desolate, at which time the gentile nations trample the city until the times of the gentiles are fulfilled. (Luke 21:24b)		The gentile nations will trample Jerusalem for 42 months. (Rev 11:2)		

428

CHART SHOWING THE COMPLETE RECONCILIATION OF THE SIX SEQUENCES

Reconciliation of the Six Sequences

The Sequence	Seq. 1 & 2 Thess	Seq. Olivet Discourse	1st Seq. Rev: Abomination to Eternal State	2nd Seq. Rev: 2 Witnesses	3rd Seq. Rev: Woman, Child, and Dragon	4th Seq. Rev: Heaven's War to God's Throne
17. Perhaps because of his 2 recent defeats—being cast out of heaven by Michael and his failure to catch the fleeing 144,000—Satan decides to transfer his power, his throne, and his great authority to the beast.						The dragon stood on the sand of the seashore as the beast rose out of the sea. Satan then transferred his power, his authority, and his throne to the beast. (Rev 12:18—13:4)
18. The beast, who is the rider on the white horse, is allowed to exercise authority over every tribe and people and language and nation for 42 months. He is also allowed to make war on the saints and to conquer them.			Vision seen under the 1st seal: The rider on the white horse was told to go! He came out conquering and to conquer. (Rev 6:1–2)			The beast was allowed to exercise authority over every tribe and people and language and nation for 42 months. He was also allowed to make war on the saints and to conquer them. (Rev 13:5–10)

APPENDIX A

Reconciliation of the Six Sequences

The Sequence	Seq. 1 & 2 Thess	Seq. Olivet Discourse	1st Seq. Rev: Abomination to Eternal State	2nd Seq. Rev: 2 Witnesses	3rd Seq. Rev: Woman, Child, and Dragon	4th Seq. Rev: Heaven's War to God's Throne
19. The 2nd angelic rider initiates nuclear war through the 10-nation confederation, under the leadership of the beast.		Greatest suffering in the history of the world will begin. (Matt 24:21)	Vision seen under the 2nd seal: The rider on the red horse was told to go! He caused the people on the earth to slaughter one another. (Rev 6:3–4)			
20. God ends the nuclear war for the sake of the unconverted elect. If he didn't, no flesh would survive.		God will cut short the days of the greatest suffering in the history of the world for the sake of the elect. (Matt 24:22)				

430

CHART SHOWING THE COMPLETE RECONCILIATION OF THE SIX SEQUENCES

Reconciliation of the Six Sequences

The Sequence	Seq. 1 & 2 Thess	Seq. Olivet Discourse	1st Seq. Rev: Abomination to Eternal State	2nd Seq. Rev: 2 Witnesses	3rd Seq. Rev: Woman, Child, and Dragon	4th Seq. Rev: Heaven's War to God's Throne
21. The 3rd angelic rider causes famine, which initiates the nuclear aftermath as well as the second period of suffering during "the great tribulation."			Vision seen under the 3rd seal: The rider on the black horse was told to go! He caused famine, which initiated the nuclear aftermath. (Rev 6:5–6)			
22. The 4th rider and his partner—Death and Hades—are given authority to kill 1/4 of the earth's population by the initial nuclear war as well as its aftermath, i.e., famine, pestilence, and death by wild animals.			Vision seen under the 4th seal: The rider on the pale green horse was told to go! He, who is Death, and his partner, Hades, were given authority to kill 1/4 of the earth by sword, famine, pestilence, and wild animals. (Rev 6:7–8)			

APPENDIX A

Reconciliation of the Six Sequences

The Sequence	Seq. 1 & 2 Thess	Seq. Olivet Discourse	1st Seq. Rev: Abomination to Eternal State	2nd Seq. Rev: 2 Witnesses	3rd Seq. Rev: Woman, Child, and Dragon	4th Seq. Rev: Heaven's War to God's Throne
23. Along with the nuclear aftermath comes false messiahs and false prophets, causing deception by means of signs and wonders. This deception plants the seeds for "the rebellion."		Deception will be caused by false messiahs and false prophets. (Matt 24:23–28)				
24. At some point during the nuclear aftermath, the man of lawlessness emerges from among the many false messiahs and false prophets when he calls down fire from heaven in the sight of all. He now begins to exercise all the authority and power of the angelic beast.	The man of lawlessness is revealed, the one destined for destruction. (2 Thess 2:3)					A 2nd beast rose out of the earth and he exercised all of the authority of the 1st beast. He performed great signs and wonders, even calling down fire from heaven. (Rev 13:11–13)

432

CHART SHOWING THE COMPLETE RECONCILIATION OF THE SIX SEQUENCES

Reconciliation of the Six Sequences

The Sequence	Seq. 1 & 2 Thess	Seq. Olivet Discourse	1st Seq. Rev: Abomination to Eternal State	2nd Seq. Rev: 2 Witnesses	3rd Seq. Rev: Woman, Child, and Dragon	4th Seq. Rev: Heaven's War to God's Throne
25. The man of lawlessness deceives the inhabitants of the earth by telling them to make an image of the 1st beast.	The man of lawlessness will deceive the unrighteous by signs and wonders. (2 Thess 2:9–12)					The man of lawlessness deceives the inhabitants of the earth by telling them to make an image of the 1st beast. (Rev 13:14)
26. The man of lawlessness causes the image of the beast to speak. He then causes those who do not worship the image to be killed. This leads to the martyrdom of the saints.		A second period of suffering is in progress. (Matt 24:29a)				The man was allowed to cause the image of the beast to speak. He then caused those who would not worship the image to be killed. (Rev 13:15)

APPENDIX A

Reconciliation of the Six Sequences

The Sequence	Seq. 1 & 2 Thess	Seq. Olivet Discourse	1st Seq. Rev: Abomination to Eternal State	2nd Seq. Rev: 2 Witnesses	3rd Seq. Rev: Woman, Child, and Dragon	4th Seq. Rev: Heaven's War to God's Throne
27. The man causes all who worship the image of the beast to be marked on the right hand or the forehead, so that no one can buy or sell who does not have the mark. The mark is the name of the 2nd beast or the number of his name, which is 666.						The man caused all to be marked on the right hand or the forehead, so that no one could buy or sell who does not have the mark. The mark is the name of the beast or the number of its name, 666. (Rev 13:16–18)

434

CHART SHOWING THE COMPLETE RECONCILIATION OF THE SIX SEQUENCES

Reconciliation of the Six Sequences

The Sequence	Seq. 1 & 2 Thess	Seq. Olivet Discourse	1st Seq. Rev: Abomination to Eternal State	2nd Seq. Rev: 2 Witnesses	3rd Seq. Rev: Woman, Child, and Dragon	4th Seq. Rev: Heaven's War to God's Throne
28. Toward the end of the great tribulation of the saints, the souls of the martyrs in heaven ask God when he is going to judge and avenge their blood on the inhabitants of the earth. They are told to wait just a little longer—until the full number of martyrs are killed just as they have been killed.			Vision seen under the 5th seal: Martyrs are seen under the altar in heaven, asking God when he was going to avenge their blood on the inhabitants of the earth. They were told to wait until the full number of martyrs are killed just as they have been. (Rev 6:9–11)			

APPENDIX A

Reconciliation of the Six Sequences

The Sequence	Seq. 1 & 2 Thess	Seq. Olivet Discourse	1st Seq. Rev: Abomination to Eternal State	2nd Seq. Rev: 2 Witnesses	3rd Seq. Rev: Woman, Child, and Dragon	4th Seq. Rev: Heaven's War to God's Throne
29. After the full number of martyrs is reached, God sends a great earthquake, and heavenly signs: a darkened sun and moon and falling meteorites, which mark the end of the great tribulation of the saints as well as usher in the Day of the Lord.	The Day of the Lord will come like a thief in the night when they are saying "there is peace and security." (1 Thess 5:2–3a)	After a second period of suffering, heavenly signs will appear: 1. The sun was darkened 2. The moon did not give its light 3. The stars fell from heaven (Matt 24:29b; Mark 13:24–25a; Luke 21:25)	Vision seen under the 6th seal: There was a great earthquake and heavenly signs appeared: 1. The sun became black as sackcloth 2. The moon became like blood 3. The stars fell to the earth (Rev 6:12–14)			
30. The unrighteous are seen scurrying for cover at the sight of the earthquake and the heavenly signs because they know that the Day of the Lord has come.	When the Day of the Lord arrives, sudden destruction will come upon them and there will be no escape. (1 Thess 5:3b)	People will be confused by the roaring of the sea and the waves and will faint from fear and foreboding of what is coming upon the world. (Luke 21:25–26)	The unrighteous hid in the caves and among the rocks of the mountains at the sight of the earthquake and the heavenly signs. (Rev 6:15–17)			

436

CHART SHOWING THE COMPLETE RECONCILIATION OF THE SIX SEQUENCES

Reconciliation of the Six Sequences

The Sequence	Seq. 1 & 2 Thess	Seq. Olivet Discourse	1st Seq. Rev: Abomination to Eternal State	2nd Seq. Rev: 2 Witnesses	3rd Seq. Rev: Woman, Child, and Dragon	4th Seq. Rev: Heaven's War to God's Throne
31. The 4 angels who stand at the 4 corners of the earth are given authority to harm the earth during the upcoming 1st 4 trumpet judgments, but are told to wait until they have marked the 144,000 Jewish remnant with the seal of God.			The 4 angels who stand at the 4 corners of the earth were given authority to harm the earth but were told to wait until they had marked the 144,000 with the seal of God. (Rev 7:1–3)			
32. Because the 144,000 (a number determined to be symbolic) have just confessed Christ at the appearance of the heavenly signs, they are marked with a seal by God's angels, by which they are physically protected from the upcoming wrath of God that will be dispersed during the Day of the Lord.			The 144,000 Jewish remnant was marked with a seal by the angels of God. (Rev 7:4–8)			

APPENDIX A

Reconciliation of the Six Sequences

The Sequence	Seq. 1 & 2 Thess	Seq. Olivet Discourse	1st Seq. Rev: Abomination to Eternal State	2nd Seq. Rev: 2 Witnesses	3rd Seq. Rev: Woman, Child, and Dragon	4th Seq. Rev: Heaven's War to God's Throne
33. A great multitude of righteous souls from every nation, tribe, people, and language who died during the great tribulation—from the nuclear war, the nuclear aftermath, and martyrdom—are seen worshiping around the throne of God because the great tribulation of the saints has ended. Nevertheless, the saints on earth will continue to suffer a lesser tribulation for the remainder of the beast's 42-month reign. (This part of the tribulation is "less" because it does not include the threat of martyrdom.)			A great multitude from every nation, tribe, people, and language were seen worshiping around the throne of God. An elder told John these were they who have come out of the great tribulation. (Rev 7:9–17)			

CHART SHOWING THE COMPLETE RECONCILIATION OF THE SIX SEQUENCES

Reconciliation of the Six Sequences

The Sequence	Seq. 1 & 2 Thess	Seq. Olivet Discourse	1st Seq. Rev: Abomination to Eternal State	2nd Seq. Rev: 2 Witnesses	3rd Seq. Rev: Woman, Child, and Dragon	4th Seq. Rev: Heaven's War to God's Throne
34. Now that the Day of the Lord has arrived, the 7 angels who stand before God are given 7 trumpets and they make ready to blow them.			Vision seen under the 7th seal: The 7 angels who stand before God were given 7 trumpets and they made ready to blow them. (Rev 8:1–6)			
35. The judgments of the Day of the Lord begin with the blowing of the 1st trumpet. A third of the trees and all grasses are burned up, doubtless from global lightning strikes.		The powers of heaven will be shaken. (Matt 24:29c)	1st trumpet was blown: A third of the trees and all grasses were burned up on the earth. (Rev 8:7)			

APPENDIX A

Reconciliation of the Six Sequences

The Sequence	Seq. 1 & 2 Thess	Seq. Olivet Discourse	1st Seq. Rev: Abomination to Eternal State	2nd Seq. Rev: 2 Witnesses	3rd Seq. Rev: Woman, Child, and Dragon	4th Seq. Rev: Heaven's War to God's Throne
36. At the 2nd trumpet blast, 1/3 of the sea becomes blood, 1/3 of the living creatures in the sea die, and 1/3 of all ships are destroyed, perhaps from global volcanic activity affecting the seas.			2nd trumpet was blown: A third of the sea became blood, 1/3 of the living creatures in the sea died, and 1/3 of all ships were destroyed. (Rev 8:8–9)			
37. At the 3rd trumpet blast, 1/3 of the freshwater becomes poisoned when the earth is struck with the asteroid Wormwood.			3rd trumpet was blown: A third of the fresh waters became wormwood and many died from the water because it was bitter. (Rev 8:10–11)			

CHART SHOWING THE COMPLETE RECONCILIATION OF THE SIX SEQUENCES

Reconciliation of the Six Sequences

The Sequence	Seq. 1 & 2 Thess	Seq. Olivet Discourse	1st Seq. Rev: Abomination to Eternal State	2nd Seq. Rev: 2 Witnesses	3rd Seq. Rev: Woman, Child, and Dragon	4th Seq. Rev: Heaven's War to God's Throne
38. At the 4th trumpet blast, 1/3 of the sun, the moon, and the stars are darkened, and 1/3 of the day and night are kept from shining probably from dust clouds caused by the impact of the asteroid Wormwood.			4th trumpet was blown: A third of the sun, the moon, and the stars were darkened, and 1/3 of the day and night were kept from shining. (Rev 8:12)			
39. Just after the blowing of the 4th trumpet, an angel warns the inhabitants of the earth of the next 3 judgments. Instead of targeting the earth they will directly target the inhabitants of the earth.			An eagle appeared, warning the inhabitants of the earth of the next 3 judgments. They are called "the 3 woes." (Rev 8:13)			

APPENDIX A

Reconciliation of the Six Sequences

The Sequence	Seq. 1 & 2 Thess	Seq. Olivet Discourse	1st Seq. Rev: Abomination to Eternal State	2nd Seq. Rev: 2 Witnesses	3rd Seq. Rev: Woman, Child, and Dragon	4th Seq. Rev: Heaven's War to God's Throne
40. At the 5th trumpet blast, evil spirits are released out of the bottomless pit and are allowed to torture the inhabitants of the earth for 5 months. Their king is the angel of the bottomless pit, a.k.a. the beast.			5th trumpet was blown: Locust-appearing demonic spirits were released out of the bottomless pit and were allowed to torture the inhabitants of the earth for 5 months. Their king is the angel of the bottomless pit. (Rev 9:1–11)			

442

CHART SHOWING THE COMPLETE RECONCILIATION OF THE SIX SEQUENCES

Reconciliation of the Six Sequences

The Sequence	Seq. 1 & 2 Thess	Seq. Olivet Discourse	1st Seq. Rev: Abomination to Eternal State	2nd Seq. Rev: 2 Witnesses	3rd Seq. Rev: Woman, Child, and Dragon	4th Seq. Rev: Heaven's War to God's Throne
41. At the 6th trumpet blast, 4 evil angels are released from the area of the Euphrates River. They orchestrate the killing of 1/3 of the inhabitants of the earth by fire, smoke, and sulfur, using the same demons seen during the 5th trumpet judgment.			6th trumpet was blown: Four angels were released from the area of the Euphrates River and they orchestrated the killing of 1/3 of the inhabitants of the earth, by fire, smoke, and sulfur, using an army of 200,000,000. (Rev 9:13–21)			

APPENDIX A

Reconciliation of the Six Sequences

The Sequence	Seq. 1 & 2 Thess	Seq. Olivet Discourse	1st Seq. Rev: Abomination to Eternal State	2nd Seq. Rev: 2 Witnesses	3rd Seq. Rev: Woman, Child, and Dragon	4th Seq. Rev: Heaven's War to God's Throne
42. At the 7th trumpet blast, the kingdom of the world becomes the kingdom of the Lord and his Messiah. The blast marks the end of 1. the 42-month reign of the beast, 2. the 42-month trampling of Jerusalem, and 3. the 1,260-day exile of the 144,000 Jewish remnant. The ark of the covenant is seen within the open temple.			7th trumpet was blown: Celebration and worship were heard in heaven because the kingdom of the world had become the kingdom of the Lord and his Messiah. The ark of the covenant was seen within the open temple. (Rev 11:15–19)			

444

CHART SHOWING THE COMPLETE RECONCILIATION OF THE SIX SEQUENCES

Reconciliation of the Six Sequences

The Sequence	Seq. 1 & 2 Thess	Seq. Olivet Discourse	1st Seq. Rev: Abomination to Eternal State	2nd Seq. Rev: 2 Witnesses	3rd Seq. Rev: Woman, Child, and Dragon	4th Seq. Rev: Heaven's War to God's Throne
43. After the blast of the 7th trumpet, which ended the 1,260-day exile of the 144,000 Jewish remnant in the wilderness, the remnant returns home where they are seen standing on Mount Zion with Christ.						The 144,000 Jewish remnant were seen on Mount Zion with the Lamb, and a voice was heard from heaven that sounded like harpists playing and singing a new song before the throne and the 4 living creatures and the elders. (Rev 14:1–5)

APPENDIX A

Reconciliation of the Six Sequences

The Sequence	Seq. 1 & 2 Thess	Seq. Olivet Discourse	1st Seq. Rev: Abomination to Eternal State	2nd Seq. Rev: 2 Witnesses	3rd Seq. Rev: Woman, Child, and Dragon	4th Seq. Rev: Heaven's War to God's Throne
44. The 7 angels with the 7 plagues exit the open temple doorway and each are given a golden bowl full of the wrath of God by 1 of the living creatures.			The 7 angels with the 7 plagues exited the opened temple and were each given a golden bowl full of the wrath of God by 1 of the living creatures. (Rev 15:5–8)			
45. After receiving the golden bowls full of the wrath of God, the 7 angels are told to pour them upon the inhabitants of the earth.			The 7 angels were told to pour the 7 golden bowls full of the wrath of God upon the inhabitants of the earth. (Rev 16:1)			

CHART SHOWING THE COMPLETE RECONCILIATION OF THE SIX SEQUENCES

Reconciliation of the Six Sequences

The Sequence	Seq. 1 & 2 Thess	Seq. Olivet Discourse	1st Seq. Rev: Abomination to Eternal State	2nd Seq. Rev: 2 Witnesses	3rd Seq. Rev: Woman, Child, and Dragon	4th Seq. Rev: Heaven's War to God's Throne
46. At the pouring of the 1st bowl, a painful sore appears on those who have the mark of the beast and who have worshiped the image of the beast.			1st bowl was poured: A painful sore appeared on those who had the mark of the beast and who had worshiped the image of the beast. (Rev 16:2)			
47. At the pouring of the 2nd bowl, the sea becomes like the blood of a corpse and every living thing in the sea dies.			2nd bowl was poured: The sea became like the blood of a corpse and every living thing in the sea died. (Rev 16:3)			
48. At the pouring of the 3rd bowl, the rivers and springs of water become like blood.			3rd bowl was poured: The rivers and springs of water became like blood. (Rev 16:4–7)			

APPENDIX A

Reconciliation of the Six Sequences

The Sequence	Seq. 1 & 2 Thess	Seq. Olivet Discourse	1st Seq. Rev: Abomination to Eternal State	2nd Seq. Rev: 2 Witnesses	3rd Seq. Rev: Woman, Child, and Dragon	4th Seq. Rev: Heaven's War to God's Throne
49. At the pouring of the 4th bowl, the sun's heat scorches the inhabitants of the earth with fire.			4th bowl was poured: The sun's heat scorched the inhabitants of the earth with fire. (Rev 16:8–9)			
50. At the pouring of the 5th bowl, the residual throne and kingdom of the beast that he had originally received from Satan is plunged into darkness.			5th bowl was poured: The throne of the beast and its kingdom were plunged into darkness. (Rev 16:10–11)			

448

CHART SHOWING THE COMPLETE RECONCILIATION OF THE SIX SEQUENCES

Reconciliation of the Six Sequences

The Sequence	Seq. 1 & 2 Thess	Seq. Olivet Discourse	1st Seq. Rev: Abomination to Eternal State	2nd Seq. Rev: 2 Witnesses	3rd Seq. Rev: Woman, Child, and Dragon	4th Seq. Rev: Heaven's War to God's Throne
51. At the pouring of the 6th bowl, the River Euphrates is dried up in order to prepare the way for the kings from the east. Three demons then come from the mouths of the dragon, the beast, and the false prophet, and lure the kings from the whole world and assemble them at a place called Armageddon.			6th bowl was poured: The River Euphrates was dried up in order to prepare the way for the kings from the east. Then 3 demons came from the mouths of the dragon, the beast, and the false prophet, and lured the kings from the whole world and assembled them at a place called Armageddon. (Rev 16:12–16)			

449

APPENDIX A

Reconciliation of the Six Sequences

The Sequence	Seq. 1 & 2 Thess	Seq. Olivet Discourse	1st Seq. Rev: Abomination to Eternal State	2nd Seq. Rev: 2 Witnesses	3rd Seq. Rev: Woman, Child, and Dragon	4th Seq. Rev: Heaven's War to God's Throne
52. At the pouring of the 7th bowl comes the greatest earthquake in the history of the world. All the cities of the nations are destroyed, and every island and mountain disappear. Hundred-pound hailstones fall upon the inhabitants of the earth.			7th bowl was poured: There came the greatest earthquake in the history of the world. All the cities of the nations were destroyed, and every island and mountain on the earth disappeared. Hundred-pound hailstones fell upon the inhabitants of the earth. (Rev 16:17–21)			

450

CHART SHOWING THE COMPLETE RECONCILIATION OF THE SIX SEQUENCES

Reconciliation of the Six Sequences

The Sequence	Seq. 1 & 2 Thess	Seq. Olivet Discourse	1st Seq. Rev: Abomination to Eternal State	2nd Seq. Rev: 2 Witnesses	3rd Seq. Rev: Woman, Child, and Dragon	4th Seq. Rev: Heaven's War to God's Throne
53. After the pouring of the 7 bowls of wrath, 3 angels appear in the midheaven with 3 announcements. The 1st angel announces that the hour of God's judgment has come, which is a reference to the upcoming Battle of Armageddon.						Three angels appeared in the midheaven with 3 announcements. The 1st angel announced that the hour of God's judgment had come. (Rev 14:6-7)
54. The 2nd angel announces that Babylon the great has fallen, which is a reference to God remembering great Babylon during the 7th bowl judgment.			An angel announced that fallen, fallen is Babylon the great! (Rev 18:1-3)			The 2nd angel announced that fallen, fallen is Babylon the great! (Rev 14:8)

APPENDIX A

Reconciliation of the Six Sequences

The Sequence	Seq. 1 & 2 Thess	Seq. Olivet Discourse	1st Seq. Rev: Abomination to Eternal State	2nd Seq. Rev: 2 Witnesses	3rd Seq. Rev: Woman, Child, and Dragon	4th Seq. Rev: Heaven's War to God's Throne
55. The 3rd angel announces that those who worship the beast and receive its mark will drink the wine of God's wrath and suffer eternal punishment.						The 3rd angel announced that those who worship the beast and receive the mark will drink the wine of God's wrath and suffer eternal punishment. (Rev 14:9–11)
56. After the 3 angelic announcements, heaven celebrates because Babylon the great has fallen, and because the marriage of the Lamb has come, which is a reference to the upcoming resurrection and rapture of the saints.			Heaven was heard celebrating because Babylon the great had fallen and because the marriage of the Lamb has come. (Rev 19:1–8)			

Reconciliation of the Six Sequences

The Sequence	Seq. 1 & 2 Thess	Seq. Olivet Discourse	1st Seq. Rev: Abomination to Eternal State	2nd Seq. Rev: 2 Witnesses	3rd Seq. Rev: Woman, Child, and Dragon	4th Seq. Rev: Heaven's War to God's Throne
57. Jesus is seen seated on a white cloud just as he is about to descend for the Battle of Armageddon.						The Son of Man was seen seated on a white cloud. He was told to use his sickle for the hour to reap had come because the harvest of the earth was fully ripe. (Rev 14:14–16)
58. Christ appears to the world.	The Lord will return. (1 Thess 4:15a; 2 Thess 1:6–10 and 2:1, 8)	The Son of Man will appear. (Matt 24:30; Mark 13:26; Luke 21:27)	The rider on a white horse, called Faithful and True, appeared from heaven. (Rev 19:11–16)			
59. Christ descends to the earth and engages the armies of the world who have assembled against him on the plains of Armageddon.			The rider descended from heaven and fought the armies in the Battle of Armageddon. (Rev 19:17–19)			The clusters of the vine of the earth were gathered and thrown into the great wine press of the wrath of God. (Rev 14:17–20)

APPENDIX A

Reconciliation of the Six Sequences

The Sequence	Seq. 1 & 2 Thess	Seq. Olivet Discourse	1st Seq. Rev: Abomination to Eternal State	2nd Seq. Rev: 2 Witnesses	3rd Seq. Rev: Woman, Child, and Dragon	4th Seq. Rev: Heaven's War to God's Throne
60. The beast and the false prophet are captured alive.	The man of lawlessness will be taken away at Christ's *parousia*. (2 Thess 2:8)		The beast and the false prophet were captured alive. (Rev 19:20a)			
61. The beast and the man of lawlessness are brought before the Father in heaven for judgment, at which time the man is made to take a seat. The man then begins speaking arrogantly and defiantly, declaring that he is God.	The man of lawlessness will enter the temple of God and be made to take a seat. He will then declare that he is God. (2 Thess 2:4)					

454

CHART SHOWING THE COMPLETE RECONCILIATION OF THE SIX SEQUENCES

Reconciliation of the Six Sequences

The Sequence	Seq. 1 & 2 Thess	Seq. Olivet Discourse	1st Seq. Rev: Abomination to Eternal State	2nd Seq. Rev: 2 Witnesses	3rd Seq. Rev: Woman, Child, and Dragon	4th Seq. Rev: Heaven's War to God's Throne
62. The beast and the man of lawlessness are judged, found guilty, and cast into the lake of fire. The rest of the armies at the battle have already been killed.			The beast and the false prophet were cast into the lake of fire. The rest of those at the battle were killed. (Rev 19:20b–21)			
63. Satan is seized and cast into the bottomless pit for 1,000 years.			Satan was seized and cast into the bottomless pit for 1,000 years. (Rev 20:1–3)			
64. Those who are seated on the thrones are given authority to judge.			Those who were seated on the thrones were given authority to judge. (Rev 20:4a)			

APPENDIX A

Reconciliation of the Six Sequences

The Sequence	Seq. 1 & 2 Thess	Seq. Olivet Discourse	1st Seq. Rev: Abomination to Eternal State	2nd Seq. Rev: 2 Witnesses	3rd Seq. Rev: Woman, Child, and Dragon	4th Seq. Rev: Heaven's War to God's Throne
65. The 7 angels who poured the 7 bowls of wrath appear in heaven around God's throne with the martyrs who had conquered the beast, its image, and the number of its name. The martyrs were seen standing beside a sea of glass mixed with fire, as they sang the Song of Moses and the Song of the Lamb.			The souls of those who had been beheaded for their testimony to Jesus and the word of God, who had not worshiped the beast or its image and had not received its mark on their foreheads or their hands, were seen standing around the throne worshiping the Lord. (Rev 20:4b)			The 7 angels with the 7 plagues appeared in heaven with the martyrs who had conquered the beast, its image, and the number of its name. The martyrs were seen standing beside a sea of glass mixed with fire, as they sang the Song of Moses and the Song of the Lamb. (Rev 15:1–4)

456

Chart Showing the Complete Reconciliation of the Six Sequences

Reconciliation of the Six Sequences

The Sequence	Seq. 1 & 2 Thess	Seq. Olivet Discourse	1st Seq. Rev: Abomination to Eternal State	2nd Seq. Rev: 2 Witnesses	3rd Seq. Rev: Woman, Child, and Dragon	4th Seq. Rev: Heaven's War to God's Throne
66. After Jesus is presented before the Ancient of Days and is given the dominion of the world, he descends with the souls of all the saints who have died in Christ for the first resurrection and rapture of the saints.	With a cry of command, the archangel's call, and the sound of God's trumpet, the saints will be resurrected and raptured. (1 Thess 4:13–17a)	The elect are gathered from one end of heaven to the other. (Matt 24:31; Mark 13:27; Luke 21:28)	The martyrs from the great tribulation came to life. This is the 1st resurrection. (Rev 20:4c–6a)			
67. Jesus begins his millennial reign on the earth.	The resurrected and raptured will then be with the Lord forever. (1 Thess 4:17b)		The saints of the 1st resurrection will be priests of God and Jesus, and they will reign with him 1,000 years. (Rev 20:6b)			

APPENDIX A

Reconciliation of the Six Sequences

The Sequence	Seq. 1 & 2 Thess	Seq. Olivet Discourse	1st Seq. Rev: Abomination to Eternal State	2nd Seq. Rev: 2 Witnesses	3rd Seq. Rev: Woman, Child, and Dragon	4th Seq. Rev: Heaven's War to God's Throne
68. At the end of Christ's millennial reign, the rebellious and jealous nations of the earth, with the prodding of the just released Satan, come up against Jerusalem, at which time God rains fire down from heaven and destroys them.			When the 1,000 years are ended and Satan is released, the nations at the 4 corners of the earth will gather against the saints in Jerusalem for the Battle of Gog and Magog. (Rev 20:7–10)			
69. God assembles all of the unrighteous who have died from the beginning of time up through the millennial reign of Christ. All are judged, found guilty, and cast into the lake of fire.			All the dead were gathered and judged according to what they had done, at the Great White Throne Judgment. (Rev 20:11–15)			

458

CHART SHOWING THE COMPLETE RECONCILIATION OF THE SIX SEQUENCES

Reconciliation of the Six Sequences

The Sequence	Seq. 1 & 2 Thess	Seq. Olivet Discourse	1st Seq. Rev: Abomination to Eternal State	2nd Seq. Rev: 2 Witnesses	3rd Seq. Rev: Woman, Child, and Dragon	4th Seq. Rev: Heaven's War to God's Throne
70. The millennial souls descend from heaven for the second resurrection, accompanied by the Father and the Son. Then the Father, the Son, and the Holy Spirit will dwell on earth with the elect for eternity.			The New Jerusalem, which represents the bride of Christ, i.e., the elect of God, was seen descending out of heaven. (Rev 21:1—22:5)			

APPENDIX B

Proof That Daniel's Seventieth Week Has Nothing to Do with End Times

WITH THE KNOWLEDGE THAT the murder of the two witnesses by the beast comprises the abomination that will drive the Jewish remnant into the wilderness leaving Jerusalem desolate, let's revisit the Lord's words on the Mount of Olives surrounding the event. When Jesus stopped addressing the disciples about their future perils and then began directing all of his attention to the future "reader," warning them of the pandemonium that would accompany the abomination of desolation, no doubt the disciples may have initially thought this was a brand new prophecy until, that is, he referenced the prophet Daniel. And, as it turns out, even Daniel wasn't the only prophet who knew about the event, or at least the "desolation" part of it. Zechariah, Joel, and several other Old Testament prophets already knew of the remnant's escape from Jerusalem in the last days that would leave the city desolate. But as Jesus pointed out, it was Daniel who revealed the reason why the Jewish inhabitants would one day escape Jerusalem, and that was because of the mysterious "abomination":

"So when you see the desolating sacrilege standing in the holy place, as was spoken by the prophet Daniel (let the reader understand), then those in Judea must flee to the mountains; the one on the housetop must not go down to take what is in the house; the one in the field must not turn back to get a coat. Woe to those who are pregnant and to those who are nursing infants in those days! Pray that your flight may not be in winter or on a sabbath" (Matt 24:15–20).

The issue that presents itself to us is that Daniel referenced "an abomination of desolation" on three separate occasions: 9:27, 11:29–31, and 12:11–13. Here they are (italics used for emphasis):

1. "He shall make a strong covenant with many for one week, and for half of the week he shall make sacrifice and offering cease; and in their place shall be *an abomination that desolates*, until the decreed end is poured out upon the desolator" (Dan 9:27).

2. "At the time appointed he shall return and come into the south, but this time it shall not be as it was before. For ships of Kittim shall come against him, and he shall lose heart and withdraw. He shall be enraged and take action against the holy covenant. He shall turn back and pay heed to those who forsake the holy covenant. Forces sent by him shall occupy and profane the temple and fortress. They shall abolish the regular burnt offering and set up *the abomination that makes desolate*" (Dan 11:29–31).

3. "From the time that the regular burnt offering is taken away and *the abomination that desolates* is set up, there shall be one thousand two hundred ninety days. Happy are those who persevere and attain the thousand three hundred thirty-five days. But you, go your way, and rest; you shall rise for your reward at the end of the days" (Dan 12:11–13).

So, which of the three is the one that Jesus referenced in the Olivet Discourse? Fortunately, the task of choosing the correct one is not as daunting as it may first appear. For instance, if the abomination in question was coupled with a still standing temple, then that abomination could not have been the one Jesus was referencing, because as you know, a future temple will not be in existence at the time of the last-days abomination of desolation. Secondly, if the abomination itself is described as lasting more than three and a half days, then that particular abomination could not have been the one Jesus was referencing, because the future abomination will only last three and a half days according to Rev 11:7–9. And, thirdly, if the desolation caused by the abomination in question lasts more than three and a half years, then that abomination cannot be the future abomination because the future desolation of Jerusalem will last exactly 1,260 days according to Rev 12:6. Of course, there are many other reasons that two of the three cannot be the one that Jesus referenced, and in order to prove that's the case, let's analyze each abomination beginning with the one in 9:27.

APPENDIX B

First Abomination of Desolation: Daniel 9:27

Toward the end of Judah's Babylonian captivity (586–516 BC), Daniel determined from studying the book of Jeremiah that the length of Israel's captivity would be seventy years (Jer 29:10). The moment he made that determination he turned and prayed to the Lord, confessing his sins and the sins of the people. Daniel's prayer contrasted the righteousness of God with the iniquity of the people of Judah. He told the Lord that the people had transgressed the law and were now receiving the deserved curses for their disobedience laid out in the law of Moses. Daniel affirmed that God was right in all that he did but still appealed to God, "not on the ground of our righteousness, but on the ground of your great mercies." He prayed that God's anger and wrath would turn away from the city of Jerusalem and his holy mountain, and that God would let his face shine once again upon the desolated sanctuary. While Daniel was still in prayer, the archangel Gabriel appeared, bringing the prophet a message from the Lord. It is one of the most glorious messages recorded in all of Scripture, as it foretells the coming of the Messiah. Gabriel indicated to Daniel that by the end of seventy weeks, six accomplishments will be fulfilled on behalf of his people and the holy city because of the Messiah's arrival. Here's the beginning of the message:

> Seventy weeks are decreed for your people and your holy city: to finish the transgression, to put an end to sin, and to atone for iniquity, to bring in everlasting righteousness, to seal both vision and prophet, and to anoint a most holy place. (Dan 9:24)

Here's the list of the six accomplishments; the first three relate to the removal of sin, while the second three concern the establishment of righteousness:[1]

Table Appendix B.1. The Six Requirements Decreed to Be Accomplished within Seventy Weeks	
1. To finish transgression	4. To bring in everlasting righteousness
2. To put an end to sin	5. To seal both vision and prophet
3. To atone for iniquity	6. To anoint a most holy place (or, a most holy one)

---

1. Archer, *Daniel*, 112.

What's the explanation for these wonders? God is implementing *a new covenant* between him and his people! Finally, they will miraculously have the opportunity of standing in a right relationship with the Lord, once and for all. Of course, the people will be helpless to fulfill any of the six accomplishments on their own, and for that reason, God must take it upon himself to accomplish all six by sending the Messiah, Christ Jesus, within the seventy-week time frame.

The Decree

If Daniel's people were to be expectant of the future seventy-week time frame, then it's only reasonable that Gabriel reveal the starting date. And so he does:

> Know therefore and understand: from the time that the word went out to restore and rebuild Jerusalem until the time of an anointed prince, there shall be seven weeks; and for sixty-two weeks it shall be built again with streets and moat, but in a troubled time. (Dan 9:25)

Gabriel said the countdown to the Messiah would begin at "the time that the word goes out to restore and rebuild Jerusalem."[2] Which word was that? Let's determine: Before the seventy-year sentence had been completely served, two of three decrees were sent out for the captives to rebuild the walls of Jerusalem, but only the last of those three specifically spoke about resuming the everyday activities in the city, i.e., temple worship, government activities, marriages, etc., which seemed to correspond to Gabriel's declaration that a decree will go out "to restore and rebuild Jerusalem" rather than just rebuild the walls around the city. Here are the three decrees, their approximate dates, and their scriptural references:

1. Cyrus's decree, ca. 537 BC (Ezra 4)
2. Darius's decree, ca. 518 BC (Ezra 6)
3. Artaxerxes's decree, ca. 457 BC (Ezra 7)

---

2. In the following, ones sees Philip (one of the twelve) as an example of those who were counting down the days until the coming of the Messiah: "We have found him about whom Moses in the law and also the prophets wrote, Jesus son of Joseph from Nazareth" (John 1:45b).

APPENDIX B

As indicated, it was the third decree, the one by Artaxerxes, that specifically spoke about resuming life and the daily activities in the city, and thereby appears to be the one that Gabriel was referencing.

Next question: Was Gabriel speaking of seventy weeks of days (490 days) or seventy weeks of years (490 years)? If it were days, that meant the seventy-week time frame would end at 455 BC (457 BC + 490 days), which one knows is nowhere near the time of Christ's arrival. Therefore, one knows that Gabriel could only have been speaking of seventy weeks of years, or 490 years, which brings the seventy-week time frame up to the approximate time of Christ (457 BC + 490 years = AD 33).

The Anointed Prince

The archangel indicated that beginning with the decree, after seven weeks plus sixty-two weeks (49 years + 434 years = 483 years), an anointed prince would come, and for the first seven weeks (49 years), Jerusalem would be rebuilt with streets and a moat, but in troubled time. Notice that Gabriel did not say that after 483 years an anointed prince would be "born," but rather, there would be 483 years "until the time of the anointed prince." In other words, there would be 483 years until the prince is "anointed." If one accepts the consensus of historians that Jesus was born in approximately 4 BC[3] and crucified 33 years later, in AD 29, that would place the start of Christ's ministry, which was the time he was "baptized" by John the Baptist in the River Jordan as well as the time the Holy Spirit descended upon Jesus like a dove (Luke 3:22), in approximately AD 26. Then, to confirm this date of the anointing by the Holy Spirit, if one adds 7 weeks + 62 weeks (483 years) to the year of Artaxerxes's decree in 457 BC, the result is AD 26, which is the exact year Christ became the "anointed prince."

The Seventieth Week

Now that one knows the identity of "an anointed prince" is Jesus, Gabriel next confirms our knowledge of the time of Christ's crucifixion:

> After the sixty-two weeks, an anointed one shall be cut off and shall have nothing . . . (Dan 9:26a)

---

3. Metzger, *New Testament*, 124.

Here, Gabriel revealed that after the sixty-two-week time frame (which is actually after the sixty-nine-week time frame, i.e., 7 weeks + 62 weeks), that Jesus will be "cut off and shall have nothing." The phrase immediately reminds one of Isaiah's prophecy that Jesus will be "cut off" from the land of the living (italics used for emphasis):

"By a perversion of justice he was taken away. Who could have imagined his future? *For he was cut off from the land of the living*, stricken for the transgression of my people. They made his grave with the wicked and his tomb with the rich, although he had done no violence, and there was no deceit in his mouth" (Isa 53:8–9).

With the knowledge that Jesus was crucified approximately three years after he was baptized by John the Baptist in the River Jordan, placing the crucifixion in AD 29, one can see that that date falls well within the seventieth week of the seventy-week time frame. Observe:

Table Appendix B.2. The Seventy Weeks			
Artaxerxes's decree 457 BC	First 7 weeks (of years) 457–408 BC	Next 62 weeks (of years) 408 BC–AD 26	70th week (of years) AD 26–33
Decree to restore and rebuild Jerusalem	Jerusalem is rebuilt for 49 years	Christ anointed by the Holy Spirit by the end of 483 years, in AD 26	Christ is crucified after the 483 years, during the 70th week in AD 29

Next, and quite unexpectedly, Gabriel introduces a second personality in the message:

> ... and the troops of the prince who is to come shall destroy the city and the sanctuary. Its end shall come with a flood, and to the end there shall be war. Desolations are decreed. (Dan 9:26b)

Gabriel said after Jesus is crucified, the troops of the prince who is to come shall destroy the city and the sanctuary. Its end shall come with a flood, and to the end there shall be war; and desolations are decreed. And what does history record? After Christ was crucified in AD 29, Roman troops destroyed Jerusalem and the temple in AD 70, just as Gabriel foretold.

Concerning the phrase "the troops of the prince who is to come," whether Gabriel was speaking of the coming sixth angelic prince who

APPENDIX B

would eventually rule over the Roman Empire[4] or whether he was speaking of the coming human prince, Titus, who would serve as the military leader at the time of the destruction of Jerusalem and the temple in AD 70 is totally irrelevant. The pertinent facts are that Roman troops did come in like a flood and destroy the city and the temple after Jesus was crucified, and then, after that destruction, just as Gabriel further indicated, Jerusalem became desolate, from approximately AD 70 to AD 130.

Now, to the last verse of Gabriel's message, which has needlessly brought about much confusion:

> He shall make a strong covenant with many for one week, and for half of the week he shall make sacrifice and offering cease. (Dan 9:27a)

First things first: Who is the "he" that shall make or confirm a covenant with many for one week? The answer can be only one of the two personalities that Gabriel has referenced in the message: The "he" is either "the anointed prince" or "the prince who is to come" whose troops will destroy Jerusalem and the temple. That's it. Furthermore, since Gabriel doesn't indicate whether "the prince who is to come," i.e., the prince over the future Roman troops who will destroy the city and the temple, was an angel or human, the identity of the "he" in 9:27 can only be one of three personalities:

1. The anointed one, i.e., Christ.
2. The "human" Roman prince who is to come, whose troops will destroy Jerusalem and the temple, i.e., Titus.
3. The "angelic" Roman prince who is to come, whose troops will destroy Jerusalem and the temple, i.e., the angelic prince over the Roman Empire.

Looking at the options, one can quickly eliminate option #3. I think we can all safely agree that the angelic prince that ruled over the Roman Empire will never make or confirm a strong covenant with anyone! That leaves Jesus or Titus. As to Titus, could he have been the one who made or confirmed a covenant with "many" during the years of the seventieth week (AD 26–33)? Hardly! Titus wasn't even born until six years after the seventieth week ended, namely, December 30, AD 39. Therefore, it

---

4. Remember, of the seven angelic princes that were subservient to Satan, the sixth one was the angelic prince over the Roman Empire (see pp. 288–293).

is quickly and easily proven that the "he" in Dan 9:27a could only have been Jesus Christ. Now, with that determination, one has the following:

"He [Jesus] shall make a strong covenant with many for one week, and for half of the week he shall make sacrifice and offering cease" (Dan 9:27a).

Knowing that Jesus' earthly ministry lasted approximately three years (AD 26–29), why does Gabriel say that "Jesus shall make a covenant with many for one week," implying that Jesus' ministry will last seven years? Answer: Gabriel didn't say that. As one might expect, the problem is found within the translation, and in this case it's the translation of the Hebrew *ehād šābūa* as "one week." The word translated "one" (*ehād*) is found hundreds of times in the OT, and is often translated "same" instead of "one." Had the word been correctly translated as "same" in this context instead of "one," the following would be the result:

"He [Jesus] shall confirm a covenant with many the *same* week, and for half of the week he shall make sacrifice and offering cease."

In other words, Jesus didn't confirm a covenant for seven years; rather he confirmed the new covenant in "the same week" that he was crucified, which was the seventieth week, and for half of that same week, "he shall make sacrifice and offering cease." And how exactly will Christ make sacrifice and offering cease for half of the seventieth week? The answer is obvious: The sacrifice of Christ on the cross will not only put into effect "the new covenant" in the middle of the seventieth week, but it will simultaneously make "the old covenant" obsolete the last half of the week, including its required sacrifices and offerings.[5]

Finally, Gabriel concludes God's message to Daniel by revealing what will happen after the sacrifices and offerings are made to cease:

> ... and in their place shall be an abomination that desolates, until the decreed end is poured out upon the desolator. (Dan 9:27b)

In place of the sacrifices and offerings prescribed by the old covenant, Gabriel said that there shall be "abominations that desolate" (Hebrew: *mešōmêm šiqqūsîm*), as opposed to just one "abomination of desolation" (Hebrew: *mešōwmêm haššiqqūs*), until the decreed end is poured out upon the desolator. Whether these "abominations," which began immediately after Christ's sacrifice on the cross and continued until Jerusalem's destruction and desolation forty years later, consisted of

---

5. Concerning the old and new covenants, the author of Hebrews put it this way: "He abolishes the first in order to establish the second" (Heb 10:9b).

the now-obsolete animal sacrifices offered in front of the still-standing, obsolete temple, or whether it was simply the continual presence of the Roman armies atop God's holy Temple Mount, armies that would later wear insignias of eagles and images of Tiberius, all of which were considered blasphemous by the Jews, is, again, totally irrelevant. What is relevant was the message: God was going to send the Lord Jesus who would single-handedly replace the old covenant with the new covenant by his crucifixion on the cross, and he would do this wonderful feat within seventy weeks of the decree that will go out to restore and rebuild Jerusalem. The words of Jeremiah come to mind (italics used for emphasis):

"The days are surely coming, says the Lord, when I will make *a new covenant* with the house of Israel and the house of Judah. It will not be like the covenant that I made with their ancestors when I took them by the hand to bring them out of the land of Egypt—a covenant that they broke, though I was their husband, says the Lord. But this is the covenant that I will make with the house of Israel after those days, says the Lord: I will put my law within them, and I will write it on their hearts; and I will be their God, and they shall be my people. No longer shall they teach one another, or say to each other, 'Know the Lord,' for they shall all know me, from the least of them to the greatest, says the Lord; for I will forgive their iniquity and remember their sin no more" (Jer 31:31–34).

The new "covenant" (Hebrew: *berît*) in Jer 31:31 is the same "covenant" (*berît*) in Dan 9:27a. Whether the people of God learned of this new covenant through the Lord's words recorded in Jeremiah or through Gabriel's message of the seventy weeks, the archangel's message was always about Jesus Christ and the new covenant and had nothing to do with "an imaginary signed piece of paper" in the last days; speaking of which, there remains some unfinished business.

A Far-Fetched Teaching Revisited

What if I told you that there is an interpretation of Gabriel's message of the seventy weeks floating out there that doesn't place the seventieth week where one would expect it (AD 26–33), but transports it over two thousand years into the future, to the time of the angelic beast and the false prophet in the book of Revelation; would you believe it? Unfortunately, it's true. Although the theory was briefly mentioned back in chapter 7 of this study, it's now time to look at it a little more closely.[6] The theory goes as follows:

Instead of understanding that Gabriel brought a message to Daniel foretelling the coming of the Messiah and the new covenant within the time frame of seventy weeks, many well-meaning Christians have been regrettably led astray into believing that the seventieth week of this seventy-week time frame centers around the dastardly deeds of the future beast and his signing of a seven-year peace treaty with Israel, who will later break the treaty at the midway point by setting up an abomination of some sort in a newly rebuilt temple in Jerusalem. Of course, as the reader knows by now, every part of the theory is far-fetched: The end-time abomination of desolation will not consist of some unclean object being placed in a newly constructed temple, but rather will be fulfilled when the beast comes up from the bottomless pit and kills the two witnesses on the Temple Mount. Furthermore, the beast is an angel and angels don't sign peace treaties. But what about the false prophet? Since he's obviously a man, could he possibly sign a peace treaty three and a half years prior to the beast killing the two witnesses? In other words, isn't there some way one can make this beloved theory work? Not a chance. Three and a half years prior to the killing of the two witnesses, the true abomination, the angelic beast and his human false prophet, will be nowhere to be found: The angelic beast will be imprisoned in the bottomless pit and his false prophet, also known as the man of lawlessness, will be living a life of complete anonymity until he is revealed to the world during the nuclear aftermath, which is well after the murders of the two witnesses.

In retrospect, even if someone could somehow separate the seventieth week from the seventy-week time frame and miraculously transport it, as it stands now, over two thousand years in the future to the time of the two witnesses, to the dismay of many, there would be no temple, no beast, no man of lawlessness, and last but not least, no one would care about an imaginary seven-year treaty. Instead, all eyes will only be focused upon the 1,260-day ministry of the two witnesses. During those days, they will be busy proclaiming the message that Jesus is the Messiah, with the following results: Christians will love it; the 144,000 Jewish remnant will ponder it; some will receive it; but the overwhelming majority will reject it. Needless to say, a signed piece of paper will be the last thing on anyone's mind. Of course, all of these facts are in direct opposition to

---

6. See pp. 226–227.

the "The Seven-Year-Treaty Theory," as well they should be, since that theory has always been an ill-conceived and far-fetched misinterpretation from, shall we say, less than stellar biblical scholarship.

Second Abomination of Desolation: Daniel 11:31

The second abomination of desolation is found toward the end of a rather lengthy prophetic message, that once again is delivered from an angel to Daniel, and is so detailed, so accurate, that many biblical commentators and historians can only throw up their hands in frustration and disbelief, claiming that the author could only have known this kind of information about certain events had they already occurred. (To them, perhaps the Lord is not quite so omniscient after all.) Here's the second abomination of desolation:

> At the time appointed he shall return and come into the south, but this time it shall not be as it was before. For ships of Kittim shall come against him, and he shall lose heart and withdraw. He shall be enraged and take action against the holy covenant. He shall turn back and pay heed to those who forsake the holy covenant. Forces sent by him shall occupy and profane the temple and fortress. They shall abolish the regular burnt offering and set up the abomination that makes desolate. (Dan 11:29–31)

In order to arrive at the proper time frame of this abomination, one will need to determine who the individual is that comes into the south, is confronted by ships of Kittim, becomes discouraged before becoming enraged, takes action against God's covenant, pays heed to those who forsake the covenant, sends his forces to occupy the temple, and, finally, abolishes the regular burnt offerings and sacrifices and replaces them with a specific abomination of desolation. Whoever the scoundrel is, he's left quite a trail.

The fact that the angel indicated that a temple is still standing lets one know that this abomination of desolation occurred before the last temple was destroyed in AD 70, and therefore cannot be the end-time abomination referenced by Christ in the Olivet Discourse. Nevertheless, although it's not the one that we are looking for, let's identify the time frame when this abomination was perpetrated and thereby identify its perpetrator.

At the beginning of the narrative, starting in Dan 10:1, an angel appeared to Daniel after the prophet had prayed and fasted for twenty-one days and told him that the answer to his prayer was delayed because of hindrance from the angelic prince of Persia (10:13), and that he must soon return and confront the angelic prince of Greece (10:20). But before returning to the battle, the angel gave Daniel a detailed narrative describing the end of the current Persian Empire as well as the beginning of the upcoming Grecian Empire. As the angel proceeded to describe how the Grecian Empire would eventually split into four kingdoms (11:4), Daniel soon realized that the angel seemed only concerned with two of the four kingdoms: the northern kingdom of Syria with its Seleucid Dynasty (312–63 BC), and the southern kingdom of Egypt with its Ptolemy Dynasty (323–30 BC).[7] Only with these two dynasties did the angel trace their interactions up until the time of the aforementioned abomination. Armed with this information alone, one at least knows that Daniel's second abomination of desolation occurred between 323 BC and 30 BC.

Antiochus Epiphanies

So, did an abomination of desolation occur between 323 BC and 30 BC? Absolutely! Antiochus IV perpetrated the most infamous and heinous abomination of desolation in Jewish history to date, giving impetus to the Maccabean Revolt (167–160 BC), which in turn gave rise to the Festival of Hanukkah, which, as many may know, was a festival observed by Christ himself (John 10:22–23). One will soon learn that Antiochus IV, also known as Antiochus Epiphanies, was indeed the one confronted by the ships of Kittim, disheartened by the Romans, and enraged at the people of Israel just before committing an abomination whereby the carcass of a swine was placed upon the temple's altar in 168 BC. For the reader's perusal, the following is a short compilation of some of the leaders of the two dynasties, leading up to the man at the center of our attention:[8]

---

7. Walton, *Chronological and Background Charts*, 32.
8. Walton, *Chronological and Background Charts*, 32.

APPENDIX B

Table Appendix B.3. Corresponding Kings from the Seleucid and Ptolemy Dynasties Leading Up to Antiochus Epiphanies	
The Seleucid Dynasty (312–63 BC)	The Ptolemy Dynasty (323–30 BC)
Seleucus I 312–281 BC	Ptolemy I Soter 323–285 BC
Antiochus I 281–261 BC	Ptolemy II Philadelphus 285–247 BC
Antiochus II 261–246 BC	
Seleucus II 246–226 BC	Ptolemy III Euergetes 247–222 BC
Seleucus III 226–223 BC	
Antiochus III 223–187 BC	Ptolemy IV Philapator 222–205 BC
	Ptolemy V Epiphanies 205–182 BC
Seleucus IV Philapator 187–175 BC	Ptolemy VI Philometer 182–146 BC
Antiochus IV Epiphanies 175–163 BC	

After the angel had disclosed to Daniel several of the future interactions between kings of the two dynasties—including how a particular king of the south (Ptolemy II, 285–247 BC) will one day offer his daughter (Berenice) to a king of the north (Antiochus II, 261–246 BC) in an attempt to procure an alliance (Dan 11:6),[9] and then later, how another king of the south (Ptolemy V, 205–182 BC) will act similarly by offering his daughter (Cleopatra II) to the opposing king of the north (Antiochus III, 223–187 BC) for the same type of alliance (Dan 11:17)[10]—the angel of God eventually zeroed in on the man behind the abomination in question, Antiochus Epiphanies:

> In his place shall arise a contemptible person on whom royal majesty had not been conferred; he shall come in without warning and obtain the kingdom through intrigue. Armies shall be

---

9. Montgomery, *Commentary on the Book of Daniel*, 428.
10. Montgomery, *Commentary on the Book of Daniel*, 441.

utterly swept away and broken before him, and the prince of the covenant as well. (Dan 11:21–22)

When the oldest son of Antiochus III, Seleucid IV, was murdered, the next in line to the throne was Seleucid's son Demetrius. But as the above text indicates, *"In his place shall arise a contemptible person on whom royal majesty had not been conferred."* That "contemptible" person was none other than Antiochus Epiphanies (175–163 BC).[11]

Epiphanies's first order of business was to ensure that all lands conquered by the Seleucid Dynasty were hellenized, including Israel, while simultaneously keeping an eye out for any new opportunities to expand the dynasty, including Egypt. The following are just a few of the highlights:

In the first year of his reign (175 BC), Epiphanies set out to Hellenize the already-conquered Jewish people by disposing of their Jewish high priest, Onias III, and replacing him with one of his own choosing, which turned out to be Onias's brother, Jason. Then, five years later, when Epiphanies' sister Cleopatra died, the tyrant believed that was the perfect opportunity for him to invade Egypt (170 BC), with the pretense of securing the Egyptian kingdom for her son and his nephew, Ptolemy VI Philometor (182–146 BC).[12] Along the way, however, he entered Jerusalem a second time in order to reinforce his initial efforts to hellenize the Jewish people. After exiting the city and subsequently completing his expedition to Egypt, Antiochus prepared to return home:

> He shall return to his land with great wealth, but his heart shall be set against the holy covenant. He shall work his will, and return to his own land. (Dan 11:28)

On the way back, Antiochus heard rumors that some in Jerusalem had revolted against his most recent effort to hellenize the city, and in the heat of the moment, he returned to Jerusalem once again, massacred many in the city, entered the temple, and stole many of the sacred objects of gold and silver. From this moment forward, *"his heart shall be set against the holy covenant."*[13]

---

11. Montgomery, *Commentary on the Book of Daniel*, 446.
12. Montgomery, *Commentary on the Book of Daniel*, 446.
13. Montgomery, *Commentary on the Book of Daniel*, 454.

APPENDIX B

The Circle in the Sand

After the massacre, and having returned home, Antiochus eventually prepared once again to invade Egypt, thinking just as before, victory was his for the taking:

> At the time appointed he shall return and come into the south, but this time it shall not be as it was before. For ships of Kittim shall come against him, and he shall lose heart and withdraw. He shall be enraged against the holy covenant. He shall turn back and pay heed to those who forsake the holy covenant. (Dan 11:29–30)

But this time, as he journeyed toward Egypt, Antiochus was unexpectedly intercepted by an envoy of Roman ships, i.e., the *"ships of Kittim."* Leading the envoy was a Roman legate named Popillius Laenas. After disembarking from his ship, he approached Antiochus and issued the ultimatum from Rome that he turn back from his intention of invading Egypt. Antiochus insisted on delaying his decision on whether to comply or not with the demand, but Popillius drew a circle around Antiochus in the sand and demanded a decision before he left the circle. Humiliated and frustrated, Antiochus acquiesced and withdrew, i.e., *"he shall lose heart and withdraw."*[14] But just as the last trip, he headed toward Jerusalem with the intention of taking out his frustration upon the Jews. Once he arrived, he fell mercilessly upon God's people, i.e., *"He shall be enraged against the holy covenant."* It was at this time that Antiochus committed the unspeakable:

> Forces sent by him shall occupy and profane the temple and fortress. They shall abolish the regular burnt offering and set up the abomination that makes desolate. (Dan 11:31)

He turned God's temple into a sanctuary of Zeus, as swine's flesh and unclean animal sacrifices were continually offered upon the temple's altar. The abomination took place in December of 168 BC and the ensuing desolation lasted approximately three years.[15]

Of Daniel's three references to an abomination of desolation, the events leading up to the second one have the distinct characteristic of being almost completely substantiated by extra-canonical sources. To not recognize these events as specifically transpiring between the Seleucid

---

14. Montgomery, *Commentary on the Book of Daniel*, 455.
15. Archer, *Daniel*, 139.

and Ptolemy Dynasties during the twilight of the Grecian Empire, which include the bribe of Berenice, the bribe of Cleopatra, the murder of Seleucid IV, the theft of Demetrius's right to the throne, the ships of Kittim, and the heinous acts committed by the psychotic Antiochus Epiphanies against God's people and the holy covenant in 168 BC, and instead, assign them to an entirely different, last-days time frame with an entirely different cast of characters is incomprehensible to say the least, and can only be explained by one's lack of familiarity with the history of the intertestamental period. Suffice to say, the abomination of desolation of Dan 11:31 has already occurred and will never be repeated again.

Third Abomination of Desolation: Daniel 12:11

Since the two previous abominations have already occurred, one now knows that the abomination of desolation in Dan 12:11 is the one referenced by Jesus in the Olivet Discourse. Beginning in Dan 12:1, the same angel who had disclosed to Daniel the events leading up to the abomination perpetrated by Antiochus Epiphanies here picks up at the moment immediately subsequent to the end-time abomination of desolation, which we now know is composed of the murder of the two witnesses. In the following, notice the similarity between the words of the angel and the words of Christ concerning the worldwide suffering that will immediately follow the end-time abomination:

> At that time Michael, the great prince, the protector of your people, shall arise. There shall be a time of anguish, such as has never occurred since nations first came into existence. But at that time your people shall be delivered, everyone who is found written in the book. (Dan 12:1)

And here is Christ's description of the same post-abomination suffering:
"For at that time there will be great suffering, such as has not been from the beginning of the world until now, no, and never will be" (Matt 24:21).

The pronouncements are identical. Despite the great suffering, which has been determined to be caused by a global nuclear war, the angel promised Daniel that "his" people shall be delivered. And how will they be delivered? After the two witnesses are raised to life and caught back up to heaven, the 144,000 Jewish remnant, i.e., Daniel's people, will

APPENDIX B

flee to a place prepared for them in the wilderness where they will be nourished and protected for 1,260 days. And to ensure that all goes according to plan, God will first have Michael cast Satan to the earth (Rev 12:9), knowing that Satan will then chase the 144,000 out of Jerusalem. Next, the Lord will send an earthquake that splits the Mount of Olives, thereby providing a pathway for the remnant to safely reach the wilderness (compare Rev 11:13, 12:6, and 12:13–16). After assuring Daniel of his people's deliverance, the angel tells him of their blessed reward:

> Many of those who sleep in the dust of the earth shall awake, some to everlasting life, and some to shame and everlasting contempt. Those who are wise shall shine like the brightness of the sky, and those who lead many to righteousness, like the stars forever and ever. (Dan 12:2–3)

Here, the angel gives the best and clearest reference in the Old Testament to the resurrection of the saints. This verse alone proves that this is the abomination that Jesus referenced in the Olivet Discourse because, of the three abominations, i.e., 9:27, 11:31, and 12:11, this is the only one that is followed by the resurrection of the saints.

The Angel's Question

I'm sure all would agree when the angel told Daniel that God's people would one day be resurrected, that would have been a fitting way for the angelic visitation to have ended. But Daniel wasn't quite finished. The prophet still had a question or two for "the man clothed in linen." In fact, even one of the angels accompanying the man clothed in linen had a question:

> Then I, Daniel, looked, and two others appeared, one standing on this bank of the stream and one on the other. One of them said to the man clothed in linen, who was upstream, "How long shall it be until the end of these wonders?" The man clothed in linen, who was upstream, raised his right hand and his left hand toward heaven. And I heard him swear by the one who lives forever that it would be for a time, two times, and half a time, and that when the shattering of the power of the holy people comes to an end, all these things would be accomplished. (Dan 12:5–7)

As the man in linen stood next to the stream and revealed to Daniel a few of the end-time events that will follow the abomination of desolation, e.g., the greatest tribulation in world history, the deliverance of

PROOF THAT DANIEL'S SEVENTIETH WEEK

Daniel's people, and the resurrection of the saints, one of the accompanying angels asked the man in linen how long shall it be until the end of these wonders. The angel said:

"... it would be for a time, two times, and half a time, and that when the shattering of the power of the holy people comes to an end, all these things would be accomplished" (Dan 12:7b).

If you recall, we addressed this same passage when we were discussing the angel who approached John in the third conversation, recorded in Rev 10. As a reminder, here was the table showing the comparison of the two angels:[16]

Table 5.1. The Two Who Swore by the One Who Lives Forever	
The Angel in Rev 10	**The Angel in Dan 12**
1. The mighty angel was wrapped in a cloud.	1. The angel was clothed in linen.
2. He raised his right hand to heaven.	2. He raised his right and left hands to heaven.
3. He swore by him who lives forever.	3. He swore by him who lives forever.
4. He said that in the days that the seventh angel is to blow his trumpet the mystery of God will be fulfilled.	4. He said that after a time, two times, and half a time, the shattering of the power of the holy people will come to an end and then all these things will be accomplished.

When attempting to reconcile the words of both angels, it was earlier surmised that perhaps the angel's phrase in Revelation "in the days that the seventh angel is to blow his trumpet the mystery of God will be fulfilled" coincided with the angel's phrase in Daniel "for a time, two times, and half a time, and that when the shattering of the power of the holy people comes to an end, all these things would be accomplished." They do. At the seventh trumpet, the kingdom of the world will become the kingdom of the Lord and his Messiah, which means that the forty-two-month kingdom of the beast will then be stripped away by the Lord. Not only will this turn of events allow the 144,000 Jewish remnant to return home, but it will also officially end the beast's reign of terror over all the saints worldwide, which does indeed coincide with the angel's phrase in Daniel, "the shattering of the power of the holy people comes to an end." Then, according to the man in linen, all things will be accomplished: the

---

16. See pp. 138–139.

remainder of the Day of the Lord, which includes the seven bowls of wrath leading up to the return of Christ, and the resurrection and rapture of the saints.[17]

Daniel's Question

Curiously, after listening to the exchange between the two angels, Daniel then basically asked the same question as did the angel:

> I heard but could not understand; so I said, "My lord, what shall be the outcome of these things?" He said, "Go your way, Daniel, for the words are to remain secret and sealed until the time of the end. Many shall be purified, cleansed, and refined, but the wicked shall continue to act wickedly. None of the wicked shall understand, but those who are wise shall understand." (Dan 12:8–10)

Daniel's question was superfluous. But the man in linen was patient with Daniel and told him to go his way and rest. It seems that the angel's instruction "Go your way" may have anticipated the prophet's soon approaching death, as the angel soon repeats the phrase but adds that the prophet will rise for his reward at the end of days (Dan 12:13). Nevertheless, before finally dismissing Daniel, the angel unexpectedly reveals the lengths of two particular time frames:

> From the time that the regular burnt offering is taken away and the abomination that desolates is set up, there shall be one thousand two hundred ninety days. Happy are those who persevere and attain the thousand three hundred thirty-five days. But you, go your way, and rest; you shall rise for your reward at the end of the days. (Dan 12:11–13)

Now, we must address the elephant in the room: Why did the angel say "From the time the regular burnt offering is taken away" which is a clear implication of an offering associated with Judaism and the temple? That sounds strange, especially since we have proven unequivocally throughout this entire study that a rebuilt temple will never exist prior to Christ's return and therefore hasn't any connection with the end-time abomination of desolation. What burnt offering could the man in linen have possibly been referencing? In order to unravel this apparent conundrum, we must first, as usual, address the translation of the Hebrew text.

---

17. The man was not indicating that at the seventh trumpet all things "have been accomplished," but rather, after the seventh trumpet all these things "will finally become accomplished." There's a distinction.

What's Taken Away?

First and foremost, let's establish the fact that the angel did not say "From the time that the regular burnt offering is taken away," which is the translation in the above text. Instead, the Hebrew word *hattāmîd* is better translated "the continual" or "the daily." There's quite a difference between "From the time the regular burnt offering is taken away"[18] and "From the time the continual is taken away." One requires the presence of a temple and one doesn't. The man clothed in linen knew that a temple would not be present in the last days, including any burnt offerings or sacrifices associated with it, especially since Gabriel, the angel who brought Daniel the message of the seventy weeks, had revealed the details of the future destruction of Jerusalem and the temple, as well as the end of all sacrifices and offerings associated with the temple (italics used for emphasis):

"He [*Christ*] shall confirm a strong covenant [*the new covenant*] with many the same week [*the seventieth week*], and in the middle of the week he shall make sacrifice and offering cease [*Christ's sacrifice on the cross shall make all other sacrifice and offering cease*]" (Dan 9:27a).

Gabriel specifically indicated that the "sacrifice and offering" (Hebrew: *zebah ūminhāh*) of the old covenant were going to end because the one sacrifice of the Anointed One was going to single-handedly render all other sacrifices and offerings meaningless. And just as Gabriel foretold, those animal sacrifices and burnt offerings did cease once and for all when the temple was razed to the ground in AD 70. But these are not the words that the angel spoke in Dan 12:11. Instead of animal sacrifices and burnt offerings (*zebah ūminhāh* and *qorban ʻōlā*) being taken away, the angel said "the continual" (*hattāmîd*) would be taken away. The word *hattāmîd* simply implies an offering to God that is present day after day, such as was the case when the bread of the Presence was to be continually placed on the table in the Holy Place before God, in the Old Testament (Exod 25:30), or when believers are to continually offer themselves as a living sacrifice, holy and acceptable to God, in the New Testament (Rom 12:1). As one can clearly see, the "continual" (Hebrew: *hattāmîd*) has nothing to do with "a burnt" offering; the word simply indicates a day-after-day, continual sacrifice and service to God.

Now, to the all important question: In the last days, what "continual" will be taken away just before the abomination of desolation is set up?

---

18. The Hebrew phrase for "burnt offering" is *qorban ʻōlā*, which is never used by the man in linen in Dan 12.

In other words, what "continual" will be taken away just as the two witnesses are murdered and displayed on the Temple Mount? Of course, it's the 1,260 day-after-day, continual ministry of the two witnesses. When the angel said, "From the time the continual is taken away and the abomination that desolates is set up," he was specifically referencing the time when the 1,260-day ministry of the two witnesses is taken away and the murdered bodies of the two are set up as some type of a trophy-display on the Temple Mount for three and a half days. Then curiously, the angel said that from the time the abomination is set up, there shall be 1,290 days.

Day 1,290

By now, one knows about the several implications of 1,260 days, but the 1,290-day time frame is new territory. Nevertheless, because of the closeness of the two numbers, one would assume that there is some type of relationship between the two time frames. In order to determine, let's quickly review the parameters of the 1,260-day time frame and compare them to the newfound parameters of the 1,290-day time frame:

1. 1,260 Days: It was determined that the forty-two-month reign of the beast will begin at the moment when one of the living creatures commands the beast to go forth (Rev 6:1–2), and it will end at the seventh trumpet blast.

2. 1,290 Days: But now, the man in linen comes along and says that from the time that the "daily" is taken away (the ministry of the two witnesses is taken away) and the abomination that desolates is set up (the two witnesses are murdered and their bodies are set up on the Temple Mount) there shall be 1,290 days; 1,290 days until what? Remember, the man in linen was in the process of answering Daniel's question, "What shall be the outcome of these things?" which was the same question posed earlier by the man's accompanying angel, "How long shall it be until the end of these wonders?" By combining the man-in-linen's two responses given to Daniel and the angel, one has the following, more complete answer to their questions: There will be 1,290 days from the time the abomination is set up until the shattering of the power of the holy people comes to an end, which is at the seventh trumpet.

And therein lies the explanation of the thirty-day discrepancy between Day 1,260 and Day 1,290! Although both time frames have the same end-date (the seventh trumpet), they have different starting points. The 1,260-day time frame begins at the moment the living creature commands the beast "to go," but the 1290-day time frame begins thirty days earlier at the setting up of the abomination of desolation, which is when the two witnesses are murdered by the beast. Observe:

Table Appendix B.4. 1,290-Day Time Frame: From the Abomination to the Seventh Trumpet

		The Great Tribulation		The Day of the Lord		
1,260-Day Ministry of the 2 Witnesses	30 Days	Nuclear War Human Assist. Needed: The 10 Kings	1. Nuclear Aftermath 2. Deception of the Unrighteous 3. Martyrdom of the Saints	7 Trumpets		
			Human Assistance Needed: The Man of Lawlessness	Lesser Tribulation		
			Beast's 42-Month Reign			
			1,260-Day Exile of the 144,000 Jewish Remnant	7 Bowls	Unknown Time Frame	Millennium
			42-Month Trampling of Jerusalem			
< Abomination		< Command to the Beast "to Go"	< Revealing of Man of Sin (during the nuclear aftermath)	< 7th Trumpet	< Lord's Return	< Resurrection
		<------------------- 1,260 Days ------------------->				
<-------------------------------- 1290 Days -------------------------------->						

One always knew that the beast's murder of the two witnesses occurred prior to the moment that the living creature will command the beast "to go," but until now, one never knew how much earlier. Now one knows: The murders of the two witnesses will occur thirty days prior to the living creature's command.

Day 1,335

Finally, the angel told Daniel, "Happy are those who persevere and attain the thousand three hundred thirty-five days." In other words, the angel said that if the saints "persevere" they will attain "something" 1,335 days after the abomination of desolation that will make them happy. Question: After the seventh trumpet, which falls on either Day 1,260 or Day 1,290, depending on the start-date, what are the two preeminent events that will make the saints happy? Of course, it's the return of Christ and the gathering of the saints. Now, with that simple assessment, compare the angel's words of happiness, perseverance, and attaining Day 1,335 to Paul's words of perseverance and attaining the resurrection (italics used for emphasis):

"I want to know Christ and *the power of his resurrection* and the sharing of his suffering by becoming like him in his death, if somehow I may *attain the resurrection from the dead*.

"Not that I have already obtained this or have already reached the goal; but *I press on to make it my own*, because Christ Jesus has made me his own. Beloved, I do not consider that I have made it my own; but this one thing I do: *forgetting what lies behind and straining forward to what lies ahead, I press on toward the goal for the prize* of the heavenly call of God in Christ Jesus" (Phil 3:10–14).

Paul encouraged the Philippians to press on and strain forward so that one day they might attain the resurrection from the dead. When considering the two specific days after the seventh trumpet which will cause the saints to have joy and happiness—the return of Christ and the resurrection of the saints—Paul describes the resurrection as a goal for which the saints must persevere and ultimately attain, but the apostle never describes Christ's manifestation as something for which the saints must "attain." Christ's return may be described as hoped for, waited for, and expected (compare Titus 2:13; Jas 5:7; and Phil 3:20), but never "attained." With these simple observations, the reader can be certain that Day 1,335 is none other than the day of the resurrection. Observe:

Table Appendix B.5. 1,335-Day Time Frame: From the Abomination to the Resurrection

	The Great Tribulation				The Day of the Lord			
		1. Nuclear Aftermath	7 Trumpets					
	Nuclear War	2. Deception of the Unrighteous	Lesser Tribulation		7 Bowls	Unknown Time Frame		Millennium
1,260-Day Ministry of the 2 Witnesses	Human Assist. Needed: The 10 Kings	3. Martyrdom of the Saints						Resurrection
	30 Days	Human Assistance Needed: The Man of Lawlessness				<---45 Days--->		
		Beast's 42-Month Reign					Lord's Return	
		1,260-Day Exile of the 144,000 Jewish Remnant						
		42-Month Trampling of Jerusalem						
	<	<		<		<	<	
	Abomination	Command to the Beast "to Go"	Revealing of Man of Sin (during the nuclear aftermath)			7th Trumpet		
			<----------1,260 Days---------->					
	<----------1290 Days---------->							
	<--------------------------1,335 Days-------------------------->							

When analyzing the juxtaposition of Day 1,290 and Day 1,335, one sees that not only will the resurrection of the saints occur 1,335 days after the murder of the two witnesses, but it will occur forty-five days after the seventh trumpet. This necessitates that the seven bowls of wrath as well as the Battle of Armageddon transpire within a forty-five-day period. Nonetheless, because God has kept secret the day of

APPENDIX B

Christ's manifestation, the time frame of the seven bowls as well as the time frame between Christ's return and the resurrection of the saints remains unknown.

Bibliography

Archer, Gleason L., Jr. *Daniel.* The Expositor's Bible Commentary. Edited by Frank E. Gaebelein. Grand Rapids, MI: Zondervan, 1985.
Barker, Kenneth L. *Zechariah.* The Expositor's Bible Commentary. Edited by Frank E. Gaebelein. Grand Rapids, MI: Zondervan, 1985.
Beale, G. K., with David H. Campbell. *Revelation: A Shorter Commentary.* Grand Rapids, MI: Eerdmans, 2015.
Best, Ernest. *The First and Second Epistles to the Thessalonians.* Black's New Testament Commentary 13. Edited by Henry Chadwick. Peabody, MA: Hendrickson, 2003.
Blaising, Craig A., et al. *Three Views on the Millennium and Beyond.* Counterpoint Series. General editor: Darrell L. Bock. Series editor: Stanley N. Gundry. Grand Rapids, MI: Zondervan, 1999.
Charles, R. H. *The Revelation of St. John.* International Critical Commentary. 2 vols. Edited by Samuel R. Driver et al. Edinburgh: T. & T. Clark, 1985.
Frame, James Everett. *A Critical and Exegetical Commentary on the Epistles of St. Paul to the Thessalonians.* International Critical Commentary. Edited by Samuel R. Driver et al. Edinburgh: T. & T. Clark, 1988.
Goodwin, Frank J. *A Harmony of the Life of St. Paul according to the Acts of the Apostles and the Pauline Epistles.* Grand Rapids, MI: Baker, 1994.
Harris, Murray J. *2 Corinthians.* The Expositor's Bible Commentary. Edited by Frank E. Gaebelein. Grand Rapids, MI: Zondervan, 1976.
Jerusalem Post Staff. "Jerusalem Remains Israel's Biggest City with Nearly 1 M. Residents." *Jerusalem Post,* May 17, 2023.
Kampen, Robert Van. *The Sign.* Wheaton, IL: Crossway, 1992.
Lewis, C. S. *The World's Last Night and Other Essays.* San Diego: Harvest, 2002.
Metzger, Bruce M. *The Bible in Translation.* Grand Rapids, MI: Baker Academic, 2001.
———. *Breaking the Code: Understanding the Book of Revelation.* Nashville: Abingdon, 1993.
———. *The New Testament: Its Background, Growth, and Content, Third Edition.* Revised and enlarged. Nashville: Abingdon, 2003.
Montgomery, James A. *A Critical and Exegetical Commentary on the Book of Daniel.* International Critical Commentary. Edited by Samuel R. Driver et al. Edinburgh: T. & T. Clark, 1989.
Rhodes, Ron. *The End Times in Chronological Order.* Eugene, OR: Harvest House, 2012.

Sproul, R. C. *The Last Days according to Jesus*. Grand Rapids, MI: Baker, 1998.
Schweitzer, Albert. *The Quest of the Historical Jesus: A Critical Study of Its Progress from Reimarus to Wrede*. Translated by W. Montgomery. 2nd ed. London: Adam and Charles Black, 1911.
Walton, John H. *Chronological and Background Charts of the Old Testament*. Grand Rapids, MI: Baker Academic, 1978.
Walvoord, John F. *The Rapture Question, Revised and Enlarged Edition*. Grand Rapids, MI: Zondervan, 1979.
Wright, N. T. *Revelation for Everyone*. New Testament for Everyone. Louisville, KY: Westminster John Knox, 2011.

www.ingramcontent.com/pod-product-compliance
Lightning Source LLC
Chambersburg PA
CBHW071432300426
44114CB00013B/1400